USNA.

The United States of North America

A time in the future when our two great countries, Canada and the United States, have amalgamated. Within the U.S.N.A. and especially in parts of the former country of Canada, there is a growing discontent. Family farms have been replaced by huge corporate farms that exploit the bulging prison populations as labour. Severe drought has lead to food shortages and rationing in the cities. The young people are being conscripted to fight in the Cent-Am wars. The groundswell of rebellion is building and the rebels are planning the return of their leader, the exiled ex-prime minister of Canada, Samuel Stern. To combat this threat, a new organization has been created by the administrative council of USNA. It's a covert homeland security force: the Strategic Home Alliance Defense Organization (S.H.A.D.O.). Operating on the fringes of the law, their mission is simple: locate and eliminate any rebel activity, using deadly force if necessary.

USNA: The United States of North America is the story of the people's fight against tyranny. It takes place in our own backyard.

This book is dedicated to the following people whose wit, energy,
creativity and heart helped in the creation of this graphic novel:

Kathy Chan, Cordell Wynne, Craig Laven and Linden Banks.
With a special thank-you to Dr. Larry Stanleigh, Calgary's foremost and wittiest dentist,
whose sense of humour, keen business sense, intellect, love and support literally
saved this project.

For Jill Ann Moreton, who provided the pen and paper to Davy so that he could record
the original thoughts exploding in his awareness, the seeds of the story, USNA.

For John 'Man Bear' Curtis, whose support and inspiration helped in
the creation of this project and who is the model for the character, Solo.

For Blu Mankuma, Vancouver B.C. actor, for his inspiration for the character, Conrad.

Dave Casey wishes to thank his family and friends for their support.
You know who you are.

USNA: The United States of North America is based on an original screenplay by David Longworth and Allan Stanleigh.
The graphic novel, USNA: The United States of North America, written by Harry Kalensky, Davy Longworth and Allan
Stanleigh. Artwork, book design and visual concepts by Dave Casey www.dave-casey.com

USNA Publications Inc.
Vancouver, B.C. Canada
www.usna.ca

"Whether you think the story is fact or fiction, there's no denying that USNA is an entertaining yarn that focuses on a rebel movement that springs up after the amalgamation."

– Eric Volmers – Calgary Herald

"USNA is a meaty read, full of blood and bullets. (...) The story is a clever, thought provoking look at the real ways in which such a country clashing future could emerge."

– Bryn Evans – FFWD Magazine

"It's something that has long persisted within the Canadian mythos, of being slowly taken over by American influence."

– Russell Bowers – CBC Radio

USNA is a book I have been waiting for most of my life, a comic book that manages to be entertaining, thought provoking and fierce. This book confronts us with the difficult notions of sacrifices that must be made to provide the freedoms that we take for granted. Unafraid, the story moves at a pulse pounding pace, yet still allowing for moments of reflection and pause so that we, the audience, can feel the intimacy of characters caught in the middle of a conflict that is as personal as it is relevant to our rapidly evolving society. Easily the best independent comic I've read in years.

– Axel Matfin – author of 'The Bartender: Darkness on the Edge of Town'

USNA: the United States of North America

Words by David Longworth, Harry Kalensky, and Allan Stanleigh
Pictures and Design by Dave Casey

with foreword by Will Ferguson

ALASKAN
NORTH CENTRAL
PACIFIC
SOUTH CENTRAL
ATLANTIC

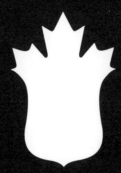

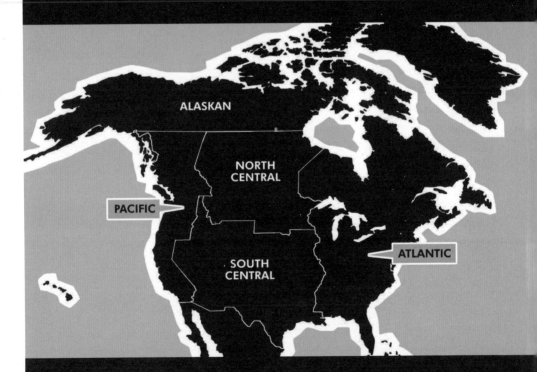

FOREWORD

"Living next door to the United States," Pierre Trudeau famously observed, "is like sleeping next to an elephant. No matter how friendly and even-tempered is the beast, one is affected by every twitch and grunt."

Canadians have long learned to sleep with one eye open. Indeed, it is one of the great myths of history that Canada's divergent destiny in North America was one charted peaceably. Far from it. Canada was founded on conquest. From the exile of the Acadians, scattered as far afield as Louisiana (where they are known now as 'Cajuns), to the Fall of New France and the Native uprisings led by Pontiac, it is a story soaked in bloodshed.

It is also worth remembering that the American Revolution was, above all, a civil war, one that split the continent down the middle along lines of loyalty. One of the first acts of the newly minted United States of America was to invade the northern colonies. "To the inhabitants of Canada," George Washington's army proclaimed, "Come, unite with us in an indissoluble Union!" The Americans were rebuffed, and the invasion of Canada was turned back in a howling snow storm at the very gates of Quebec City.

The Americans would try again in 1812, with yet another bombastic proclamation, this one issued by an invading general who warned Canadians "The United States offers you Peace, Liberty, and Security. Your choice lies between these and War, Slavery, and Destruction. Choose then, but choose wisely . . ."

But once again, the Canadian colonies stood firm. The American invasion was thwarted by ragtag Canadian militias and disciplined British troops, who counterattacked with a raid on Washington D.C that set both the capital — and the White House — ablaze.

From Canada's failed republican rebellions in 1837 to the Fenian raids launched by Irish radicals thirty years later — covertly supported by American interests — to the Aroostook Cold War in northern New Brunswick and the "Pig War" on San Juan Island south of Victoria, B.C. (wherein the two sides almost went to war over a single slain swine), the Canada-U.S. border has long been an arena of competing claims and looming threats.

These conflicts were fuelled by an American belief in "Manifest Destiny," a doctrine that claimed the entire continent for the United States. It was the threat of an imminent American invasion that was one of the driving forces behind Confederation, after all. There was safety in numbers, as the union of British North America demonstrated.

Canada's central defense plans were predicated on an assumed invasion from the United States well into the 1920s. And in USNA, David Longworth, Harry Kalensky and Allan Stanleigh envision a different outcome to this history. Dave Casey's gritty illustrations, in turn, provide a vivid reimagining of manifest destiny, one in which the American Empire has solidified its grasp on the continent. It is a story in the tradition of Richard Rohmer's novels Ultimatum and Exxoneration writ large on the canvas of a graphic novel. It is a story our forebears would find eerily familiar.

Will Ferguson

Co-author of 'How to be a Canadian' and Winner of the Pierre Berton Award for History from Canada's National History Society. Will Ferguson has been named the 2012 winner of the Scotiabank Giller Prize for his novel "419". The Giller Prize is considered one of Canada's most prestigious literary honours.

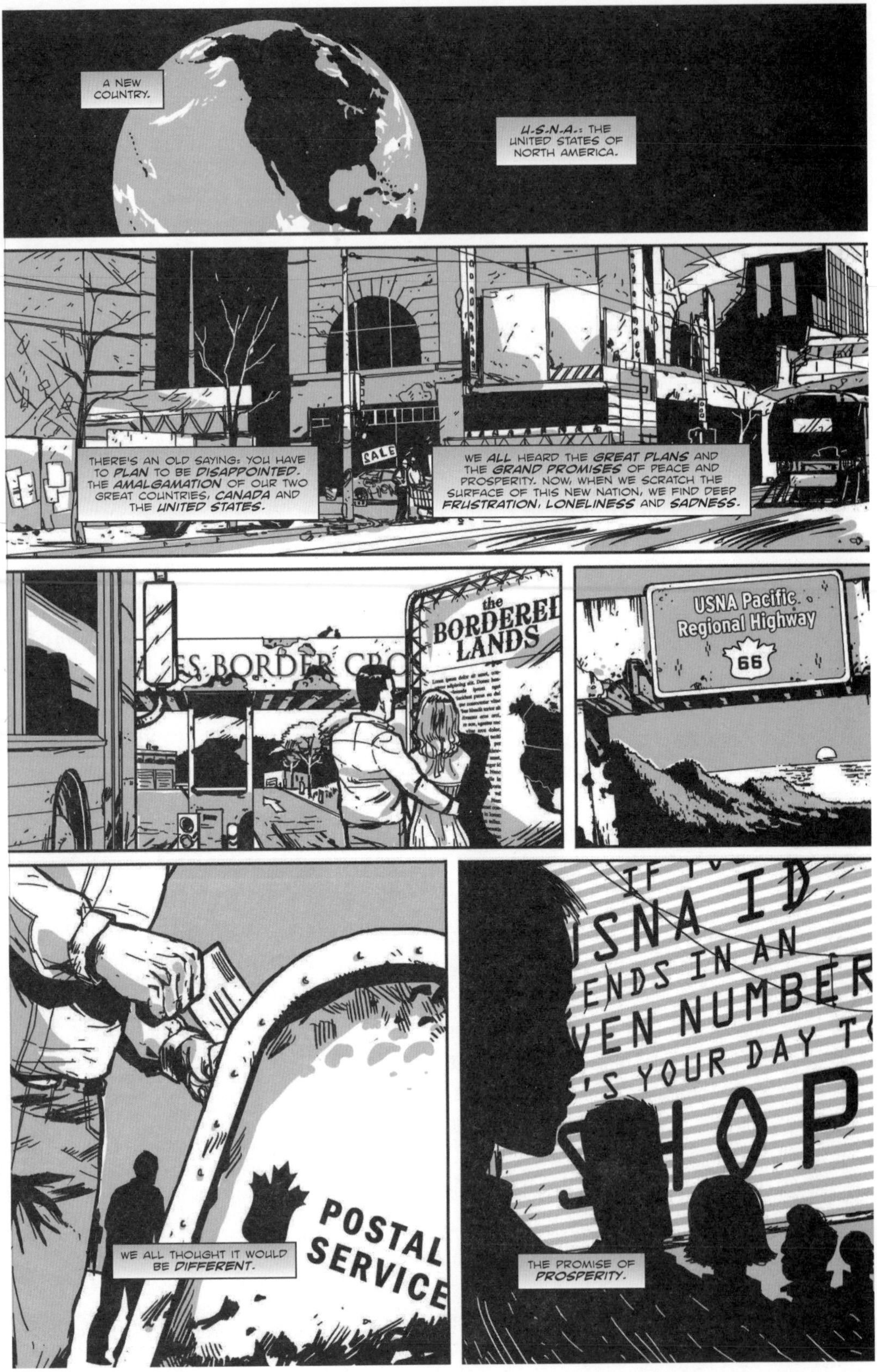
A NEW COUNTRY.
U.S.N.A.: THE UNITED STATES OF NORTH AMERICA.
THERE'S AN OLD SAYING: YOU HAVE TO PLAN TO BE DISAPPOINTED. THE AMALGAMATION OF OUR TWO GREAT COUNTRIES, CANADA AND THE UNITED STATES.
SALE
WE ALL HEARD THE GREAT PLANS AND THE GRAND PROMISES OF PEACE AND PROSPERITY. NOW, WHEN WE SCRATCH THE SURFACE OF THIS NEW NATION, WE FIND DEEP FRUSTRATION, LONELINESS AND SADNESS.
the BORDERED LANDS
USNA Pacific Regional Highway
66
POSTAL SERVICE
WE ALL THOUGHT IT WOULD BE DIFFERENT.
USNA ID
ENDS IN AN
THE PROMISE OF PROSPERITY.

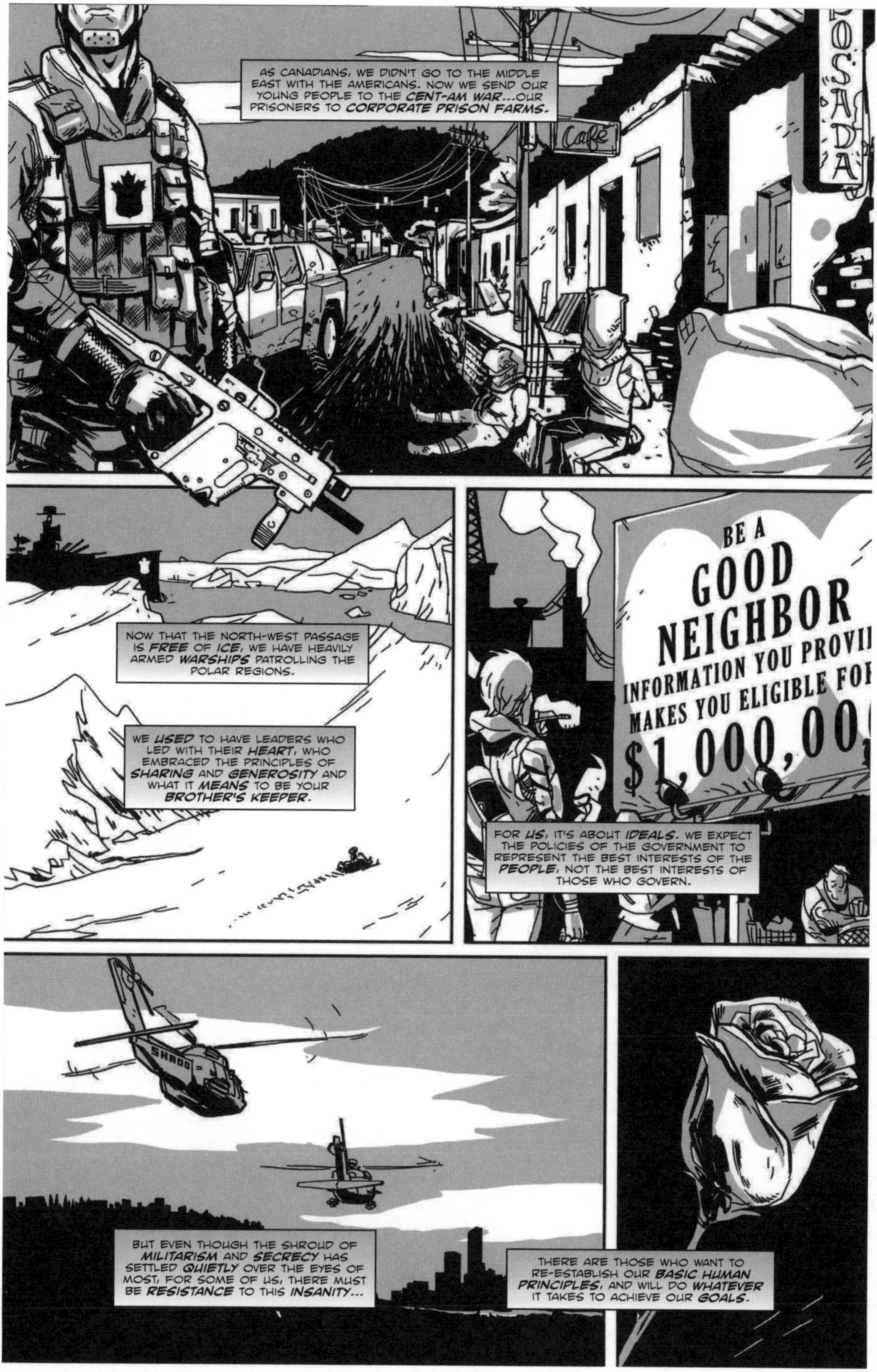

AS CANADIANS, WE DIDN'T GO TO THE MIDDLE EAST WITH THE AMERICANS. NOW WE SEND OUR YOUNG PEOPLE TO THE CENT-AM WAR...OUR PRISONERS TO CORPORATE PRISON FARMS.
Café
POSADA
NOW THAT THE NORTH-WEST PASSAGE IS FREE OF ICE, WE HAVE HEAVILY ARMED WARSHIPS PATROLLING THE POLAR REGIONS.
WE USED TO HAVE LEADERS WHO LED WITH THEIR HEART, WHO EMBRACED THE PRINCIPLES OF SHARING AND GENEROSITY AND WHAT IT MEANS TO BE YOUR BROTHER'S KEEPER.
BE A GOOD NEIGHBOR
INFORMATION YOU PROVI
MAKES YOU ELIGIBLE FO
$1,000,00
FOR US, IT'S ABOUT IDEALS. WE EXPECT THE POLICIES OF THE GOVERNMENT TO REPRESENT THE BEST INTERESTS OF THE PEOPLE, NOT THE BEST INTERESTS OF THOSE WHO GOVERN.
SHROO
BUT EVEN THOUGH THE SHROUD OF MILITARISM AND SECRECY HAS SETTLED QUIETLY OVER THE EYES OF MOST, FOR SOME OF US, THERE MUST BE RESISTANCE TO THIS INSANITY...
THERE ARE THOSE WHO WANT TO RE-ESTABLISH OUR BASIC HUMAN PRINCIPLES, AND WILL DO WHATEVER IT TAKES TO ACHIEVE OUR GOALS.

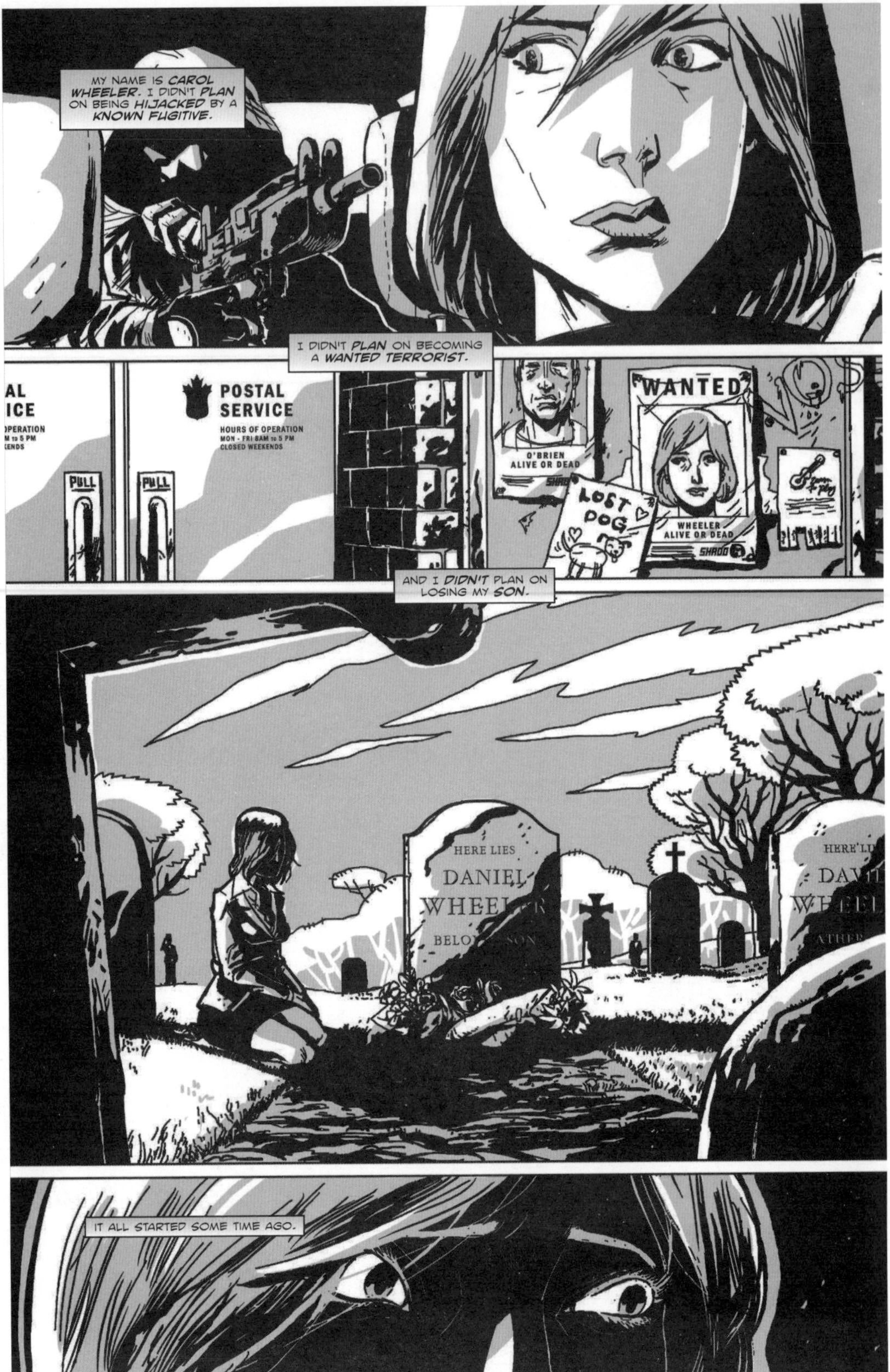
MY NAME IS CAROL WHEELER. I DIDN'T PLAN ON BEING HIJACKED BY A KNOWN FUGITIVE.
I DIDN'T PLAN ON BECOMING A WANTED TERRORIST.
POSTAL SERVICE
HOURS OF OPERATION
MON - FRI 8AM to 5 PM
CLOSED WEEKENDS
PULL
PULL
O'BRIEN
ALIVE OR DEAD
WANTED
WHEELER
ALIVE OR DEAD
LOST DOG
AND I DIDN'T PLAN ON LOSING MY SON.
HERE LIES
DANIEL
IT ALL STARTED SOME TIME AGO.

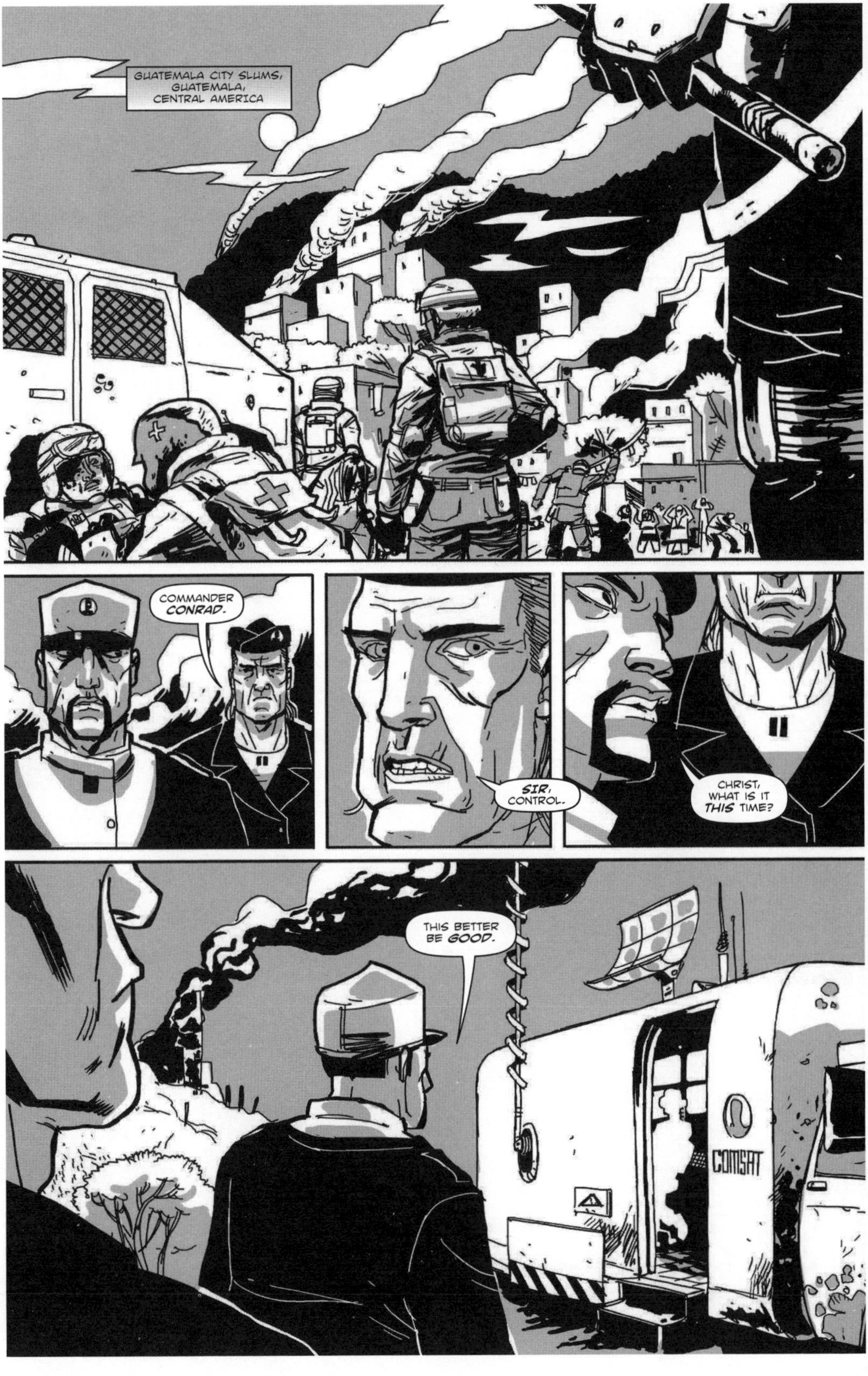
GUATEMALA CITY SLUMS, GUATEMALA, CENTRAL AMERICA
COMMANDER CONRAD.
SIR, CONTROL.
CHRIST, WHAT IS IT THIS TIME?
THIS BETTER BE GOOD.
COMSAT

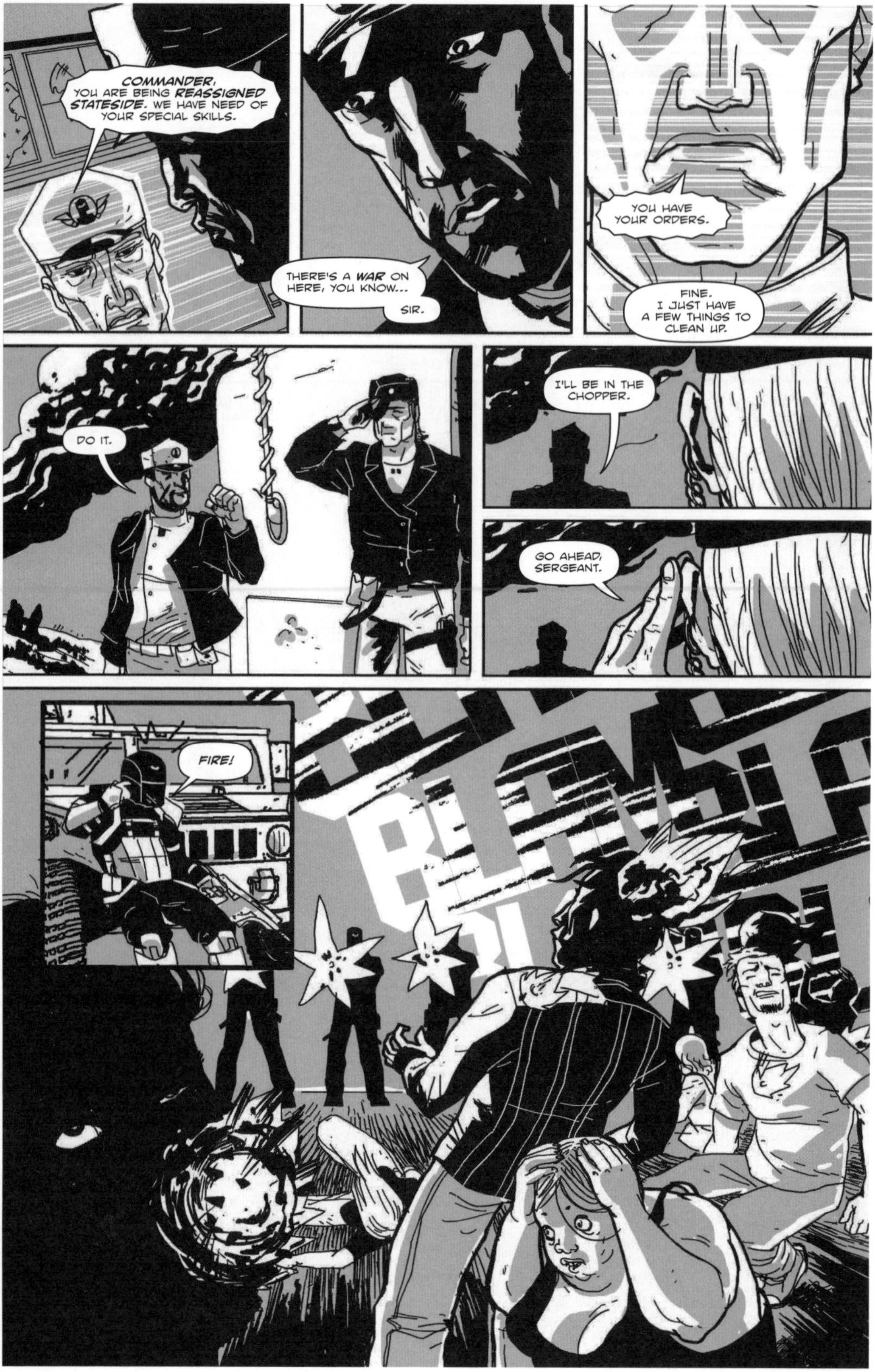
COMMANDER, YOU ARE BEING REASSIGNED STATESIDE. WE HAVE NEED OF YOUR SPECIAL SKILLS.
THERE'S A WAR ON HERE, YOU KNOW...
SIR.
YOU HAVE YOUR ORDERS.
FINE. I JUST HAVE A FEW THINGS TO CLEAN UP.
DO IT.
I'LL BE IN THE CHOPPER.
GO AHEAD, SERGEANT.
FIRE!

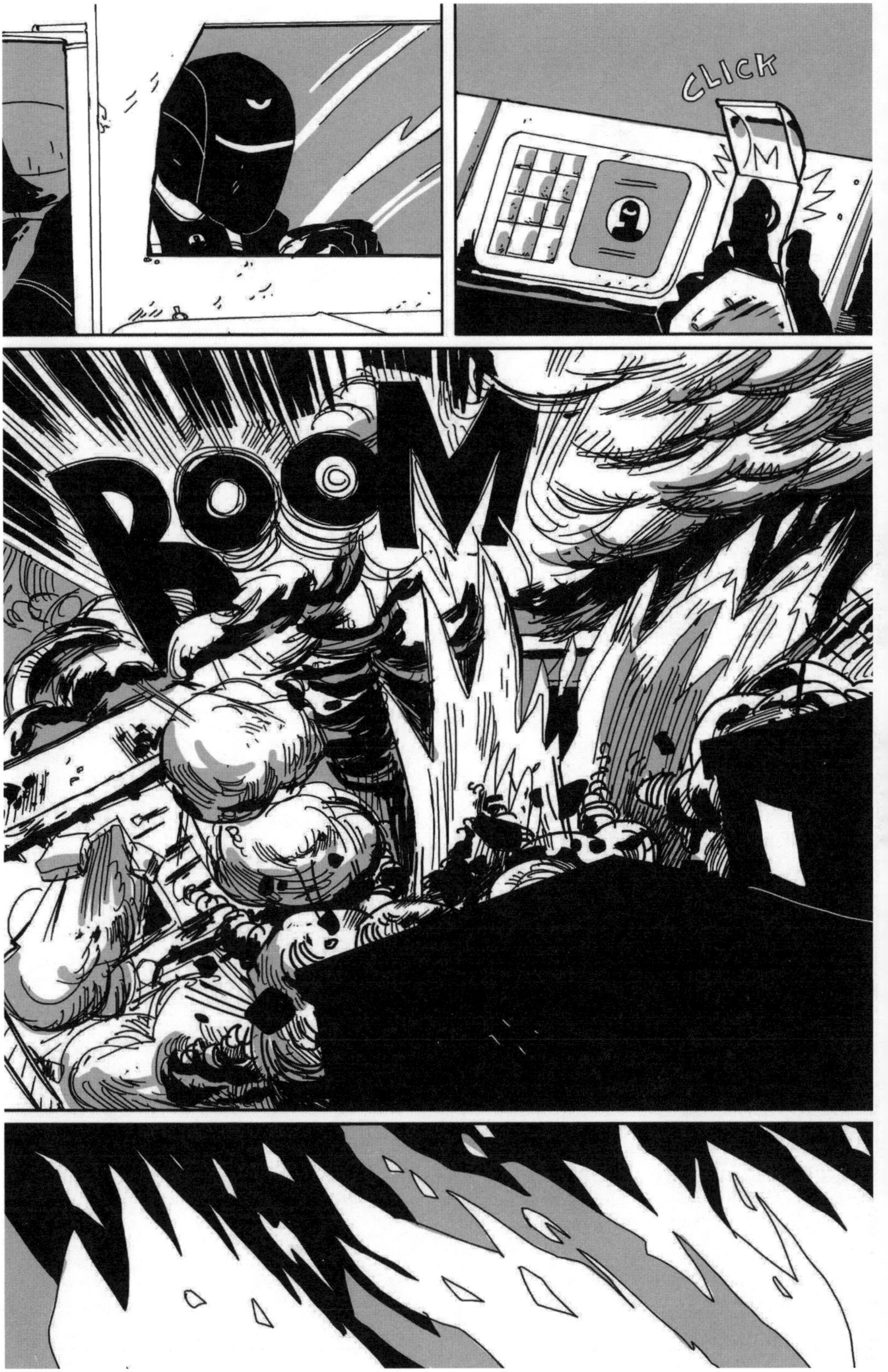
CLICK
BOOM

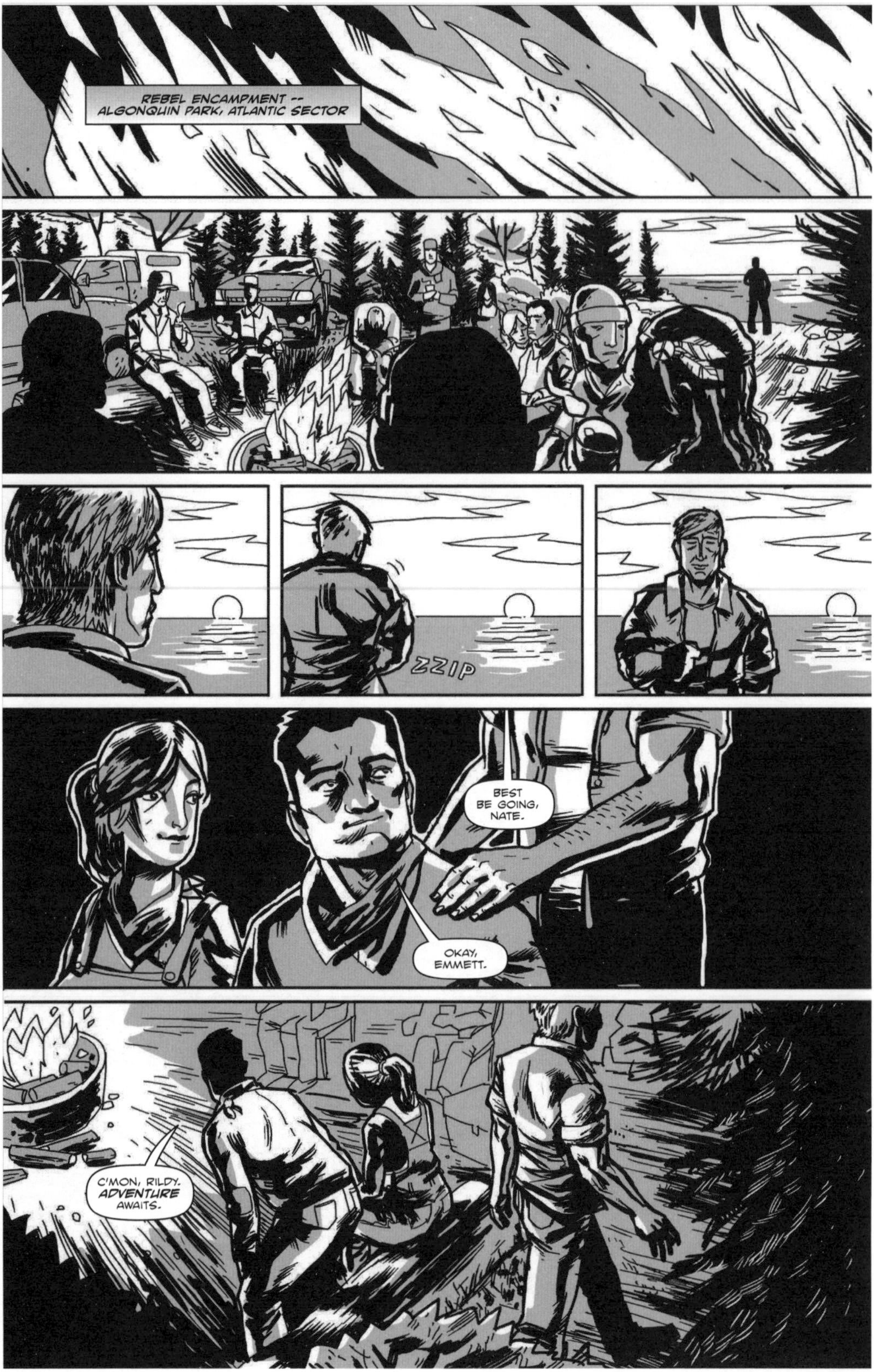
REBEL ENCAMPMENT -- ALGONQUIN PARK, ATLANTIC SECTOR
ZZIP
BEST BE GOING, NATE.
OKAY, EMMETT.
C'MON, RILDY. ADVENTURE AWAITS.

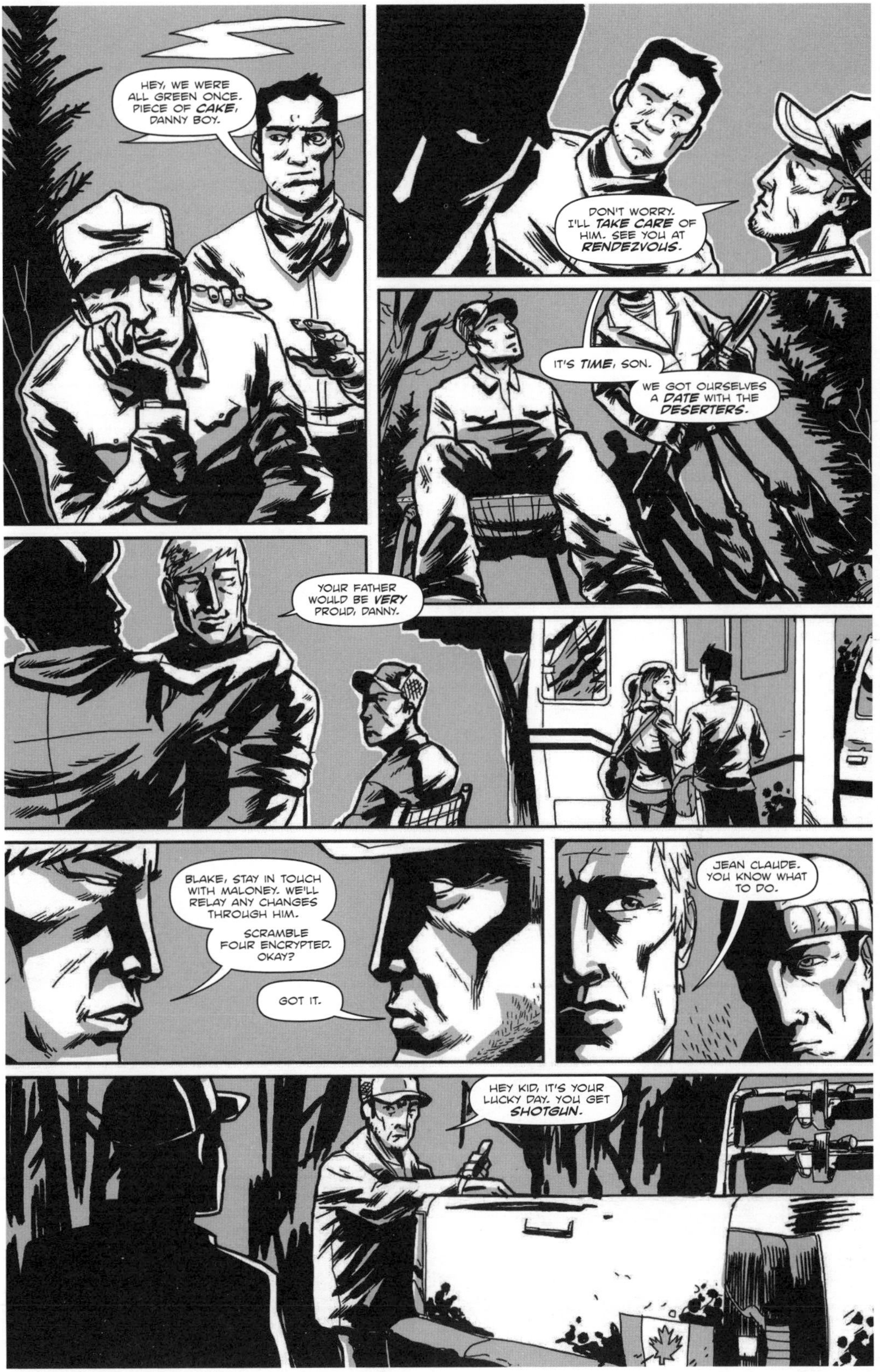
HEY, WE WERE ALL GREEN ONCE. PIECE OF CAKE, DANNY BOY.
DON'T WORRY. I'LL TAKE CARE OF HIM. SEE YOU AT RENDEZVOUS.
IT'S TIME, SON.
WE GOT OURSELVES A DATE WITH THE DESERTERS.
YOUR FATHER WOULD BE VERY PROUD, DANNY.
BLAKE, STAY IN TOUCH WITH MALONEY. WE'LL RELAY ANY CHANGES THROUGH HIM.
SCRAMBLE FOUR ENCRYPTED. OKAY?
GOT IT.
JEAN CLAUDE. YOU KNOW WHAT TO DO.
HEY KID, IT'S YOUR LUCKY DAY. YOU GET SHOTGUN.

```
------------------------------------
From:  Mr.Carter2U@usna.net
Subject: Me First, bro
Date:  April 8 10:06:18 PM EDT
To: Dwheeler <dwheeler@usna.net>
```

Hey Danny,

    I know you said to wait until you got back from your camping trip but I couldn't wait to write. I want to hear all about your adventures. Yea, I know you couldn't take me along this time and you promised to sometime....sometime? When is sometime going to happen anyhow? You know I've never gone camping or been out in the country. Now that they have all those roadblocks and check points, no-one seems to want to venture too far out of the city. What's the problem? Is it really so dangerous? Or have the lions gone rogue? Or is it wolves? lol :)

    So anyhow, you have to email me as soon as you get back. Okay! I want to hear all about it. Where were you going again?

    Mom was a little concerned, like she always is, about the people you have been hanging with recently. You know how she gets those 'feelings' about things. Women's intuition, or some such stuff. What do I know? I ain't no woman. Anyhow, that Blake guy who picked you up. I know you said he was some friend's dad, but where was the friend? And she said she'd never met that friend before. I know she hasn't met any of your new friends at graduate school but still, it did seem a little weird that his dad picked you up. Maybe your friend is a 'she?' That would explain everything. Like you don't want mom to know you're hanging with some girl in the woods. So, just to clear up any confusion, you can tell me. With dad gone, I don't have anyone to explain to me all this dating stuff. I mean, you know how shy I can be around girls, especially the nice looking ones. You seem to have a kind of easy way about you. You're a smooth operator, man.

    So call me as soon as you're back. Okay bro?

    Carter

```
------------------------------------
```

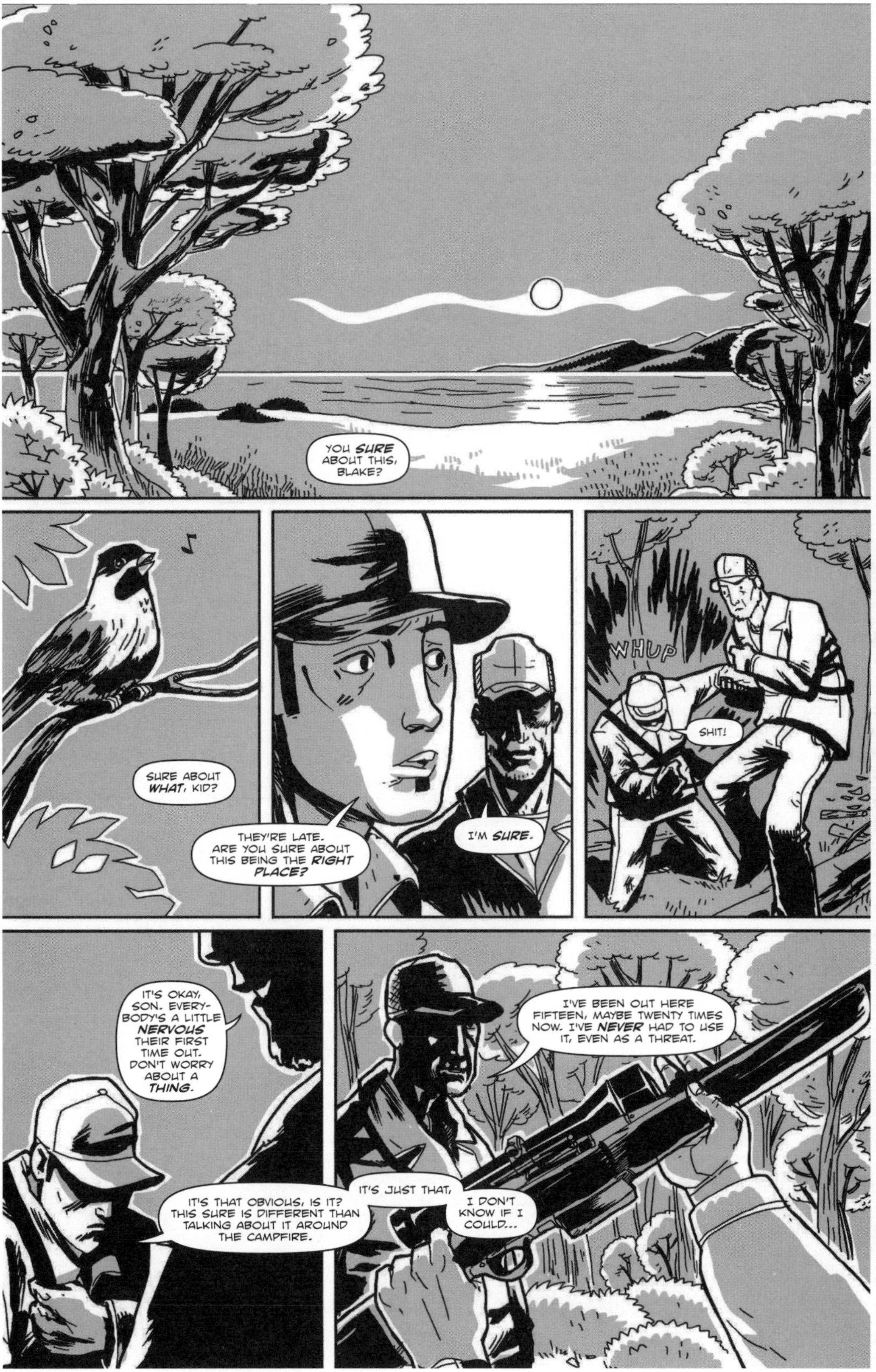
YOU SURE ABOUT THIS, BLAKE?
SURE ABOUT WHAT, KID?
THEY'RE LATE. ARE YOU SURE ABOUT THIS BEING THE RIGHT PLACE?
I'M SURE.
WHUP
SHIT!
IT'S OKAY, SON. EVERY-BODY'S A LITTLE NERVOUS THEIR FIRST TIME OUT. DON'T WORRY ABOUT A THING.
IT'S THAT OBVIOUS, IS IT? THIS SURE IS DIFFERENT THAN TALKING ABOUT IT AROUND THE CAMPFIRE.
I'VE BEEN OUT HERE FIFTEEN, MAYBE TWENTY TIMES NOW. I'VE NEVER HAD TO USE IT, EVEN AS A THREAT.
IT'S JUST THAT,
I DON'T KNOW IF I COULD...

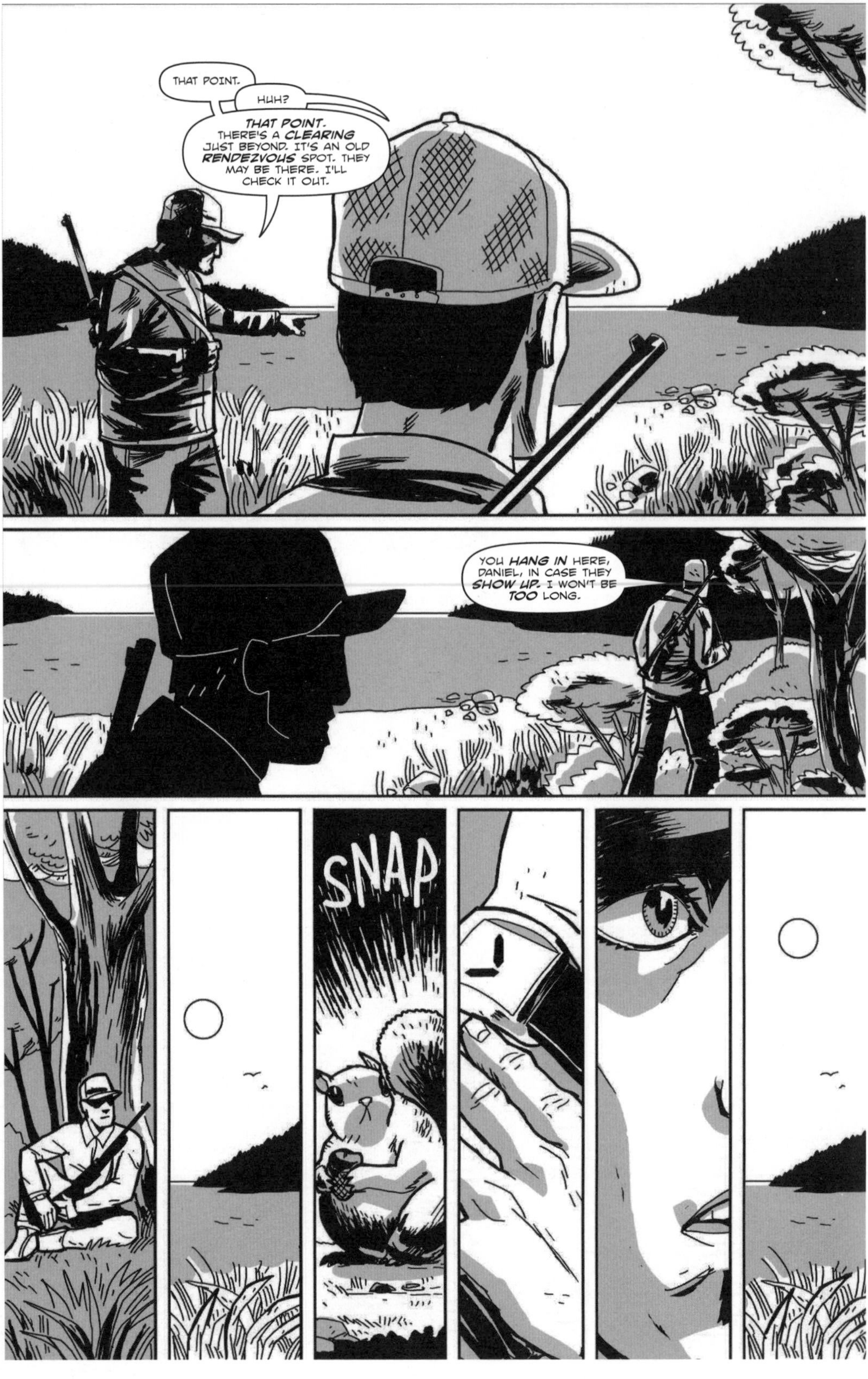
THAT POINT.
HUH?
THAT POINT. THERE'S A CLEARING JUST BEYOND. IT'S AN OLD RENDEZVOUS SPOT. THEY MAY BE THERE. I'LL CHECK IT OUT.
YOU HANG IN HERE, DANIEL, IN CASE THEY SHOW UP. I WON'T BE TOO LONG.
SNAP

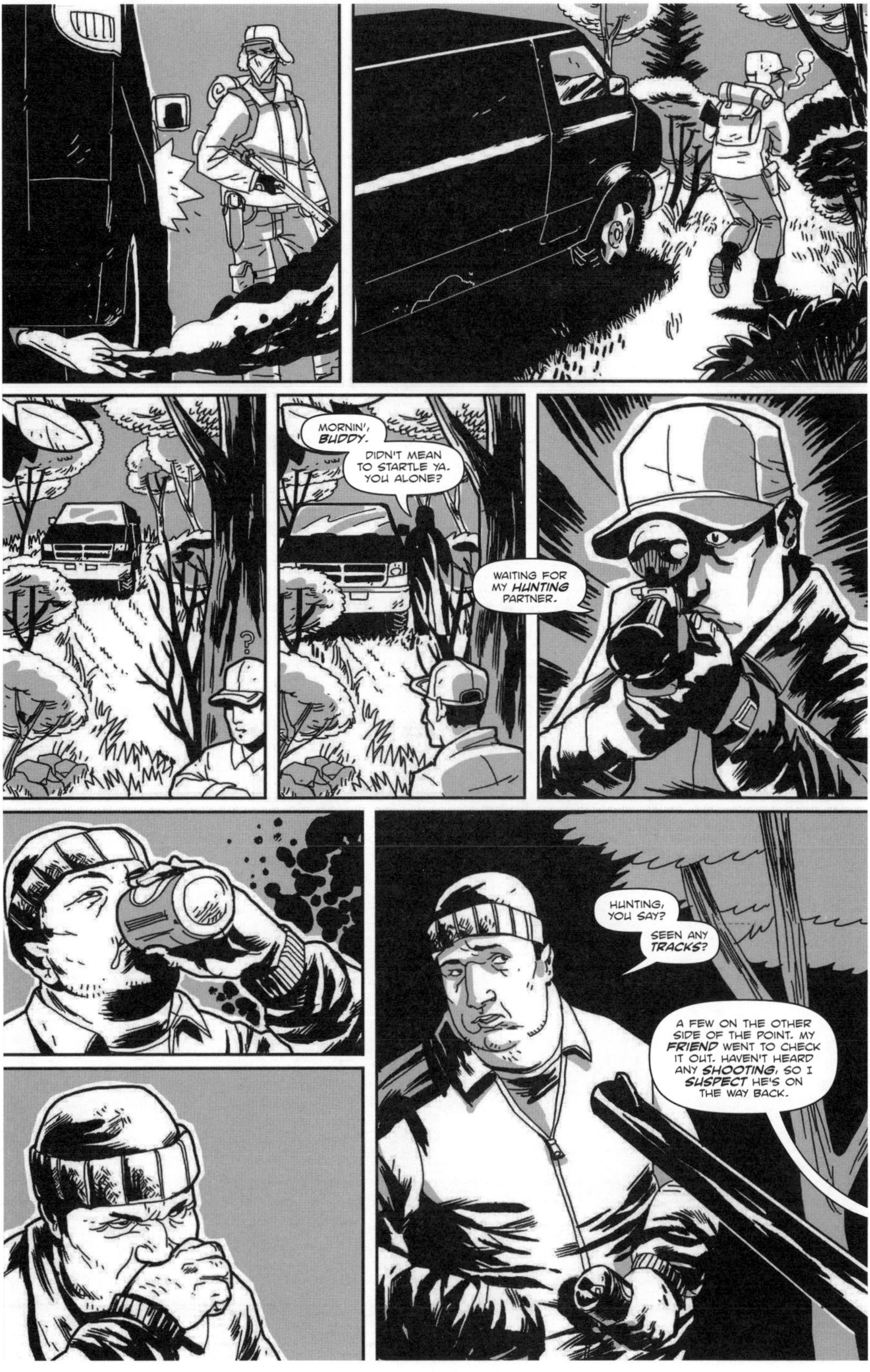
?
MORNIN', BUDDY.
DIDN'T MEAN TO STARTLE YA. YOU ALONE?
WAITING FOR MY HUNTING PARTNER.
HUNTING, YOU SAY?
SEEN ANY TRACKS?
A FEW ON THE OTHER SIDE OF THE POINT. MY FRIEND WENT TO CHECK IT OUT. HAVEN'T HEARD ANY SHOOTING, SO I SUSPECT HE'S ON THE WAY BACK.

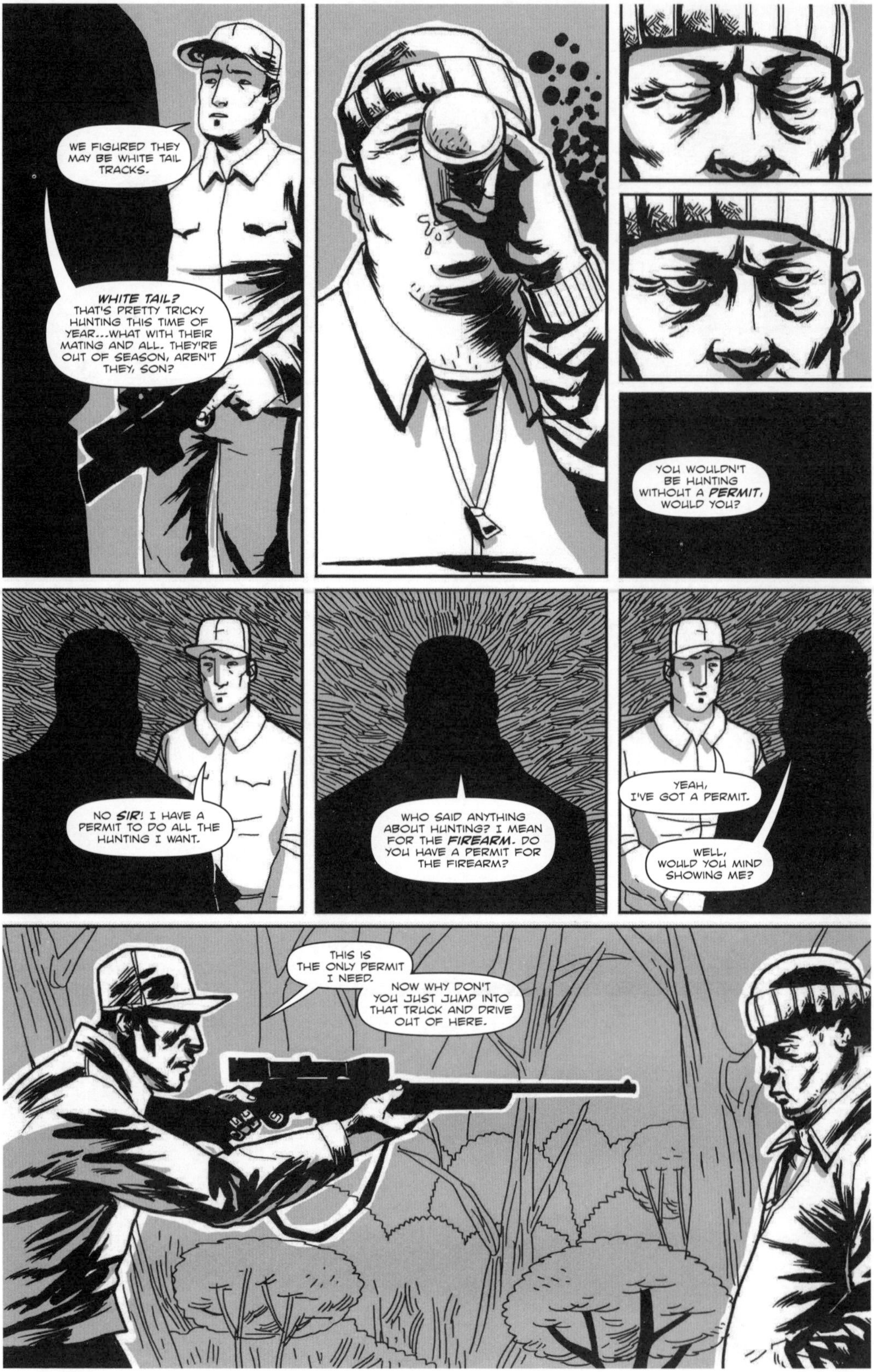
WE FIGURED THEY MAY BE WHITE TAIL TRACKS.
WHITE TAIL? THAT'S PRETTY TRICKY HUNTING THIS TIME OF YEAR...WHAT WITH THEIR MATING AND ALL. THEY'RE OUT OF SEASON, AREN'T THEY, SON?
YOU WOULDN'T BE HUNTING WITHOUT A PERMIT, WOULD YOU?
NO SIR! I HAVE A PERMIT TO DO ALL THE HUNTING I WANT.
WHO SAID ANYTHING ABOUT HUNTING? I MEAN FOR THE FIREARM. DO YOU HAVE A PERMIT FOR THE FIREARM?
YEAH, I'VE GOT A PERMIT.
WELL, WOULD YOU MIND SHOWING ME?
THIS IS THE ONLY PERMIT I NEED.
NOW WHY DON'T YOU JUST JUMP INTO THAT TRUCK AND DRIVE OUT OF HERE.

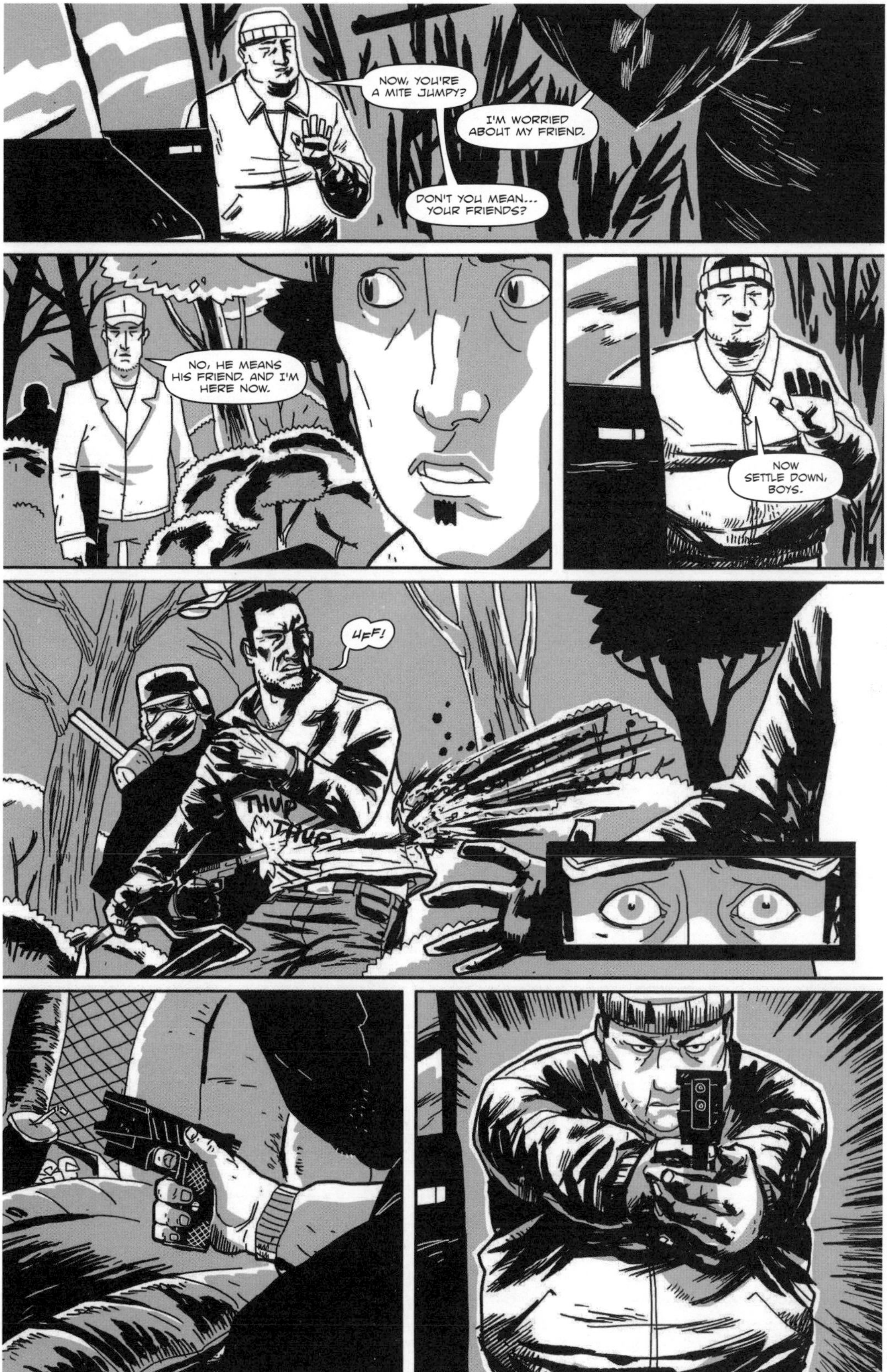
NOW, YOU'RE A MITE JUMPY?
I'M WORRIED ABOUT MY FRIEND.
DON'T YOU MEAN... YOUR FRIENDS?
NO, HE MEANS HIS FRIEND. AND I'M HERE NOW.
NOW SETTLE DOWN, BOYS.
UFF!
THUP
THUP

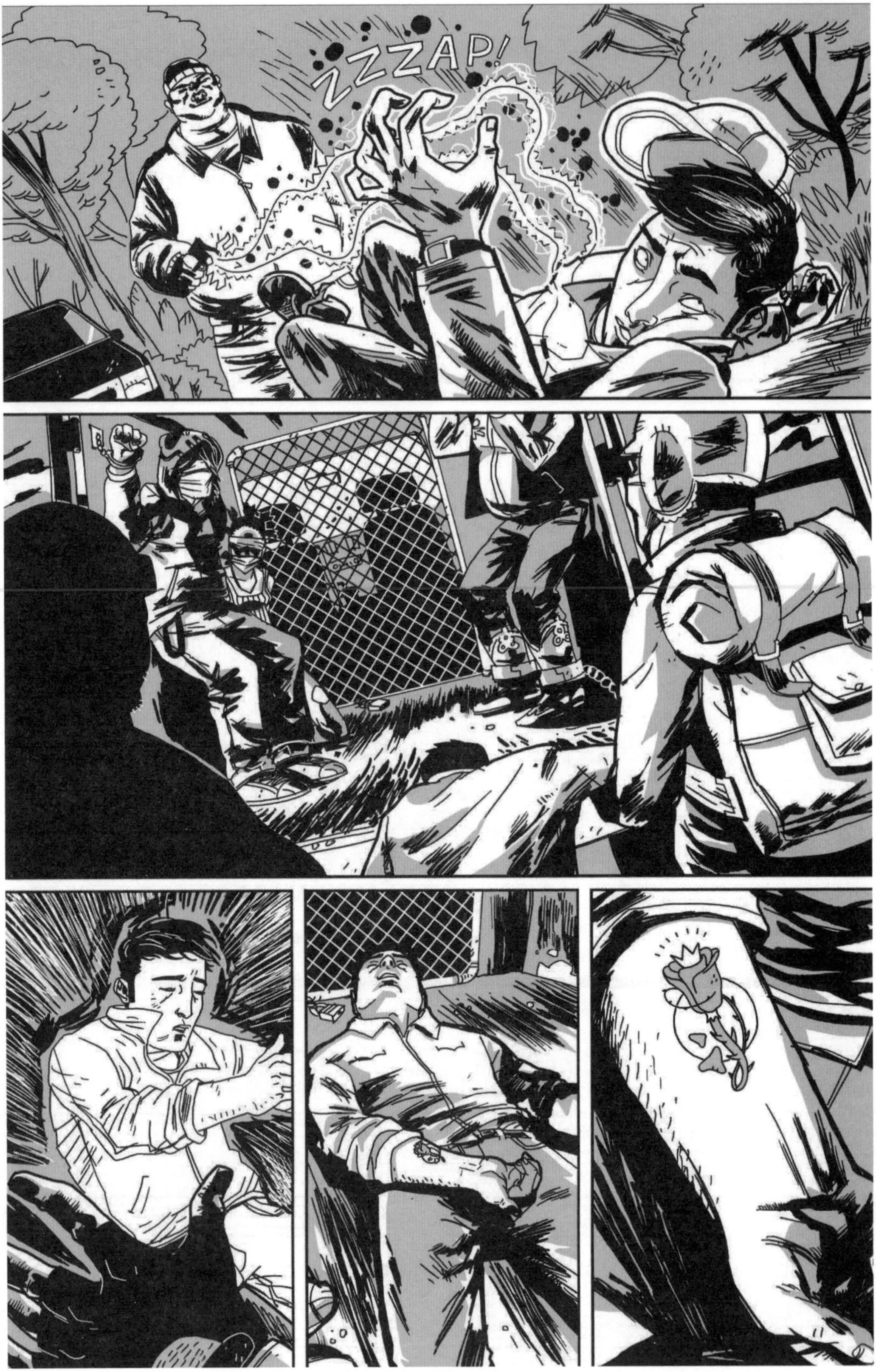
ZZZZAP!

PLEASE STAND FOR THE PLEDGE OF ALLEGIANCE.

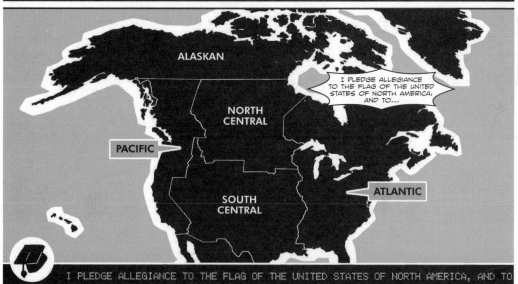

ALASKAN

NORTH CENTRAL

PACIFIC

ATLANTIC

SOUTH CENTRAL

I PLEDGE ALLEGIANCE TO THE FLAG OF THE UNITED STATES OF NORTH AMERICA, AND TO...

I PLEDGE ALLEGIANCE TO THE FLAG OF THE UNITED STATES OF NORTH AMERICA, AND TO

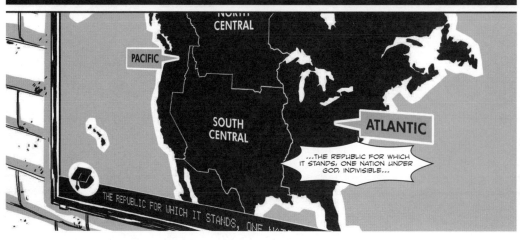

NORTH CENTRAL

PACIFIC

SOUTH CENTRAL

ATLANTIC

...THE REPUBLIC FOR WHICH IT STANDS, ONE NATION UNDER GOD, INDIVISIBLE...

THE REPUBLIC FOR WHICH IT STANDS, ONE NAT...

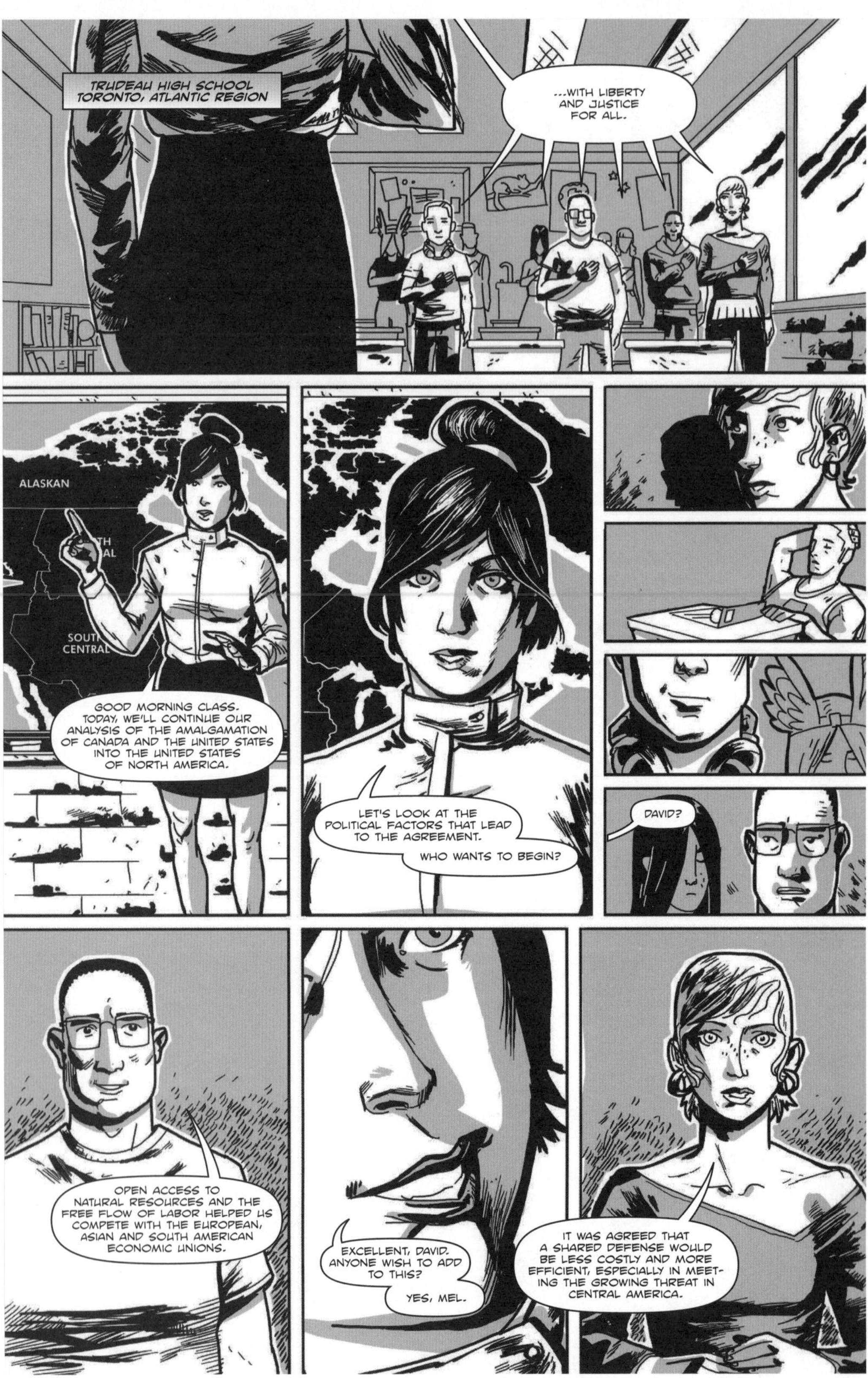
TRUDEAU HIGH SCHOOL
TORONTO, ATLANTIC REGION
...WITH LIBERTY AND JUSTICE FOR ALL.
ALASKAN
SOUTH CENTRAL
GOOD MORNING CLASS. TODAY, WE'LL CONTINUE OUR ANALYSIS OF THE AMALGAMATION OF CANADA AND THE UNITED STATES INTO THE UNITED STATES OF NORTH AMERICA.
LET'S LOOK AT THE POLITICAL FACTORS THAT LEAD TO THE AGREEMENT.
WHO WANTS TO BEGIN?
DAVID?
OPEN ACCESS TO NATURAL RESOURCES AND THE FREE FLOW OF LABOR HELPED US COMPETE WITH THE EUROPEAN, ASIAN AND SOUTH AMERICAN ECONOMIC UNIONS.
EXCELLENT, DAVID. ANYONE WISH TO ADD TO THIS?
YES, MEL.
IT WAS AGREED THAT A SHARED DEFENSE WOULD BE LESS COSTLY AND MORE EFFICIENT, ESPECIALLY IN MEETING THE GROWING THREAT IN CENTRAL AMERICA.

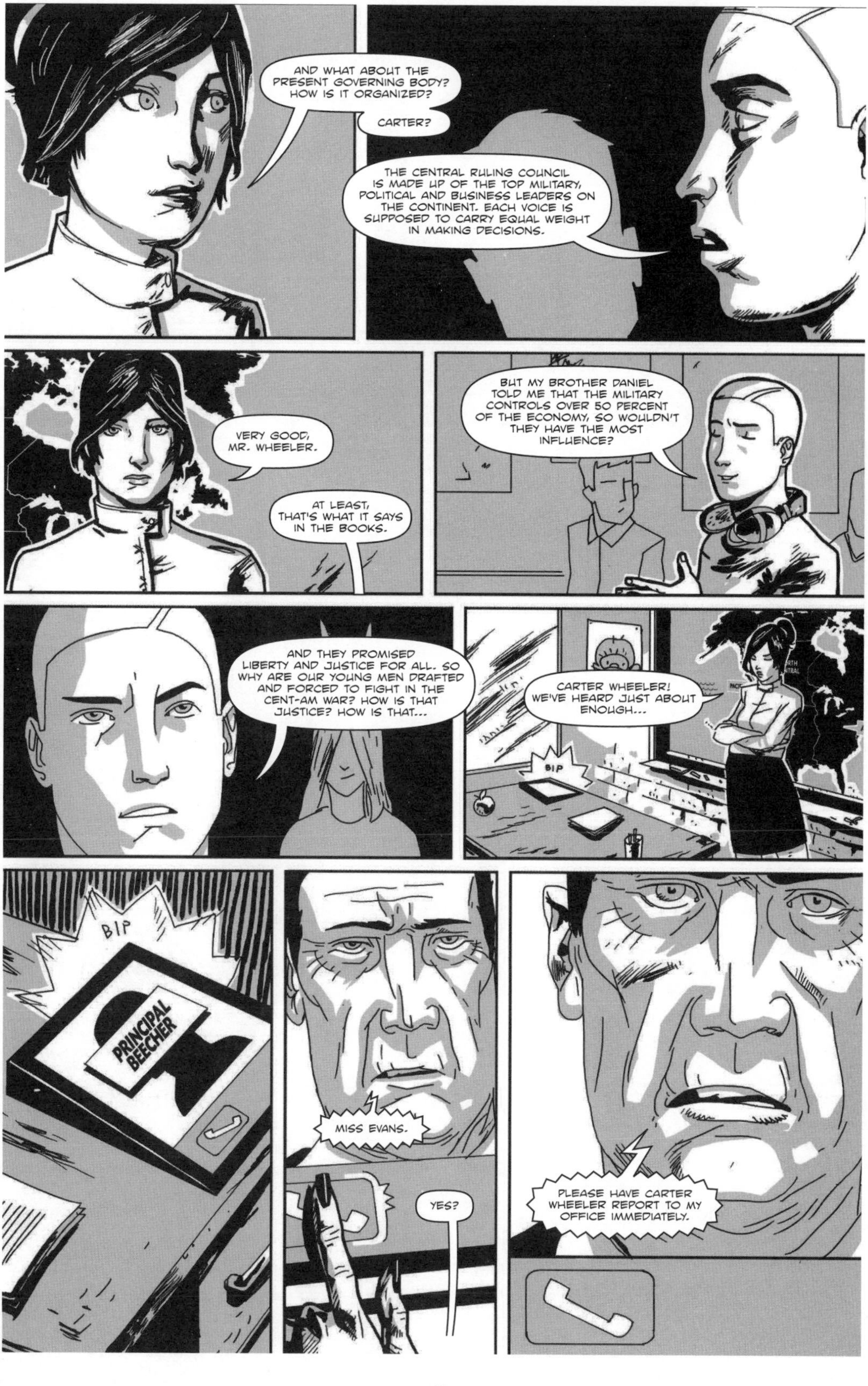
AND WHAT ABOUT THE PRESENT GOVERNING BODY? HOW IS IT ORGANIZED?
CARTER?
THE CENTRAL RULING COUNCIL IS MADE UP OF THE TOP MILITARY, POLITICAL AND BUSINESS LEADERS ON THE CONTINENT. EACH VOICE IS SUPPOSED TO CARRY EQUAL WEIGHT IN MAKING DECISIONS.
VERY GOOD, MR. WHEELER.
AT LEAST, THAT'S WHAT IT SAYS IN THE BOOKS.
BUT MY BROTHER DANIEL TOLD ME THAT THE MILITARY CONTROLS OVER 50 PERCENT OF THE ECONOMY, SO WOULDN'T THEY HAVE THE MOST INFLUENCE?
AND THEY PROMISED LIBERTY AND JUSTICE FOR ALL. SO WHY ARE OUR YOUNG MEN DRAFTED AND FORCED TO FIGHT IN THE CENT-AM WAR? HOW IS THAT JUSTICE? HOW IS THAT...
CARTER WHEELER! WE'VE HEARD JUST ABOUT ENOUGH...
BIP
BIP
PRINCIPAL BEECHER
MISS EVANS.
YES?
PLEASE HAVE CARTER WHEELER REPORT TO MY OFFICE IMMEDIATELY.

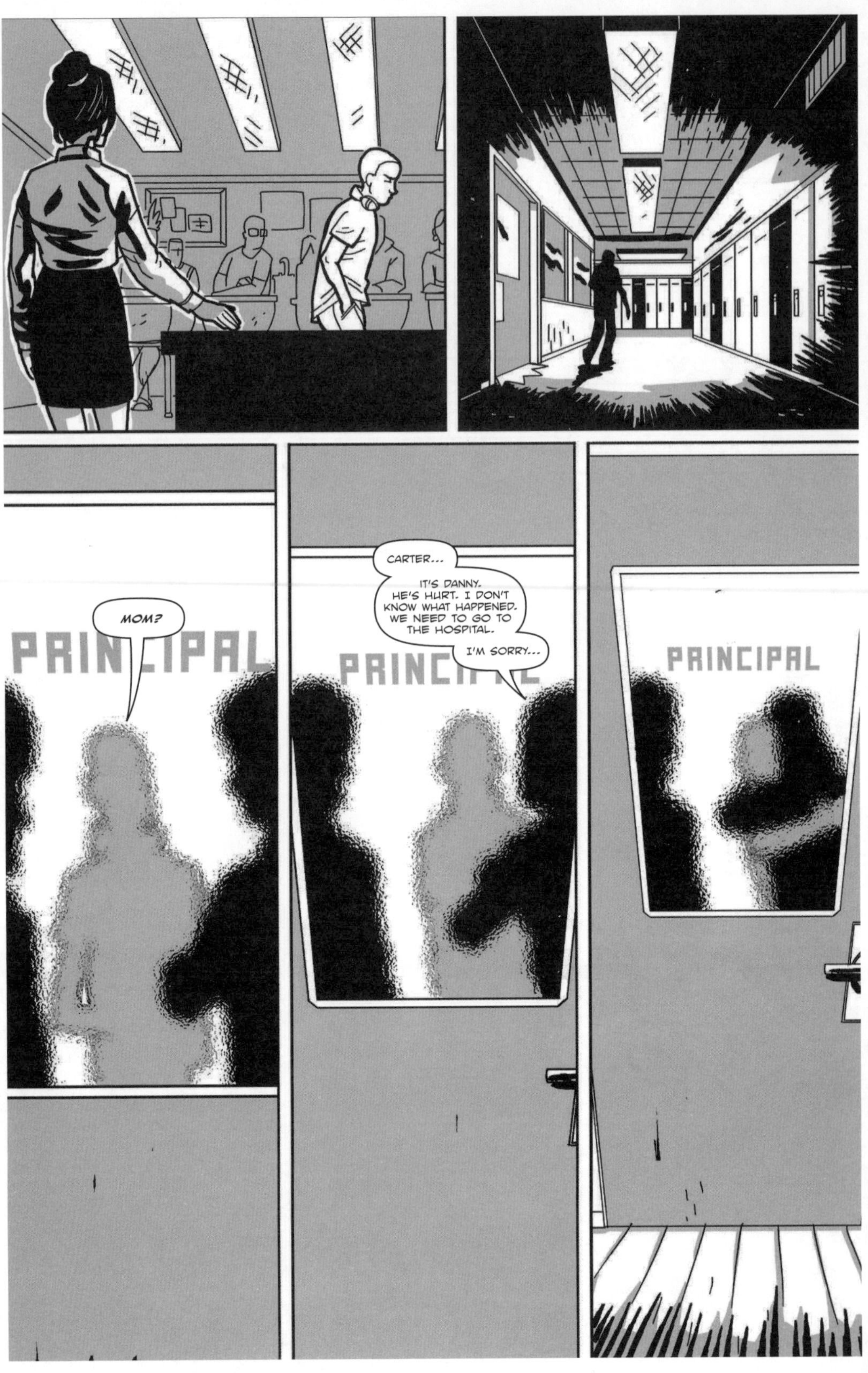
PRINCIPAL
MOM?
PRINCIPAL
CARTER...
IT'S DANNY. HE'S HURT. I DON'T KNOW WHAT HAPPENED. WE NEED TO GO TO THE HOSPITAL.
I'M SORRY...
PRINCIPAL

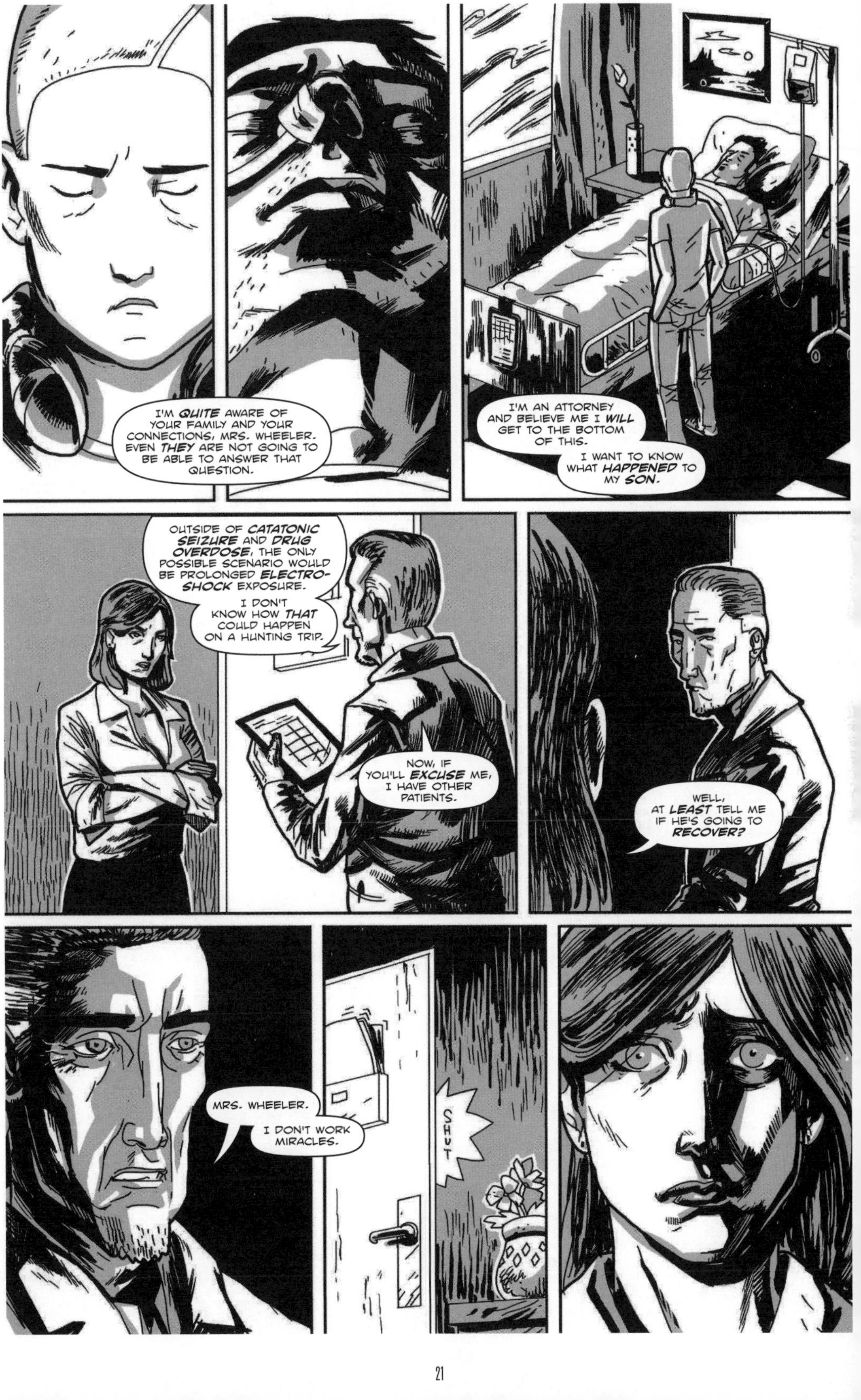
I'M QUITE AWARE OF YOUR FAMILY AND YOUR CONNECTIONS, MRS. WHEELER. EVEN THEY ARE NOT GOING TO BE ABLE TO ANSWER THAT QUESTION.
I'M AN ATTORNEY AND BELIEVE ME I WILL GET TO THE BOTTOM OF THIS.
I WANT TO KNOW WHAT HAPPENED TO MY SON.
OUTSIDE OF CATATONIC SEIZURE AND DRUG OVERDOSE, THE ONLY POSSIBLE SCENARIO WOULD BE PROLONGED ELECTRO-SHOCK EXPOSURE.
I DON'T KNOW HOW THAT COULD HAPPEN ON A HUNTING TRIP.
NOW, IF YOU'LL EXCUSE ME, I HAVE OTHER PATIENTS.
WELL, AT LEAST TELL ME IF HE'S GOING TO RECOVER?
MRS. WHEELER.
I DON'T WORK MIRACLES.
SHUT

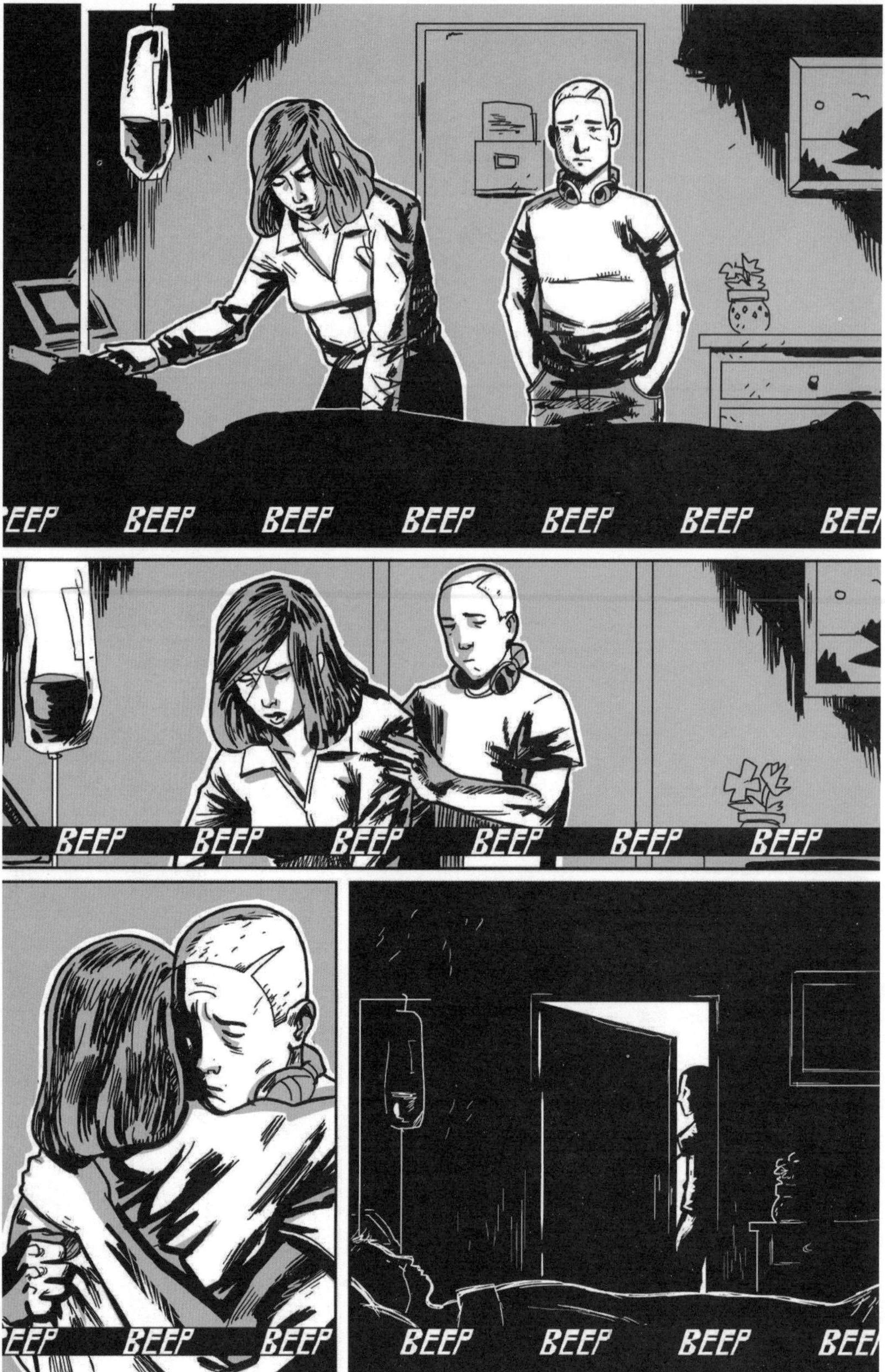
BEEP BEEP BEEP BEEP BEEP BEEP
BEEP BEEP BEEP BEEP BEEP BEEP
BEEP BEEP
BEEP BEEP BEEP

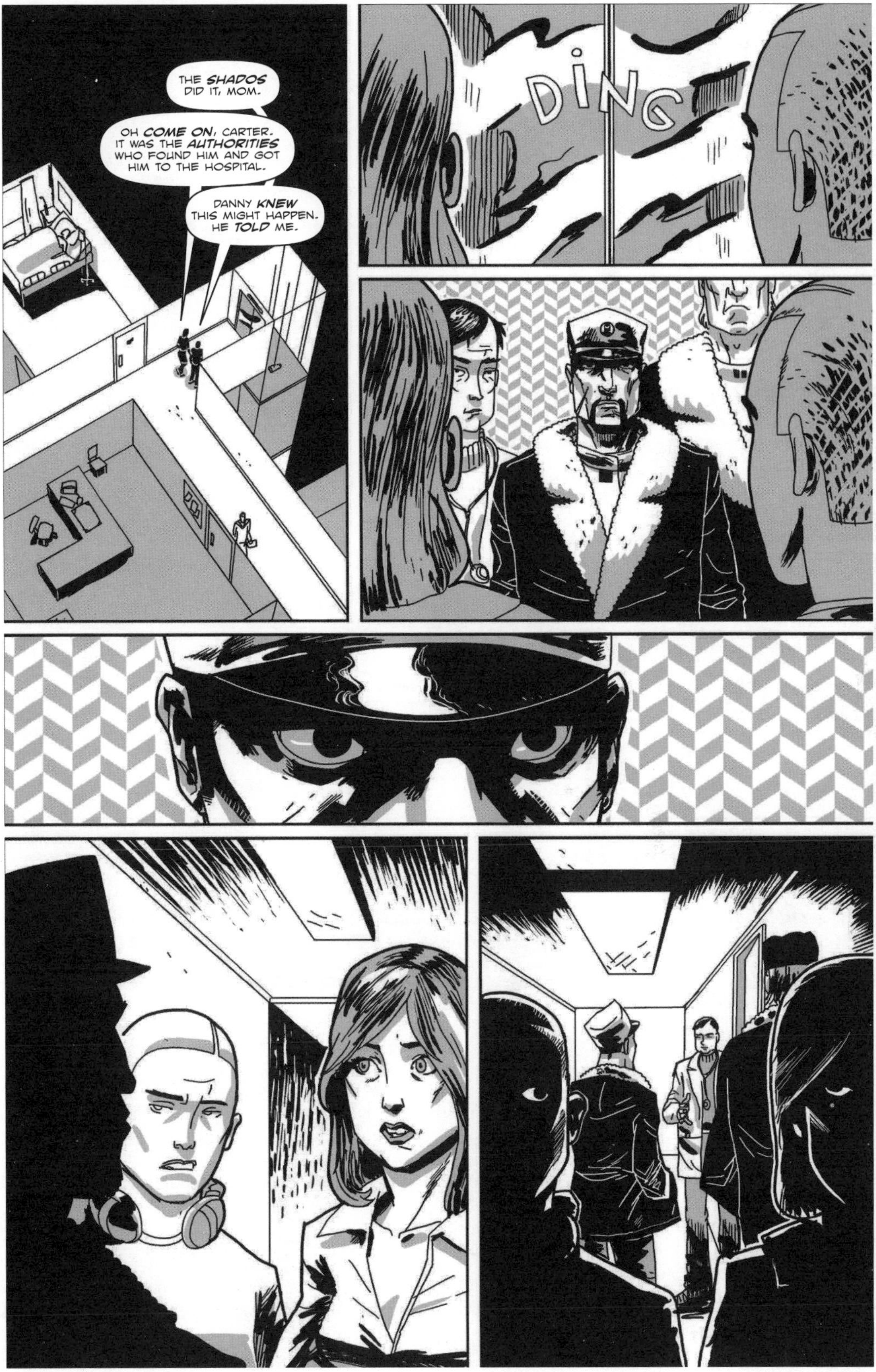
THE SHADOS DID IT, MOM.
OH COME ON, CARTER. IT WAS THE AUTHORITIES WHO FOUND HIM AND GOT HIM TO THE HOSPITAL.
DANNY KNEW THIS MIGHT HAPPEN. HE TOLD ME.
DING

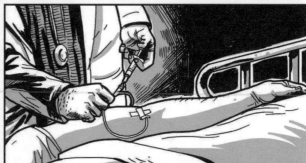

BEEP   BEEP   BEEEEEEEEEEEEEEEEEEEEEEEEEEEEEEEE

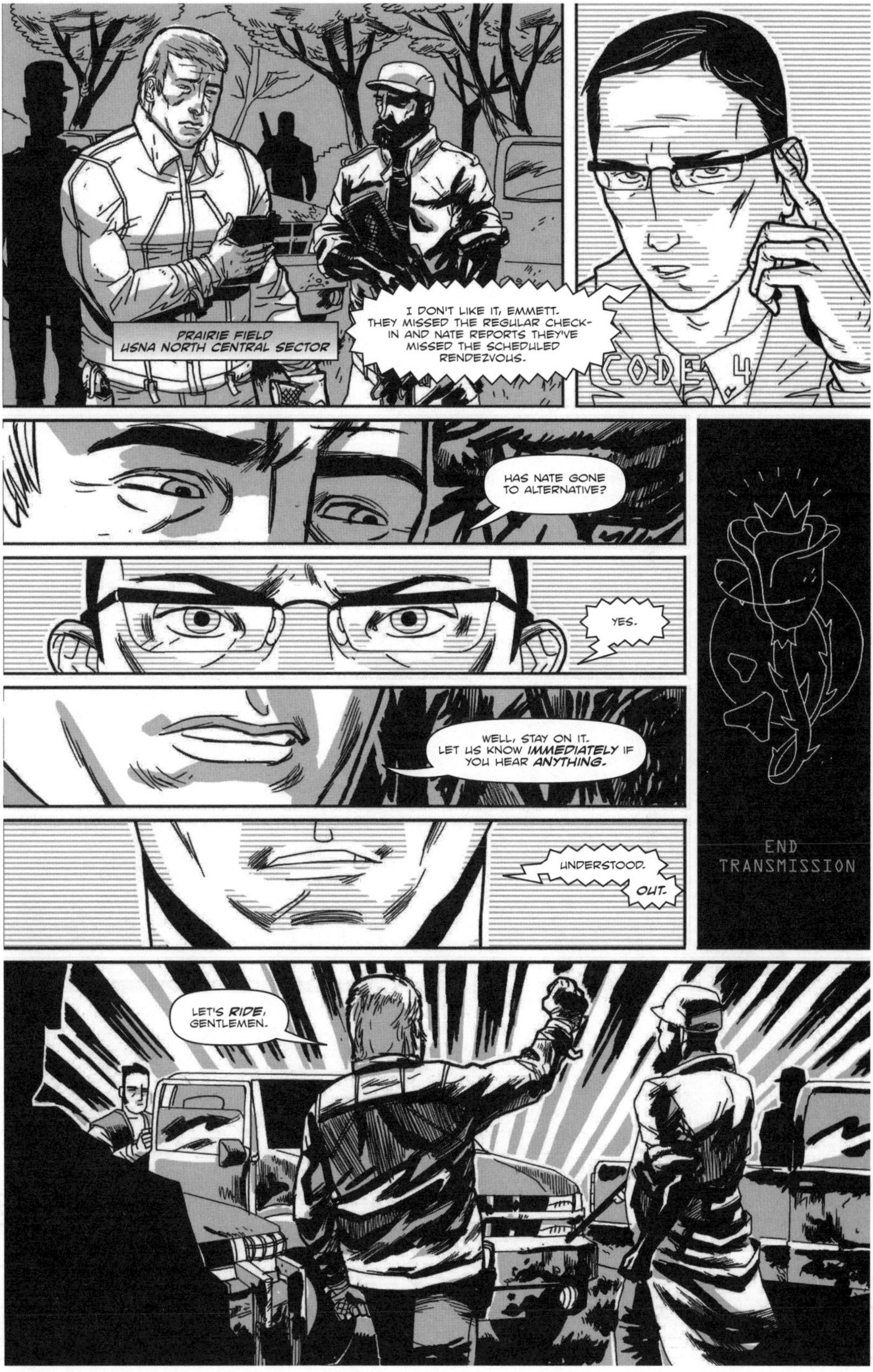

PRAIRIE FIELD
USNA NORTH CENTRAL SECTOR
I DON'T LIKE IT, EMMETT. THEY MISSED THE REGULAR CHECK-IN AND NATE REPORTS THEY'VE MISSED THE SCHEDULED RENDEZVOUS.
CODE 4
HAS NATE GONE TO ALTERNATIVE?
YES.
WELL, STAY ON IT. LET US KNOW IMMEDIATELY IF YOU HEAR ANYTHING.
UNDERSTOOD.
OUT.
END TRANSMISSION
LET'S RIDE, GENTLEMEN.

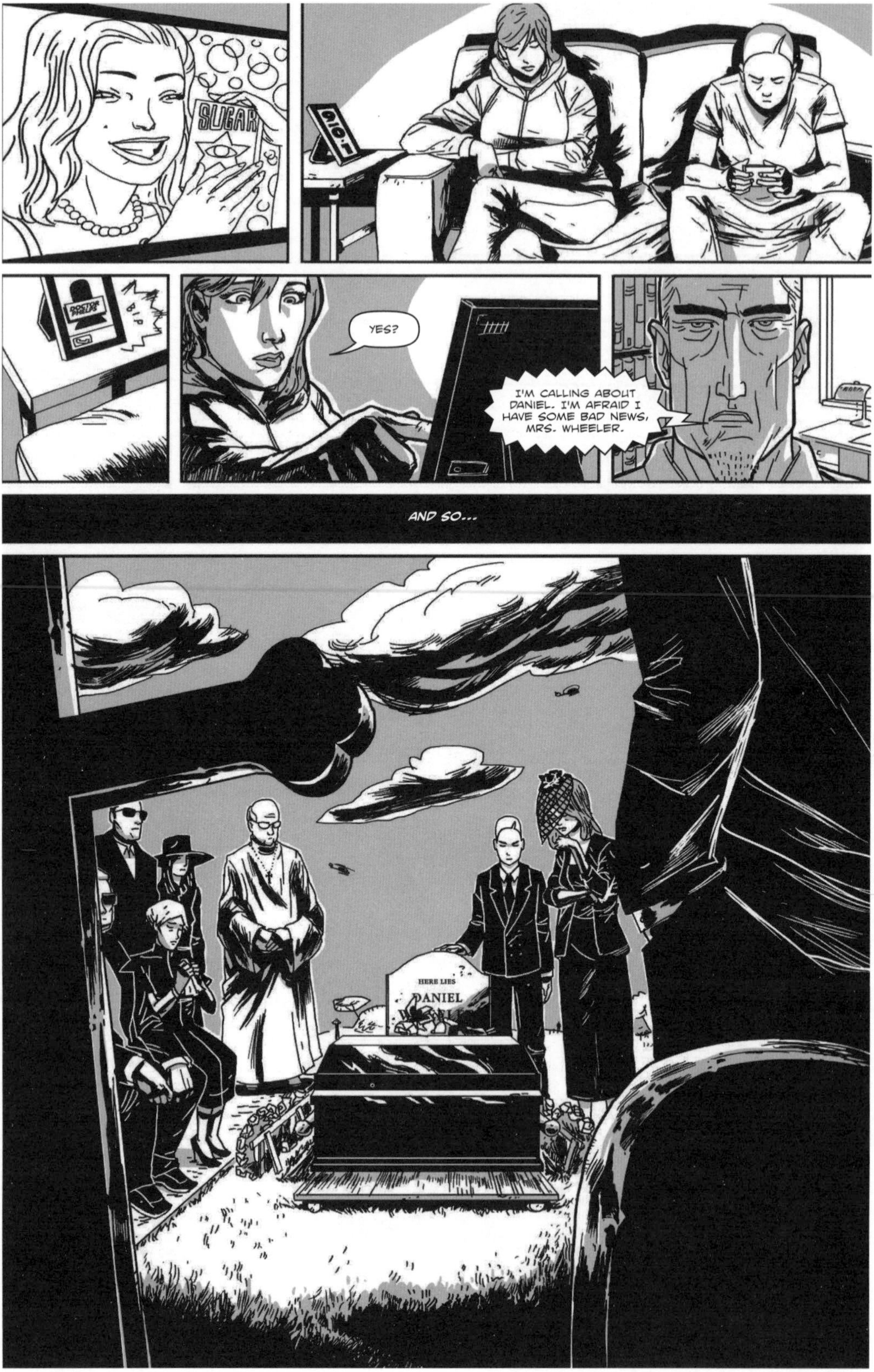
SUGAR
DOCTOR PHELPS
BIP
YES?
I'M CALLING ABOUT DANIEL. I'M AFRAID I HAVE SOME BAD NEWS, MRS. WHEELER.
AND SO...
HERE LIES
DANIEL

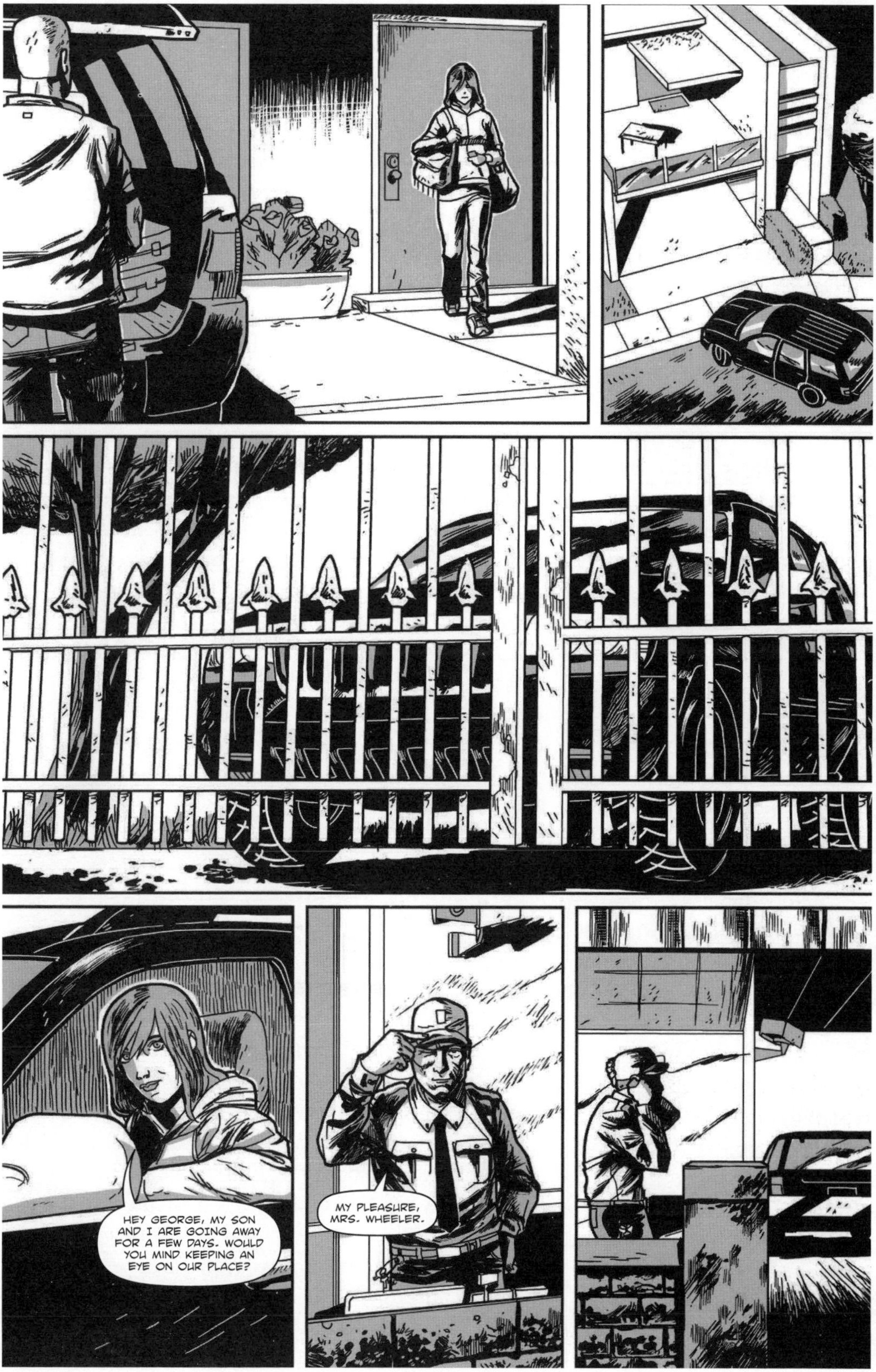
HEY GEORGE, MY SON AND I ARE GOING AWAY FOR A FEW DAYS. WOULD YOU MIND KEEPING AN EYE ON OUR PLACE?
MY PLEASURE, MRS. WHEELER.

Five Faces of the USNA

by Melissa Branigan - Staff Reporter

Every month, New Chronicle reporter Melissa Branigan presents her continuing series about the people of our new country.

Dr. Cameron Swanson drives his new all electric Cadillac Special Edition along the recently completed CS505 freeway which connects Chicago to the Eastern Seaboard. He punches his destination into his onboard computer, sets the autodrive parameters and lets go of the wheel. Electronic sensors embedded in the highway guide his vehicle safely to the outskirts of Philadelphia where he will disconnect from the grid and manually guide himself into the heart of the city. Dr. Swanson is the director of the combined Penn State and University of the Prairies team that designed the system. "By combining the talents of these universities with the financial clout of UADE (Universal Advanced Design Engineering), we were able to bring this project in under budget and months before the contracted completion date. We're very proud of what can by done without the hindrance of government controls and protections," states Dr. Swanson. This project is just one example of the advanced technology now being implemented throughout the USNA, a direct result of the amalgamation agreement.

Ben Fernie lifts a crate of apples onto the back of his aging pickup and heads from the inner city of Detroit to the Ambassador Bridge where he crosses over the Detroit River to Windsor. In the past, he would have had to undergo a thorough inspection of his vehicle and the agricultural products. Today, it's a quick trip to the growing metropolis of Windsor. A resident of Detroit, Fernie is now a farmer working his land on the site of USNA's largest urban farming community. First begun in 2010, after the recession of 2008 devastated the city's automobile industry, the shift from industrial to agriculture was accelerated with the amalgamation, as the vast markets of Southern Ontario became easily accessible without elaborate border and security protocols.

Ann Fellows is 46 years old, suffering from tuberculosis and living on the arid downtown streets of Los Angeles. Devastated by the crumbling California economy and the earthquakes that rocked the region, the downtown core has been deserted as people fled inland and north to safer locales. Many people, like Ann Fellows, were left behind. One of the most controversial elements of the amalgamation was the adoption of the old United States social model which emphasized individual responsibility for life's basics. This ran counter to the more socialist model of the former Dominion of Canada which preached the necessity of the social safety net. With the increasing population of urban homeless, there is a rising call for more government response to the growing crisis.

William Sanovich is a reluctant farmer. It's hot, backbreaking work for little pay and he's one of thousands working the industrial prison farms of the mid-west sector. The prison farm is a concept embraced by the ruling council of the USNA and reviled by those opposed to what they deem exploitation of labour. Deputy Secretary Hans Vellman oversees the prison farm network and believes the work is both healthy and necessary in rehabilitating the prisoners. "What would you have us do?" he asks. "Have them break rocks with sledge hammers and chisels? This system benefits the prisoner by teaching them useful skills and reconnecting them with the land. The consumer benefits by literally gaining the fruits of their labour. This system helps keep costs down." Sanovich disagrees. He sees little benefit in learning to pick, wash and pack lettuce, spinach and tomatoes. "Twelve hour days of kneeling in the dirt under the hot sun is about as far away from agricultural education and rehabilitation as you can get," he says. "We're slave labour for AAS (Advanced Agricultural Systems Inc.). They are the ones who benefit. Seen their stock prices lately? They ain't hurting."

Janet Michaels used to live in Denver. She now lives in Yellowknife, a city that has grown fourfold since the amalgamation. The melting ice cap and increased activity in the north has created job opportunities that didn't exist a decade ago. After a bitter divorce, Janet wanted to get as far away from her ex-husband as possible and a job in Yellowknife has proven the correct tonic to heal her emotional wounds. Trained in systems analysis and control, she heads a group coordinating the movement of goods and people north to the new mines that have opened in the past five years.
"Sure, it gets cold during the winter but it lasts half as long as it did 10 years ago and the summers are warmer than ever before." Janet is thankful she could move from Colorado to the Alaskan sector without the old travel and immigration restrictions. "It's really a free country,' she enthusiastically proclaims. "Without the amalgamation, none of this would have been possible for me."

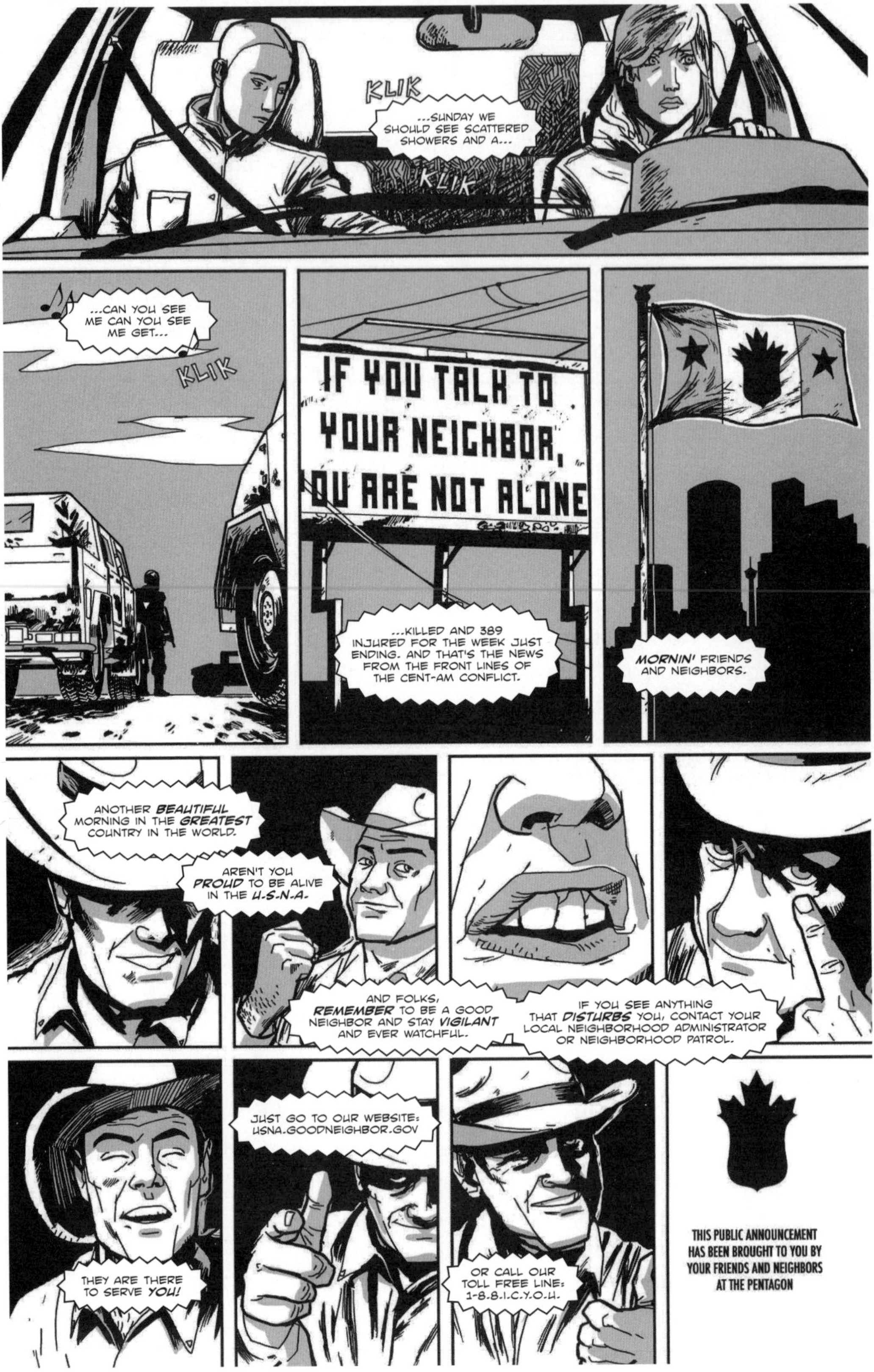
KLIK
...SUNDAY WE SHOULD SEE SCATTERED SHOWERS AND A...
KLIK
...CAN YOU SEE ME CAN YOU SEE ME GET...
KLIK
IF YOU TALK TO YOUR NEIGHBOR, YOU ARE NOT ALONE
...KILLED AND 389 INJURED FOR THE WEEK JUST ENDING. AND THAT'S THE NEWS FROM THE FRONT LINES OF THE CENT-AM CONFLICT.
MORNIN' FRIENDS AND NEIGHBORS.
ANOTHER BEAUTIFUL MORNING IN THE GREATEST COUNTRY IN THE WORLD.
AREN'T YOU PROUD TO BE ALIVE IN THE U.S.N.A.
AND FOLKS, REMEMBER TO BE A GOOD NEIGHBOR AND STAY VIGILANT AND EVER WATCHFUL.
IF YOU SEE ANYTHING THAT DISTURBS YOU, CONTACT YOUR LOCAL NEIGHBORHOOD ADMINISTRATOR OR NEIGHBORHOOD PATROL.
THEY ARE THERE TO SERVE YOU!
JUST GO TO OUR WEBSITE: USNA.GOODNEIGHBOR.GOV
OR CALL OUR TOLL FREE LINE: 1-8.8.I.C.Y.O.U.
THIS PUBLIC ANNOUNCEMENT HAS BEEN BROUGHT TO YOU BY YOUR FRIENDS AND NEIGHBORS AT THE PENTAGON

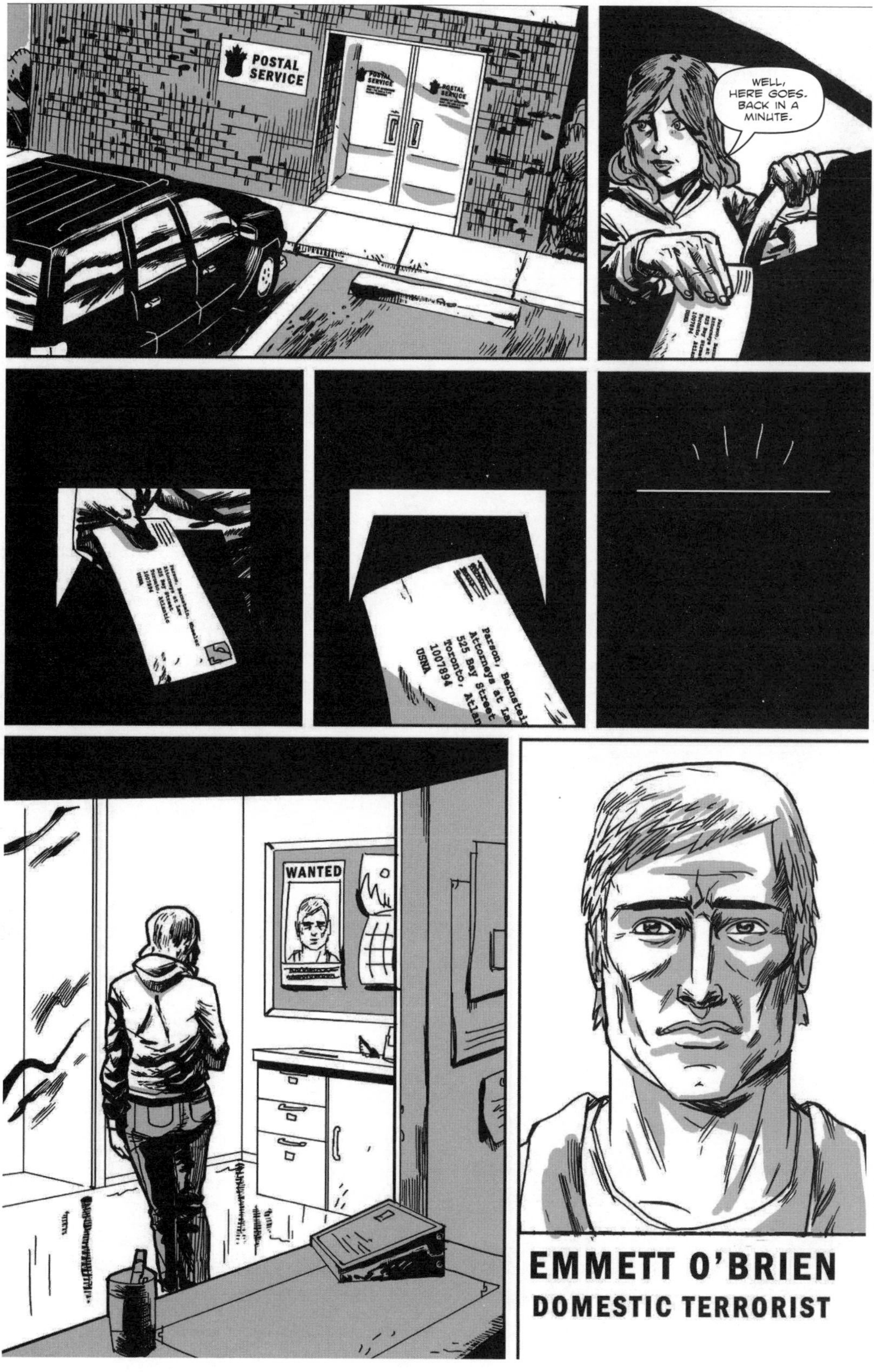
POSTAL SERVICE
WELL, HERE GOES. BACK IN A MINUTE.
525 Bay Street
1007894
USNA
WANTED
EMMETT O'BRIEN
DOMESTIC TERRORIST

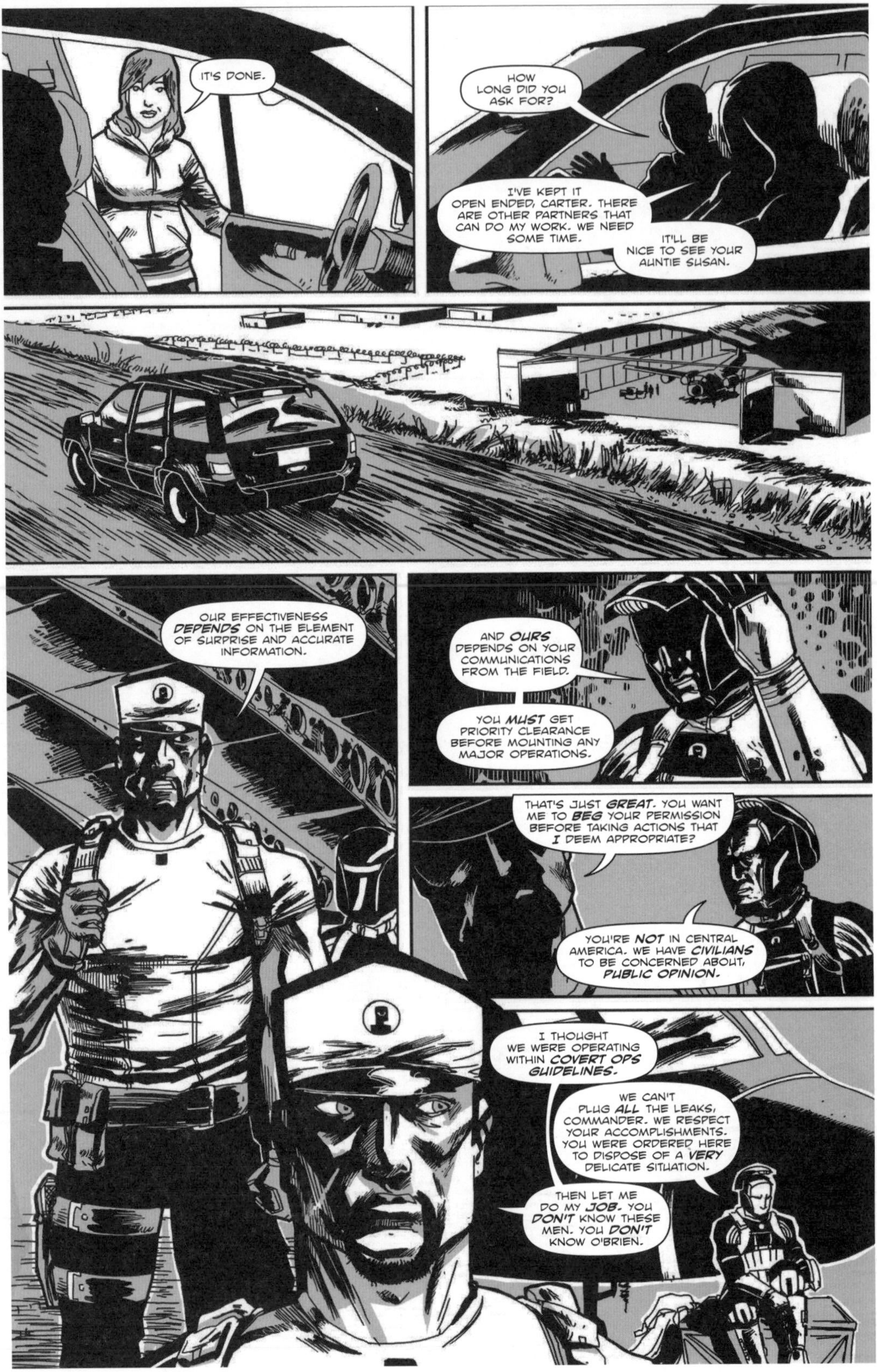
IT'S DONE.
HOW LONG DID YOU ASK FOR?
I'VE KEPT IT OPEN ENDED, CARTER. THERE ARE OTHER PARTNERS THAT CAN DO MY WORK. WE NEED SOME TIME.
IT'LL BE NICE TO SEE YOUR AUNTIE SUSAN.
OUR EFFECTIVENESS DEPENDS ON THE ELEMENT OF SURPRISE AND ACCURATE INFORMATION.
AND OURS DEPENDS ON YOUR COMMUNICATIONS FROM THE FIELD.
YOU MUST GET PRIORITY CLEARANCE BEFORE MOUNTING ANY MAJOR OPERATIONS.
THAT'S JUST GREAT. YOU WANT ME TO BEG YOUR PERMISSION BEFORE TAKING ACTIONS THAT I DEEM APPROPRIATE?
YOU'RE NOT IN CENTRAL AMERICA. WE HAVE CIVILIANS TO BE CONCERNED ABOUT, PUBLIC OPINION.
I THOUGHT WE WERE OPERATING WITHIN COVERT OPS GUIDELINES.
WE CAN'T PLUG ALL THE LEAKS, COMMANDER. WE RESPECT YOUR ACCOMPLISHMENTS. YOU WERE ORDERED HERE TO DISPOSE OF A VERY DELICATE SITUATION.
THEN LET ME DO MY JOB. YOU DON'T KNOW THESE MEN. YOU DON'T KNOW O'BRIEN.

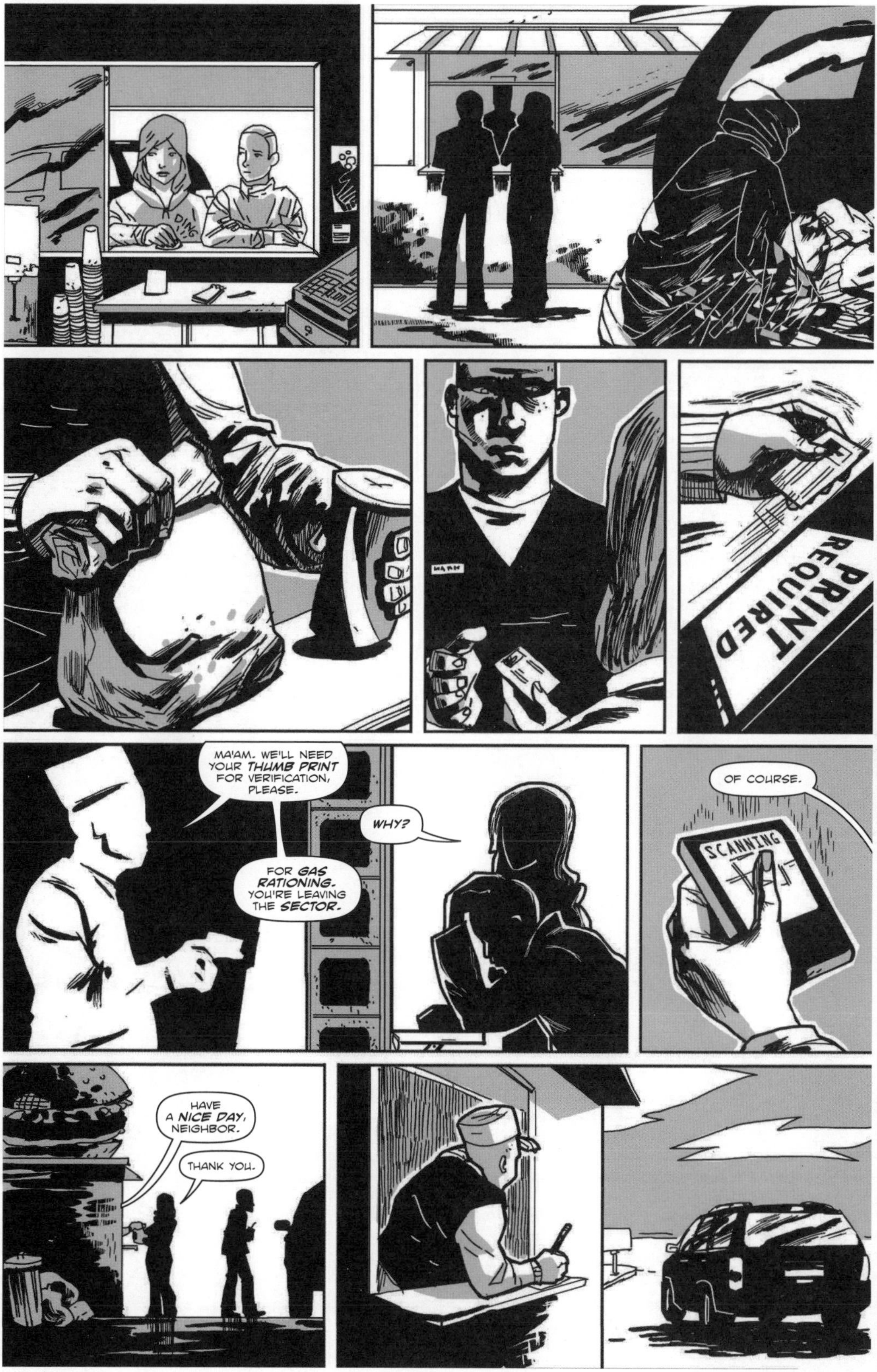
DING
PRINT REQUIRED
MA'AM. WE'LL NEED YOUR THUMB PRINT FOR VERIFICATION, PLEASE.
WHY?
FOR GAS RATIONING. YOU'RE LEAVING THE SECTOR.
OF COURSE.
SCANNING
HAVE A NICE DAY, NEIGHBOR.
THANK YOU.

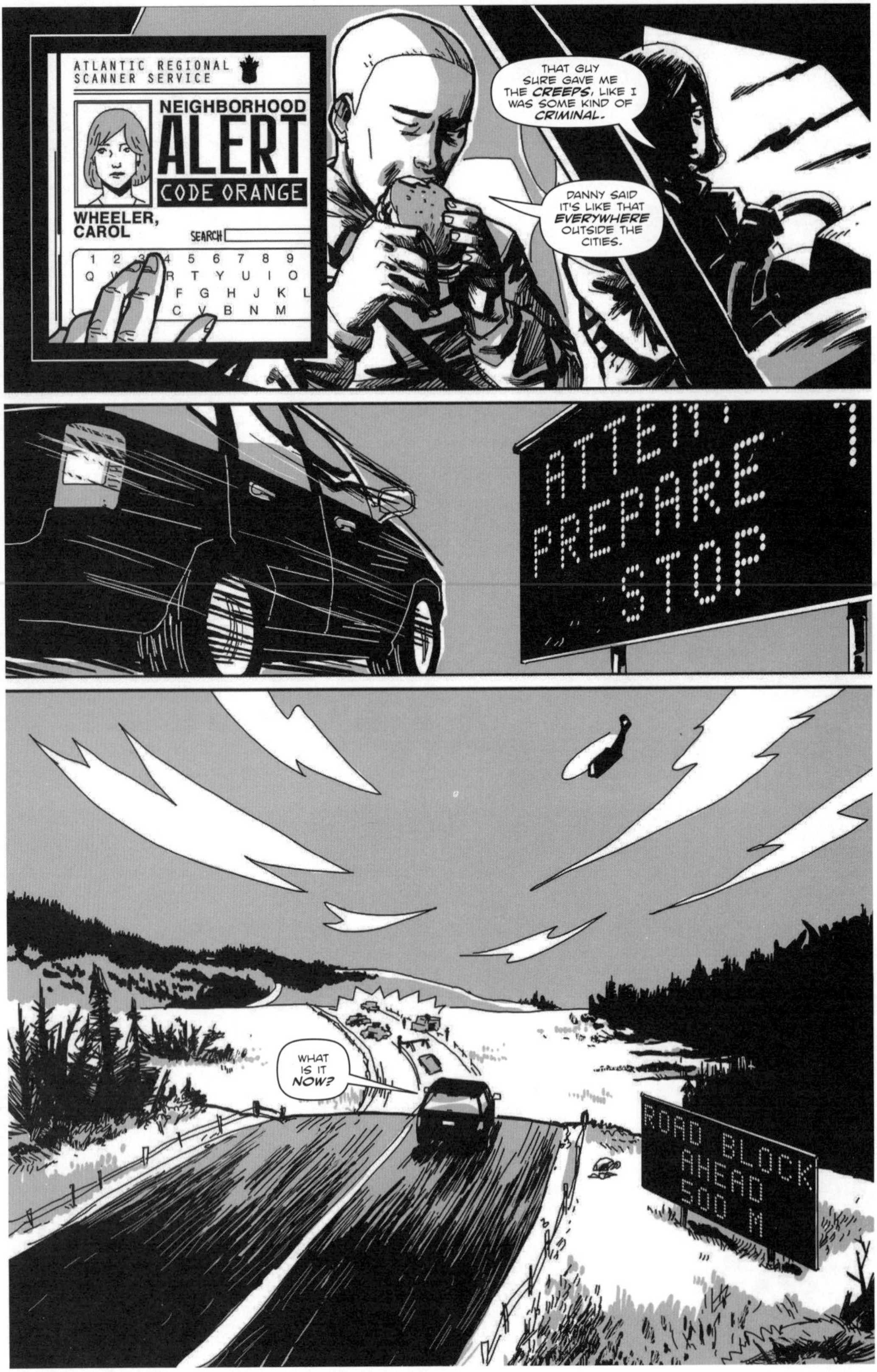
ATLANTIC REGIONAL SCANNER SERVICE
NEIGHBORHOOD ALERT
CODE ORANGE
WHEELER, CAROL
SEARCH
THAT GUY SURE GAVE ME THE CREEPS, LIKE I WAS SOME KIND OF CRIMINAL.
DANNY SAID IT'S LIKE THAT EVERYWHERE OUTSIDE THE CITIES.
PREPARE
STOP
WHAT IS IT NOW?
ROAD BLOCK AHEAD 500 M

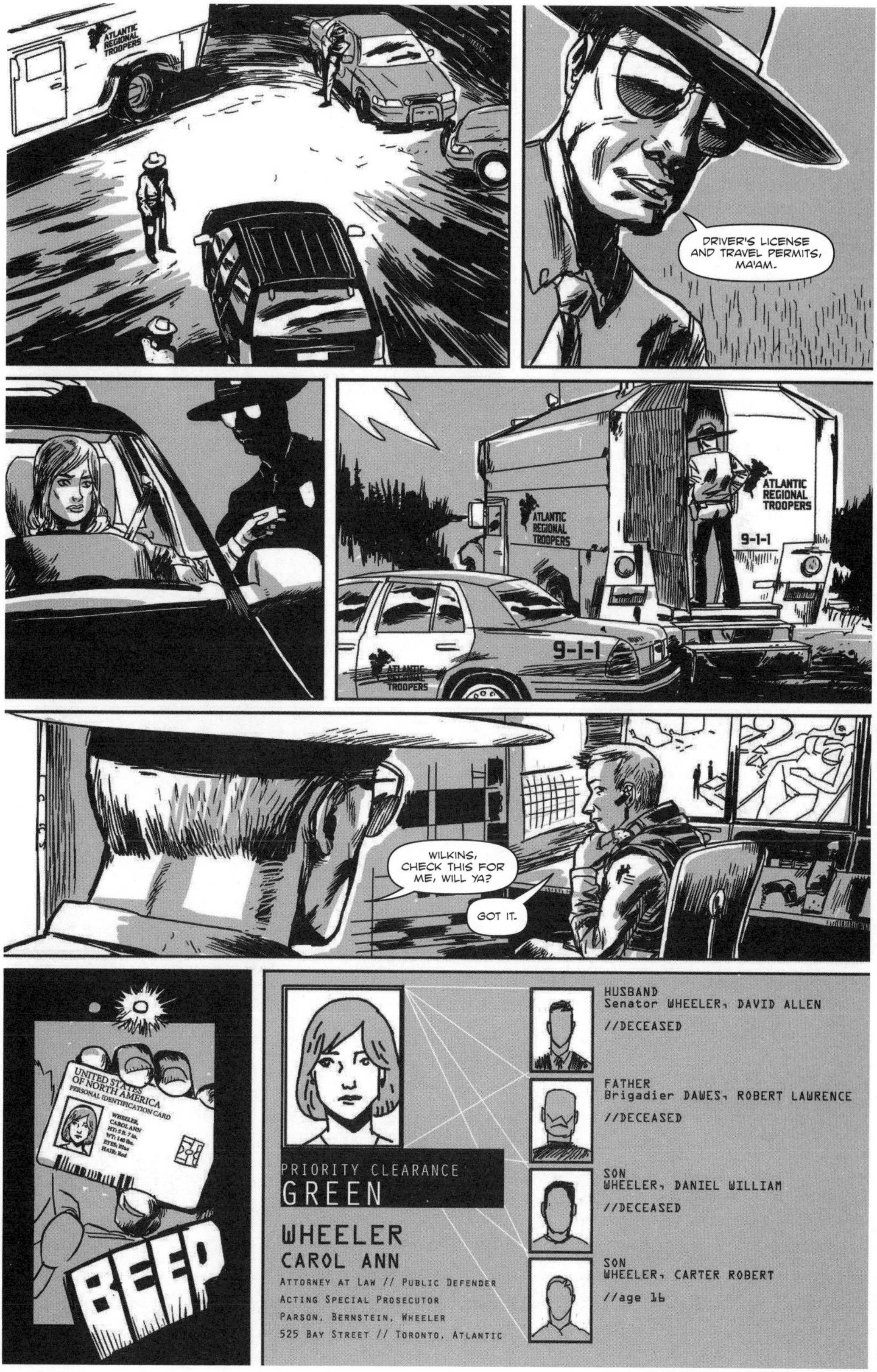
ATLANTIC REGIONAL TROOPERS
DRIVER'S LICENSE AND TRAVEL PERMITS, MA'AM.
ATLANTIC REGIONAL TROOPERS
9-1-1
ATLANTIC REGIONAL TROOPERS
9-1-1
ATLANTIC REGIONAL TROOPERS
WILKINS, CHECK THIS FOR ME, WILL YA?
GOT IT.
UNITED STATES OF NORTH AMERICA
PERSONAL IDENTIFICATION CARD
BEEP
PRIORITY CLEARANCE
GREEN
WHEELER
CAROL ANN
ATTORNEY AT LAW // PUBLIC DEFENDER
ACTING SPECIAL PROSECUTOR
PARSON, BERNSTEIN, WHEELER
525 BAY STREET // TORONTO, ATLANTIC
HUSBAND
Senator WHEELER, DAVID ALLEN
//DECEASED
FATHER
Brigadier DAWES, ROBERT LAWRENCE
//DECEASED
SON
WHEELER, DANIEL WILLIAM
//DECEASED
SON
WHEELER, CARTER ROBERT
//age 16

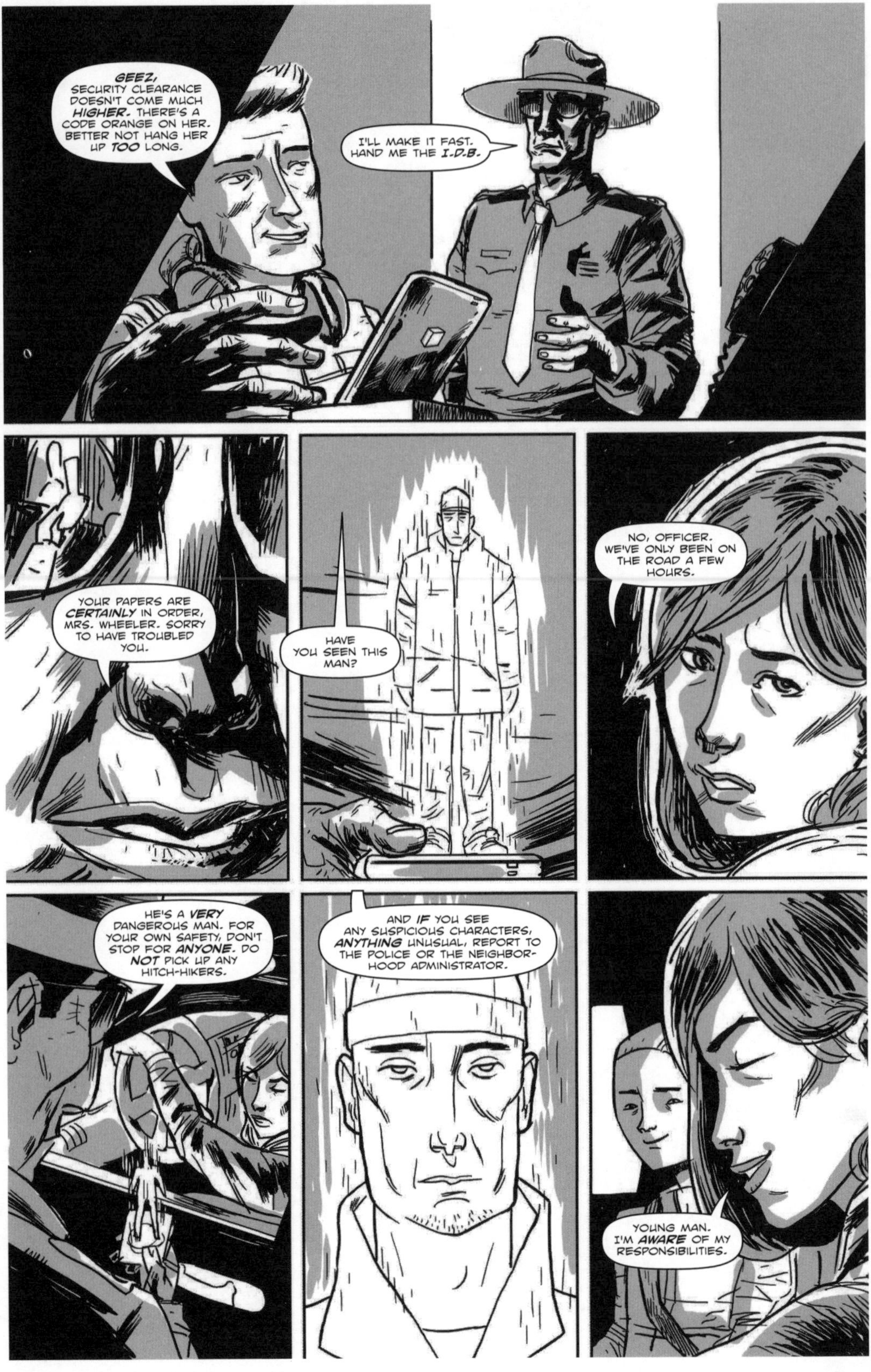
GEEZ, SECURITY CLEARANCE DOESN'T COME MUCH HIGHER. THERE'S A CODE ORANGE ON HER. BETTER NOT HANG HER UP TOO LONG.
I'LL MAKE IT FAST. HAND ME THE I.D.B.
YOUR PAPERS ARE CERTAINLY IN ORDER, MRS. WHEELER. SORRY TO HAVE TROUBLED YOU.
HAVE YOU SEEN THIS MAN?
NO, OFFICER. WE'VE ONLY BEEN ON THE ROAD A FEW HOURS.
HE'S A VERY DANGEROUS MAN. FOR YOUR OWN SAFETY, DON'T STOP FOR ANYONE. DO NOT PICK UP ANY HITCH-HIKERS.
AND IF YOU SEE ANY SUSPICIOUS CHARACTERS, ANYTHING UNUSUAL, REPORT TO THE POLICE OR THE NEIGHBOR-HOOD ADMINISTRATOR.
YOUNG MAN. I'M AWARE OF MY RESPONSIBILITIES.

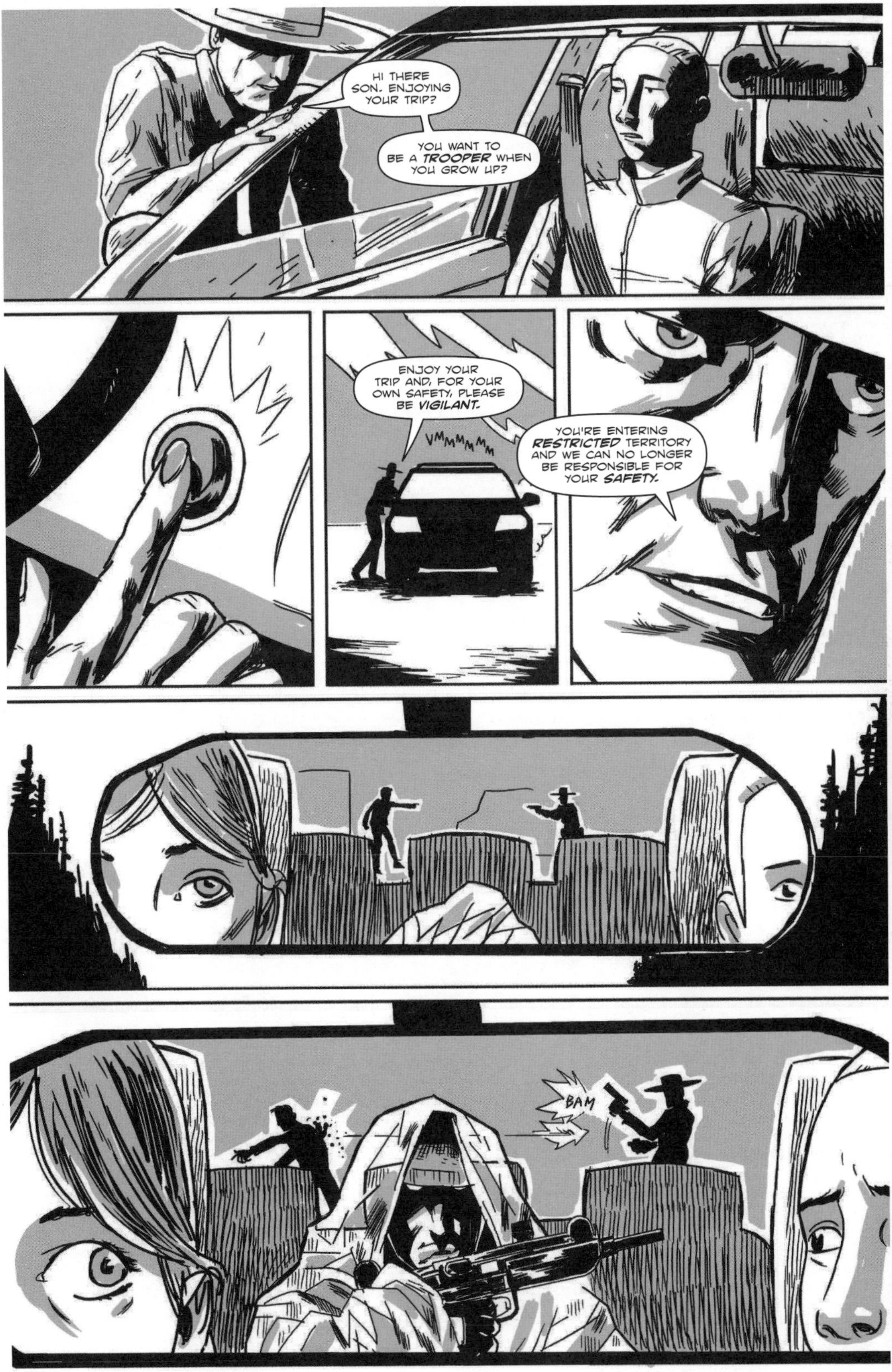
HI THERE SON. ENJOYING YOUR TRIP?
YOU WANT TO BE A TROOPER WHEN YOU GROW UP?
ENJOY YOUR TRIP AND, FOR YOUR OWN SAFETY, PLEASE BE VIGILANT.
VMMMMMM
YOU'RE ENTERING RESTRICTED TERRITORY AND WE CAN NO LONGER BE RESPONSIBLE FOR YOUR SAFETY.
BAM

From: Captain John Stanton-Mills
            Strategic Home Alliance Defense Organization
            Pentagon - Correspondence Analysis Division

To: Commander M. Conrad
            Shado Counter Insurgency Team
            Central Regional Headquarters - Calgary

Re: Analysis of Recently Intercepted eMail Between Carol Wheeler
            and Susan Parks (sister) of Calgary North Central Sector - USNA

Commander Conrad: Please find below a recently intercepted eMail from subject
Carol Wheeler sent to her sister Susan Parks of Calgary, NCS. My analysis
follows.

From: Carol Wheeler <carolwheeler@usnaserve.com>
Subject: Re: We're on the Way
Date: May 12, 2025 5:26:28 PM EST
To: Susan Parks <susanpk@usnaserve.com>

Hi Susan,

        Just wanted you to know that we're finally on our way. We're planning
to take our time. Heck, what's the hurry. We should be rolling into Calgary in
about 10 days. Carter hasn't been anywhere outside of Toronto for over 10 years
now so he's pretty excited. I must say, it is hard to travel, having just buried
Daniel. I'm taking an extended leave of absence from the firm so we'll hang
around the ranch as long as you can stand us. :)

        I gotta tell you, this country sure has changed. I never realized how
little they actually told us about life outside of Toronto. The highways are
deserted. It's as if everyone is scared to travel. They keep warning us to keep
vigilante, to not pick up strangers (like I would?). But all the checkpoints,
the burnt out cars on the side of the road make you wonder. What other
conclusion can you make but to proclaim that things have really gone downhill?
Oh well, I guess you have to hit bottom before it improves.

        I'm sorry I haven't told you much about Danny. I guess you never know
how difficult dealing with these kind of situations are until sometime after,
when you have a chance to just sit quietly and think. It's been very, very hard
for me. And so very strange. The last time I saw him, he was in a coma. All
I know is that they found Danny naked, in a park, in North York township. The
doctor said he'd been electrocuted, subjected to electric shock. The doctor was
either completely ignorant or hiding something. When I finally got to see Danny
in the hospital, he was in a bed, under covers. I didn't have a chance to look
for any wounds or marks on his body and, quite frankly, it was the last thing
on my mind. I guess, in retrospect, it would have been a good idea, if just for
peace of mind. But when you think about it, the only way someone could get an
electrical jolt would be to be tasered. But it makes no sense? He was camping
with his buds. He's a good kid, never in trouble and never looking for trouble.
It just breaks my heart.

        I contacted some of my political connections, government insiders,
friends of David's. And I asked my law partner, Allan Goodman, to try to find
out anything about the incident, the circumstances behind his injuries. All I
got was denials and apologies. You'd think my husband's best friends would be a
little more helpful. Danny was his son, after all. These days, you never know
who to trust or what to believe.

        What's happened to this country, the people, my family? It just makes
you want to try to change things, get your hands dirty.

        I look forward to seeing you and Jack and the kids. Carter and I really
need the break. I know that mountain air will help clear our heads, maybe find a
way to get centered. Are you still doing yoga? I'm thinking of getting back into
yoga and meditation. It might be helpful.

        See you soon, sis.

        Love, Carol

Analysis:

      Subject is presently traveling via car to visit her sister in Calgary.
This has been confirmed by checkpoints outside the Toronto region. Subject is
traveling west towards the Central Sector. She is accompanied by her son,
Carter, aged 16. She is presently vulnerable to detention for taking her son out
of school during term, however she is a high profile citizen, and the publicity
of such an act would be counter-productive to our goals.

      Her questions about her son Daniel Wheeler's activities and the nature
of his death are disturbing. Suffice to say her inquiries drew the inevitable
blanks but she is known to be persistent. Once she's had a chance to grieve the
loss of her son, she may become more diligent in her pursuit of the truth. She
is apparently still ignorant of his involvement in the rebel movement. Have the
records on Daniel Wheeler's death been properly sealed?

      As subject has questioned the cause of death and queried the story
of the electro-shock, we must also insure that all hospital records have been
properly sealed. Carol Wheeler's statements about the state of the highway
system, the lack of travelers and the checkpoints all point to a level of
discontent that could flourish. Coupled with the recent loss of her son and her
history of powerful political association vis a vis her husband's association
with Samuel Stern's cabinet, she becomes a person of interest to us. Her
emotional state makes her vulnerable to political sway and her statement about
wanting to make change, getting her hands dirty bears scrutiny. I recommend
that SHADO Command place her on the priority watch list with copies of all
communications diverted to your office.

                              Captain John Stanton-Mills
                              Strategic Home Alliance Defense Organization
                              Pentagon - Correspondence Analysis Division

----

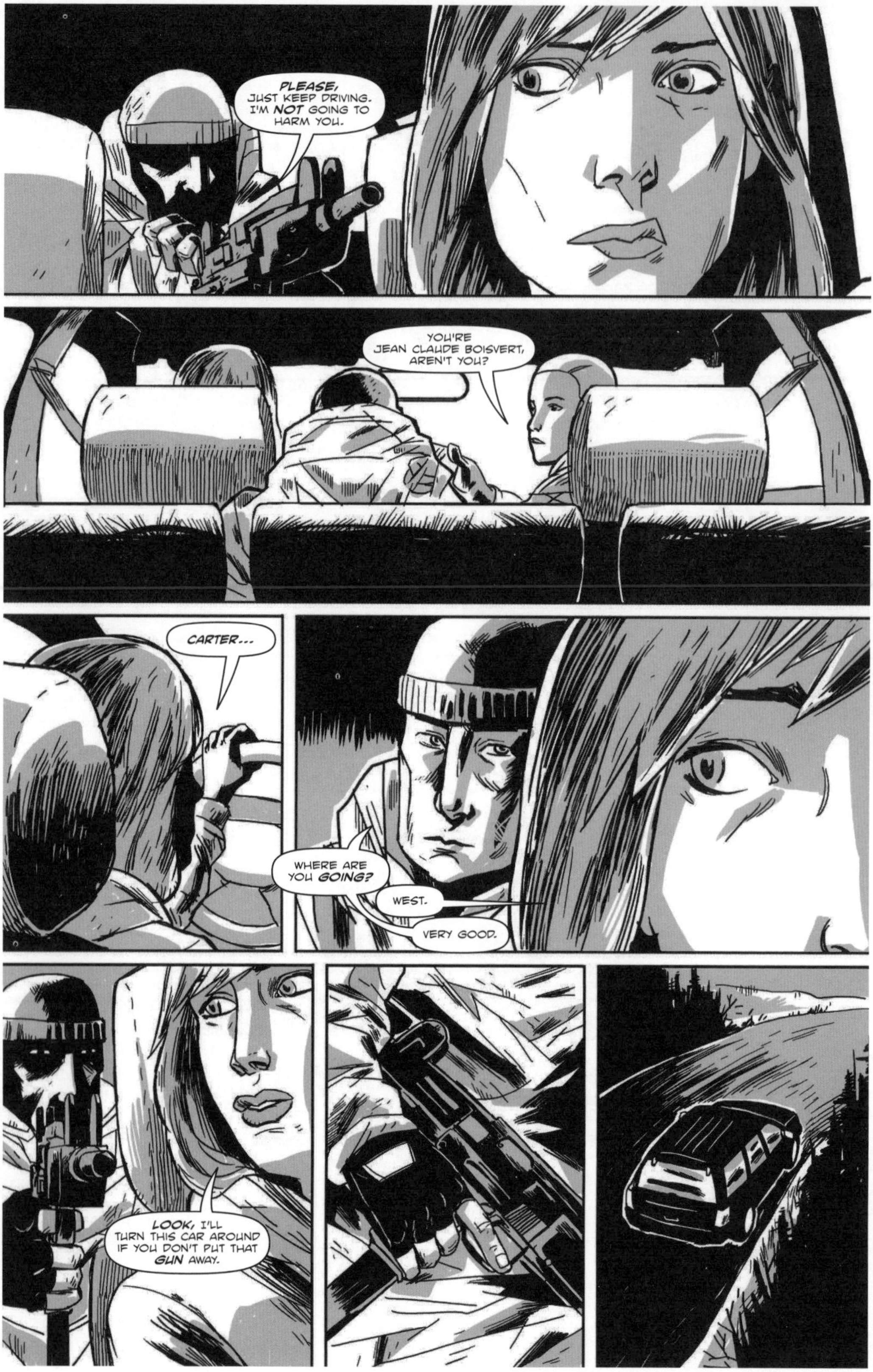
PLEASE, JUST KEEP DRIVING. I'M NOT GOING TO HARM YOU.
YOU'RE JEAN CLAUDE BOISVERT, AREN'T YOU?
CARTER...
WHERE ARE YOU GOING?
WEST.
VERY GOOD.
LOOK, I'LL TURN THIS CAR AROUND IF YOU DON'T PUT THAT GUN AWAY.

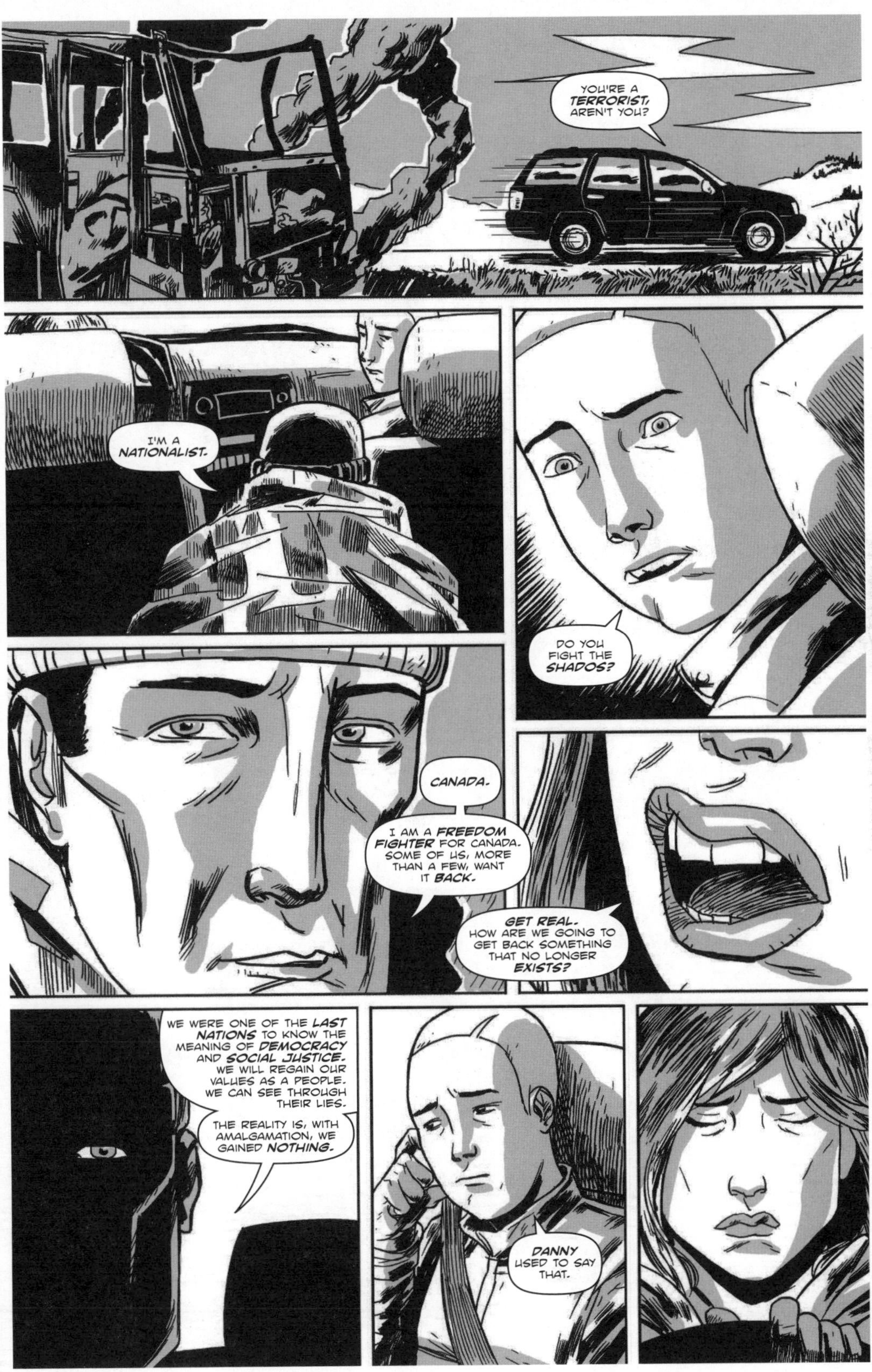
YOU'RE A TERRORIST, AREN'T YOU?
I'M A NATIONALIST.
DO YOU FIGHT THE SHADOS?
CANADA.
I AM A FREEDOM FIGHTER FOR CANADA. SOME OF US, MORE THAN A FEW, WANT IT BACK.
GET REAL. HOW ARE WE GOING TO GET BACK SOMETHING THAT NO LONGER EXISTS?
WE WERE ONE OF THE LAST NATIONS TO KNOW THE MEANING OF DEMOCRACY AND SOCIAL JUSTICE. WE WILL REGAIN OUR VALUES AS A PEOPLE. WE CAN SEE THROUGH THEIR LIES.
THE REALITY IS, WITH AMALGAMATION, WE GAINED NOTHING.
DANNY USED TO SAY THAT.

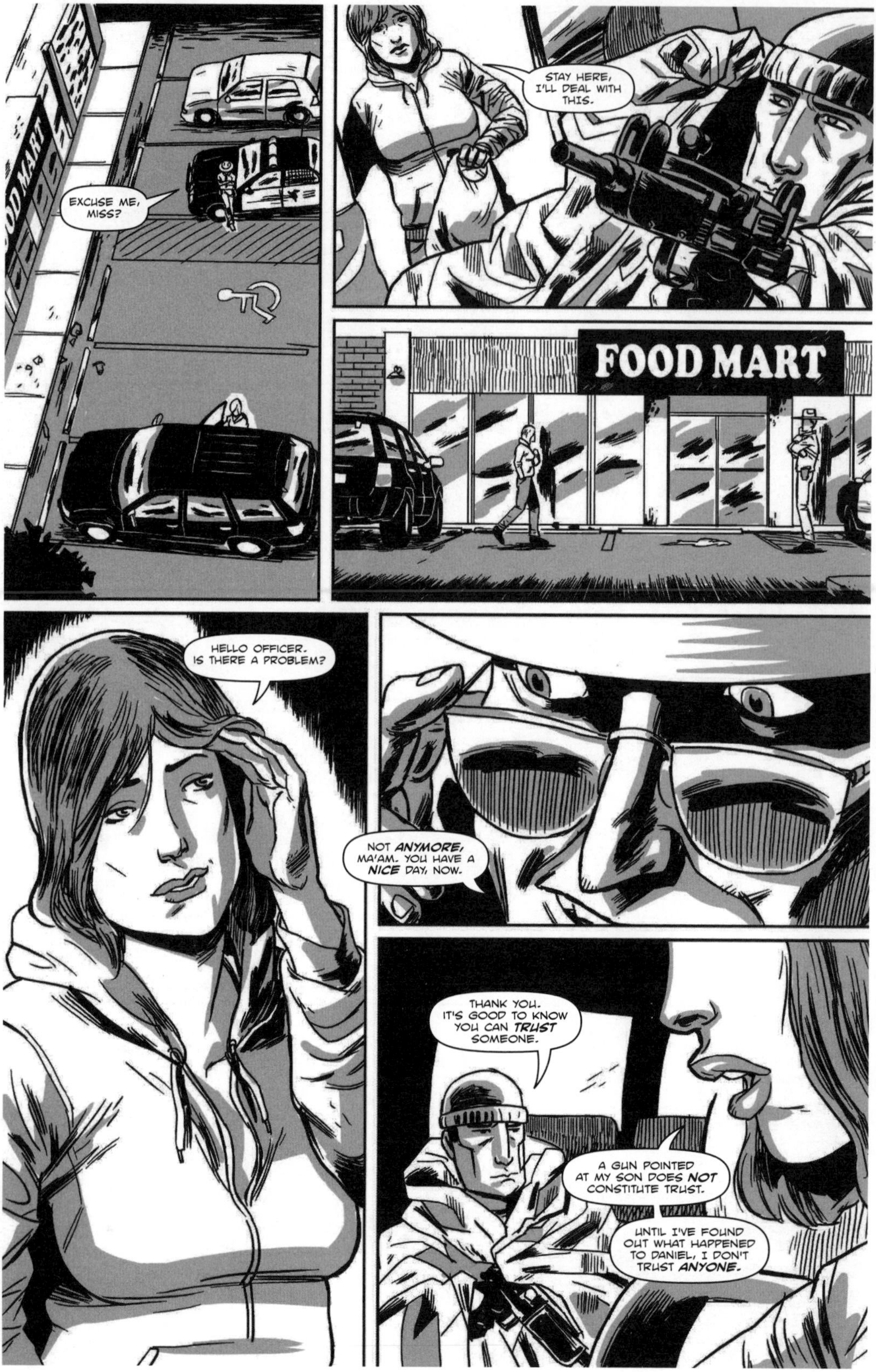
EXCUSE ME, MISS?
STAY HERE, I'LL DEAL WITH THIS.
FOOD MART
FOOD MART
HELLO OFFICER. IS THERE A PROBLEM?
NOT ANYMORE, MA'AM. YOU HAVE A NICE DAY, NOW.
THANK YOU. IT'S GOOD TO KNOW YOU CAN TRUST SOMEONE.
A GUN POINTED AT MY SON DOES NOT CONSTITUTE TRUST.
UNTIL I'VE FOUND OUT WHAT HAPPENED TO DANIEL, I DON'T TRUST ANYONE.

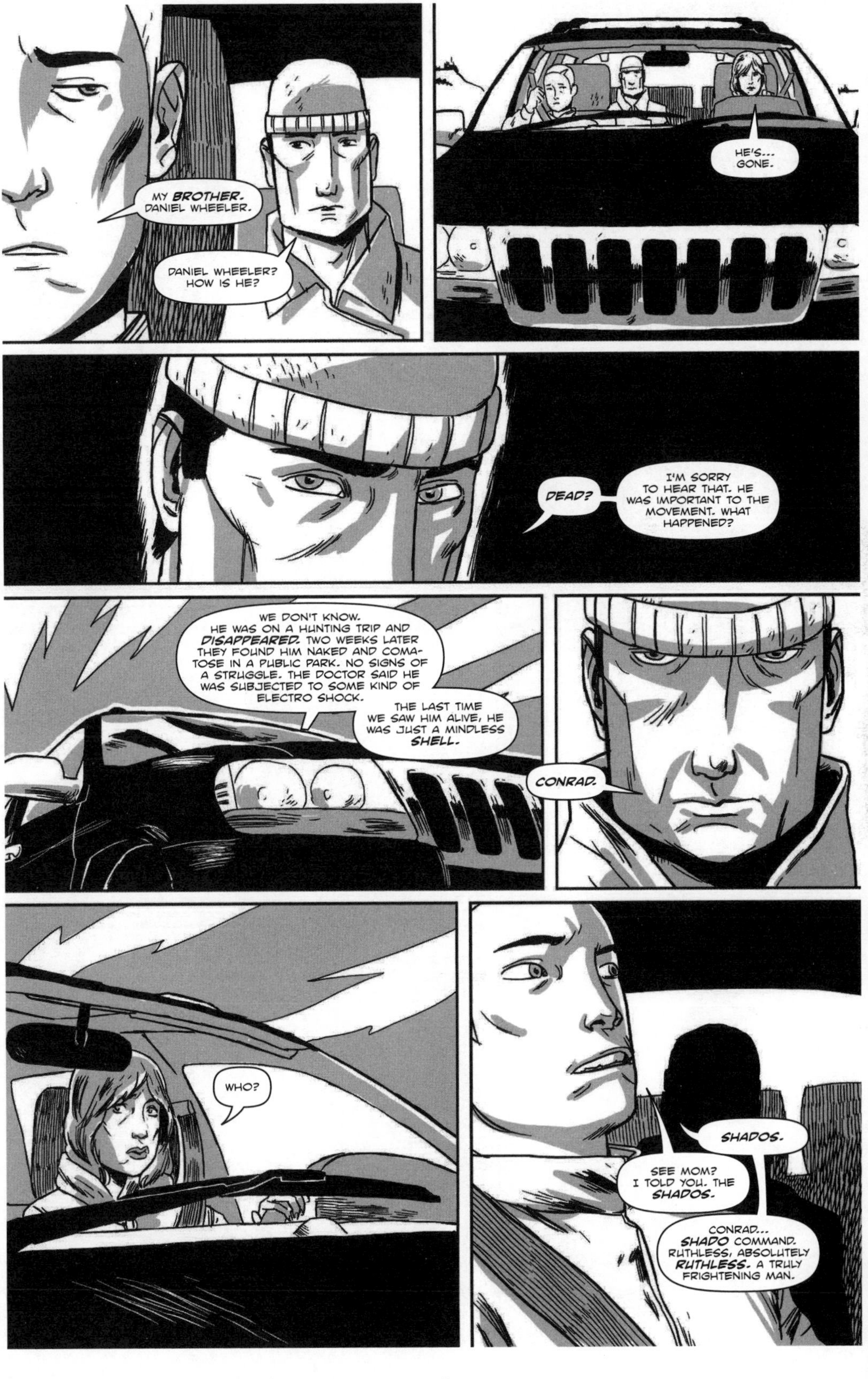
MY BROTHER. DANIEL WHEELER.
DANIEL WHEELER? HOW IS HE?
HE'S... GONE.
DEAD?
I'M SORRY TO HEAR THAT. HE WAS IMPORTANT TO THE MOVEMENT. WHAT HAPPENED?
WE DON'T KNOW. HE WAS ON A HUNTING TRIP AND DISAPPEARED. TWO WEEKS LATER THEY FOUND HIM NAKED AND COMATOSE IN A PUBLIC PARK. NO SIGNS OF A STRUGGLE. THE DOCTOR SAID HE WAS SUBJECTED TO SOME KIND OF ELECTRO SHOCK.
THE LAST TIME WE SAW HIM ALIVE, HE WAS JUST A MINDLESS SHELL.
CONRAD.
WHO?
SHADOS.
SEE MOM? I TOLD YOU. THE SHADOS.
CONRAD... SHADO COMMAND. RUTHLESS, ABSOLUTELY RUTHLESS. A TRULY FRIGHTENING MAN.

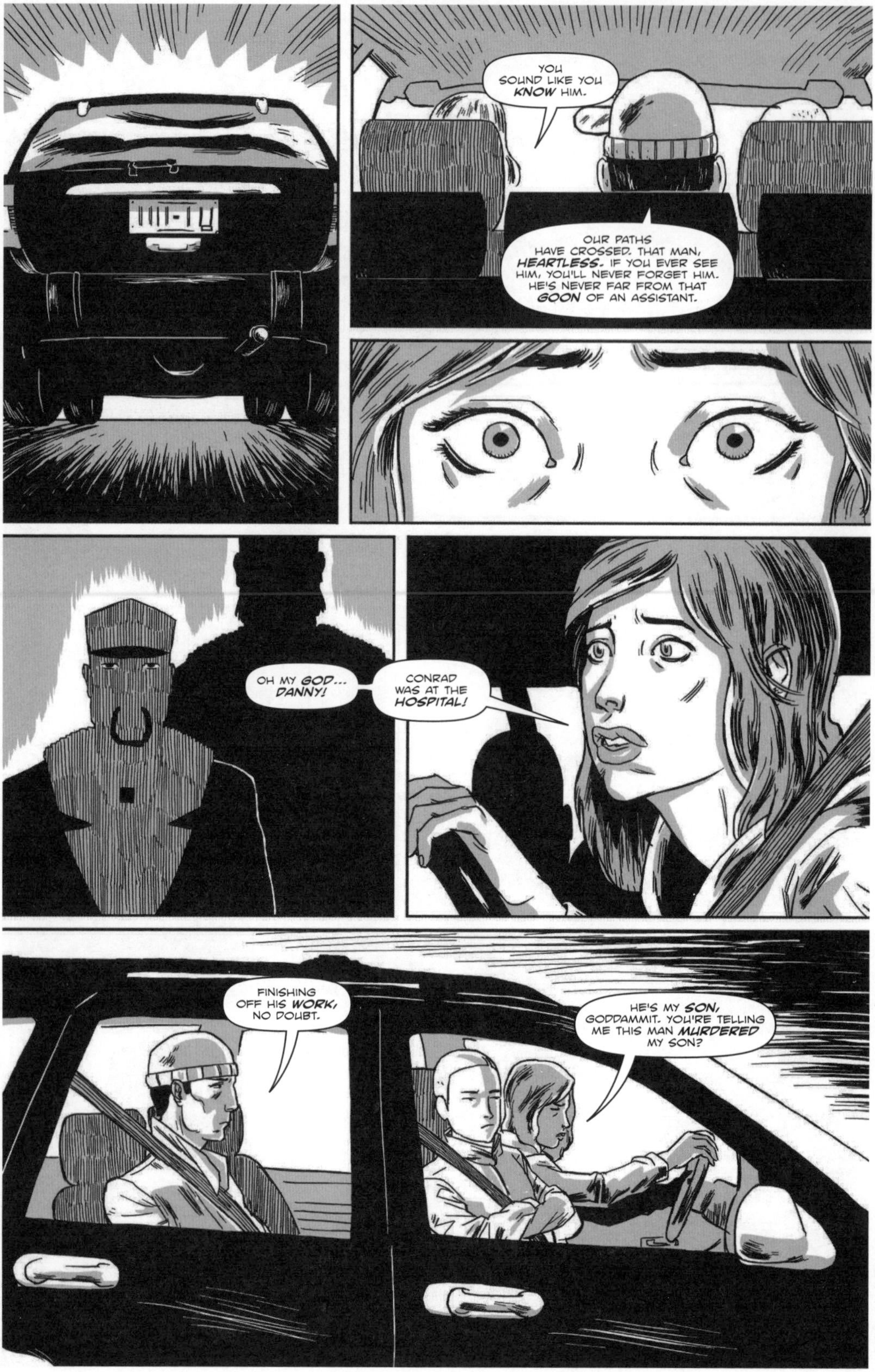
YOU SOUND LIKE YOU KNOW HIM.
OUR PATHS HAVE CROSSED. THAT MAN, HEARTLESS. IF YOU EVER SEE HIM, YOU'LL NEVER FORGET HIM. HE'S NEVER FAR FROM THAT GOON OF AN ASSISTANT.
OH MY GOD... DANNY!
CONRAD WAS AT THE HOSPITAL!
FINISHING OFF HIS WORK, NO DOUBT.
HE'S MY SON, GODDAMMIT. YOU'RE TELLING ME THIS MAN MURDERED MY SON?

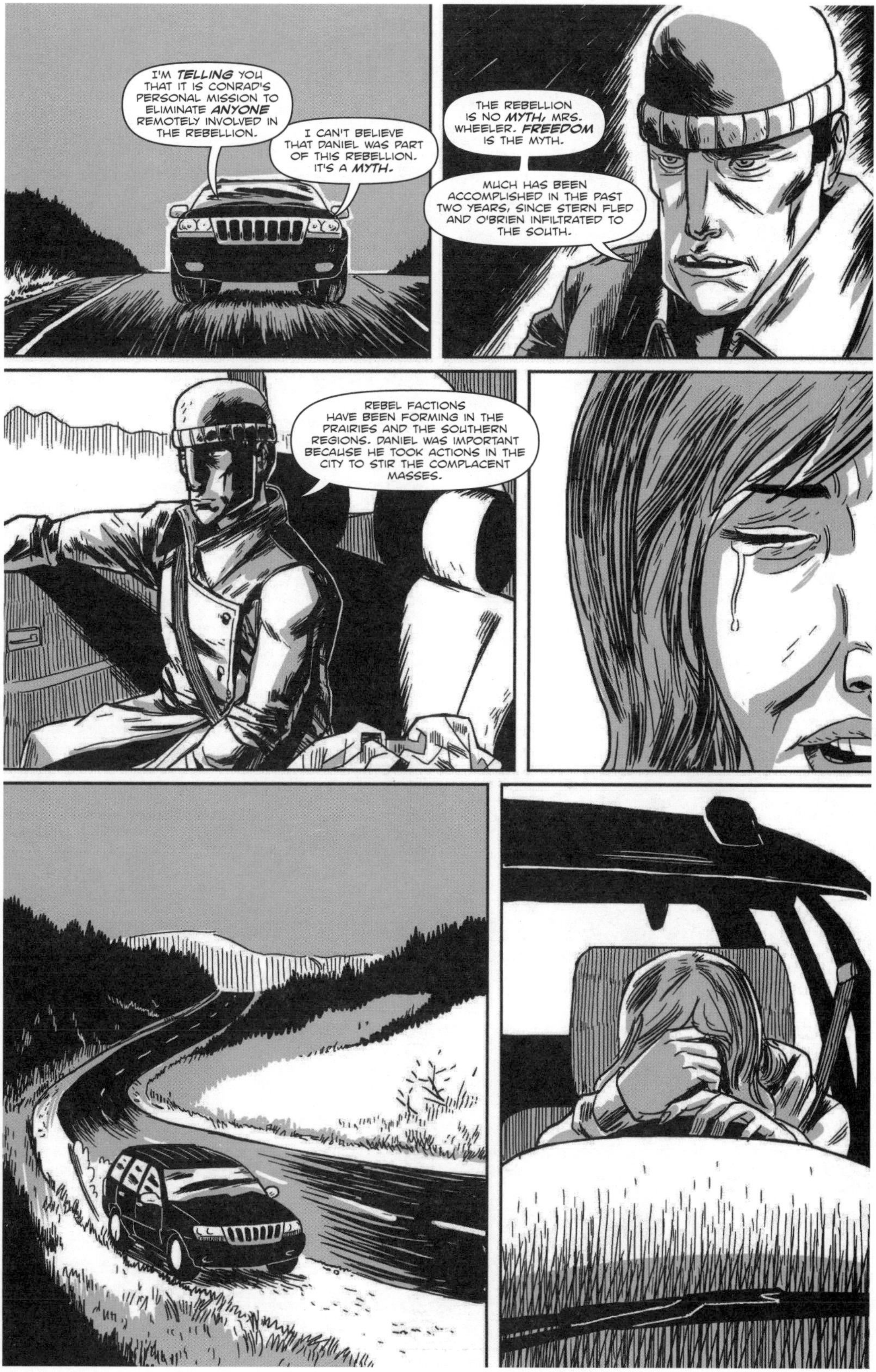
I'M TELLING YOU THAT IT IS CONRAD'S PERSONAL MISSION TO ELIMINATE ANYONE REMOTELY INVOLVED IN THE REBELLION.
I CAN'T BELIEVE THAT DANIEL WAS PART OF THIS REBELLION. IT'S A MYTH.
THE REBELLION IS NO MYTH, MRS. WHEELER. FREEDOM IS THE MYTH.
MUCH HAS BEEN ACCOMPLISHED IN THE PAST TWO YEARS, SINCE STERN FLED AND O'BRIEN INFILTRATED TO THE SOUTH.
REBEL FACTIONS HAVE BEEN FORMING IN THE PRAIRIES AND THE SOUTHERN REGIONS. DANIEL WAS IMPORTANT BECAUSE HE TOOK ACTIONS IN THE CITY TO STIR THE COMPLACENT MASSES.

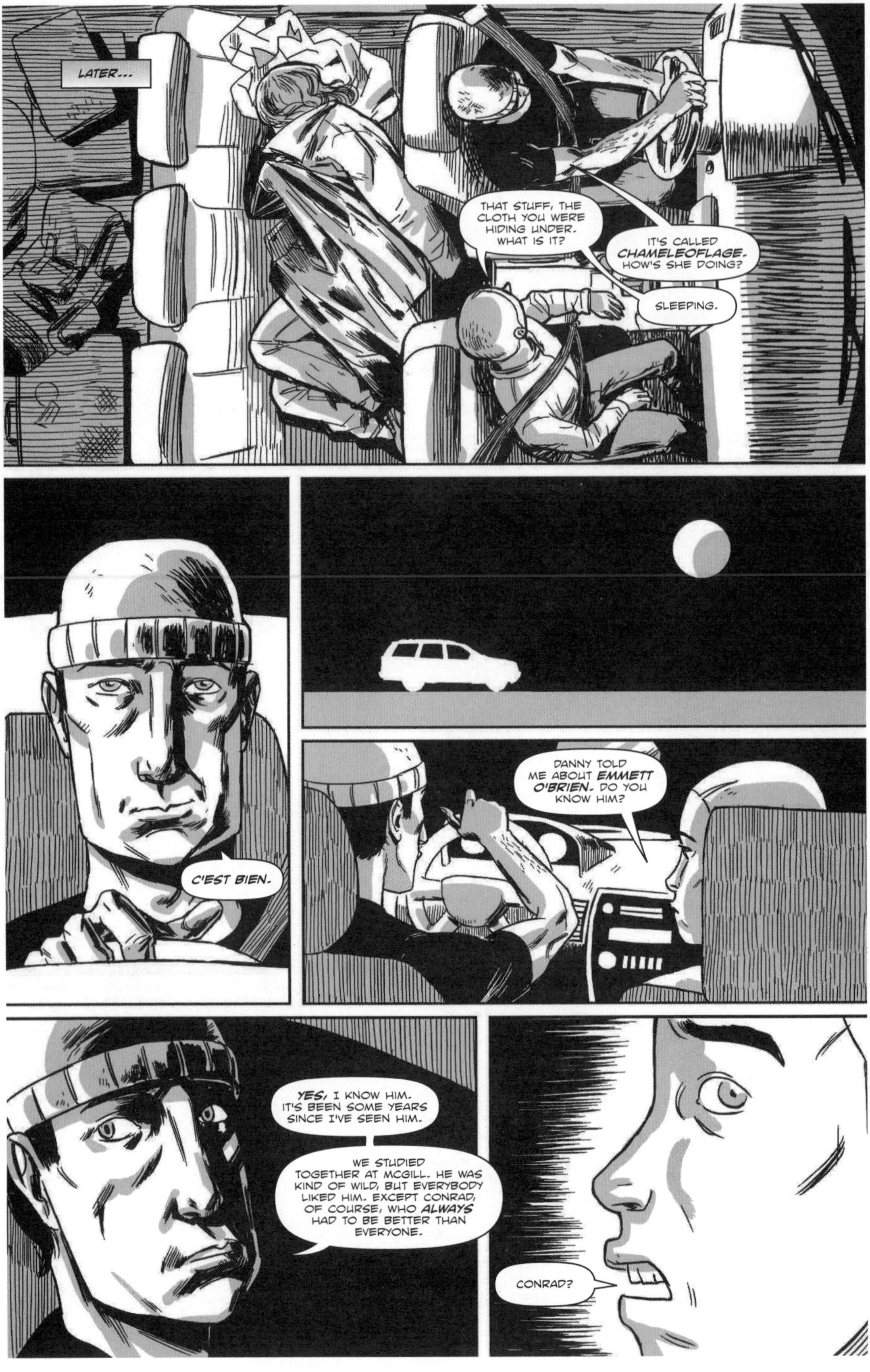
LATER...
THAT STUFF, THE CLOTH YOU WERE HIDING UNDER. WHAT IS IT?
IT'S CALLED CHAMELEOFLAGE. HOW'S SHE DOING?
SLEEPING.
C'EST BIEN.
DANNY TOLD ME ABOUT EMMETT O'BRIEN. DO YOU KNOW HIM?
YES, I KNOW HIM. IT'S BEEN SOME YEARS SINCE I'VE SEEN HIM.
WE STUDIED TOGETHER AT MCGILL. HE WAS KIND OF WILD, BUT EVERYBODY LIKED HIM. EXCEPT CONRAD, OF COURSE, WHO ALWAYS HAD TO BE BETTER THAN EVERYONE.
CONRAD?

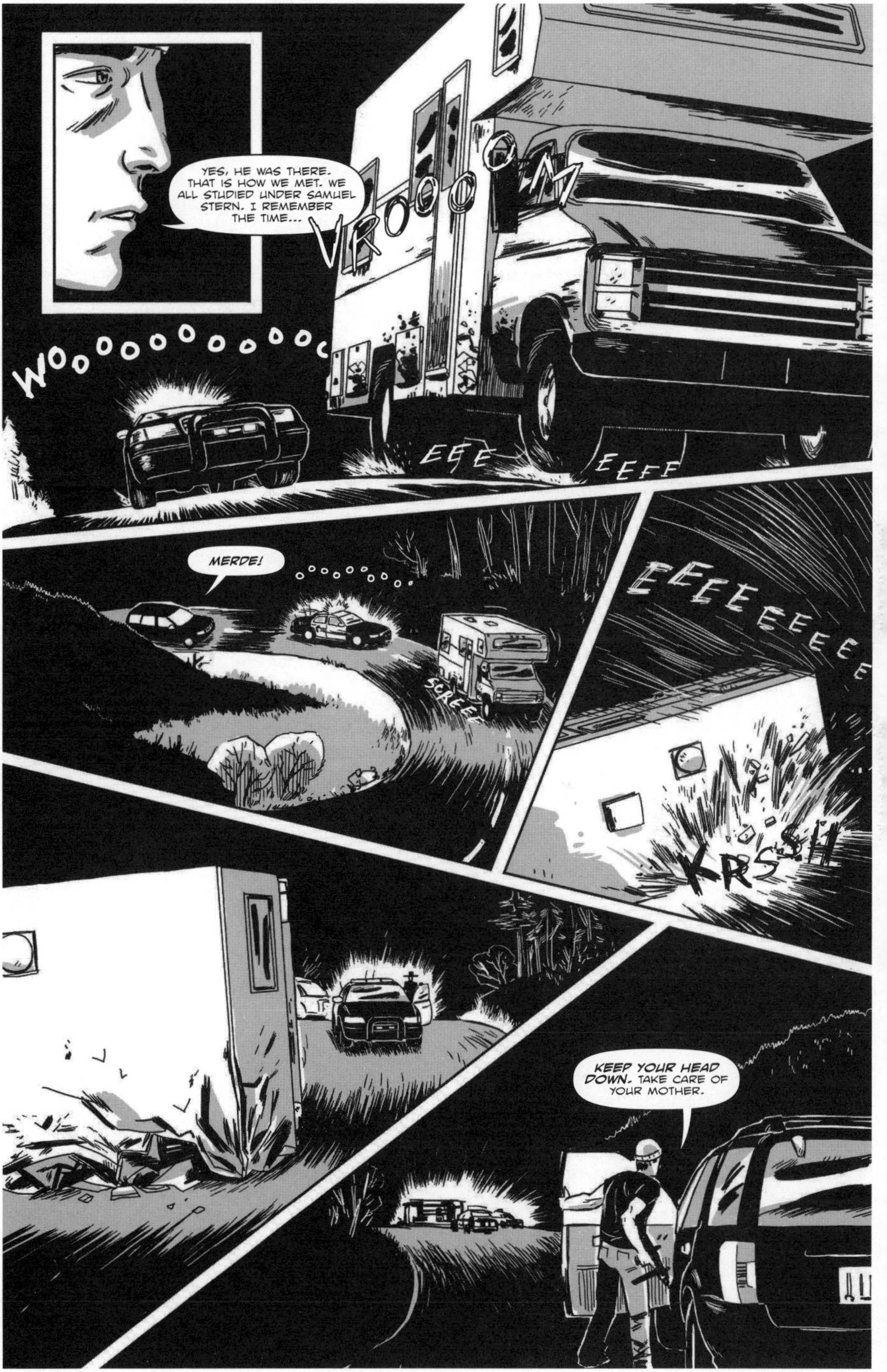
YES, HE WAS THERE. THAT IS HOW WE MET. WE ALL STUDIED UNDER SAMUEL STERN. I REMEMBER THE TIME...
VROOOOM
WOOOOOOOOOOO
EEE
EEFF
MERDE!
OOOOOOOO
SCREEE
EEEEEEEEEEE
KRSSSH
KEEP YOUR HEAD DOWN. TAKE CARE OF YOUR MOTHER.

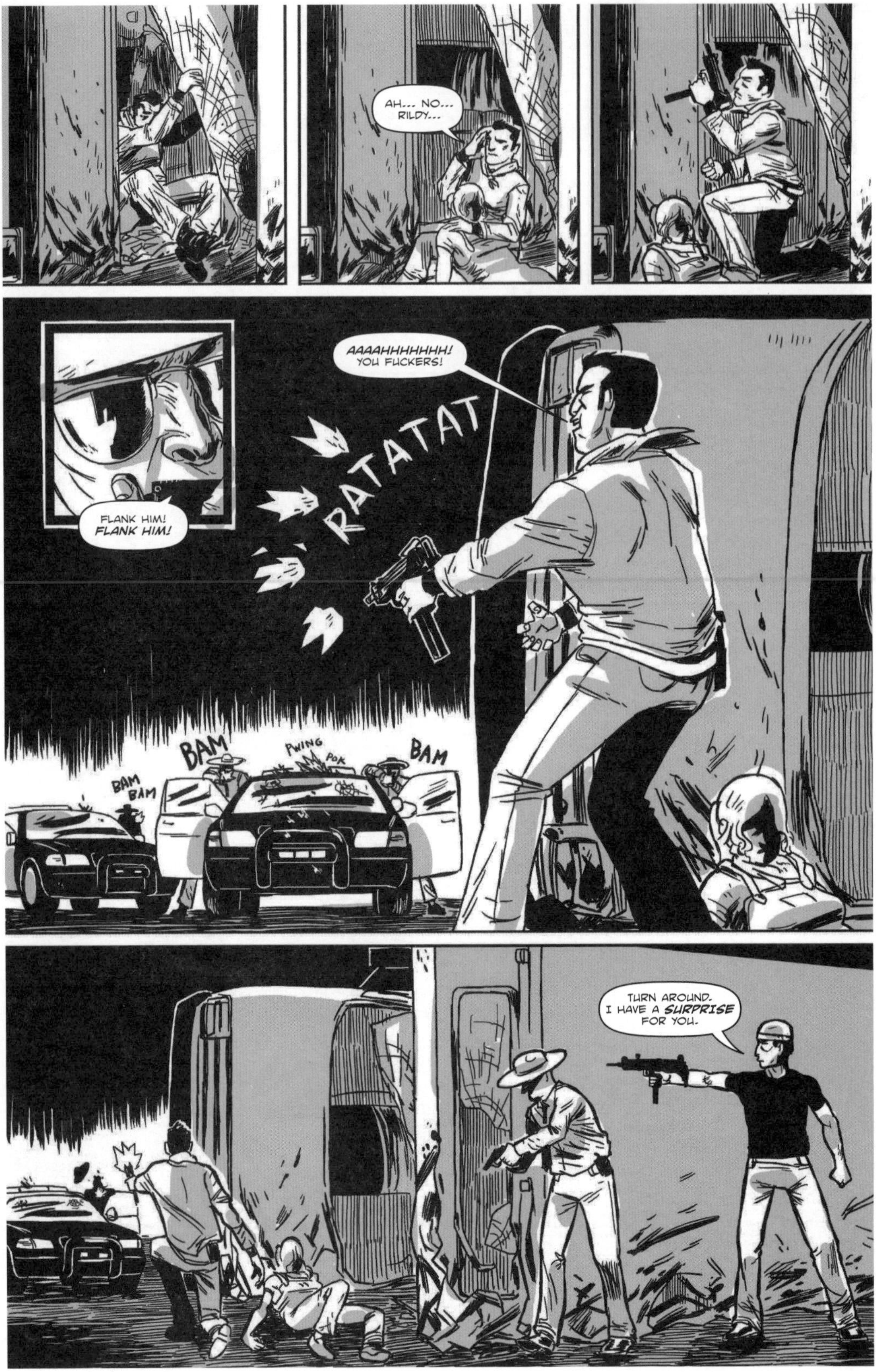

AH... NO... RILDY...
AAAAHHHHHHH! YOU FUCKERS!
FLANK HIM! FLANK HIM!
RATATAT
BAM
BAM BAM
PWING
POK
BAM
TURN AROUND. I HAVE A SURPRISE FOR YOU.

NATE.

'BOUT TIME, J.C.

GET THAT TO THE CAR. I'LL GO TO RILDY.

WHAT THE *HELL* IS GOING *ON* HERE?

THIS IS *NO* TIME FOR CHATTER. JUST GET EVERYTHING YOU CAN OUT OF THE CAMPER AND INTO THE S.U.V.

C'EST BIEN!

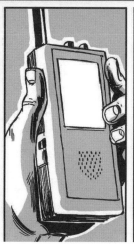

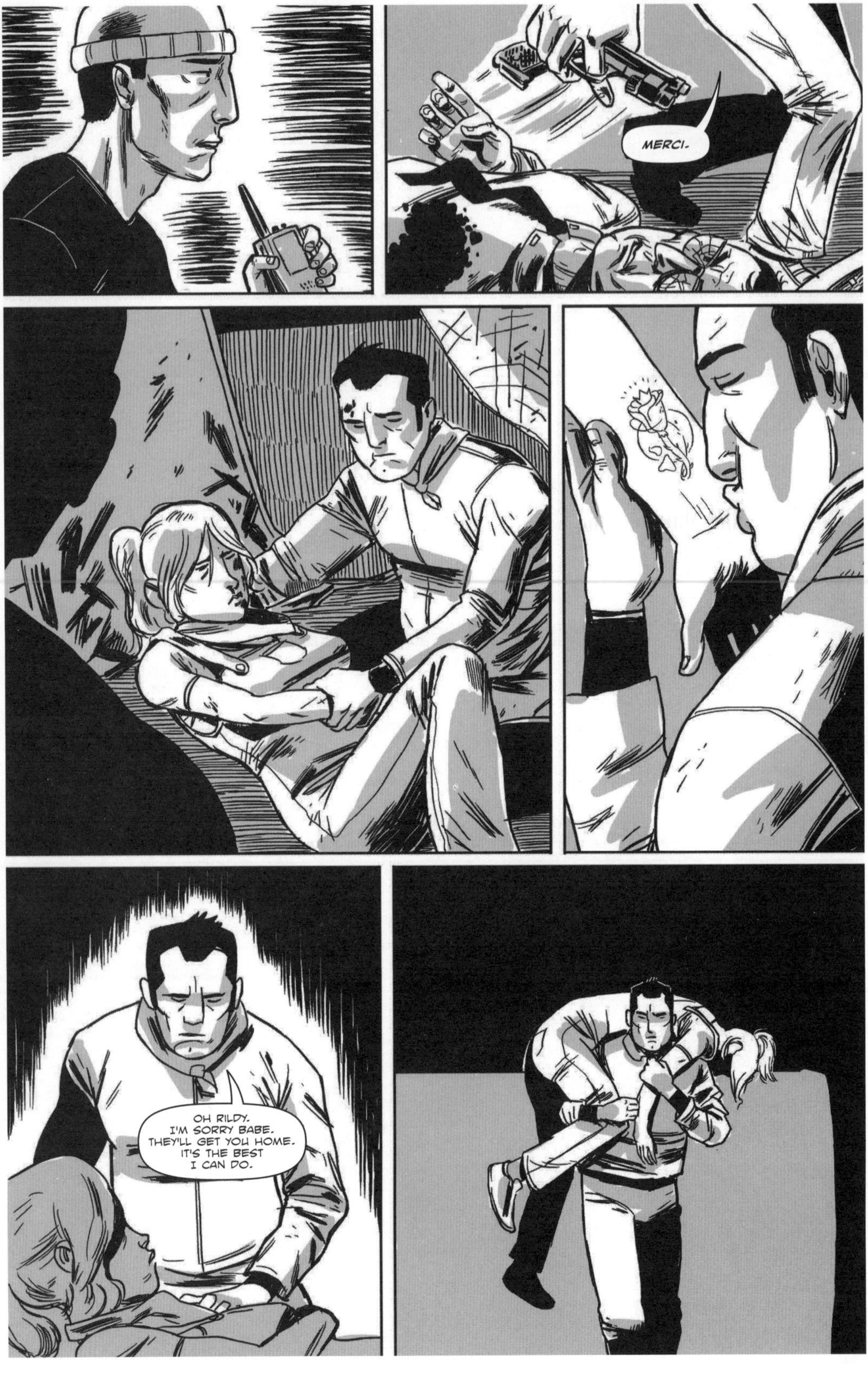
MERCI.
OH RILDY.
I'M SORRY BABE.
THEY'LL GET YOU HOME.
IT'S THE BEST
I CAN DO.

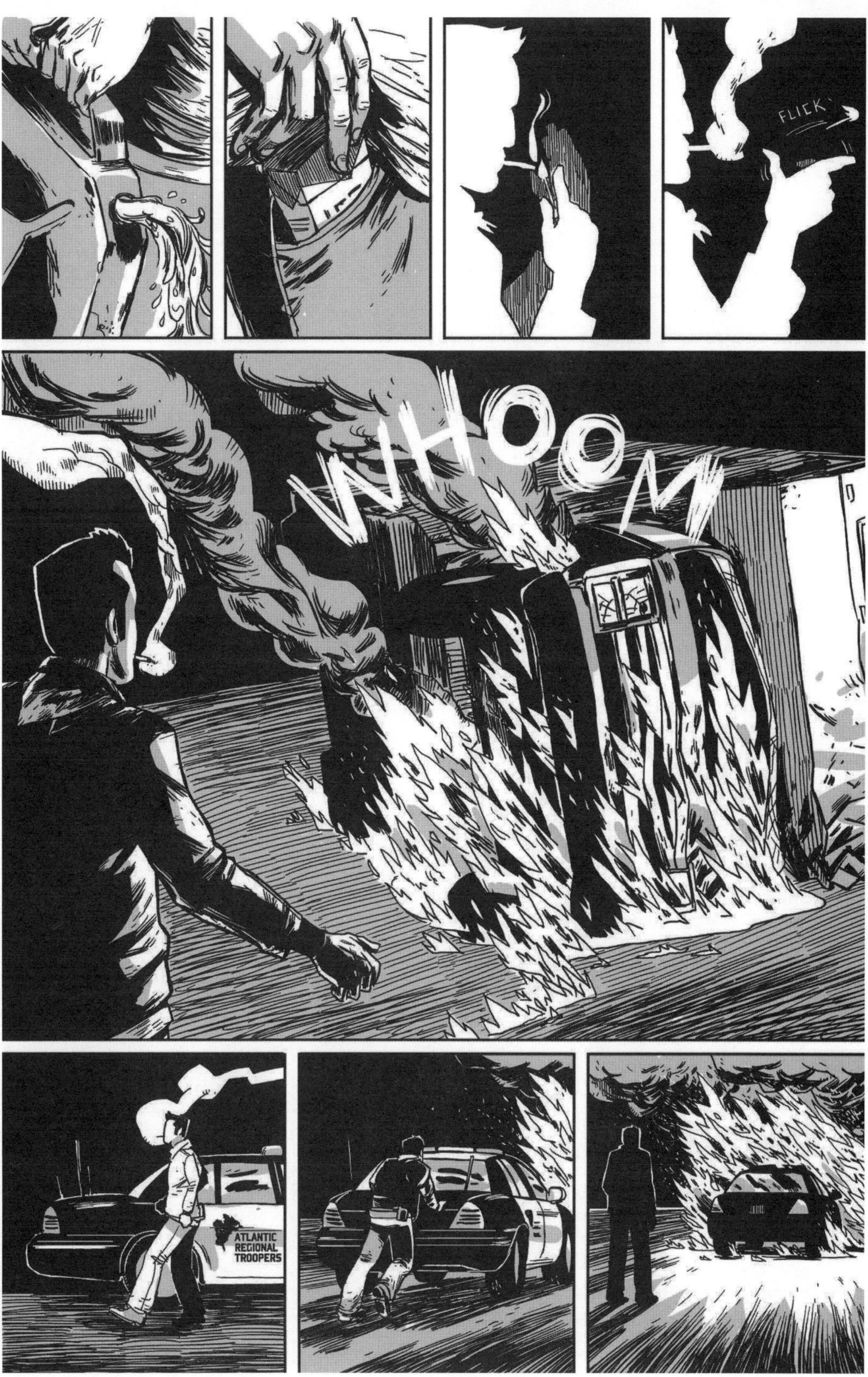
FLICK
WHOOOM
ATLANTIC
REGIONAL
TROOPERS

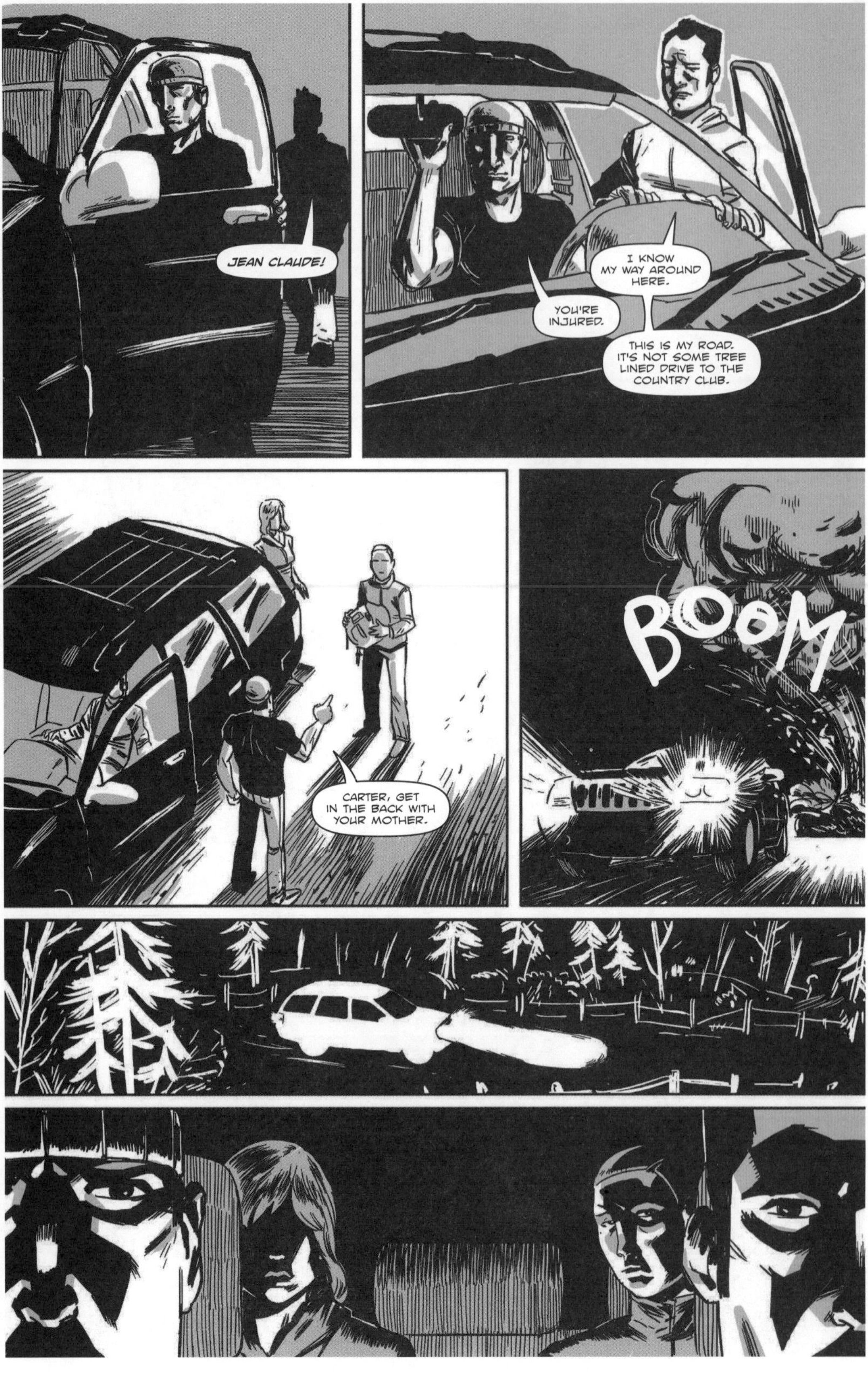
JEAN CLAUDE!
YOU'RE INJURED.
I KNOW MY WAY AROUND HERE.
THIS IS MY ROAD. IT'S NOT SOME TREE LINED DRIVE TO THE COUNTRY CLUB.
CARTER, GET IN THE BACK WITH YOUR MOTHER.
BOOM

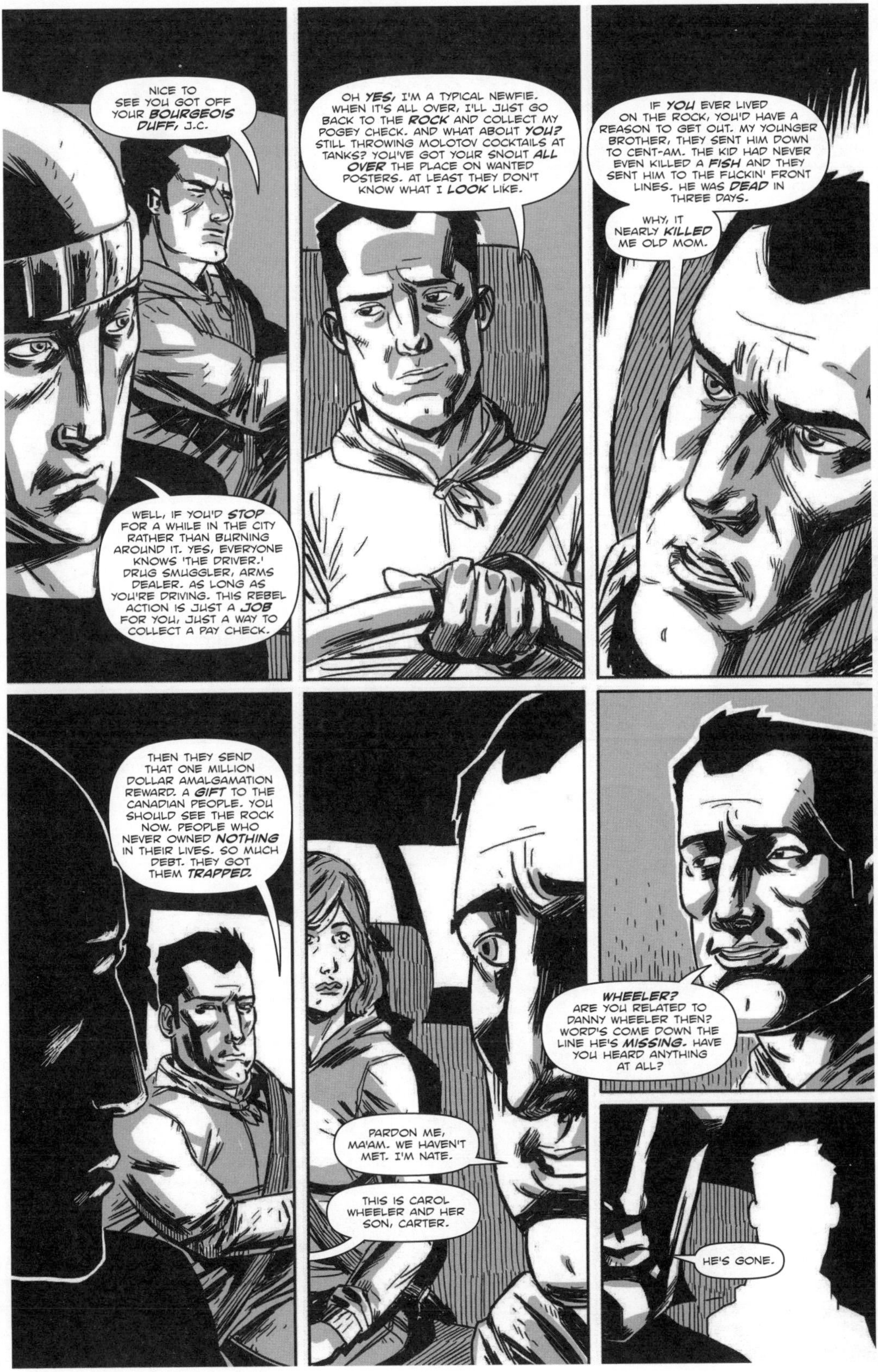
NICE TO SEE YOU GOT OFF YOUR BOURGEOIS DUFF, J.C.
WELL, IF YOU'D STOP FOR A WHILE IN THE CITY RATHER THAN BURNING AROUND IT. YES, EVERYONE KNOWS 'THE DRIVER.' DRUG SMUGGLER, ARMS DEALER. AS LONG AS YOU'RE DRIVING. THIS REBEL ACTION IS JUST A JOB FOR YOU, JUST A WAY TO COLLECT A PAY CHECK.
OH YES, I'M A TYPICAL NEWFIE. WHEN IT'S ALL OVER, I'LL JUST GO BACK TO THE ROCK AND COLLECT MY POGEY CHECK. AND WHAT ABOUT YOU? STILL THROWING MOLOTOV COCKTAILS AT TANKS? YOU'VE GOT YOUR SNOUT ALL OVER THE PLACE ON WANTED POSTERS. AT LEAST THEY DON'T KNOW WHAT I LOOK LIKE.
IF YOU EVER LIVED ON THE ROCK, YOU'D HAVE A REASON TO GET OUT. MY YOUNGER BROTHER, THEY SENT HIM DOWN TO CENT-AM. THE KID HAD NEVER EVEN KILLED A FISH AND THEY SENT HIM TO THE FUCKIN' FRONT LINES. HE WAS DEAD IN THREE DAYS.
WHY, IT NEARLY KILLED ME OLD MOM.
THEN THEY SEND THAT ONE MILLION DOLLAR AMALGAMATION REWARD. A GIFT TO THE CANADIAN PEOPLE. YOU SHOULD SEE THE ROCK NOW. PEOPLE WHO NEVER OWNED NOTHING IN THEIR LIVES. SO MUCH DEBT. THEY GOT THEM TRAPPED.
PARDON ME, MA'AM. WE HAVEN'T MET. I'M NATE.
THIS IS CAROL WHEELER AND HER SON, CARTER.
WHEELER? ARE YOU RELATED TO DANNY WHEELER THEN? WORD'S COME DOWN THE LINE HE'S MISSING. HAVE YOU HEARD ANYTHING AT ALL?
HE'S GONE.

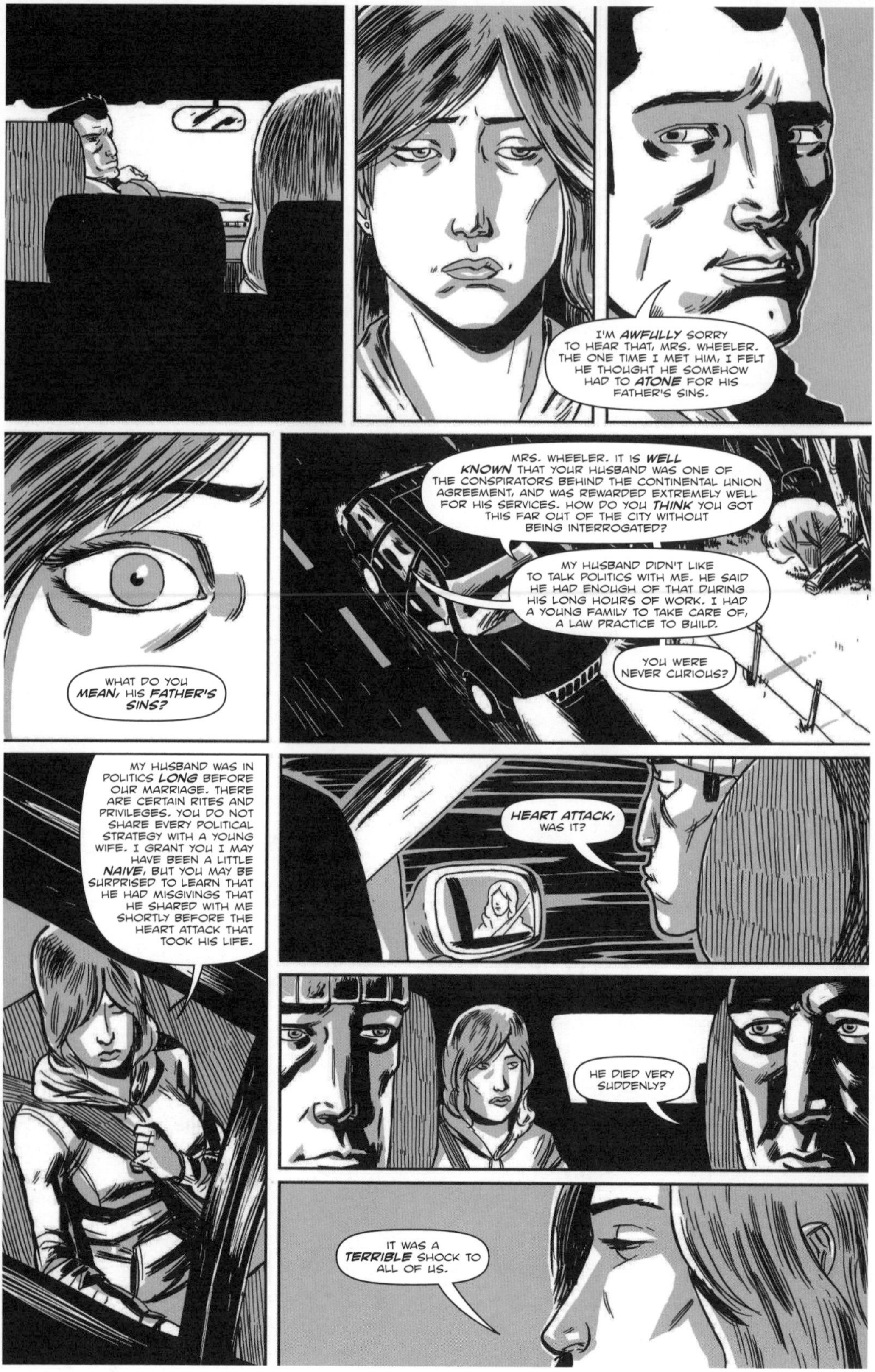
I'M AWFULLY SORRY TO HEAR THAT, MRS. WHEELER. THE ONE TIME I MET HIM, I FELT HE THOUGHT HE SOMEHOW HAD TO ATONE FOR HIS FATHER'S SINS.
WHAT DO YOU MEAN, HIS FATHER'S SINS?
MRS. WHEELER. IT IS WELL KNOWN THAT YOUR HUSBAND WAS ONE OF THE CONSPIRATORS BEHIND THE CONTINENTAL UNION AGREEMENT, AND WAS REWARDED EXTREMELY WELL FOR HIS SERVICES. HOW DO YOU THINK YOU GOT THIS FAR OUT OF THE CITY WITHOUT BEING INTERROGATED?
MY HUSBAND DIDN'T LIKE TO TALK POLITICS WITH ME. HE SAID HE HAD ENOUGH OF THAT DURING HIS LONG HOURS OF WORK. I HAD A YOUNG FAMILY TO TAKE CARE OF, A LAW PRACTICE TO BUILD.
YOU WERE NEVER CURIOUS?
MY HUSBAND WAS IN POLITICS LONG BEFORE OUR MARRIAGE. THERE ARE CERTAIN RITES AND PRIVILEGES. YOU DO NOT SHARE EVERY POLITICAL STRATEGY WITH A YOUNG WIFE. I GRANT YOU I MAY HAVE BEEN A LITTLE NAIVE, BUT YOU MAY BE SURPRISED TO LEARN THAT HE HAD MISGIVINGS THAT HE SHARED WITH ME SHORTLY BEFORE THE HEART ATTACK THAT TOOK HIS LIFE.
HEART ATTACK, WAS IT?
HE DIED VERY SUDDENLY?
IT WAS A TERRIBLE SHOCK TO ALL OF US.

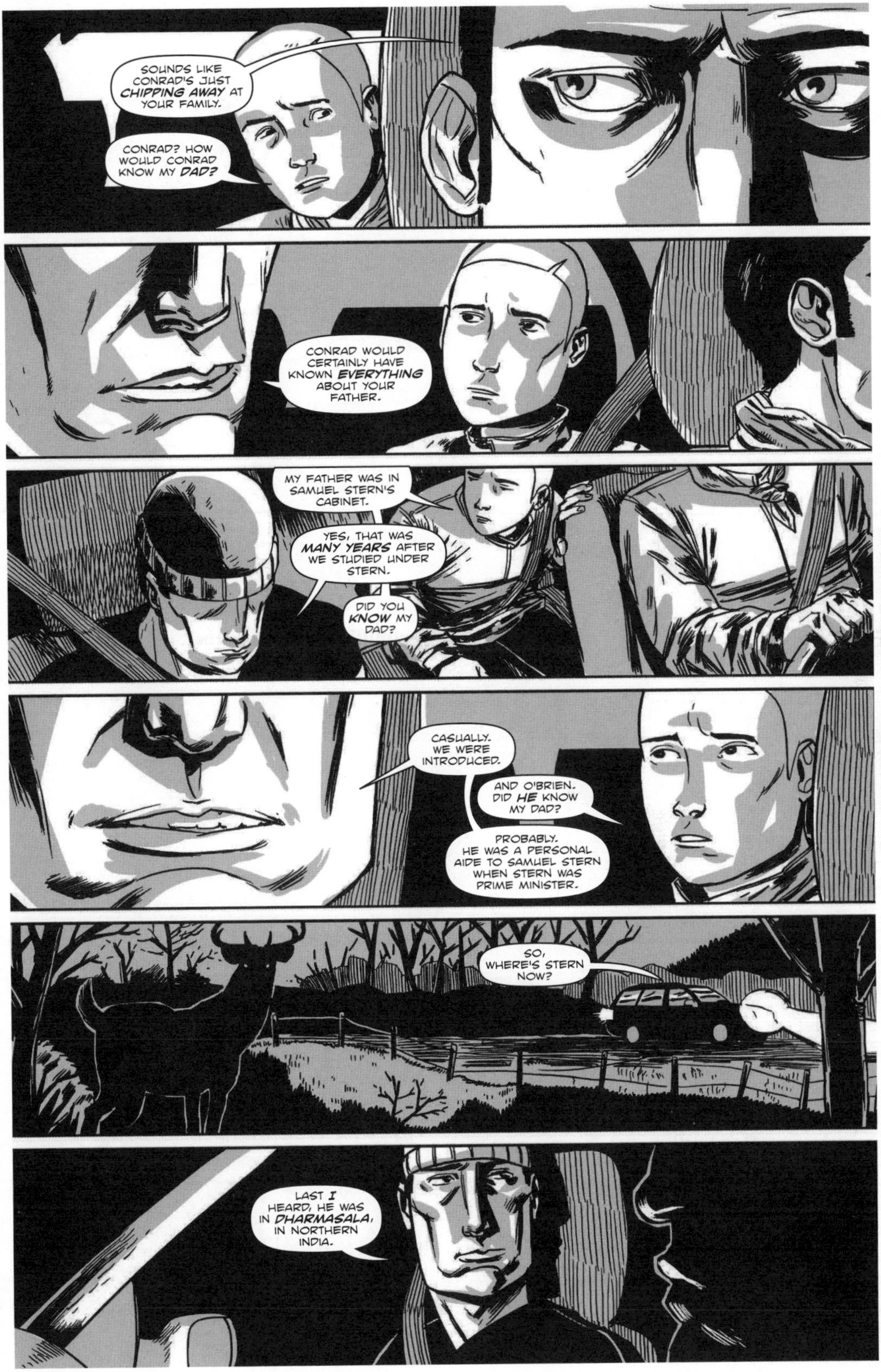
SOUNDS LIKE CONRAD'S JUST CHIPPING AWAY AT YOUR FAMILY.
CONRAD? HOW WOULD CONRAD KNOW MY DAD?
CONRAD WOULD CERTAINLY HAVE KNOWN EVERYTHING ABOUT YOUR FATHER.
MY FATHER WAS IN SAMUEL STERN'S CABINET.
YES, THAT WAS MANY YEARS AFTER WE STUDIED UNDER STERN.
DID YOU KNOW MY DAD?
CASUALLY. WE WERE INTRODUCED.
AND O'BRIEN. DID HE KNOW MY DAD?
PROBABLY. HE WAS A PERSONAL AIDE TO SAMUEL STERN WHEN STERN WAS PRIME MINISTER.
SO, WHERE'S STERN NOW?
LAST I HEARD, HE WAS IN DHARMASALA, IN NORTHERN INDIA.

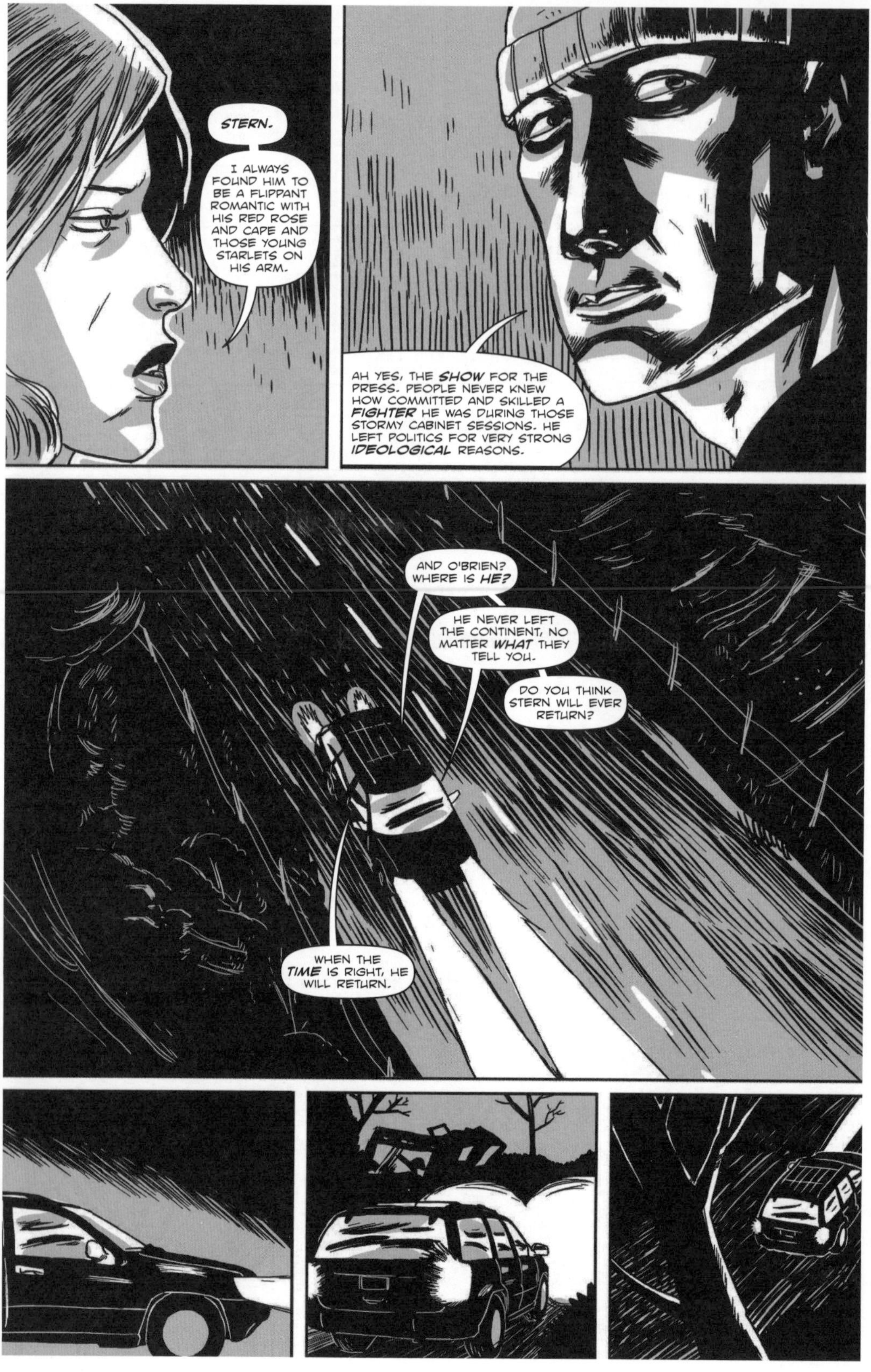
STERN.
I ALWAYS FOUND HIM TO BE A FLIPPANT ROMANTIC WITH HIS RED ROSE AND CAPE AND THOSE YOUNG STARLETS ON HIS ARM.
AH YES, THE SHOW FOR THE PRESS. PEOPLE NEVER KNEW HOW COMMITTED AND SKILLED A FIGHTER HE WAS DURING THOSE STORMY CABINET SESSIONS. HE LEFT POLITICS FOR VERY STRONG IDEOLOGICAL REASONS.
AND O'BRIEN? WHERE IS HE?
HE NEVER LEFT THE CONTINENT, NO MATTER WHAT THEY TELL YOU.
DO YOU THINK STERN WILL EVER RETURN?
WHEN THE TIME IS RIGHT, HE WILL RETURN.

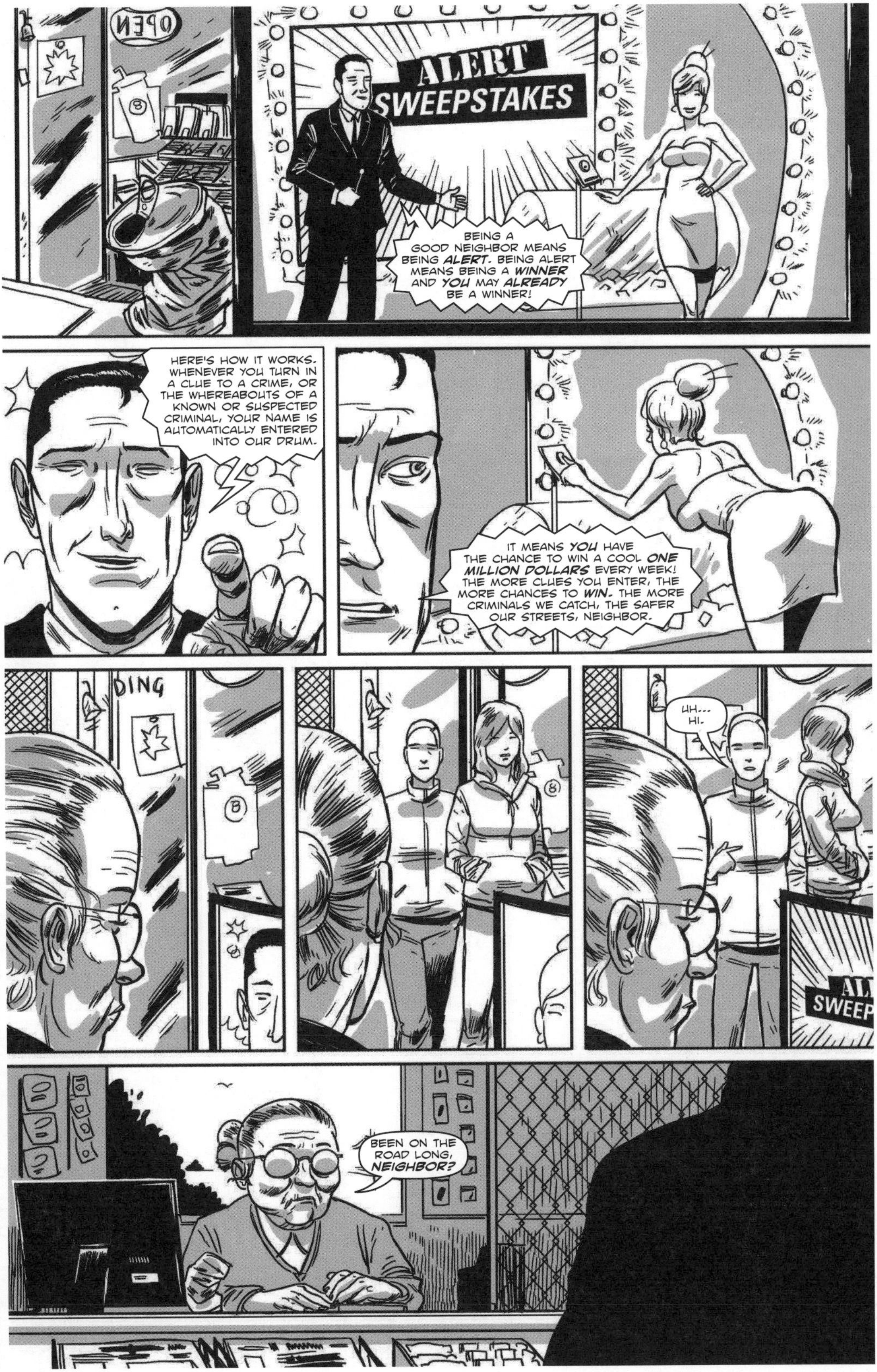
OPEN
ALERT SWEEPSTAKES
BEING A GOOD NEIGHBOR MEANS BEING ALERT. BEING ALERT MEANS BEING A WINNER AND YOU MAY ALREADY BE A WINNER!
HERE'S HOW IT WORKS. WHENEVER YOU TURN IN A CLUE TO A CRIME, OR THE WHEREABOUTS OF A KNOWN OR SUSPECTED CRIMINAL, YOUR NAME IS AUTOMATICALLY ENTERED INTO OUR DRUM.
IT MEANS YOU HAVE THE CHANCE TO WIN A COOL ONE MILLION DOLLARS EVERY WEEK! THE MORE CLUES YOU ENTER, THE MORE CHANCES TO WIN. THE MORE CRIMINALS WE CATCH, THE SAFER OUR STREETS, NEIGHBOR.
DING
UH... HI.
AL SWEEP
BEEN ON THE ROAD LONG, NEIGHBOR?

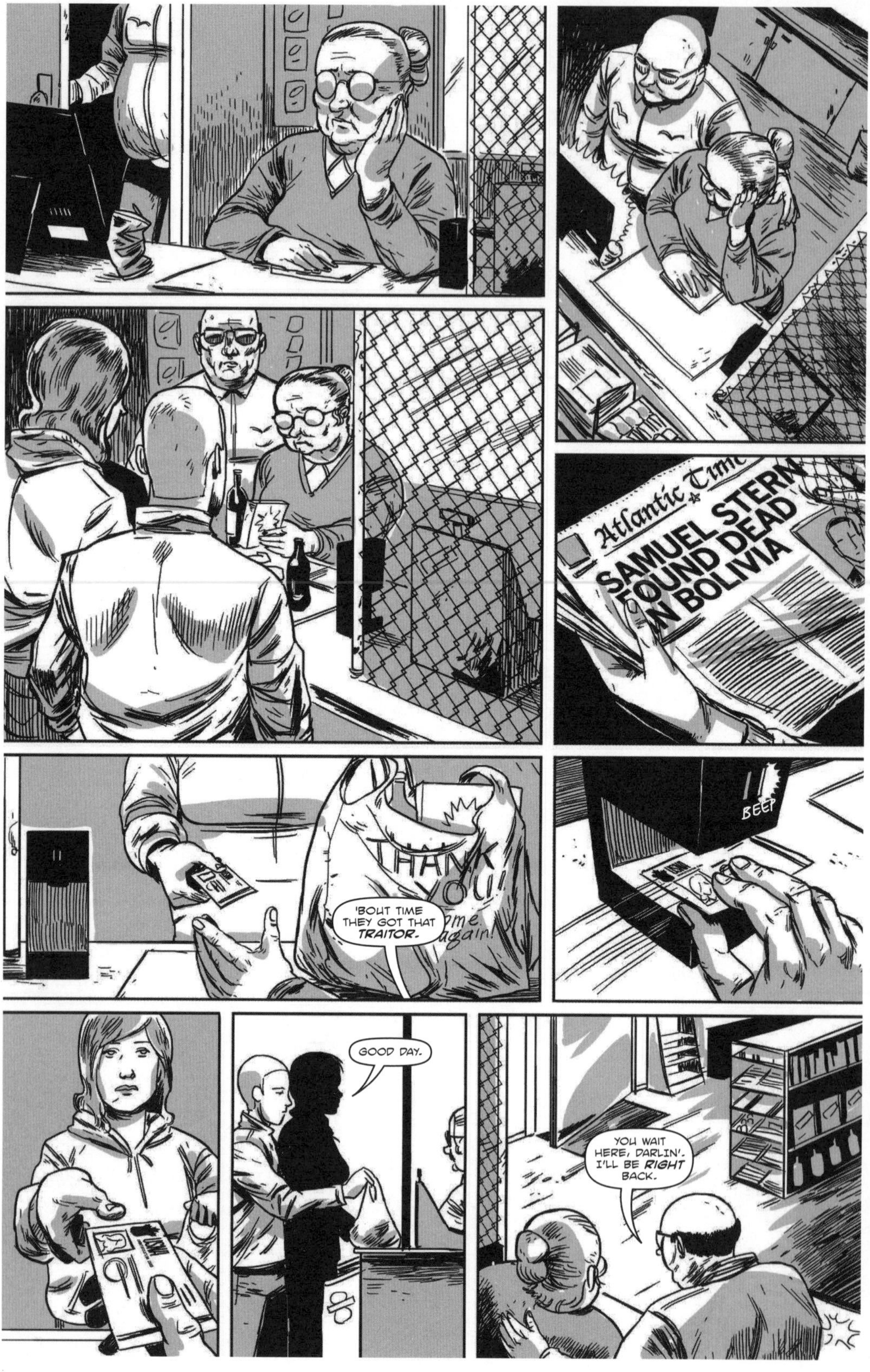
Atlantic Times
SAMUEL STERN FOUND DEAD IN BOLIVIA
THANK YOU! Come again!
'BOUT TIME THEY GOT THAT TRAITOR.
BEEP
GOOD DAY.
YOU WAIT HERE, DARLIN'. I'LL BE RIGHT BACK.

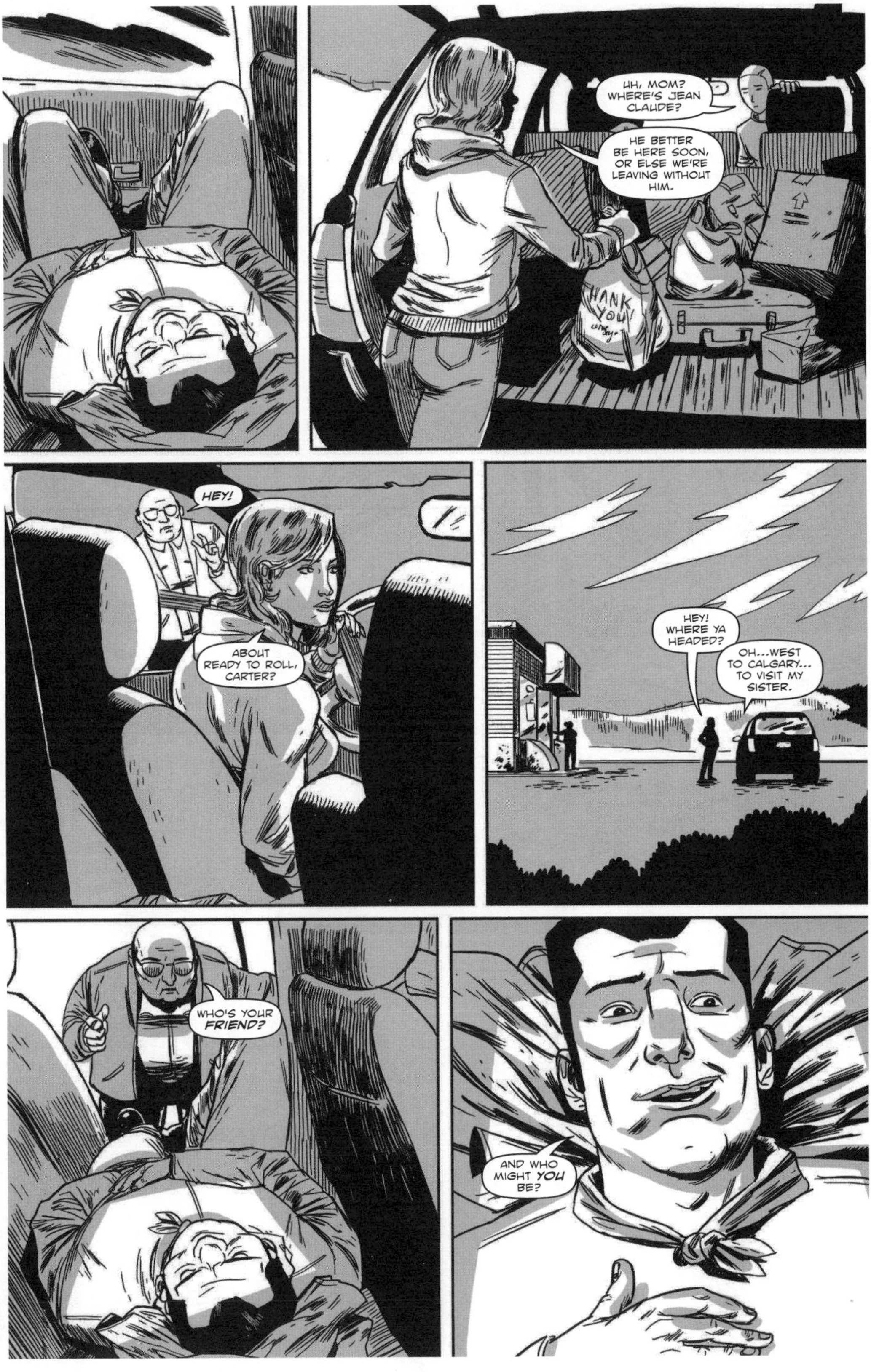
UH, MOM? WHERE'S JEAN CLAUDE?
HE BETTER BE HERE SOON, OR ELSE WE'RE LEAVING WITHOUT HIM.
HANK YOU
HEY!
ABOUT READY TO ROLL, CARTER?
HEY! WHERE YA HEADED?
OH...WEST TO CALGARY... TO VISIT MY SISTER.
WHO'S YOUR FRIEND?
AND WHO MIGHT YOU BE?

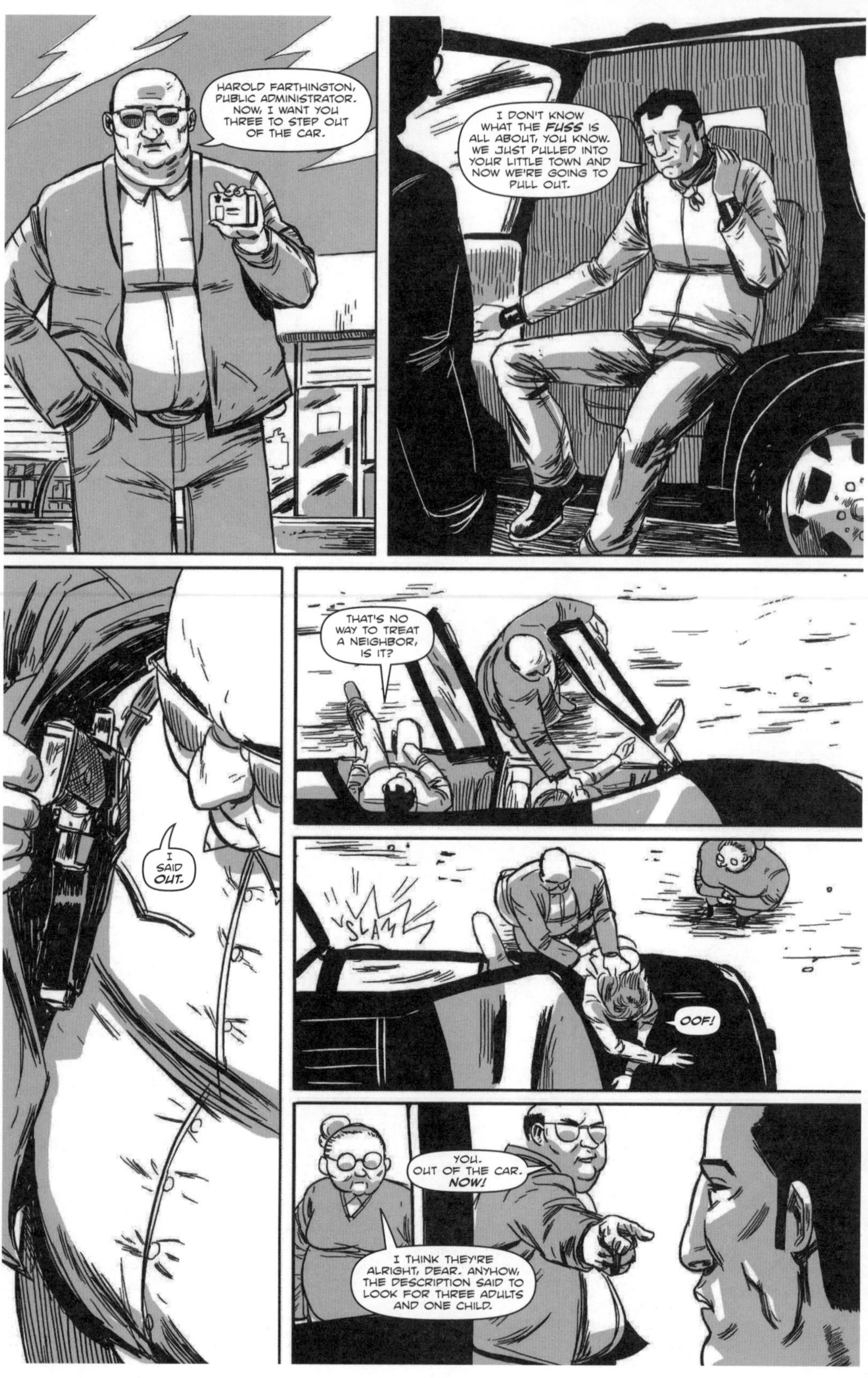
HAROLD FARTHINGTON, PUBLIC ADMINISTRATOR. NOW, I WANT YOU THREE TO STEP OUT OF THE CAR.
I DON'T KNOW WHAT THE FUSS IS ALL ABOUT, YOU KNOW. WE JUST PULLED INTO YOUR LITTLE TOWN AND NOW WE'RE GOING TO PULL OUT.
I SAID OUT.
THAT'S NO WAY TO TREAT A NEIGHBOR, IS IT?
SLAM
OOF!
YOU. OUT OF THE CAR. NOW!
I THINK THEY'RE ALRIGHT, DEAR. ANYHOW, THE DESCRIPTION SAID TO LOOK FOR THREE ADULTS AND ONE CHILD.

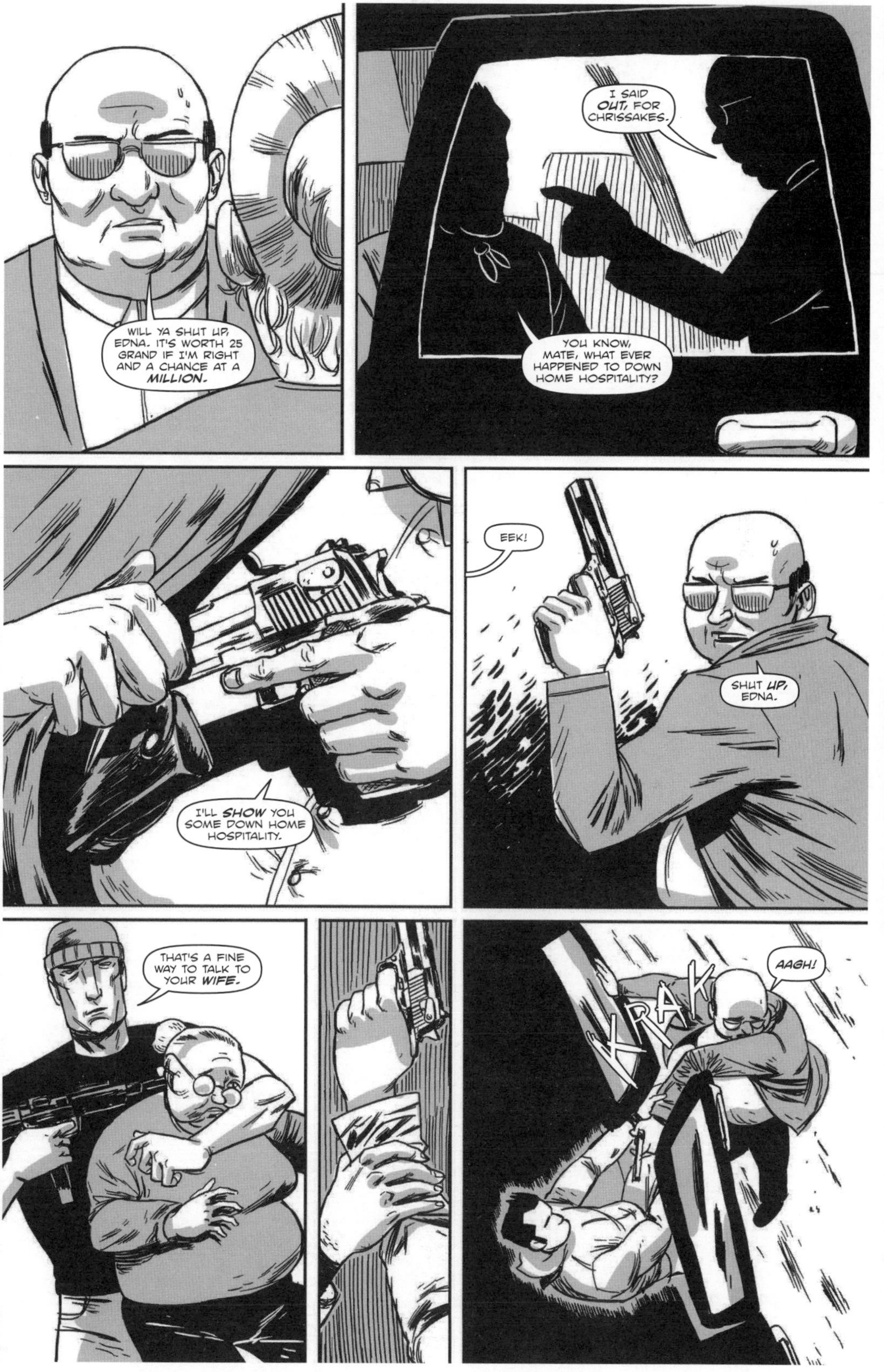
WILL YA SHUT UP, EDNA. IT'S WORTH 25 GRAND IF I'M RIGHT AND A CHANCE AT A MILLION.
I SAID OUT, FOR CHRISSAKES.
YOU KNOW, MATE, WHAT EVER HAPPENED TO DOWN HOME HOSPITALITY?
I'LL SHOW YOU SOME DOWN HOME HOSPITALITY.
EEK!
SHUT UP, EDNA.
THAT'S A FINE WAY TO TALK TO YOUR WIFE.
KRAK
AAGH!

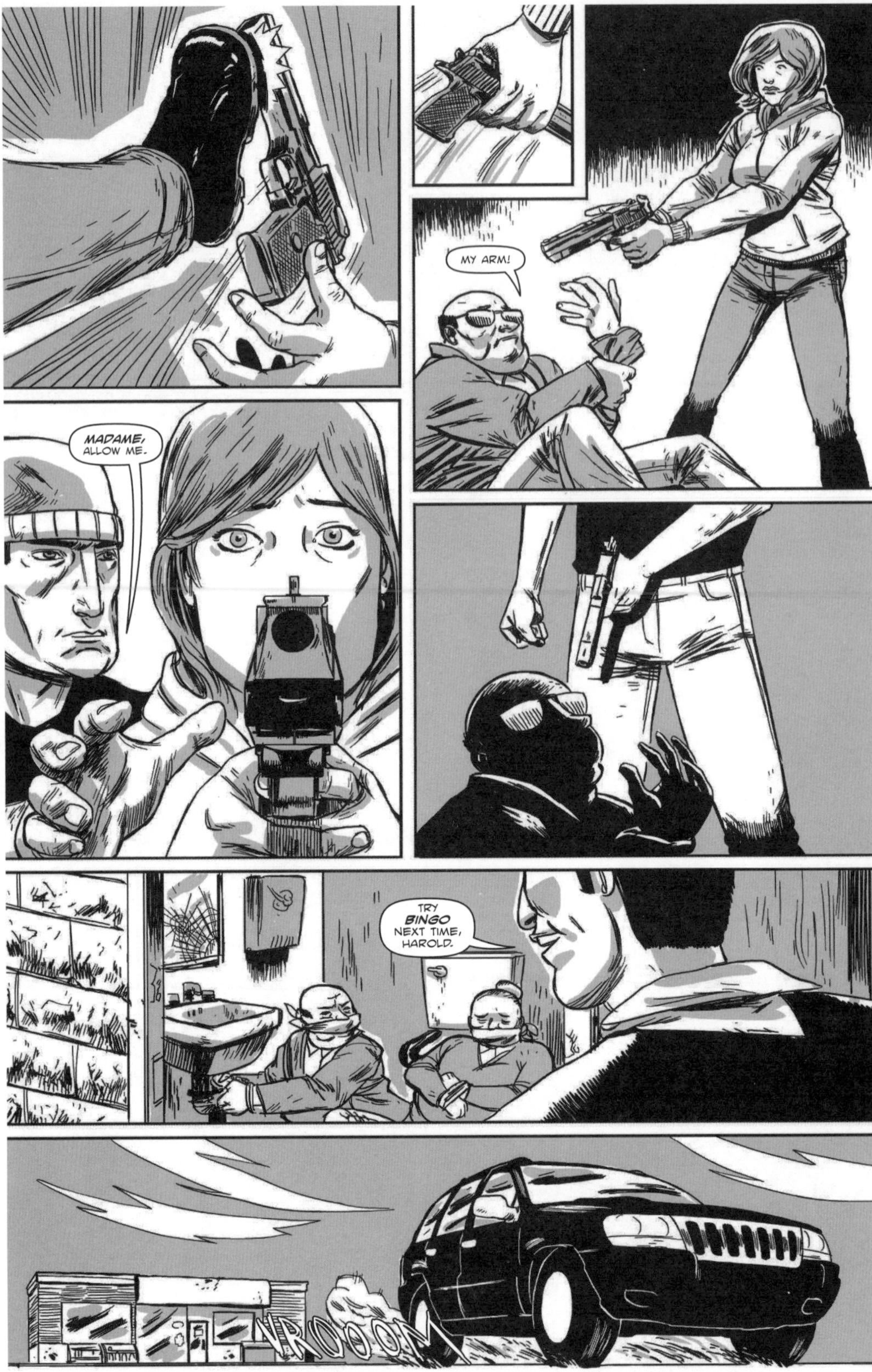
MY ARM!
MADAME, ALLOW ME.
TRY BINGO NEXT TIME, HAROLD.
VROOOM

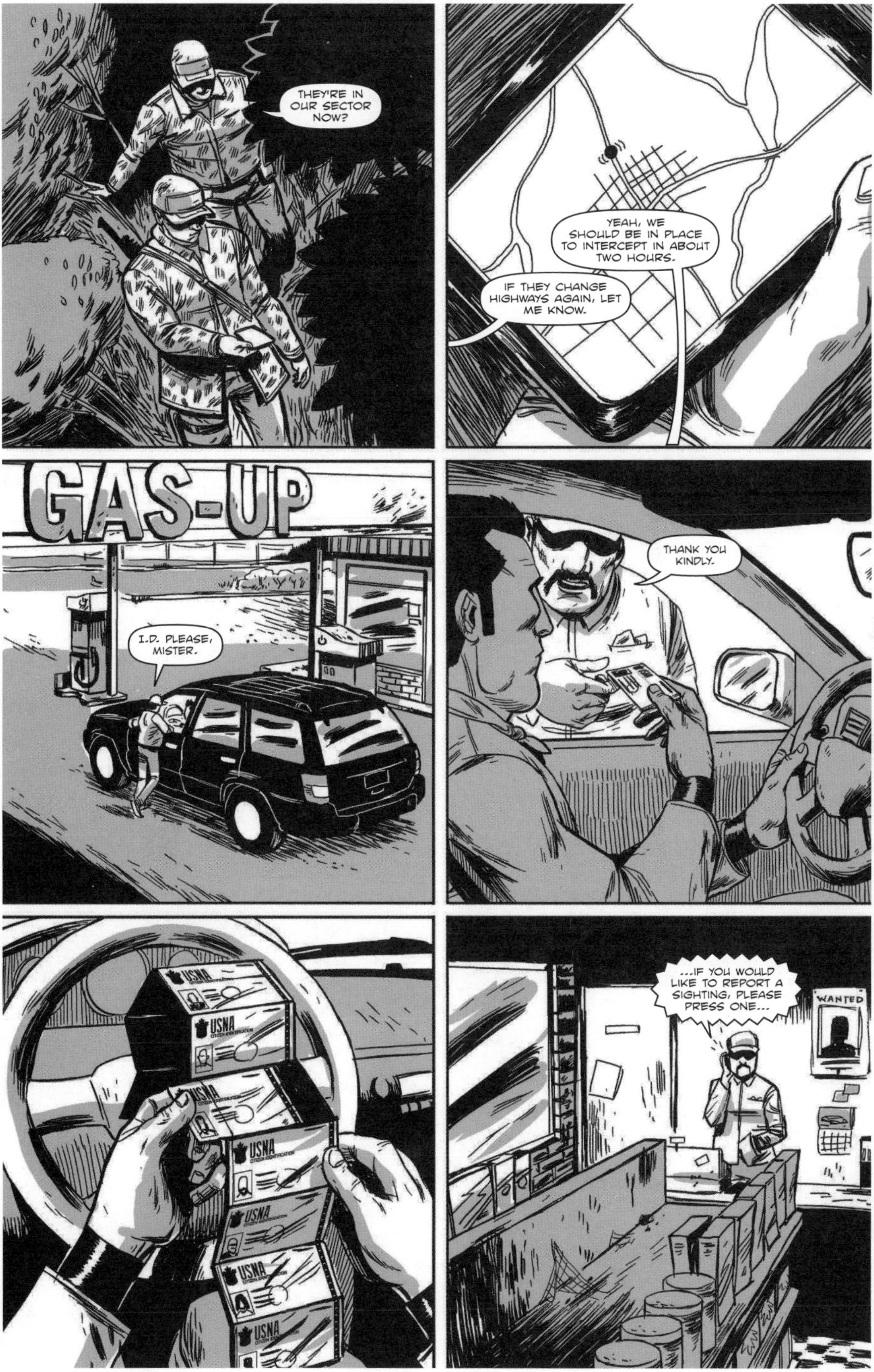
THEY'RE IN OUR SECTOR NOW?
YEAH, WE SHOULD BE IN PLACE TO INTERCEPT IN ABOUT TWO HOURS.
IF THEY CHANGE HIGHWAYS AGAIN, LET ME KNOW.
GAS-UP
I.D. PLEASE, MISTER.
THANK YOU KINDLY.
USNA
...IF YOU WOULD LIKE TO REPORT A SIGHTING, PLEASE PRESS ONE...
WANTED

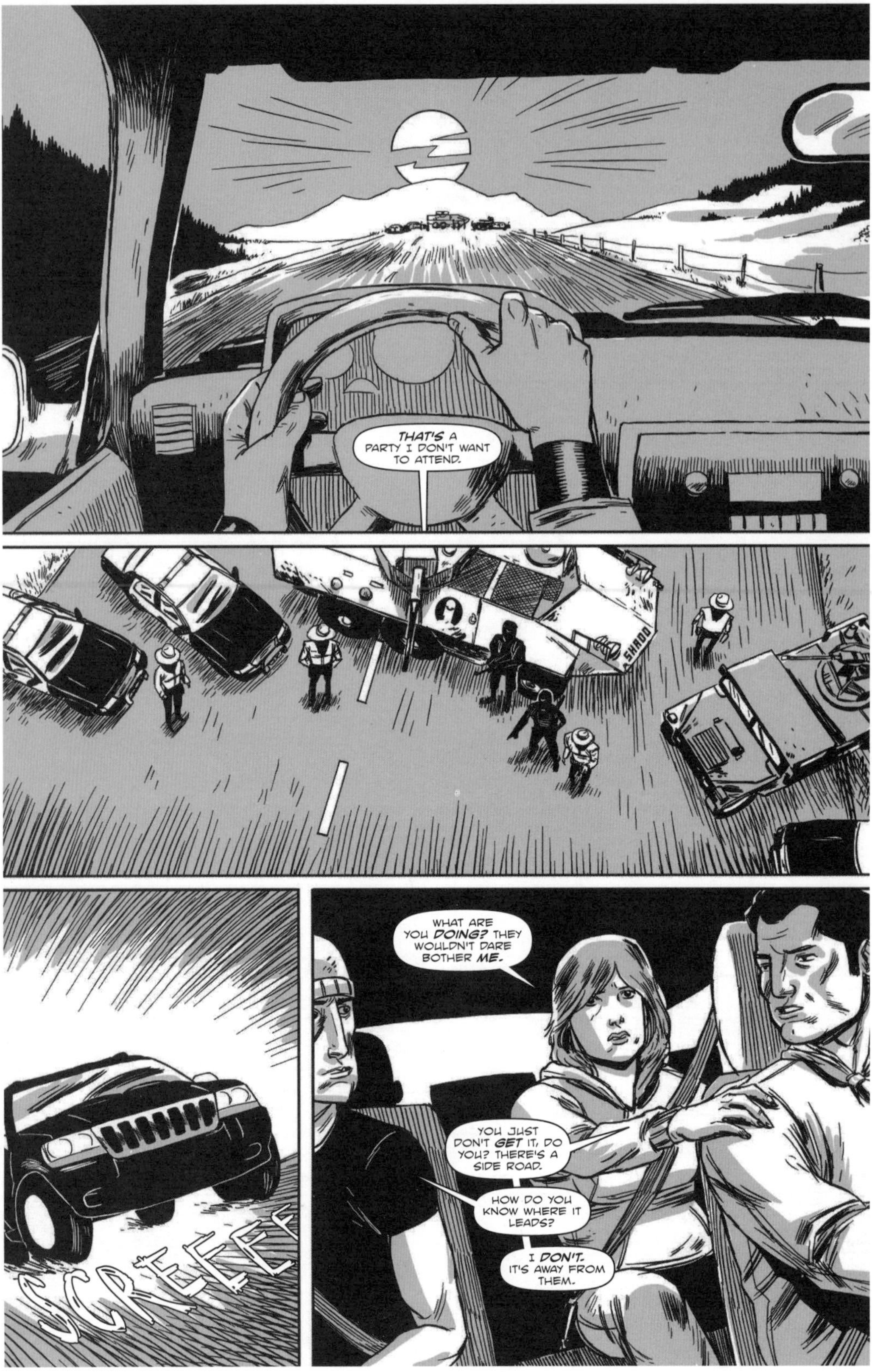
THAT'S A PARTY I DON'T WANT TO ATTEND.
SHADO
WHAT ARE YOU DOING? THEY WOULDN'T DARE BOTHER ME.
YOU JUST DON'T GET IT, DO YOU? THERE'S A SIDE ROAD.
HOW DO YOU KNOW WHERE IT LEADS?
I DON'T. IT'S AWAY FROM THEM.
SCREEEE

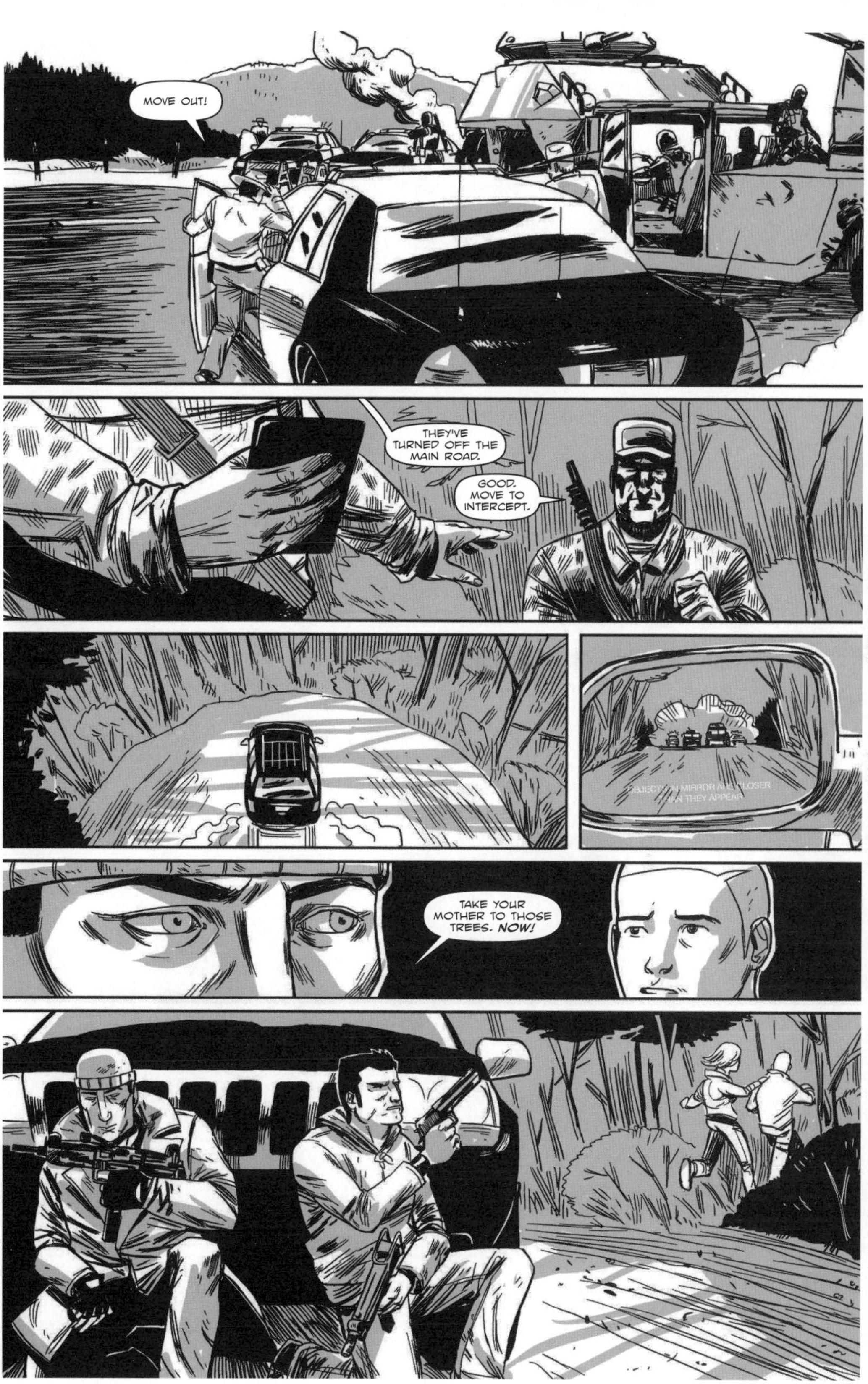
MOVE OUT!
THEY'VE TURNED OFF THE MAIN ROAD.
GOOD. MOVE TO INTERCEPT.
OBJECTS IN MIRROR ARE CLOSER
THAN THEY APPEAR
TAKE YOUR MOTHER TO THOSE TREES. *NOW!*

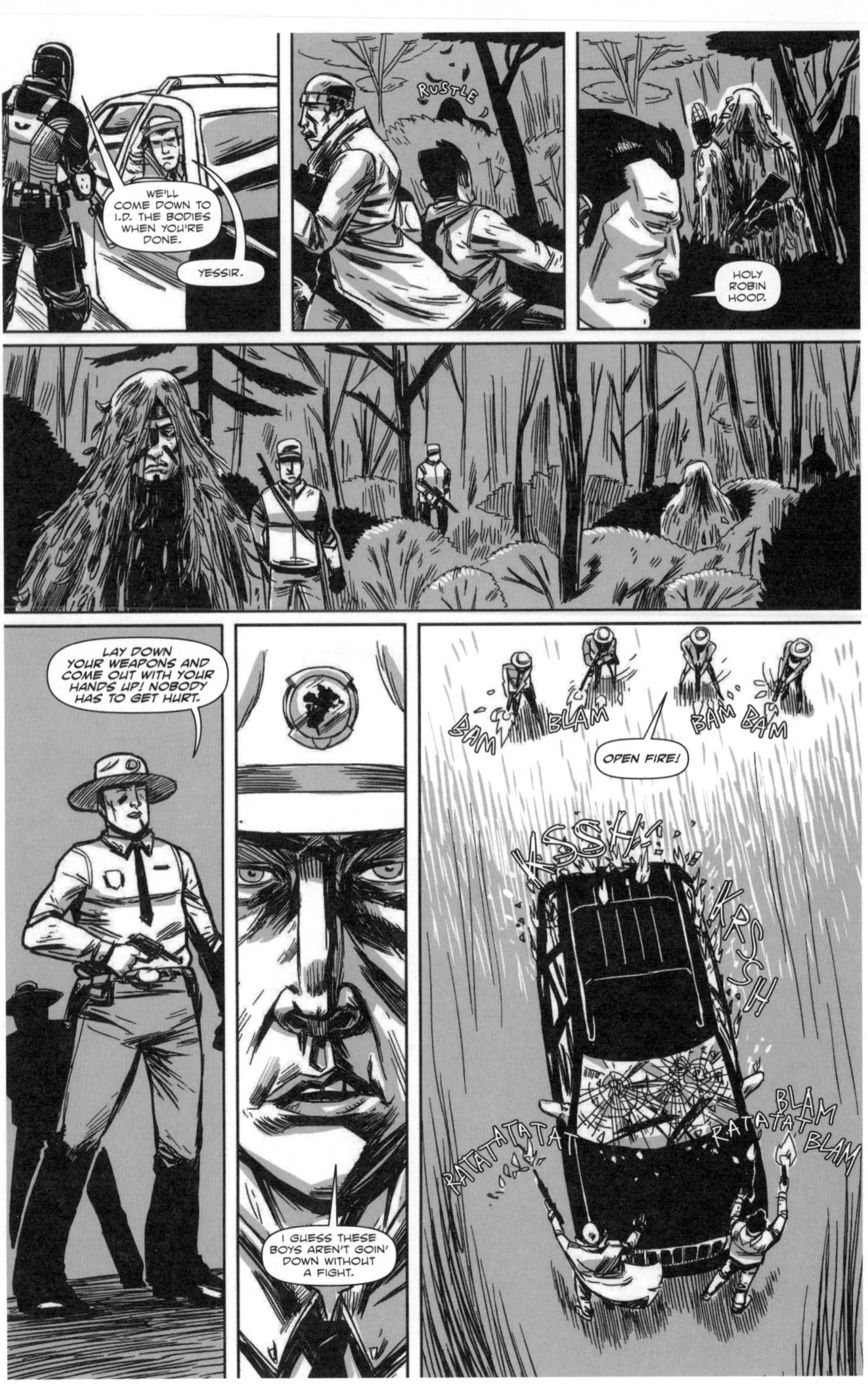
WE'LL COME DOWN TO I.D. THE BODIES WHEN YOU'RE DONE.
YESSIR.
RUSTLE
HOLY ROBIN HOOD.
LAY DOWN YOUR WEAPONS AND COME OUT WITH YOUR HANDS UP! NOBODY HAS TO GET HURT.
I GUESS THESE BOYS AREN'T GOIN' DOWN WITHOUT A FIGHT.
BAM
BLAM
BAM BAM
OPEN FIRE!
KSSH!
KRSH
RATATATATAT
RATATAT
BLAM
BLAM

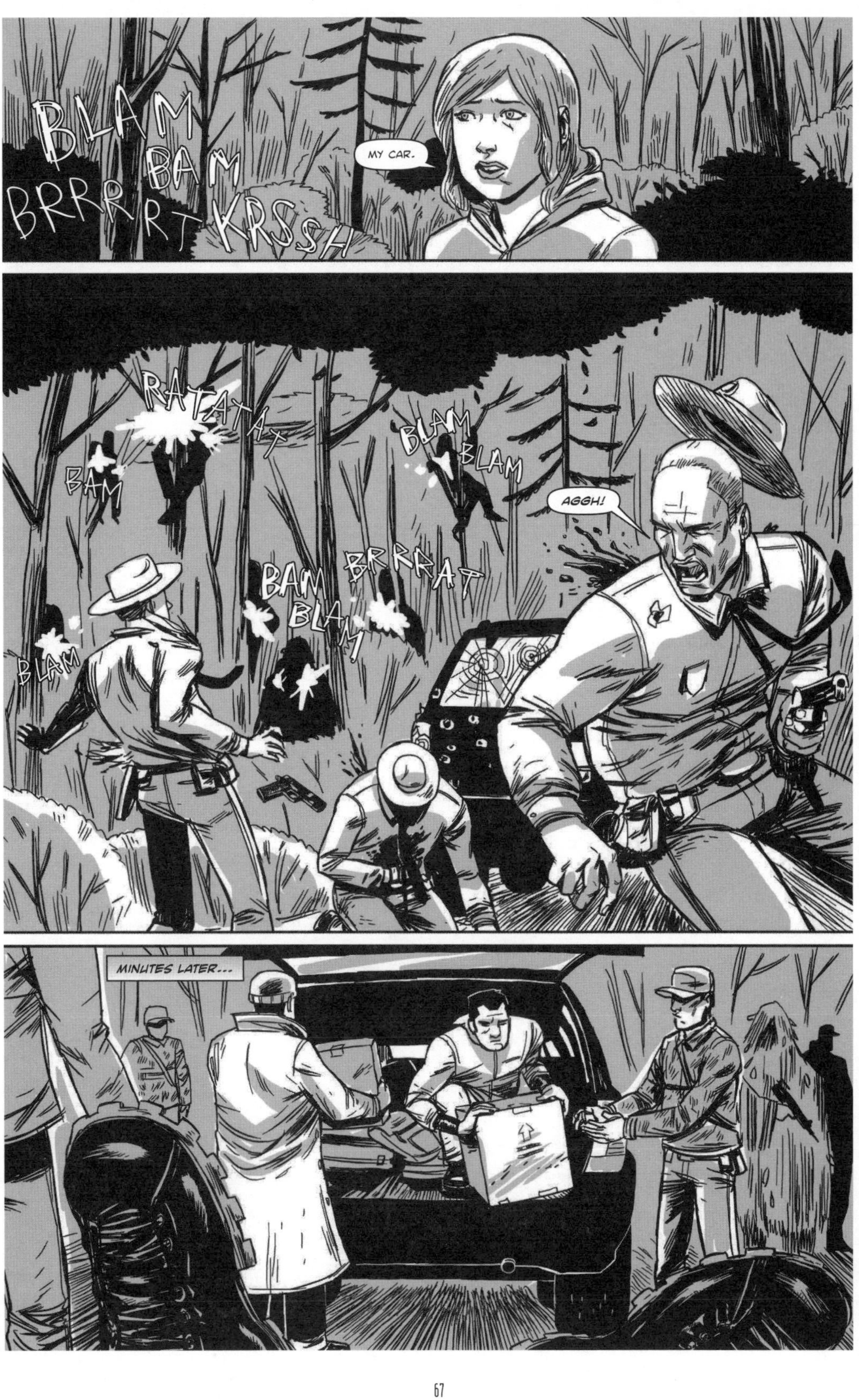
BLAM
BAM
BRRRRRT
KRSSH
MY CAR.
RATATATAT
BAM
BLAM
BLAM
AGGH!
BAM
BLAM
BRRRAT
BLAM
MINUTES LATER...

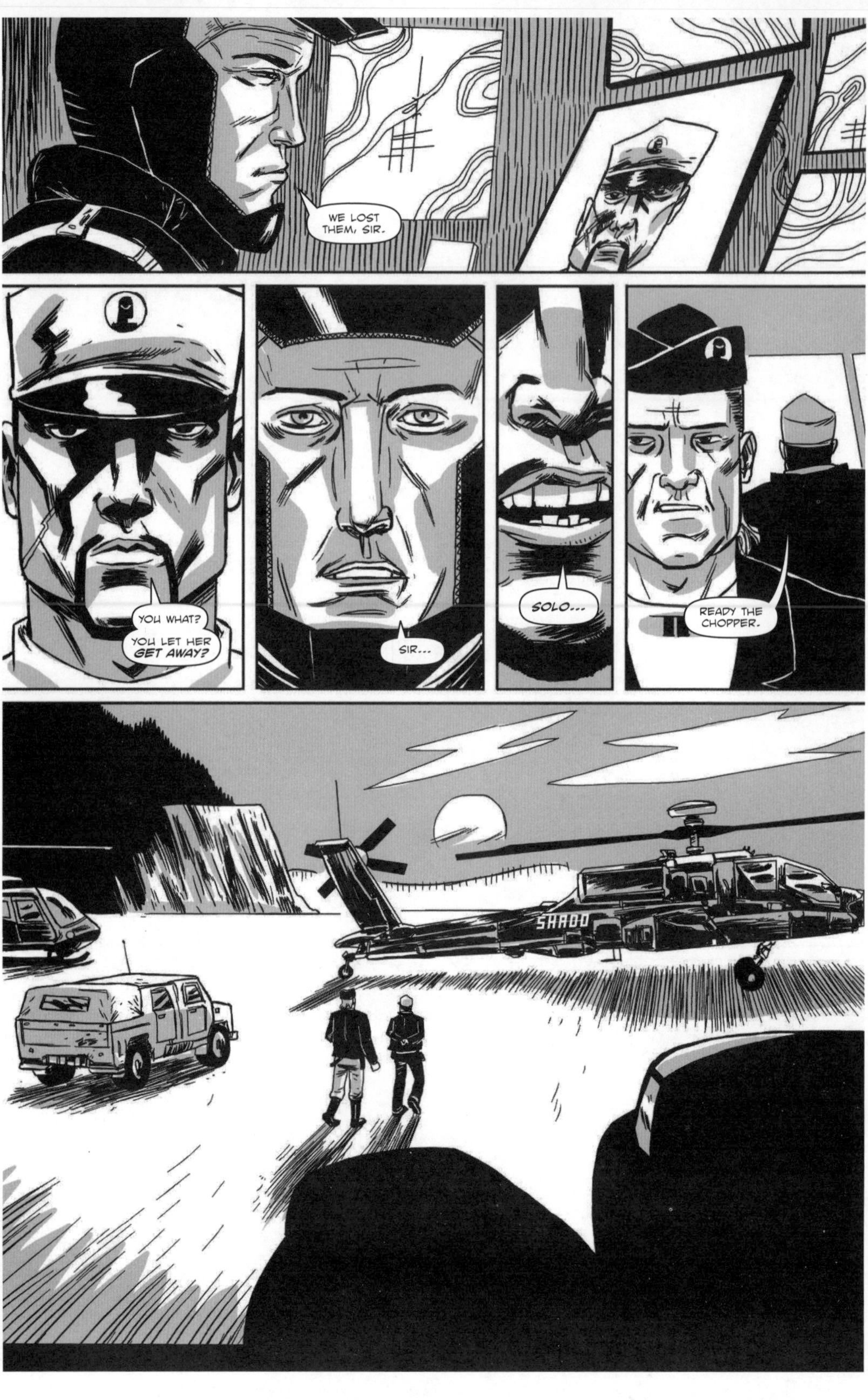
WE LOST THEM, SIR.
YOU WHAT? YOU LET HER GET AWAY?
SIR...
SOLO...
READY THE CHOPPER.
SHADO

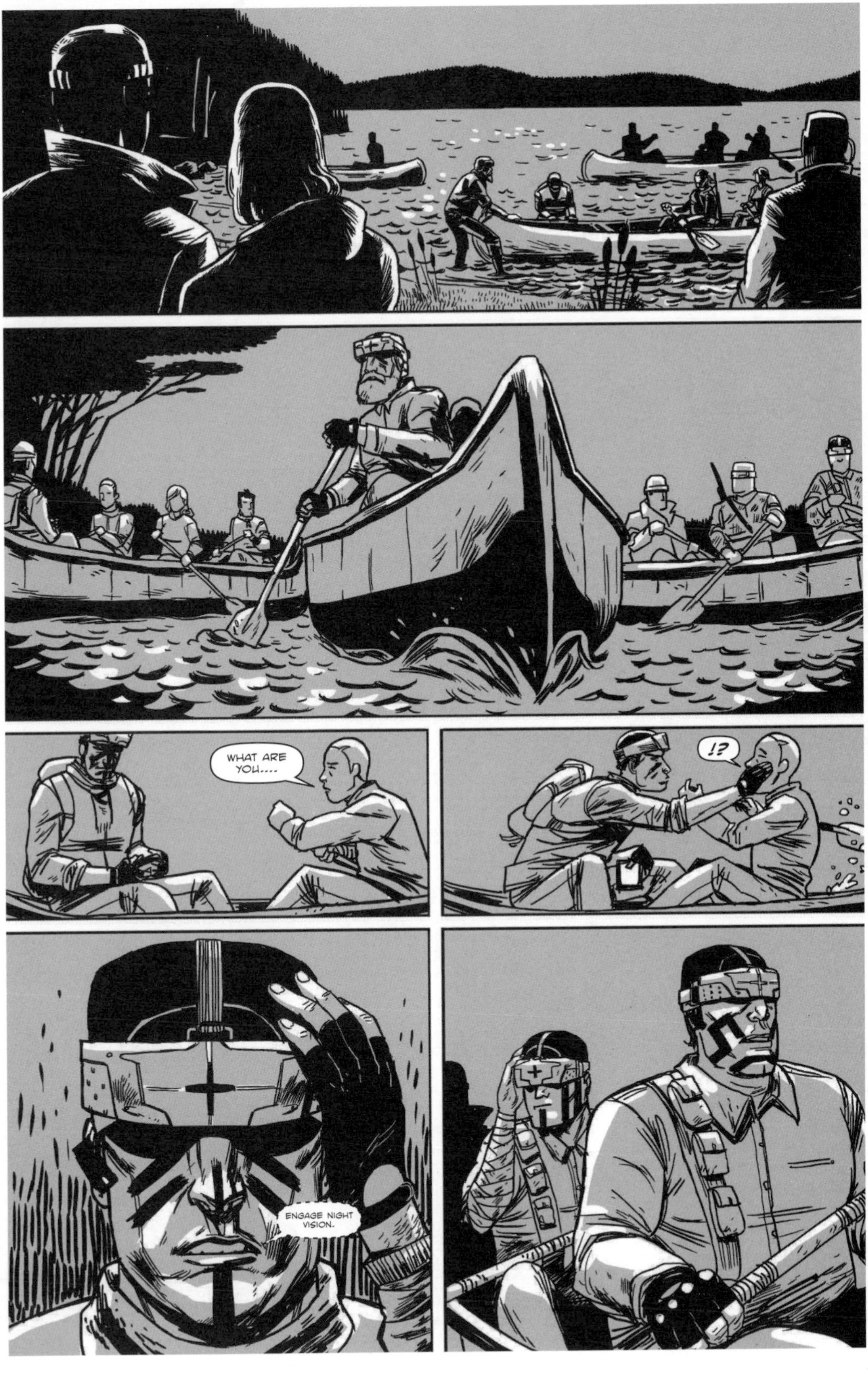
WHAT ARE YOU....
!?
ENGAGE NIGHT VISION.

TWO APPROACHING FROM SOUTHWEST. SHORELINE AND DEPLOY CHAMO.

WHUP WHUPL

WHUP WHUPWHI

WHUP WHUP WHUP WHUPL

WHUPWHUPWHUPWHL WHUPWHUP

SHADO

COME OUT COME OUT, WHEREVER YOU ARE...

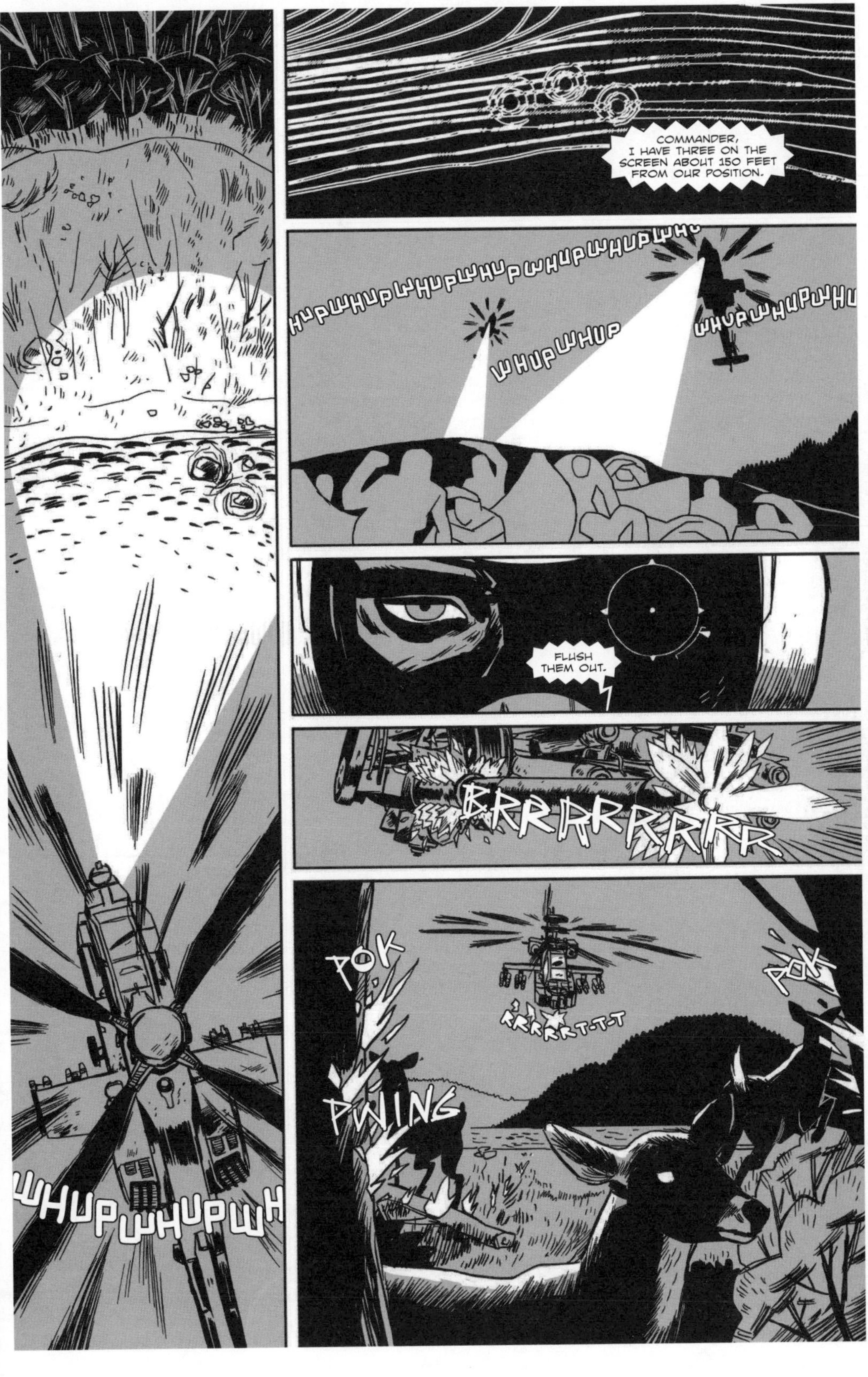
WHUPWHUPWH
COMMANDER, I HAVE THREE ON THE SCREEN ABOUT 150 FEET FROM OUR POSITION.
WHUPWHUPWHUPWHUPWHUPWHUPWHUPWHUPWHU
WHUPWHUP
WHUPWHUPWHU
FLUSH THEM OUT.
BRRRRRRRRRR
POK
POK
RRRRRRT-T-T
PWING

HOLD POSITION.

ALL CLEAR.

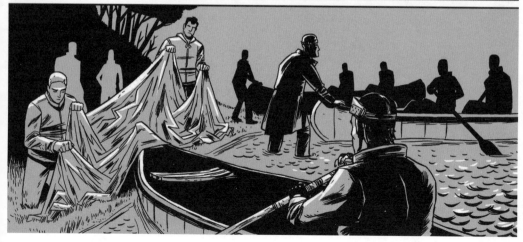

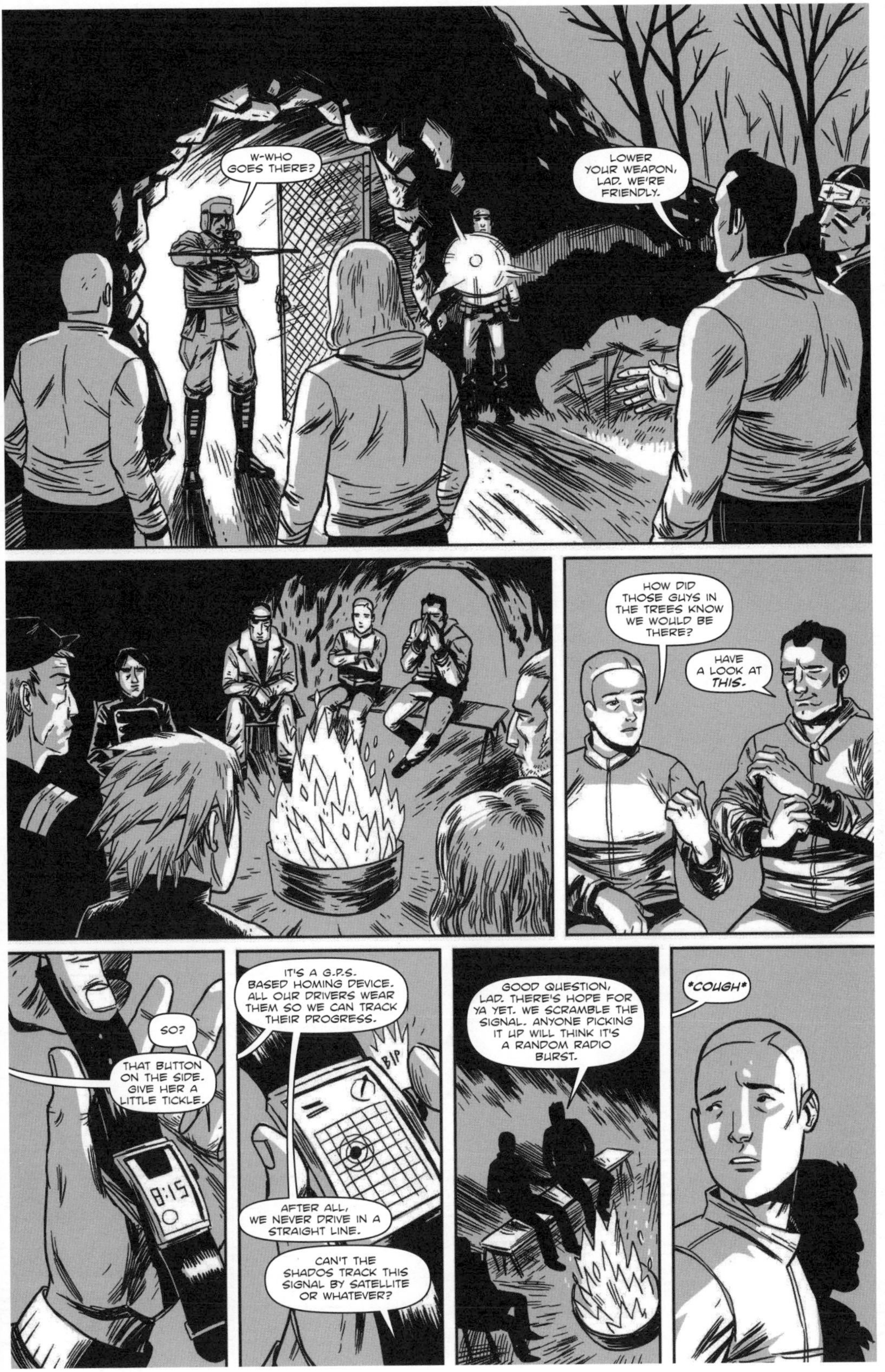

W-WHO GOES THERE?
LOWER YOUR WEAPON, LAD. WE'RE FRIENDLY.
HOW DID THOSE GUYS IN THE TREES KNOW WE WOULD BE THERE?
HAVE A LOOK AT THIS.
SO?
THAT BUTTON ON THE SIDE. GIVE HER A LITTLE TICKLE.
8:15
IT'S A G.P.S. BASED HOMING DEVICE. ALL OUR DRIVERS WEAR THEM SO WE CAN TRACK THEIR PROGRESS.
BIP
AFTER ALL, WE NEVER DRIVE IN A STRAIGHT LINE.
CAN'T THE SHADOS TRACK THIS SIGNAL BY SATELLITE OR WHATEVER?
GOOD QUESTION, LAD. THERE'S HOPE FOR YA YET. WE SCRAMBLE THE SIGNAL. ANYONE PICKING IT UP WILL THINK IT'S A RANDOM RADIO BURST.
COUGH

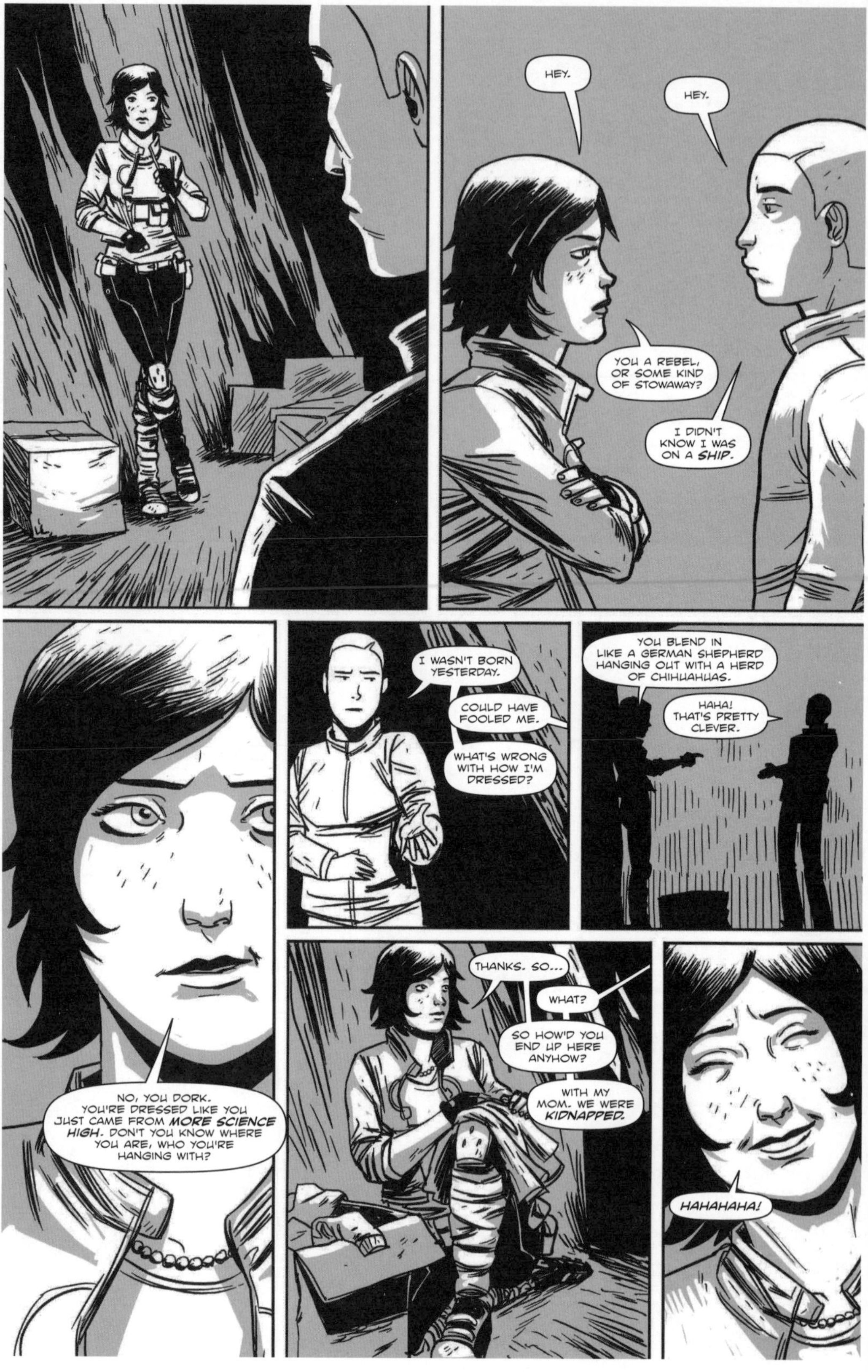
HEY.
HEY.
YOU A REBEL, OR SOME KIND OF STOWAWAY?
I DIDN'T KNOW I WAS ON A SHIP.
I WASN'T BORN YESTERDAY.
COULD HAVE FOOLED ME.
WHAT'S WRONG WITH HOW I'M DRESSED?
YOU BLEND IN LIKE A GERMAN SHEPHERD HANGING OUT WITH A HERD OF CHIHUAHUAS.
HAHA! THAT'S PRETTY CLEVER.
NO, YOU DORK. YOU'RE DRESSED LIKE YOU JUST CAME FROM MORE SCIENCE HIGH. DON'T YOU KNOW WHERE YOU ARE, WHO YOU'RE HANGING WITH?
THANKS. SO...
WHAT?
SO HOW'D YOU END UP HERE ANYHOW?
WITH MY MOM. WE WERE KIDNAPPED.
HAHAHAHA!

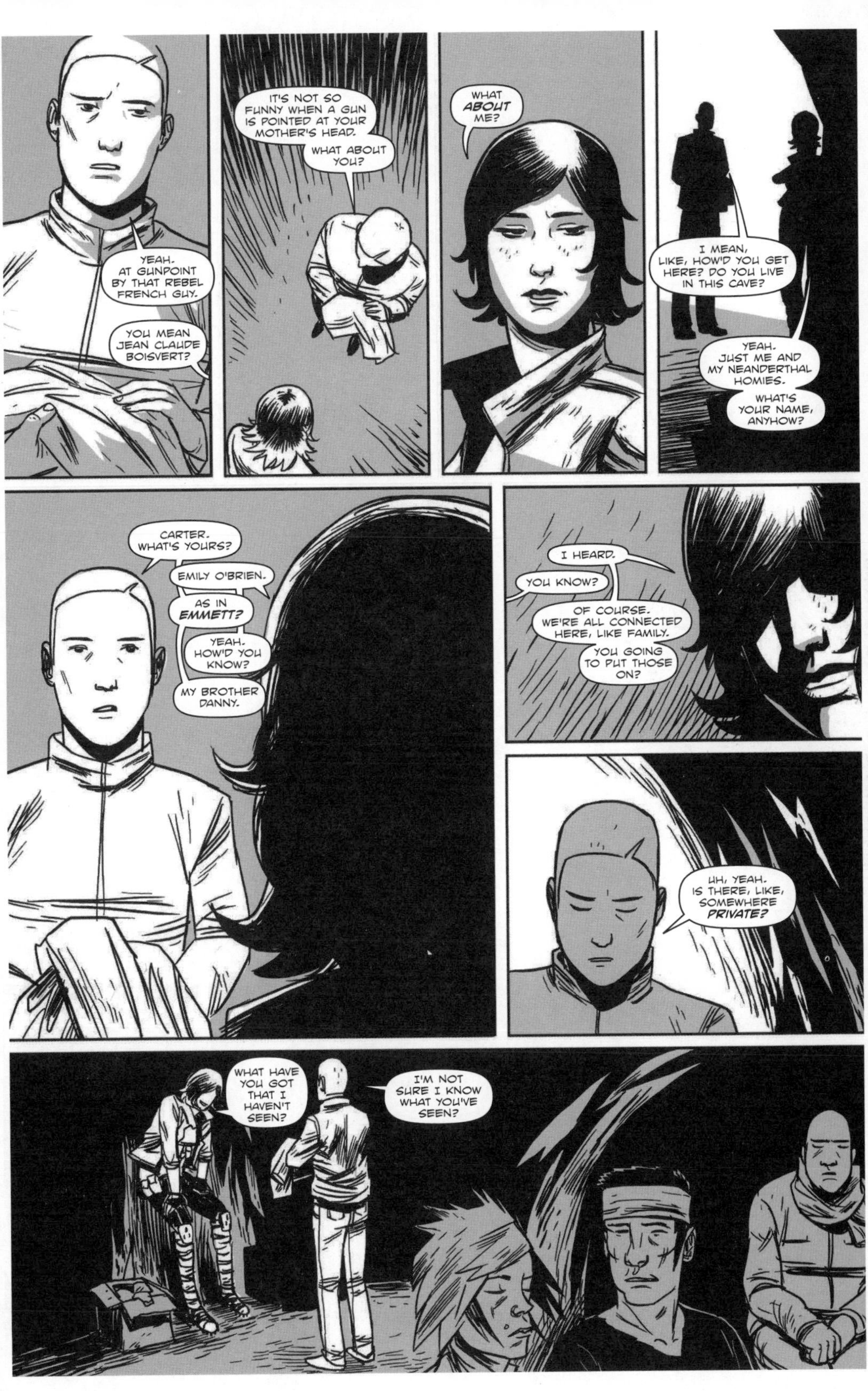
YEAH. AT GUNPOINT BY THAT REBEL FRENCH GUY.
YOU MEAN JEAN CLAUDE BOISVERT?
IT'S NOT SO FUNNY WHEN A GUN IS POINTED AT YOUR MOTHER'S HEAD.
WHAT ABOUT YOU?
WHAT ABOUT ME?
I MEAN, LIKE, HOW'D YOU GET HERE? DO YOU LIVE IN THIS CAVE?
YEAH. JUST ME AND MY NEANDERTHAL HOMIES.
WHAT'S YOUR NAME, ANYHOW?
CARTER. WHAT'S YOURS?
EMILY O'BRIEN.
AS IN EMMETT?
YEAH. HOW'D YOU KNOW?
MY BROTHER DANNY.
I HEARD.
YOU KNOW?
OF COURSE. WE'RE ALL CONNECTED HERE, LIKE FAMILY.
YOU GOING TO PUT THOSE ON?
UH, YEAH. IS THERE, LIKE, SOMEWHERE PRIVATE?
WHAT HAVE YOU GOT THAT I HAVEN'T SEEN?
I'M NOT SURE I KNOW WHAT YOU'VE SEEN?

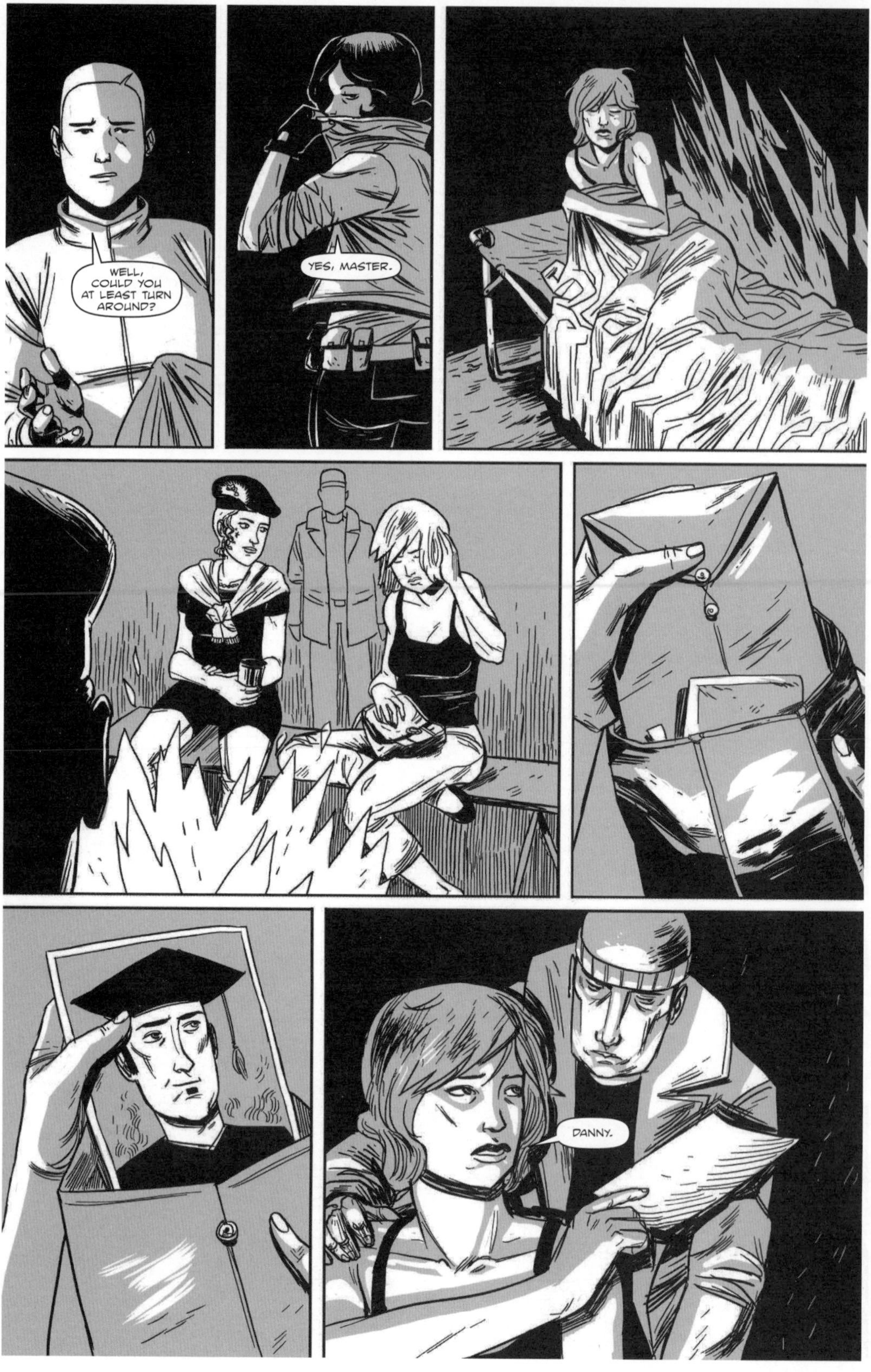
WELL, COULD YOU AT LEAST TURN AROUND?
YES, MASTER.
DANNY.

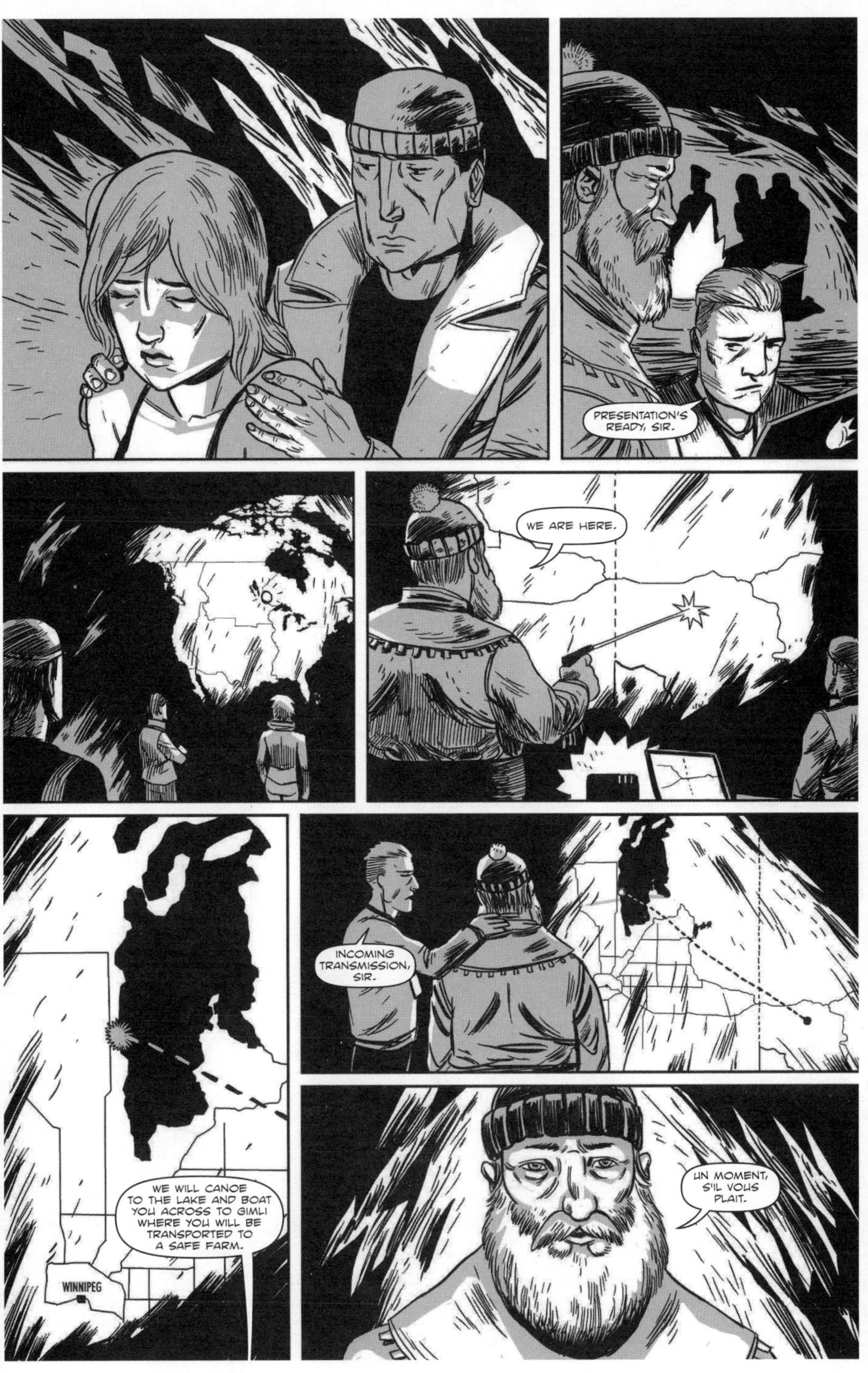
PRESENTATION'S READY, SIR.
WE ARE HERE.
WE WILL CANOE TO THE LAKE AND BOAT YOU ACROSS TO GIMLI WHERE YOU WILL BE TRANSPORTED TO A SAFE FARM.
WINNIPEG
INCOMING TRANSMISSION, SIR.
UN MOMENT, S'IL VOUS PLAIT.

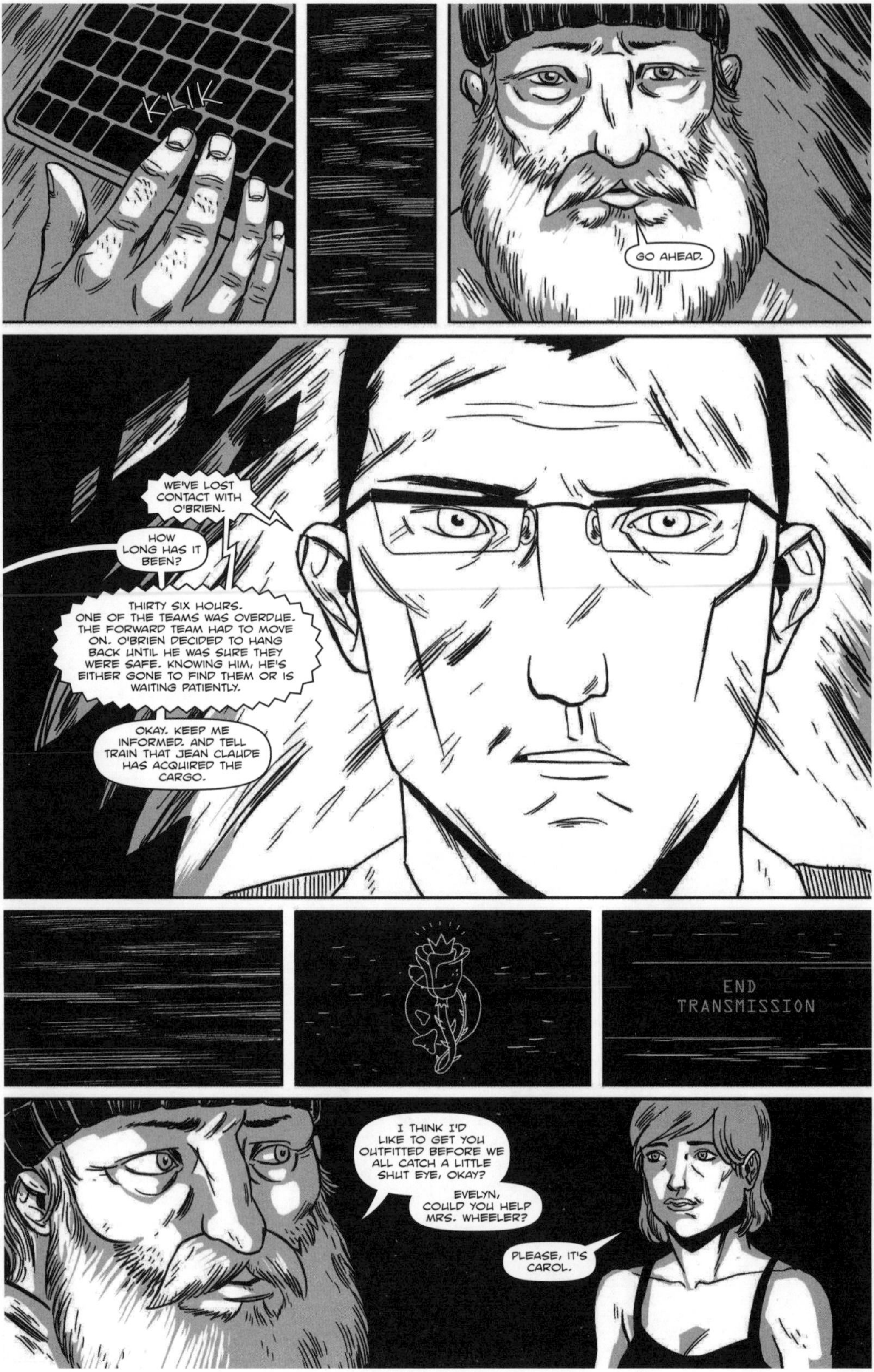

KLIK
GO AHEAD.
WE'VE LOST CONTACT WITH O'BRIEN.
HOW LONG HAS IT BEEN?
THIRTY SIX HOURS. ONE OF THE TEAMS WAS OVERDUE. THE FORWARD TEAM HAD TO MOVE ON. O'BRIEN DECIDED TO HANG BACK UNTIL HE WAS SURE THEY WERE SAFE. KNOWING HIM, HE'S EITHER GONE TO FIND THEM OR IS WAITING PATIENTLY.
OKAY. KEEP ME INFORMED. AND TELL TRAIN THAT JEAN CLAUDE HAS ACQUIRED THE CARGO.
END TRANSMISSION
I THINK I'D LIKE TO GET YOU OUTFITTED BEFORE WE ALL CATCH A LITTLE SHUT EYE, OKAY?
EVELYN, COULD YOU HELP MRS. WHEELER?
PLEASE, IT'S CAROL.

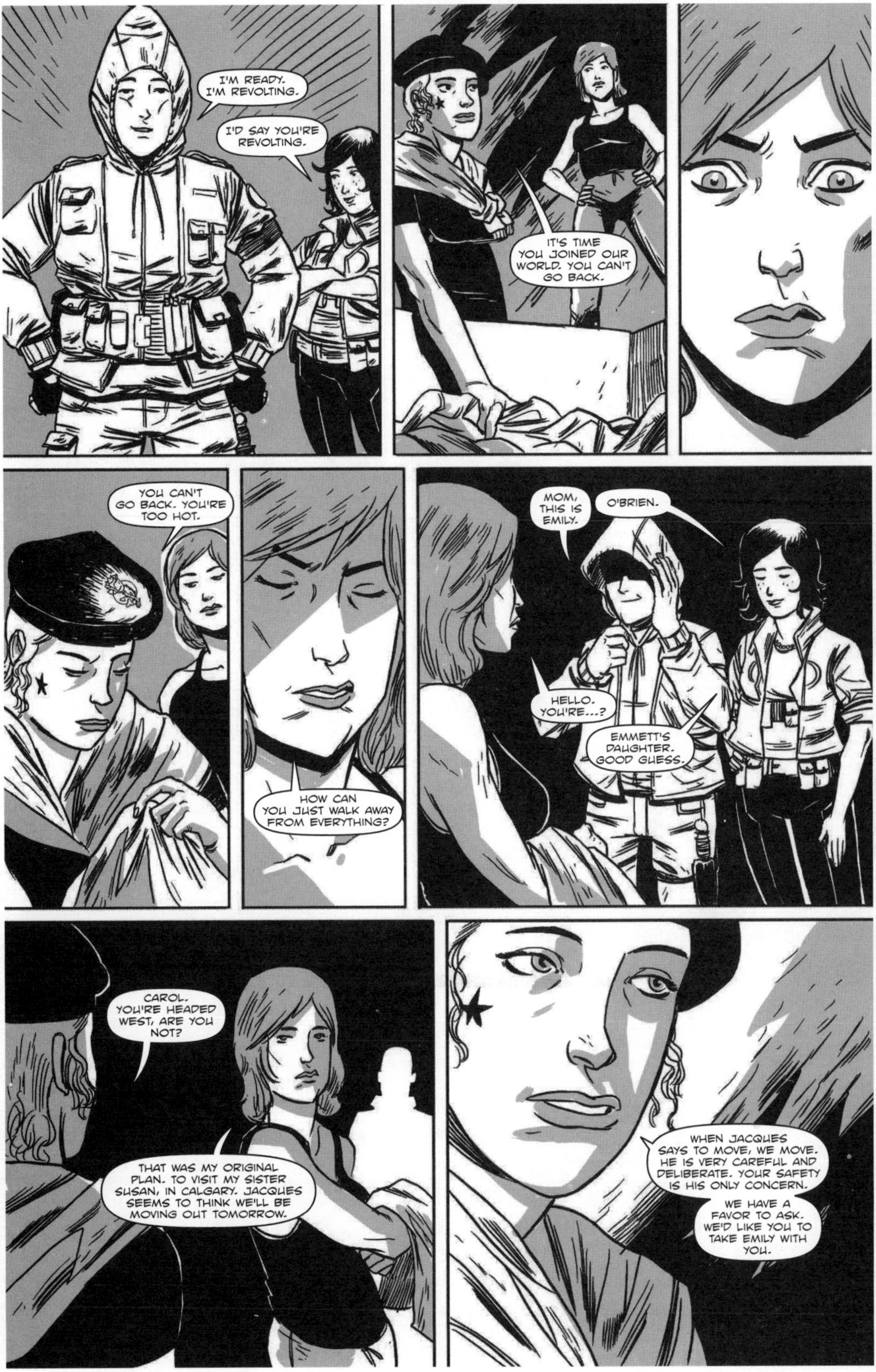
I'M READY. I'M REVOLTING.
I'D SAY YOU'RE REVOLTING.
IT'S TIME YOU JOINED OUR WORLD. YOU CAN'T GO BACK.
YOU CAN'T GO BACK. YOU'RE TOO HOT.
HOW CAN YOU JUST WALK AWAY FROM EVERYTHING?
MOM, THIS IS EMILY.
O'BRIEN.
HELLO. YOU'RE...?
EMMETT'S DAUGHTER. GOOD GUESS.
CAROL. YOU'RE HEADED WEST, ARE YOU NOT?
THAT WAS MY ORIGINAL PLAN. TO VISIT MY SISTER SUSAN, IN CALGARY. JACQUES SEEMS TO THINK WE'LL BE MOVING OUT TOMORROW.
WHEN JACQUES SAYS TO MOVE, WE MOVE. HE IS VERY CAREFUL AND DELIBERATE. YOUR SAFETY IS HIS ONLY CONCERN.
WE HAVE A FAVOR TO ASK. WE'D LIKE YOU TO TAKE EMILY WITH YOU.

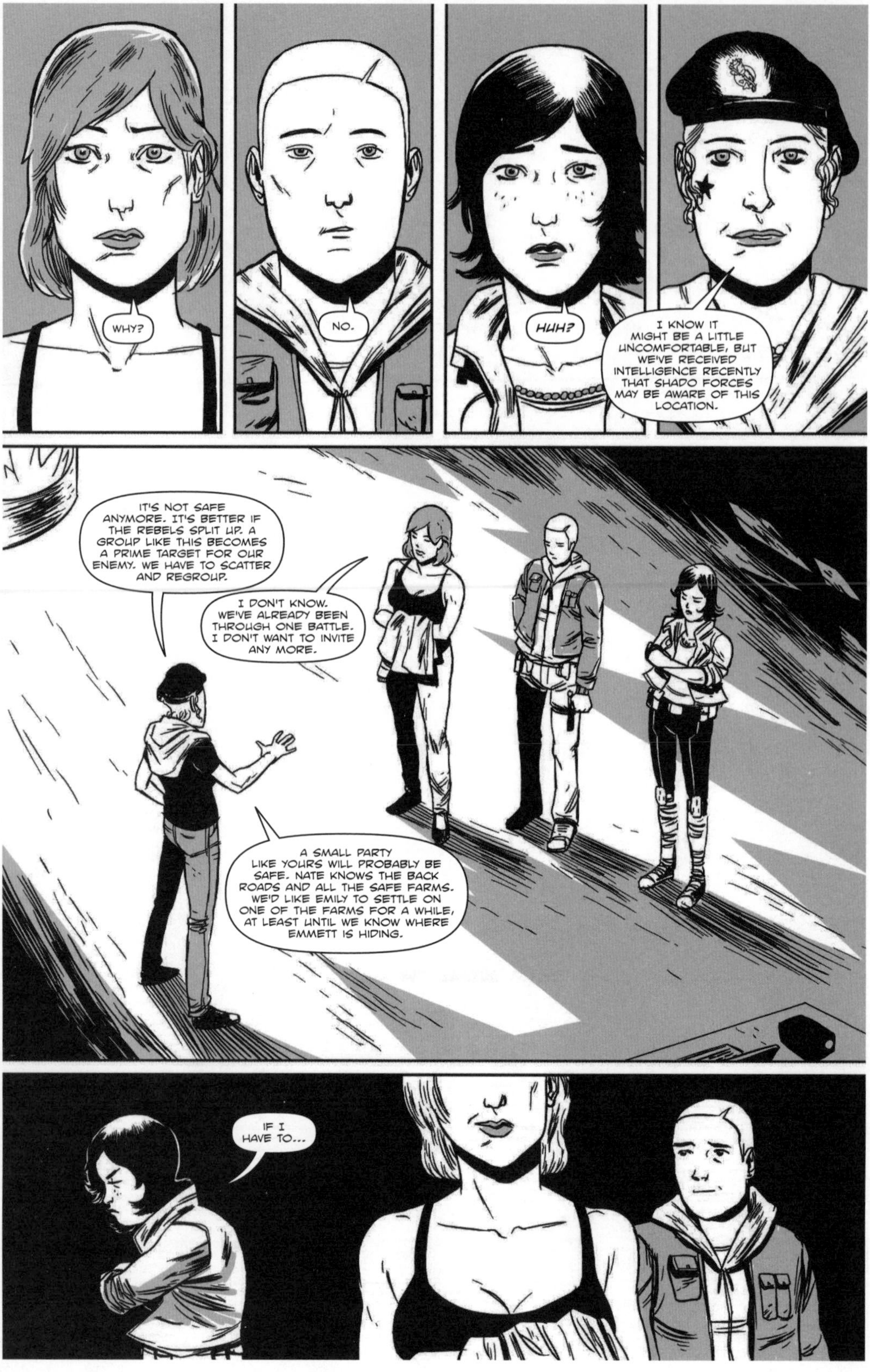
WHY?
NO.
HUH?
I KNOW IT MIGHT BE A LITTLE UNCOMFORTABLE, BUT WE'VE RECEIVED INTELLIGENCE RECENTLY THAT SHADO FORCES MAY BE AWARE OF THIS LOCATION.
IT'S NOT SAFE ANYMORE. IT'S BETTER IF THE REBELS SPLIT UP. A GROUP LIKE THIS BECOMES A PRIME TARGET FOR OUR ENEMY. WE HAVE TO SCATTER AND REGROUP.
I DON'T KNOW. WE'VE ALREADY BEEN THROUGH ONE BATTLE. I DON'T WANT TO INVITE ANY MORE.
A SMALL PARTY LIKE YOURS WILL PROBABLY BE SAFE. NATE KNOWS THE BACK ROADS AND ALL THE SAFE FARMS. WE'D LIKE EMILY TO SETTLE ON ONE OF THE FARMS FOR A WHILE, AT LEAST UNTIL WE KNOW WHERE EMMETT IS HIDING.
IF I HAVE TO...

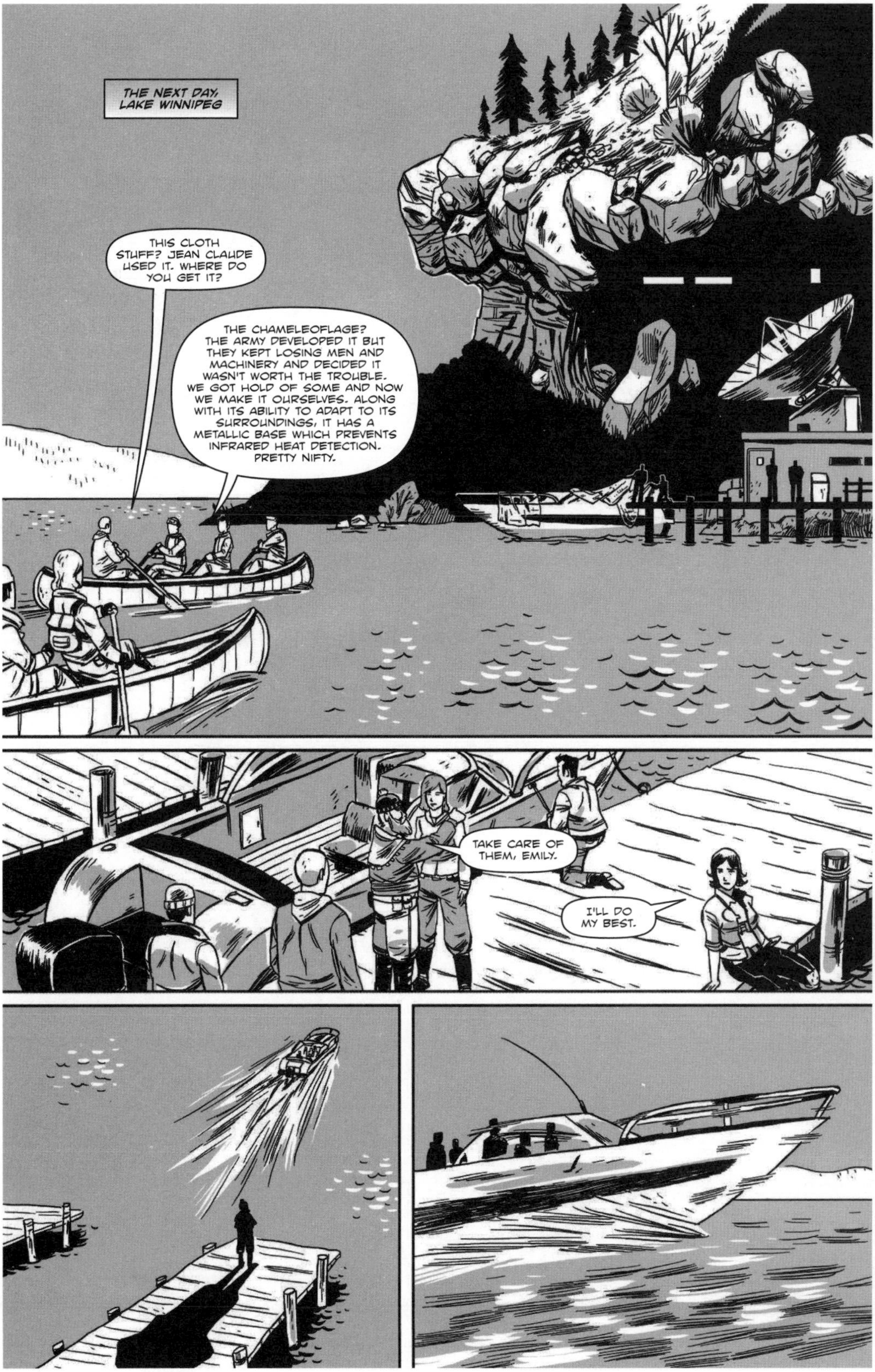
THE NEXT DAY, LAKE WINNIPEG
THIS CLOTH STUFF? JEAN CLAUDE USED IT. WHERE DO YOU GET IT?
THE CHAMELEOFLAGE? THE ARMY DEVELOPED IT BUT THEY KEPT LOSING MEN AND MACHINERY AND DECIDED IT WASN'T WORTH THE TROUBLE. WE GOT HOLD OF SOME AND NOW WE MAKE IT OURSELVES. ALONG WITH ITS ABILITY TO ADAPT TO ITS SURROUNDINGS, IT HAS A METALLIC BASE WHICH PREVENTS INFRARED HEAT DETECTION. PRETTY NIFTY.
TAKE CARE OF THEM, EMILY.
I'LL DO MY BEST.

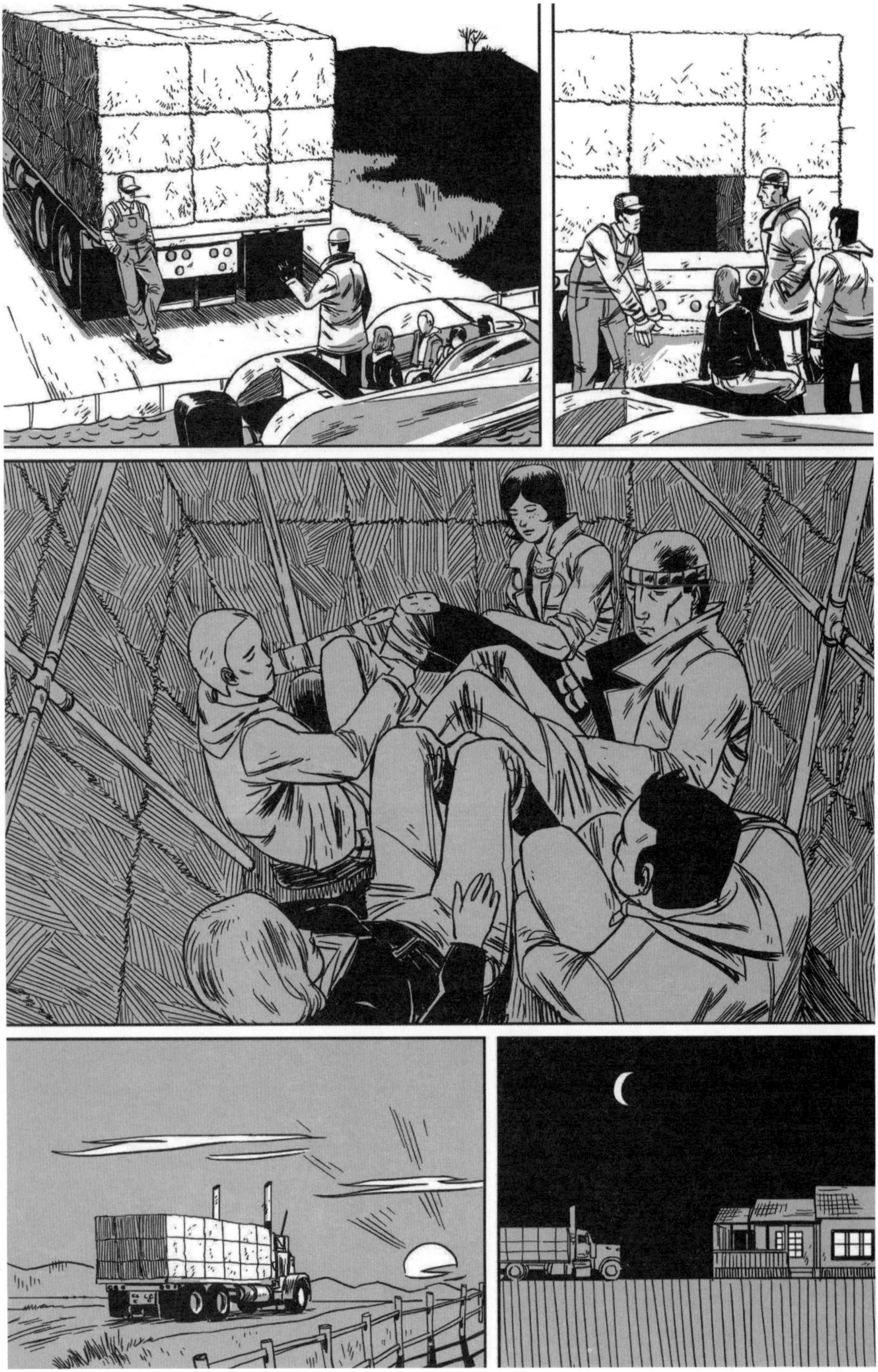

----

hey dad,

where r u?
there u go again. doin the disappearing act. don't you think it's getting
kinda....old. so things are okay with my crew. jacques tries to keep an eye on
me and evelyn has been alright. i kinda miss having kids around.
btw this woman and a dorky kid named carter showed up today with j.c. and that
driver guy, you know, from newfoundland. forget his name. sorry.
anyhow, this carter is pretty out of touch with what we're doing. he thinks it's
some kind of game, like we're playing rebels. he just doesn't get it. his mom
is some lawyer chick from toronto. kinda stuck up, city trash. thinks she knows
what's going on 'cause she watches the news. she's sure in for some surprises...
lol. i can't wait. she's upset 'cause her suv is doa from a firefight. would have
loved to c that!
seems the shados were tracking that driver guy and j.c. but jacques and his men
came to the rescue. cue the cavalry.
g2g we're heading out soon. the firefight alerted them to our presence in the area.
anyhow, can't u just send us a short message. let us know ur alright.
miss you,

lol
18r
em

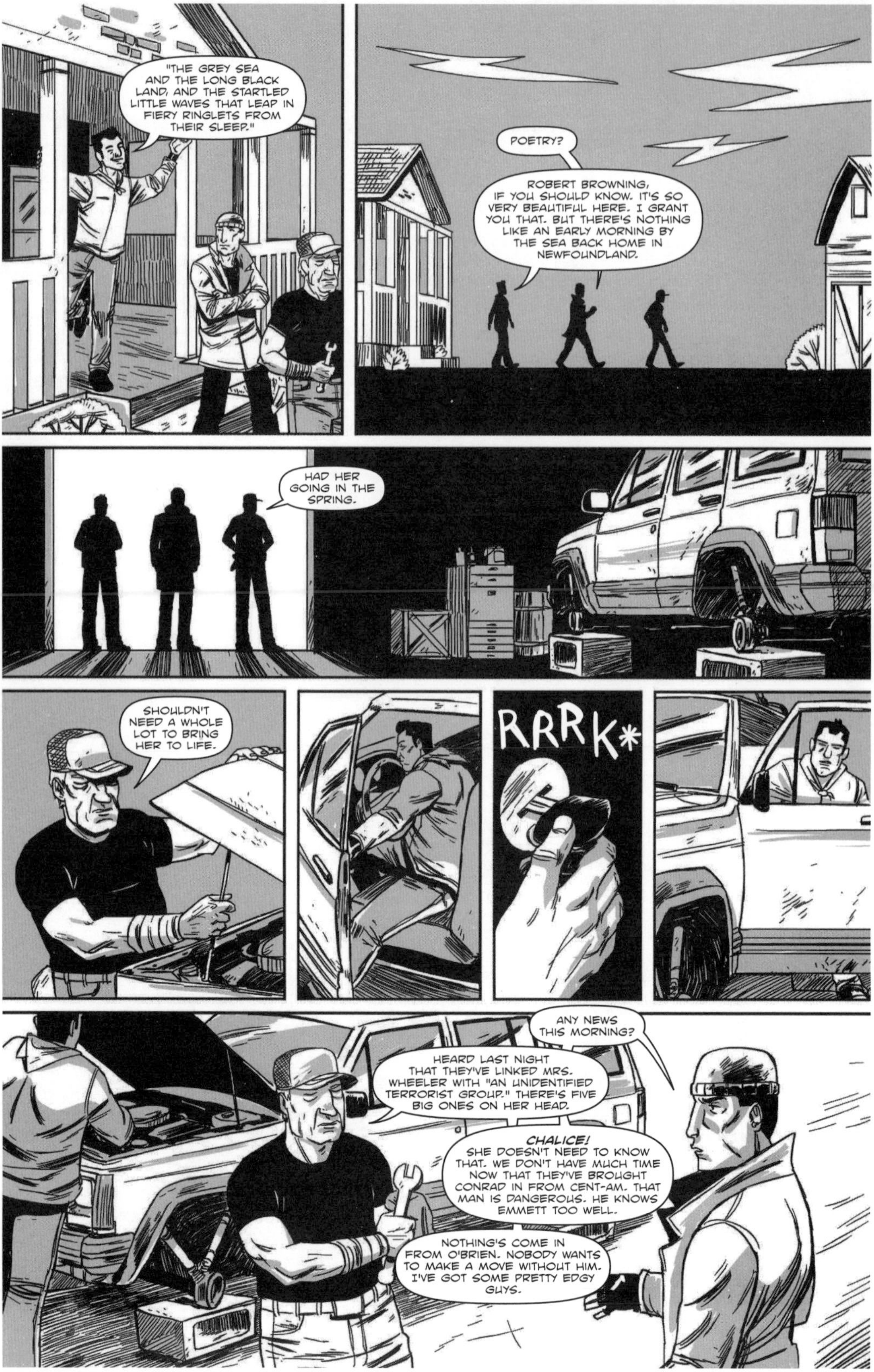
"THE GREY SEA AND THE LONG BLACK LAND, AND THE STARTLED LITTLE WAVES THAT LEAP IN FIERY RINGLETS FROM THEIR SLEEP."
POETRY?
ROBERT BROWNING, IF YOU SHOULD KNOW. IT'S SO VERY BEAUTIFUL HERE. I GRANT YOU THAT. BUT THERE'S NOTHING LIKE AN EARLY MORNING BY THE SEA BACK HOME IN NEWFOUNDLAND.
HAD HER GOING IN THE SPRING.
SHOULDN'T NEED A WHOLE LOT TO BRING HER TO LIFE.
RRRK*
ANY NEWS THIS MORNING?
HEARD LAST NIGHT THAT THEY'VE LINKED MRS. WHEELER WITH "AN UNIDENTIFIED TERRORIST GROUP." THERE'S FIVE BIG ONES ON HER HEAD.
CHALICE! SHE DOESN'T NEED TO KNOW THAT. WE DON'T HAVE MUCH TIME NOW THAT THEY'VE BROUGHT CONRAD IN FROM CENT-AM. THAT MAN IS DANGEROUS. HE KNOWS EMMETT TOO WELL.
NOTHING'S COME IN FROM O'BRIEN. NOBODY WANTS TO MAKE A MOVE WITHOUT HIM. I'VE GOT SOME PRETTY EDGY GUYS.

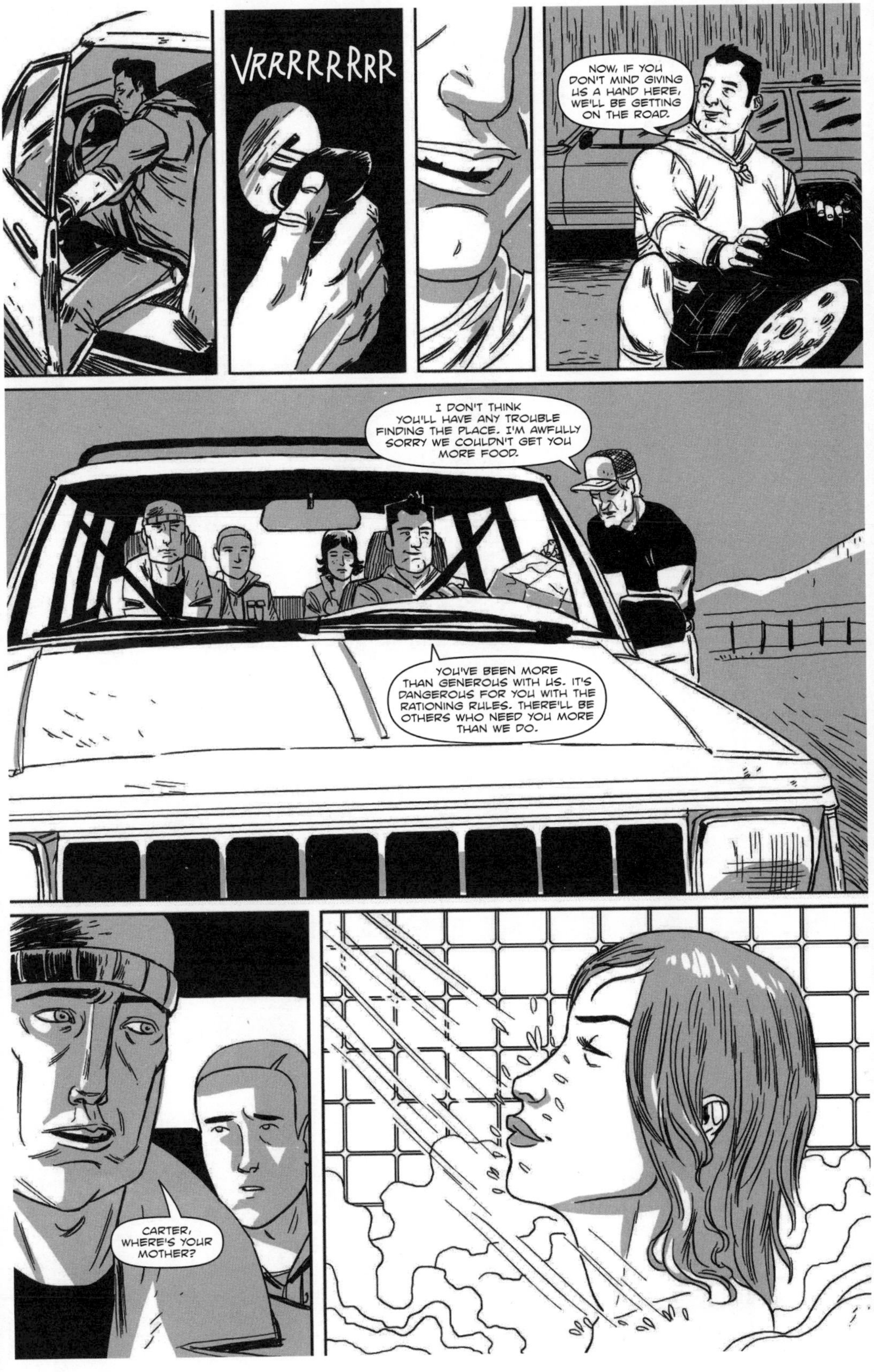
VRRRRRRRR
NOW, IF YOU DON'T MIND GIVING US A HAND HERE, WE'LL BE GETTING ON THE ROAD.
I DON'T THINK YOU'LL HAVE ANY TROUBLE FINDING THE PLACE. I'M AWFULLY SORRY WE COULDN'T GET YOU MORE FOOD.
YOU'VE BEEN MORE THAN GENEROUS WITH US. IT'S DANGEROUS FOR YOU WITH THE RATIONING RULES. THERE'LL BE OTHERS WHO NEED YOU MORE THAN WE DO.
CARTER, WHERE'S YOUR MOTHER?

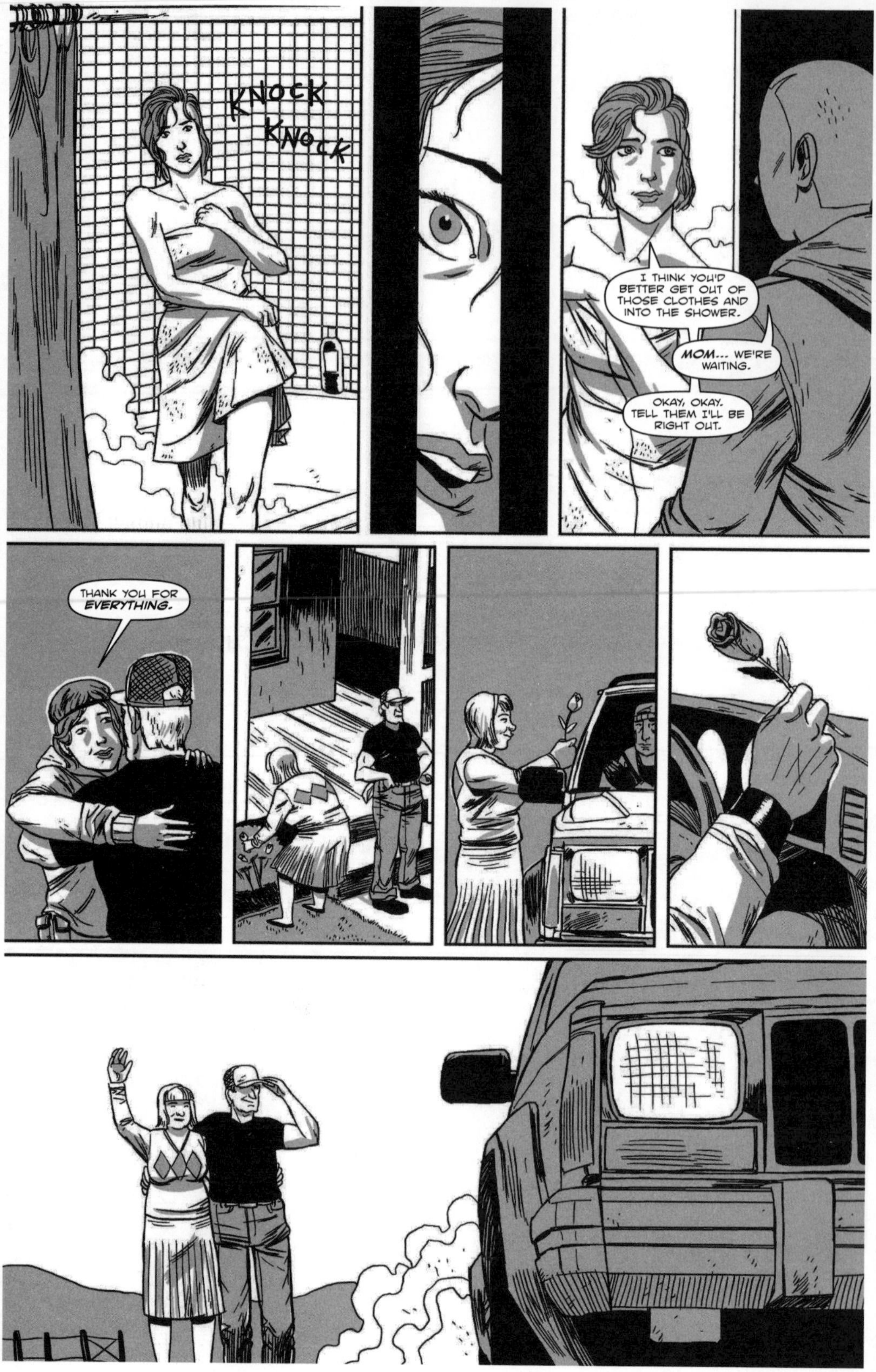
KNOCK
KNOCK
I THINK YOU'D BETTER GET OUT OF THOSE CLOTHES AND INTO THE SHOWER.
MOM... WE'RE WAITING.
OKAY, OKAY. TELL THEM I'LL BE RIGHT OUT.
THANK YOU FOR EVERYTHING.

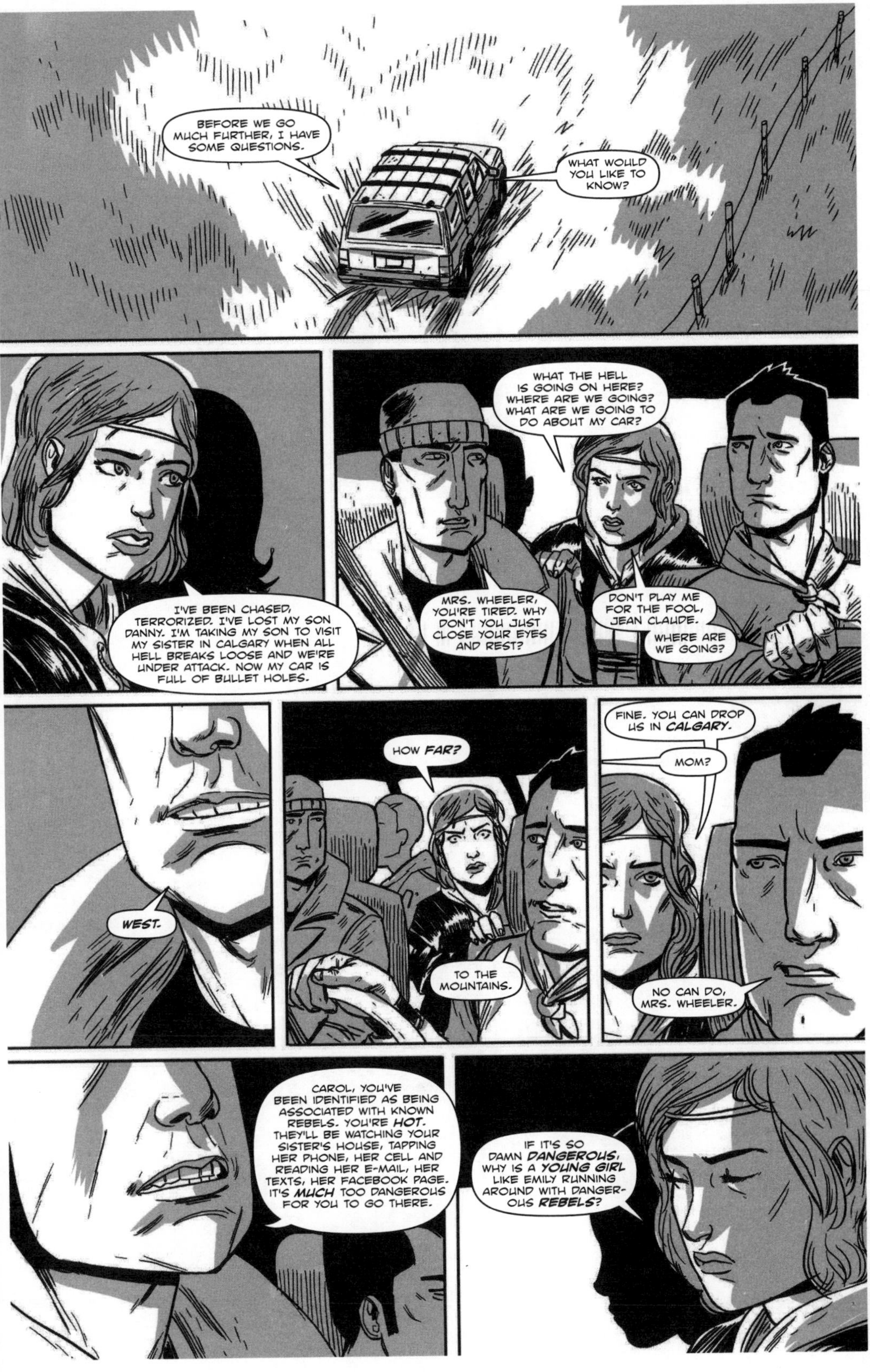
BEFORE WE GO MUCH FURTHER, I HAVE SOME QUESTIONS.
WHAT WOULD YOU LIKE TO KNOW?
I'VE BEEN CHASED, TERRORIZED. I'VE LOST MY SON DANNY. I'M TAKING MY SON TO VISIT MY SISTER IN CALGARY WHEN ALL HELL BREAKS LOOSE AND WE'RE UNDER ATTACK. NOW MY CAR IS FULL OF BULLET HOLES.
WHAT THE HELL IS GOING ON HERE? WHERE ARE WE GOING? WHAT ARE WE GOING TO DO ABOUT MY CAR?
MRS. WHEELER, YOU'RE TIRED. WHY DON'T YOU JUST CLOSE YOUR EYES AND REST?
DON'T PLAY ME FOR THE FOOL, JEAN CLAUDE.
WHERE ARE WE GOING?
WEST.
HOW FAR?
TO THE MOUNTAINS.
FINE. YOU CAN DROP US IN CALGARY.
MOM?
NO CAN DO, MRS. WHEELER.
CAROL, YOU'VE BEEN IDENTIFIED AS BEING ASSOCIATED WITH KNOWN REBELS. YOU'RE HOT. THEY'LL BE WATCHING YOUR SISTER'S HOUSE, TAPPING HER PHONE, HER CELL AND READING HER E-MAIL, HER TEXTS, HER FACEBOOK PAGE. IT'S MUCH TOO DANGEROUS FOR YOU TO GO THERE.
IF IT'S SO DAMN DANGEROUS, WHY IS A YOUNG GIRL LIKE EMILY RUNNING AROUND WITH DANGER-OUS REBELS?

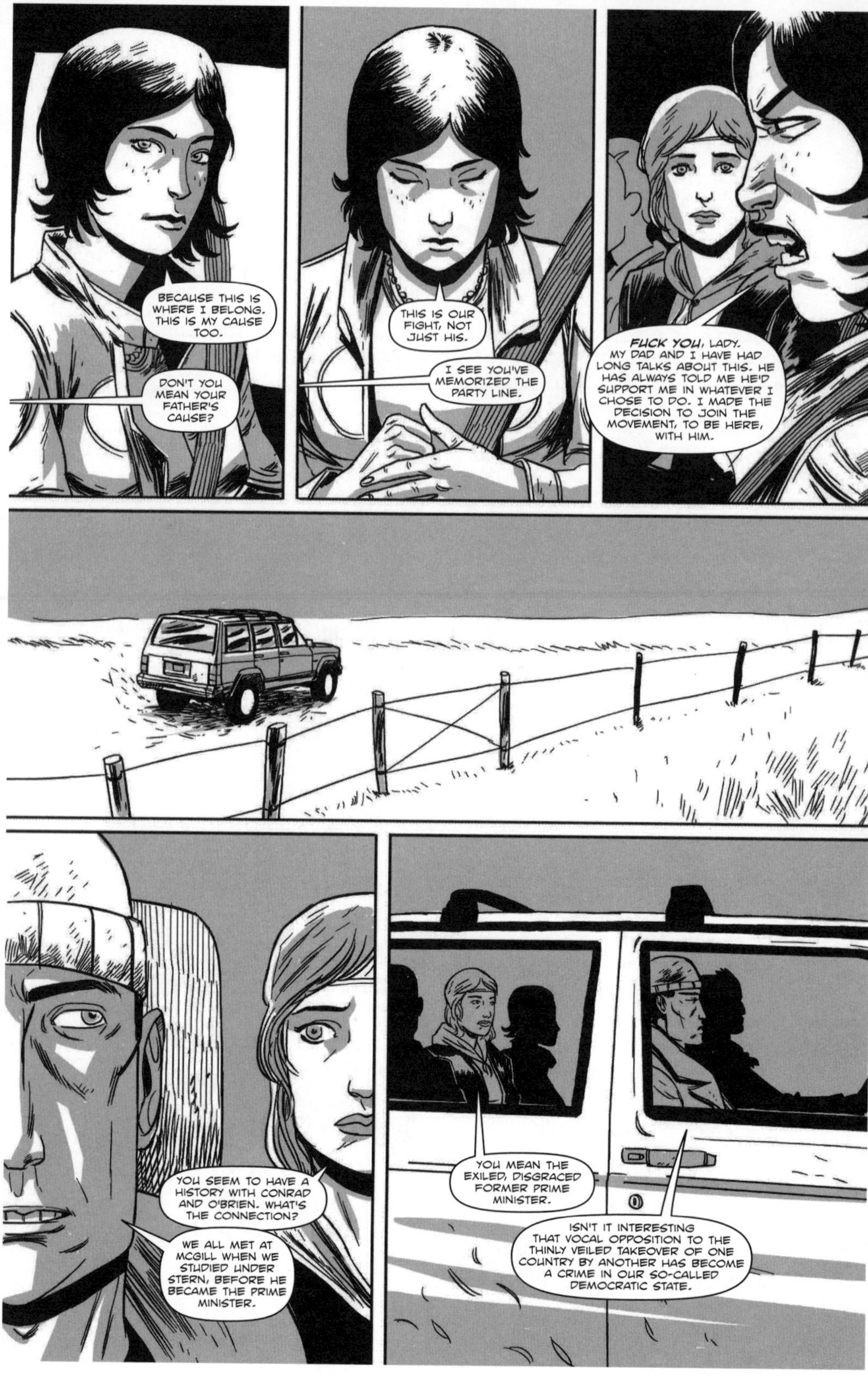
BECAUSE THIS IS WHERE I BELONG. THIS IS MY CAUSE TOO.
DON'T YOU MEAN YOUR FATHER'S CAUSE?
THIS IS OUR FIGHT, NOT JUST HIS.
I SEE YOU'VE MEMORIZED THE PARTY LINE.
FUCK YOU, LADY. MY DAD AND I HAVE HAD LONG TALKS ABOUT THIS. HE HAS ALWAYS TOLD ME HE'D SUPPORT ME IN WHATEVER I CHOSE TO DO. I MADE THE DECISION TO JOIN THE MOVEMENT, TO BE HERE, WITH HIM.
YOU SEEM TO HAVE A HISTORY WITH CONRAD AND O'BRIEN. WHAT'S THE CONNECTION?
WE ALL MET AT MCGILL WHEN WE STUDIED UNDER STERN, BEFORE HE BECAME THE PRIME MINISTER.
YOU MEAN THE EXILED, DISGRACED FORMER PRIME MINISTER.
ISN'T IT INTERESTING THAT VOCAL OPPOSITION TO THE THINLY VEILED TAKEOVER OF ONE COUNTRY BY ANOTHER HAS BECOME A CRIME IN OUR SO-CALLED DEMOCRATIC STATE.

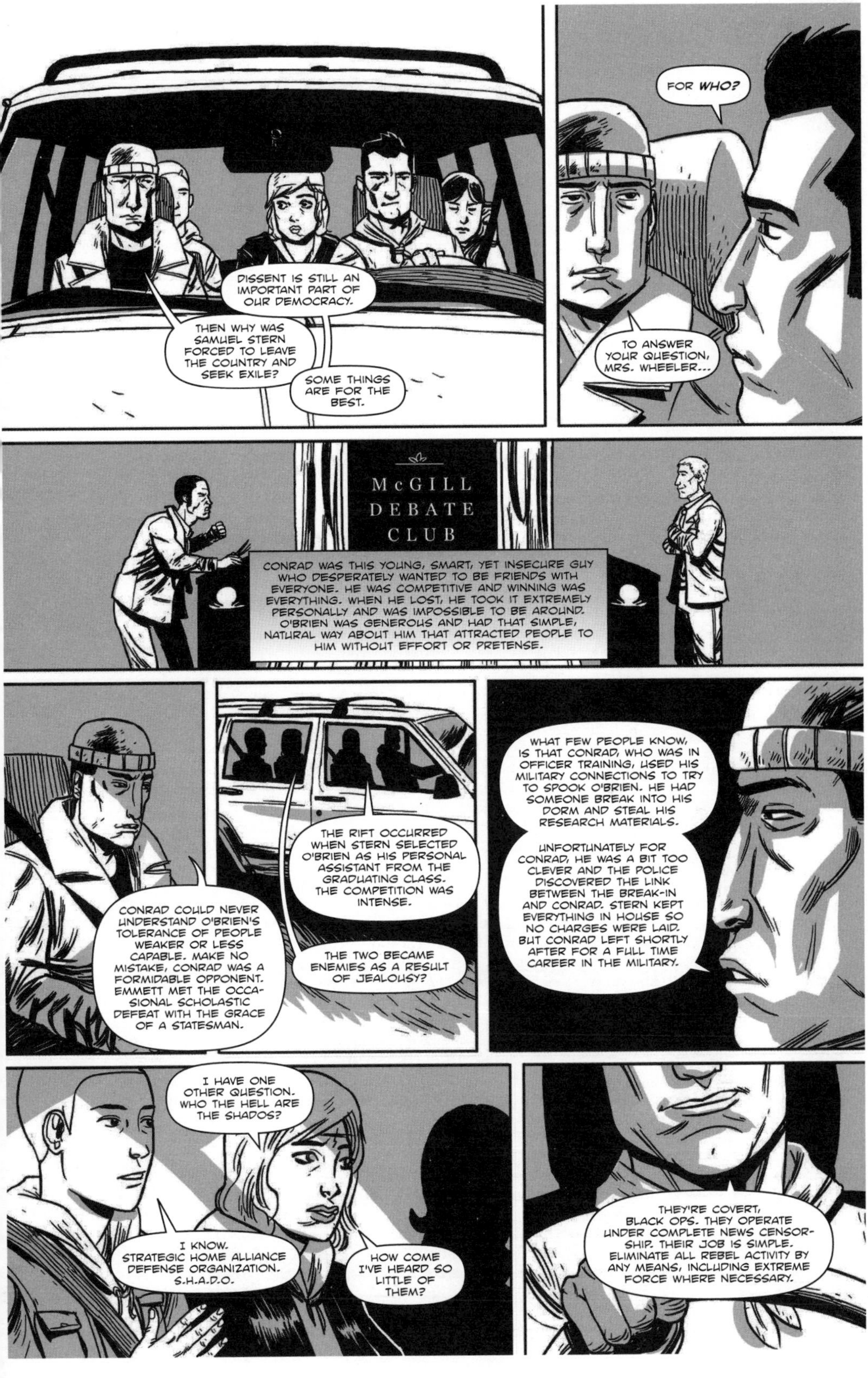
DISSENT IS STILL AN IMPORTANT PART OF OUR DEMOCRACY.
THEN WHY WAS SAMUEL STERN FORCED TO LEAVE THE COUNTRY AND SEEK EXILE?
SOME THINGS ARE FOR THE BEST.
FOR WHO?
TO ANSWER YOUR QUESTION, MRS. WHEELER...
McGILL DEBATE CLUB
CONRAD WAS THIS YOUNG, SMART, YET INSECURE GUY WHO DESPERATELY WANTED TO BE FRIENDS WITH EVERYONE. HE WAS COMPETITIVE AND WINNING WAS EVERYTHING. WHEN HE LOST, HE TOOK IT EXTREMELY PERSONALLY AND WAS IMPOSSIBLE TO BE AROUND. O'BRIEN WAS GENEROUS AND HAD THAT SIMPLE, NATURAL WAY ABOUT HIM THAT ATTRACTED PEOPLE TO HIM WITHOUT EFFORT OR PRETENSE.
CONRAD COULD NEVER UNDERSTAND O'BRIEN'S TOLERANCE OF PEOPLE WEAKER OR LESS CAPABLE. MAKE NO MISTAKE, CONRAD WAS A FORMIDABLE OPPONENT. EMMETT MET THE OCCA-SIONAL SCHOLASTIC DEFEAT WITH THE GRACE OF A STATESMAN.
THE RIFT OCCURRED WHEN STERN SELECTED O'BRIEN AS HIS PERSONAL ASSISTANT FROM THE GRADUATING CLASS. THE COMPETITION WAS INTENSE.
THE TWO BECAME ENEMIES AS A RESULT OF JEALOUSY?
WHAT FEW PEOPLE KNOW, IS THAT CONRAD, WHO WAS IN OFFICER TRAINING, USED HIS MILITARY CONNECTIONS TO TRY TO SPOOK O'BRIEN. HE HAD SOMEONE BREAK INTO HIS DORM AND STEAL HIS RESEARCH MATERIALS.
UNFORTUNATELY FOR CONRAD, HE WAS A BIT TOO CLEVER AND THE POLICE DISCOVERED THE LINK BETWEEN THE BREAK-IN AND CONRAD. STERN KEPT EVERYTHING IN HOUSE SO NO CHARGES WERE LAID. BUT CONRAD LEFT SHORTLY AFTER FOR A FULL TIME CAREER IN THE MILITARY.
I HAVE ONE OTHER QUESTION. WHO THE HELL ARE THE SHADOS?
I KNOW. STRATEGIC HOME ALLIANCE DEFENSE ORGANIZATION. S.H.A.D.O.
HOW COME I'VE HEARD SO LITTLE OF THEM?
THEY'RE COVERT, BLACK OPS. THEY OPERATE UNDER COMPLETE NEWS CENSOR-SHIP. THEIR JOB IS SIMPLE. ELIMINATE ALL REBEL ACTIVITY BY ANY MEANS, INCLUDING EXTREME FORCE WHERE NECESSARY.

```
-----------------------------------
```

INTERVIEW WITH PROFESSOR SAMUEL STERN

by Matt Clement
USNA News Services
Filed 04.09.12

Professor Samuel Stern is one of the people of whom the ruling elite wishes
would just teach his seminars and be quiet. From his office at McGill University
in Montreal, he has been a consistent voice of dissent against the perceived
blunders of the governments of both the United States and Canada. Despite the
assassination attempt last year, Professor Stern remains as vocal and passionate
as ever. I spoke to him in his office, amidst the chaos of books, papers and
computers.

Clement: I don't think it's particularly insulting to say that you have a rather
messy office, Professor Stern.

Stern: (laughs) Well, I suppose the cadence of life rises from the mists of
chaos.

Clement: Cadence is actually an important word in your lexicon.

Stern: If you study patterns, repeated sequences of events, you will find the
heart of history. For example, if you dig back into the early years of the lives
of most dictators, you find the same story, the same sequence of events. Usually
a lonely or misunderstood young man who finds a home or family or community
amongst a group of people with ideas that are far from any sense of natural
order or justice. He may not subscribe to this set of beliefs but the need
to belong supersedes any desire to follow a more humane path, especially
when the leadership, or, more appropriately, becoming the father of the
organization, becomes attainable.

Clement: Your recently published book, 'The Ascent of the Military' details what
you call the 'overt takeover of the civilian authority.' Do you find similar
cadence or patterns in what is happening now?

Stern: (laughs) Yeah, that book hasn't made me the most popular academic in
North America. The border has, in some ways, protected me from some of my more
vocal and passionate opponents from down south. There are, in a sense, two
parallel patterns at play. What I call the external and internal. The
external is the deteriorating economic conditions, the collapse of the
European economic Union, the weather disasters, the west coast earthquakes
and the central American unrest. All have lead to a destabilization of
established order and the opportunity to use fear as a weapon. This enhances
the opportunity for a tighter, smaller group to take over the power
structures and political mechanisms of government. The floundering presidency
of Jonathan Reed, a nice man, a smart man, but a man who, much like George W.
Bush, exhibits all the characteristics of a prop or puppet, led to the
Proclamation of Suspension, the so-called temporary suspension of government
allowing the forces of the military and the secret police to govern without
civilian oversight during this period of unrest and uncertainty. The internal
pattern is the combination of the weak leadership of President Reed and the
ascendency of General Karol Klusinsky. Klusinsky is the kind of aggressive,
chest thumping leader that appeals to the people who do no analysis but
accept the image and story presented to them.

Clement: His early life fits the pattern you presented earlier.

Stern: His mother was an alcoholic who looked after the boy until his 6th
birthday. His father, ex-military, was also an alcoholic and disappeared shortly
after the death of his wife. There is much speculation as to whether her death
was self induced alcoholic poisoning or something more sinister. Klusinksi
grew up in foster homes until his early teens when, in a desperate plan
to cure his chronic law breaking and drug induced violence, he was sent to
military boarding school. It was here that he found his collective family and
a place where his aggressiveness and anti-social behaviour was accepted and
nurtured.

Clement: What do you make of the rumors flying around Ottawa about secret amalgamation talks?

Stern: Let me deal with this question in two parts. First of all, the process to accepting amalgamation would require the change to our constitution and would require the acceptance of all provinces and territories plus, the government would be wise to hold a national plebiscite to insure the people were actually in support of the idea. That process would take years to organize, debate and carry out. This present government exhibits the arrogance to believe that they know what the people want and are going to give it to them. I do not put it past them to drive it down the throats of the Canadian people using fear and bullying as the tools of persuasion.

Clement: And the second?

Stern: It would be a colossal mistake. It's certainly a situation where if it actually happened, there would be no turning back, short of armed revolution. An amalgamation would lead to a more militarized society, and, I fear, a more aggressive military stance on the world stage. The United States has everything to gain, as has been pointed out many times: labour, access to market, access to natural resources, access to the Canadian north. Canada will be sold on the free flow of money, access to the US market, that sort of nonsense. Mostly, Canadians will be sold on the idea of increased personal wealth. They will also be sold on the idea of more security from outside forces. I wouldn't be surprised if there was some kind of horrific so-called terrorist incident to fuel the pro-amalgamation fires.

Clement: It's obvious that you are passionate about this issue.

Stern: As a political scientist, there is none more urgent to consider.

Clement: You have the reputation of your seminars becoming the training ground for future political talent. Any of your students worth mentioning?

Stern: Gosh, I hate to jinx my students. Well, yes there are a few worth keeping an eye on. Emmett O'Brien, who led the school's debating team at the world's this year has that rare combination of intellectual curiosity and humanity. He's much like I was 30 years ago. I'm fascinated by Jean Claude Boisvert because of his family connections in Montreal and his keen sense of timing. He just seems to know when to lay low and when to strike. A political animal who has his feet planted firmly in academia. He may not escape the cushioned university life, but if he does, watch out. Joseph A. Conrad is another. He's a wily, clever kid whose achilles' heel may be his predilection to quick decisions without complete analysis. That kind of crapshoot is effective but can also backfire in unexpected ways. He's ambitious and formidable. The one woman who shines is a gal named Judy Taylor from Sudbury who has used her physical attractiveness as a weapon against weak men who do not sense her extraordinary intellectual abilities and simple common sense. If she runs for office, as she's indicated throughout her academic career, she's a force to consider.

Clement: The leadership of the Liberal Democrat Party is coming up soon. As a former cabinet member, you are being heavily recruited to run for the leadership of the party. Are you willing to go on record and announce your candidacy?

Stern: Matt, I enjoy our chats and would love for you to have the scoop of the year, but I cannot commit at this time.

Clement: So you're literally sitting on the fence?

Stern: I cannot confirm nor deny at this time.

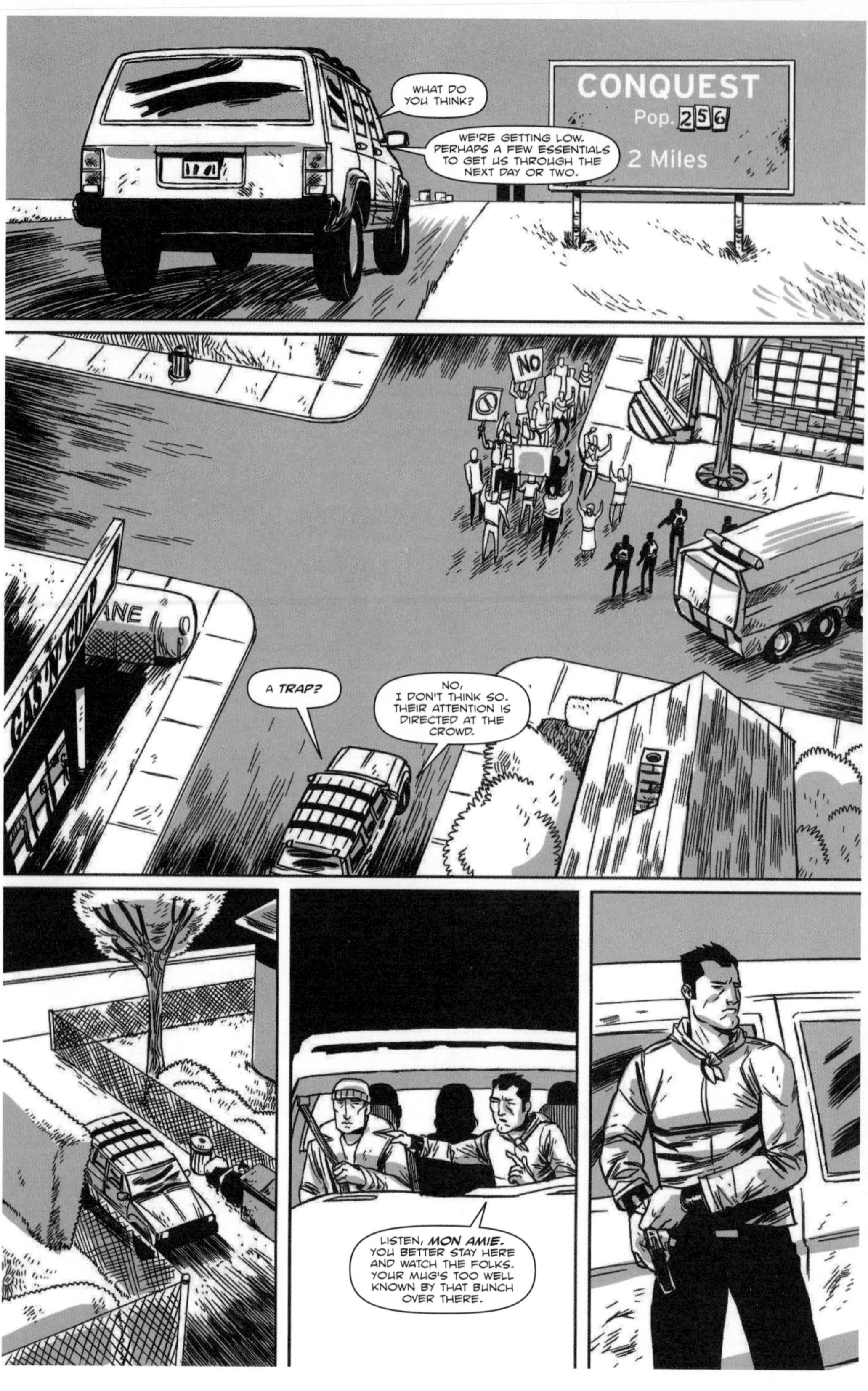
CONQUEST
Pop. 256
2 Miles
WHAT DO YOU THINK?
WE'RE GETTING LOW. PERHAPS A FEW ESSENTIALS TO GET US THROUGH THE NEXT DAY OR TWO.
NO
GAS 'N' GULP
A TRAP?
NO, I DON'T THINK SO. THEIR ATTENTION IS DIRECTED AT THE CROWD.
LISTEN, MON AMIE. YOU BETTER STAY HERE AND WATCH THE FOLKS. YOUR MUG'S TOO WELL KNOWN BY THAT BUNCH OVER THERE.

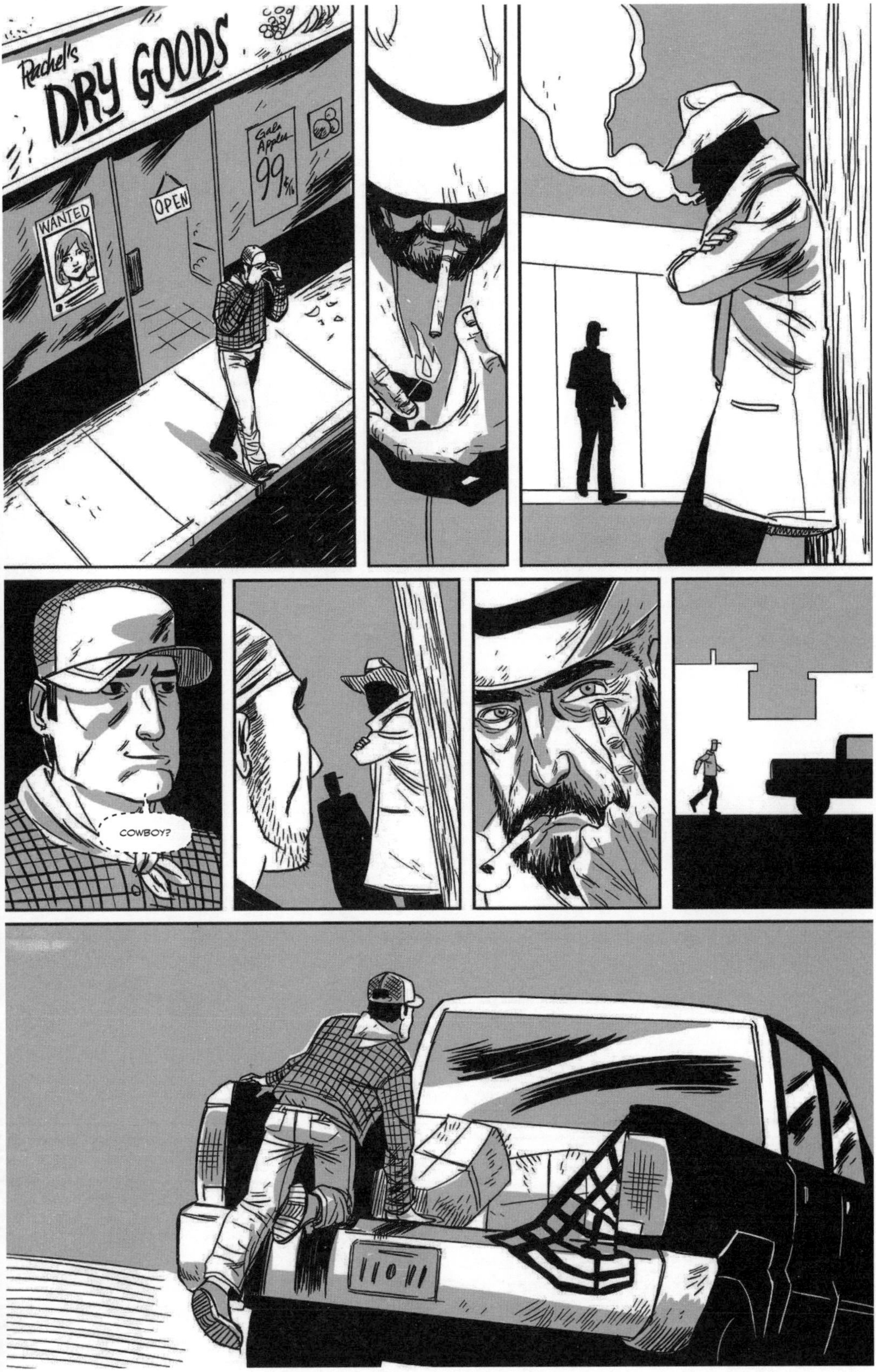
Rachel's
DRY GOODS
Gala Apples
99
WANTED
OPEN
COWBOY?

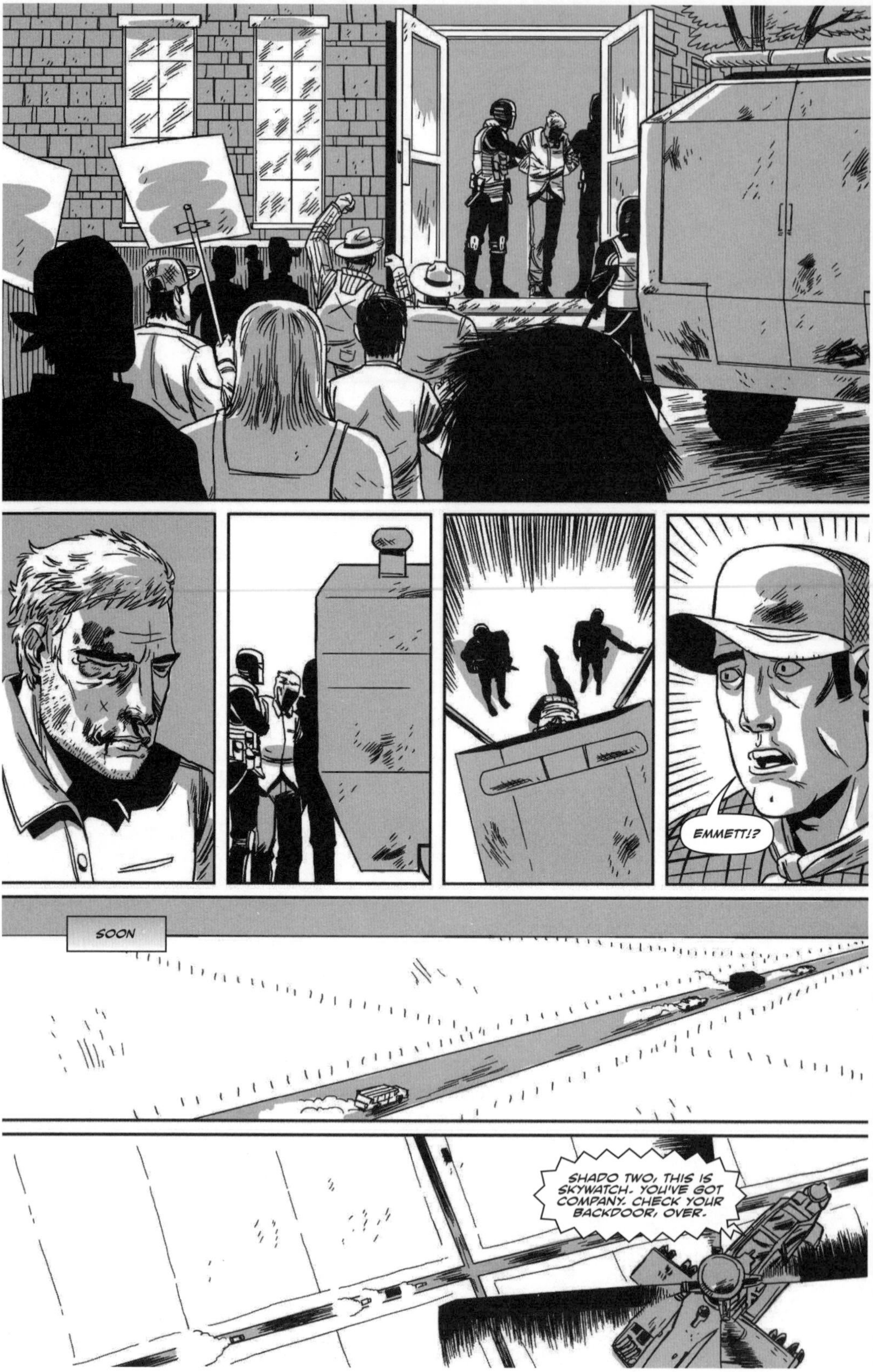
EMMETT!?
SOON
SHADO TWO, THIS IS SKYWATCH. YOU'VE GOT COMPANY. CHECK YOUR BACKDOOR, OVER.

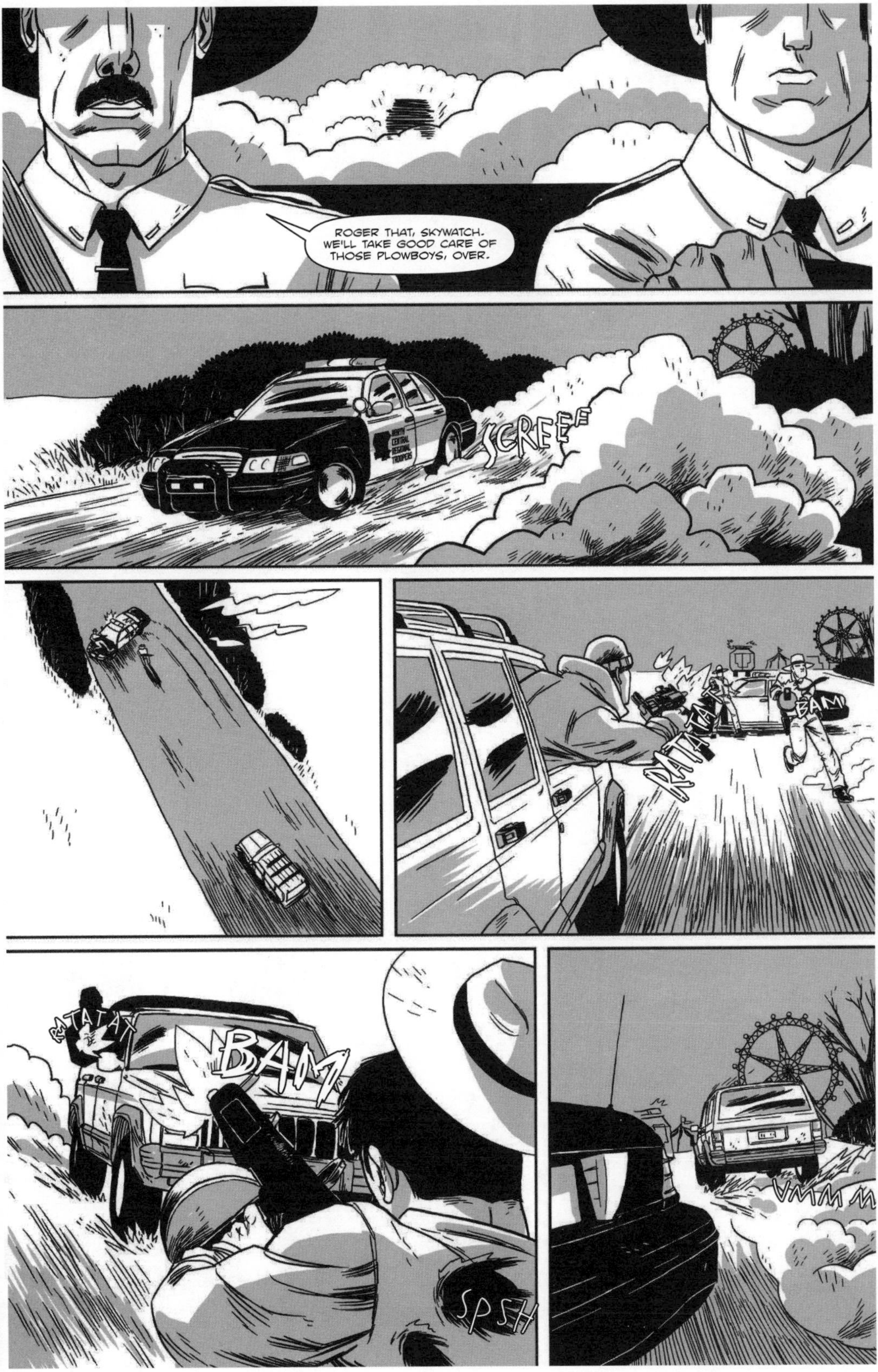
ROGER THAT, SKYWATCH. WE'LL TAKE GOOD CARE OF THOSE PLOWBOYS, OVER.
SCREEE
RATATAT
BAM
RATATAT
BAM
SPSH

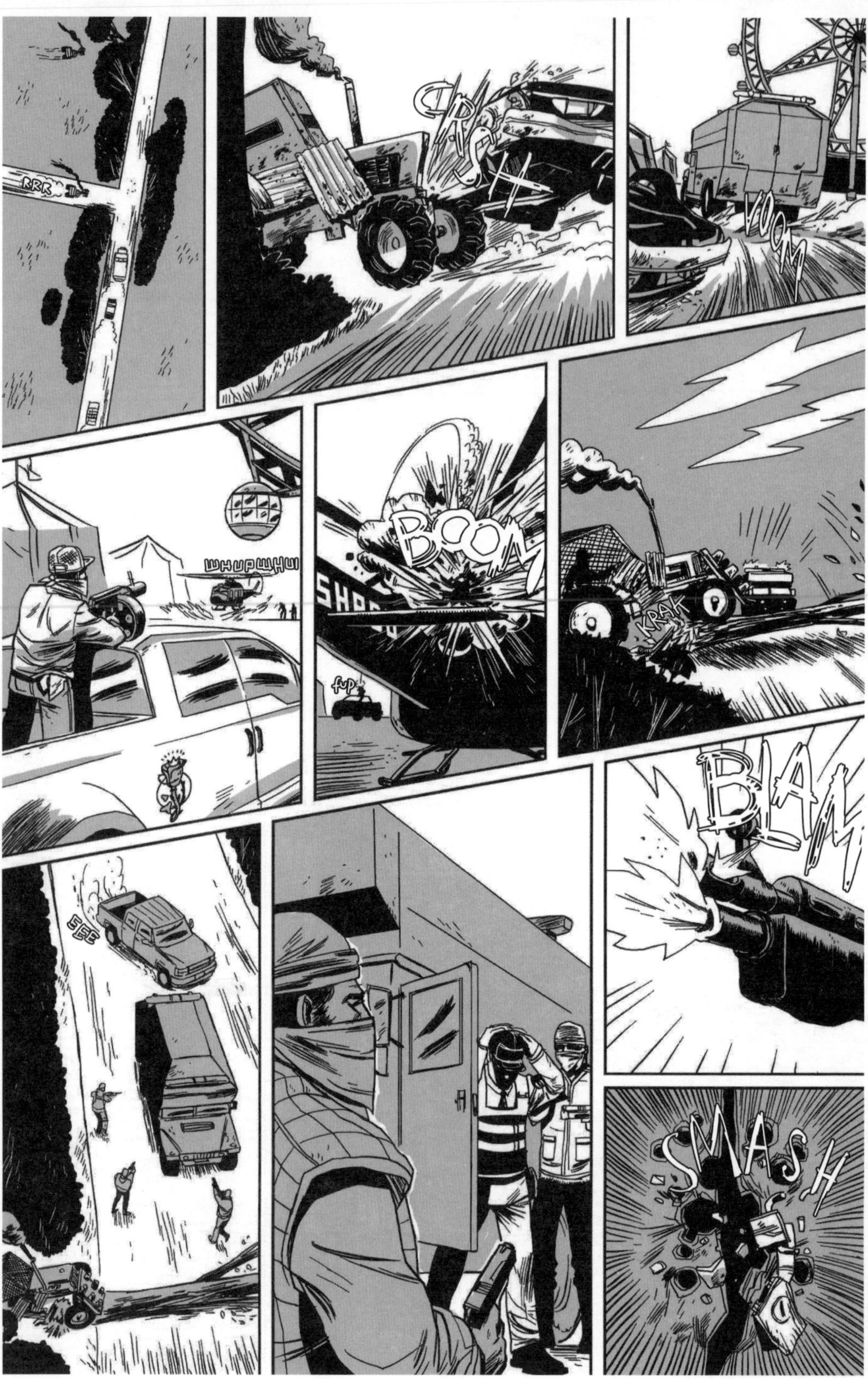
RRR
CRASH
VOOM
WHUPWHUP
BOOM
fup
KRAK
SEE
BLAM
SMASH

PUT IT DOWN, SLOWLY.

SHIT.

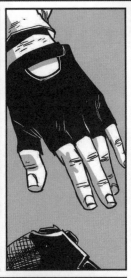

CRACK

LET'S GET YOU OUT OF HERE, EMMETT.

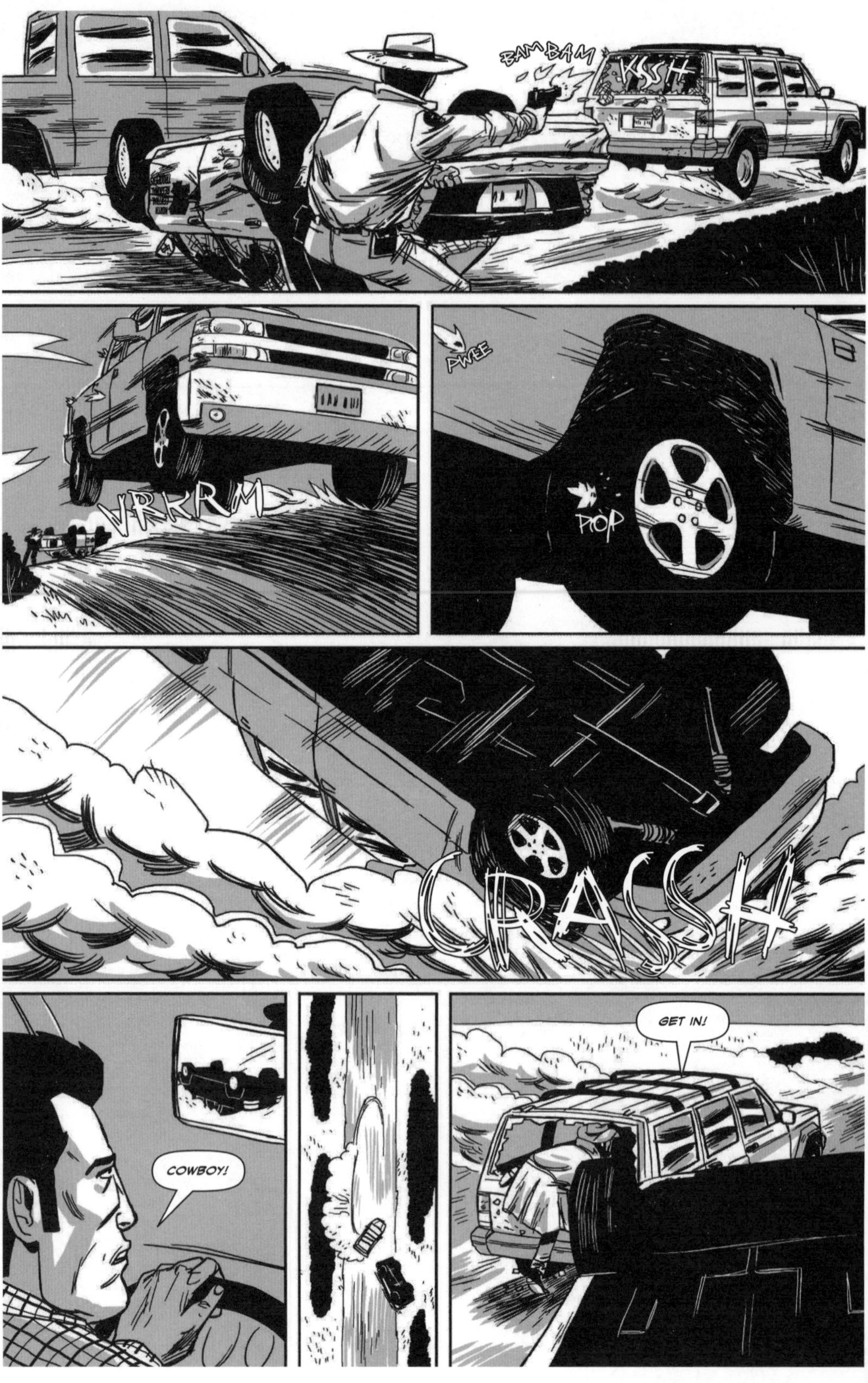
BAM BAM
KSSH
VRRRM
PWEE
POP
CRASSH
COWBOY!
GET IN!

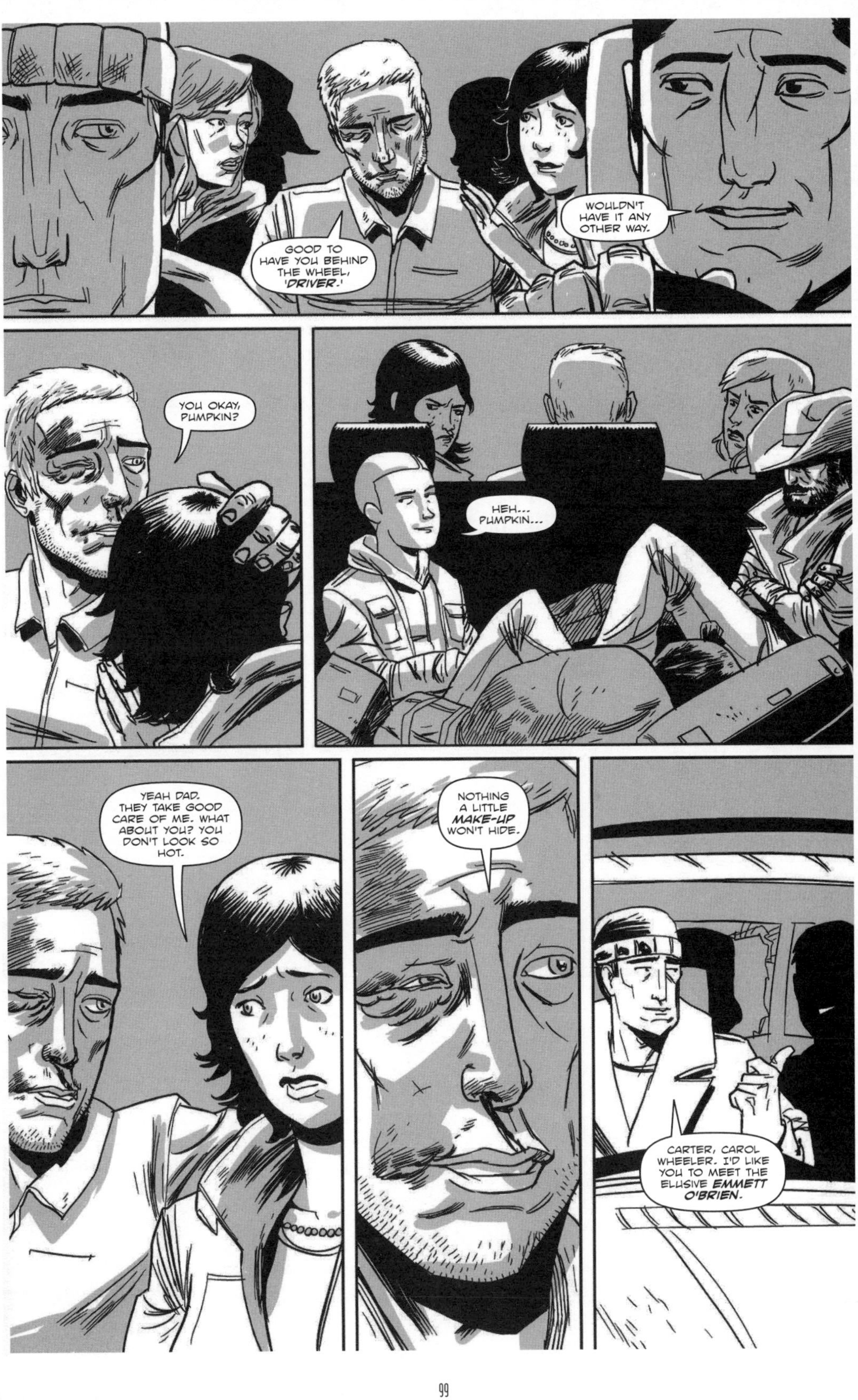
GOOD TO HAVE YOU BEHIND THE WHEEL, 'DRIVER.'
WOULDN'T HAVE IT ANY OTHER WAY.
YOU OKAY, PUMPKIN?
HEH... PUMPKIN...
YEAH DAD. THEY TAKE GOOD CARE OF ME. WHAT ABOUT YOU? YOU DON'T LOOK SO HOT.
NOTHING A LITTLE MAKE-UP WON'T HIDE.
CARTER, CAROL WHEELER. I'D LIKE YOU TO MEET THE ELUSIVE EMMETT O'BRIEN.

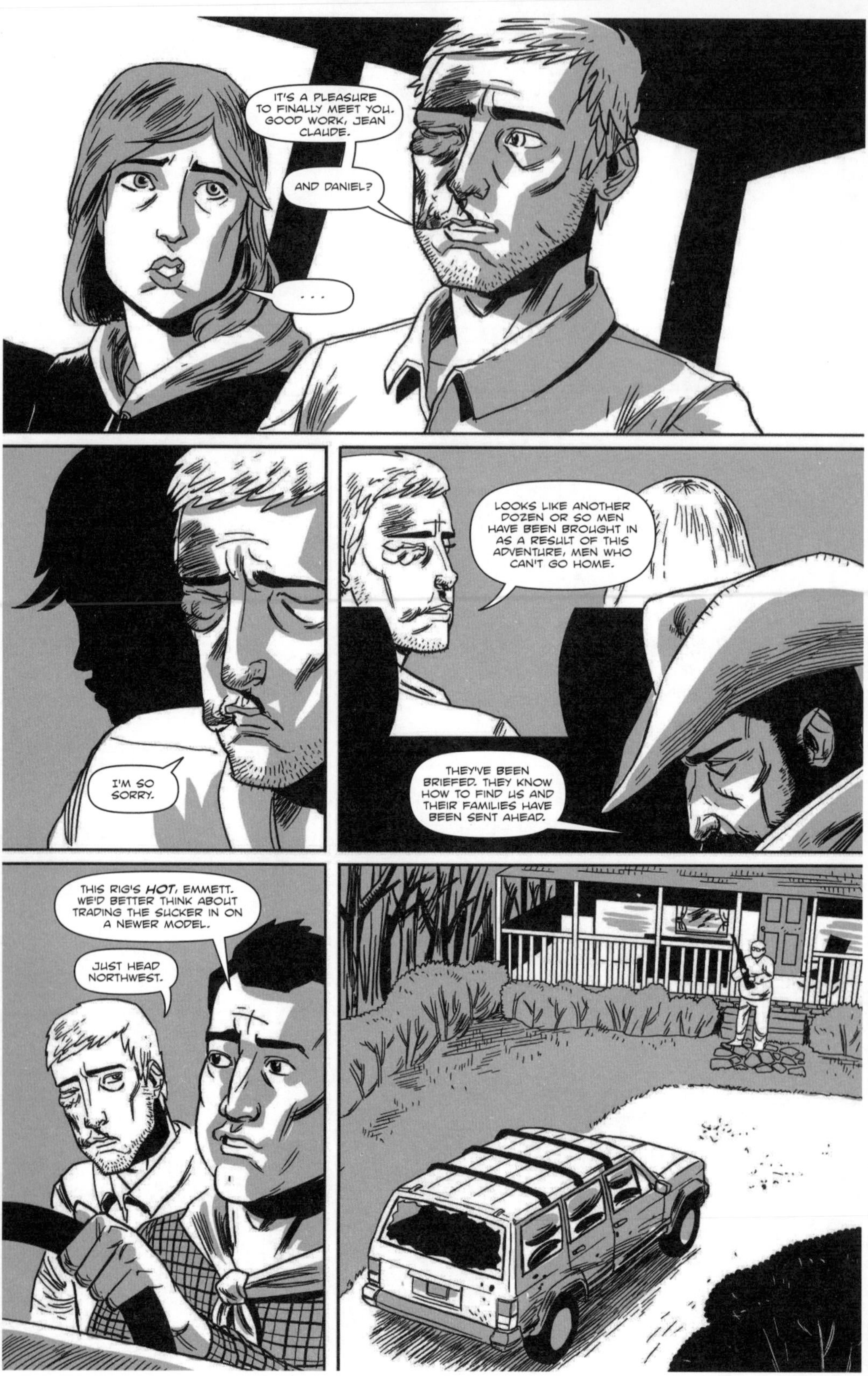
IT'S A PLEASURE TO FINALLY MEET YOU. GOOD WORK, JEAN CLAUDE.
AND DANIEL?
. . .
I'M SO SORRY.
LOOKS LIKE ANOTHER DOZEN OR SO MEN HAVE BEEN BROUGHT IN AS A RESULT OF THIS ADVENTURE, MEN WHO CAN'T GO HOME.
THEY'VE BEEN BRIEFED. THEY KNOW HOW TO FIND US AND THEIR FAMILIES HAVE BEEN SENT AHEAD.
THIS RIG'S HOT, EMMETT. WE'D BETTER THINK ABOUT TRADING THE SUCKER IN ON A NEWER MODEL.
JUST HEAD NORTHWEST.

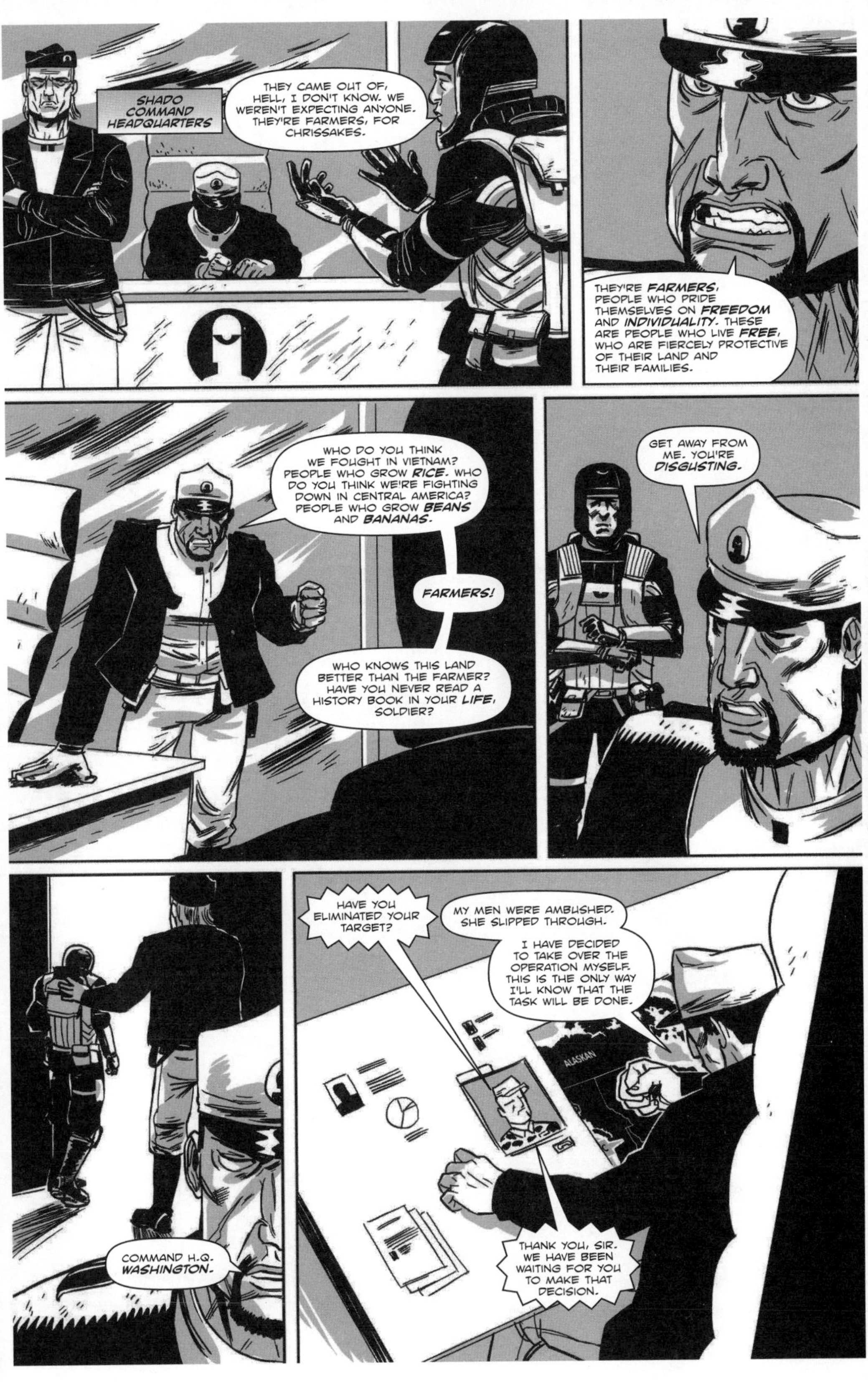
SHADO COMMAND HEADQUARTERS
THEY CAME OUT OF, HELL, I DON'T KNOW. WE WEREN'T EXPECTING ANYONE. THEY'RE FARMERS, FOR CHRISSAKES.
THEY'RE FARMERS, PEOPLE WHO PRIDE THEMSELVES ON FREEDOM AND INDIVIDUALITY. THESE ARE PEOPLE WHO LIVE FREE, WHO ARE FIERCELY PROTECTIVE OF THEIR LAND AND THEIR FAMILIES.
WHO DO YOU THINK WE FOUGHT IN VIETNAM? PEOPLE WHO GROW RICE. WHO DO YOU THINK WE'RE FIGHTING DOWN IN CENTRAL AMERICA? PEOPLE WHO GROW BEANS AND BANANAS.
FARMERS!
WHO KNOWS THIS LAND BETTER THAN THE FARMER? HAVE YOU NEVER READ A HISTORY BOOK IN YOUR LIFE, SOLDIER?
GET AWAY FROM ME. YOU'RE DISGUSTING.
COMMAND H.Q. WASHINGTON.
HAVE YOU ELIMINATED YOUR TARGET?
MY MEN WERE AMBUSHED. SHE SLIPPED THROUGH.
I HAVE DECIDED TO TAKE OVER THE OPERATION MYSELF. THIS IS THE ONLY WAY I'LL KNOW THAT THE TASK WILL BE DONE.
ALASKAN
THANK YOU, SIR. WE HAVE BEEN WAITING FOR YOU TO MAKE THAT DECISION.

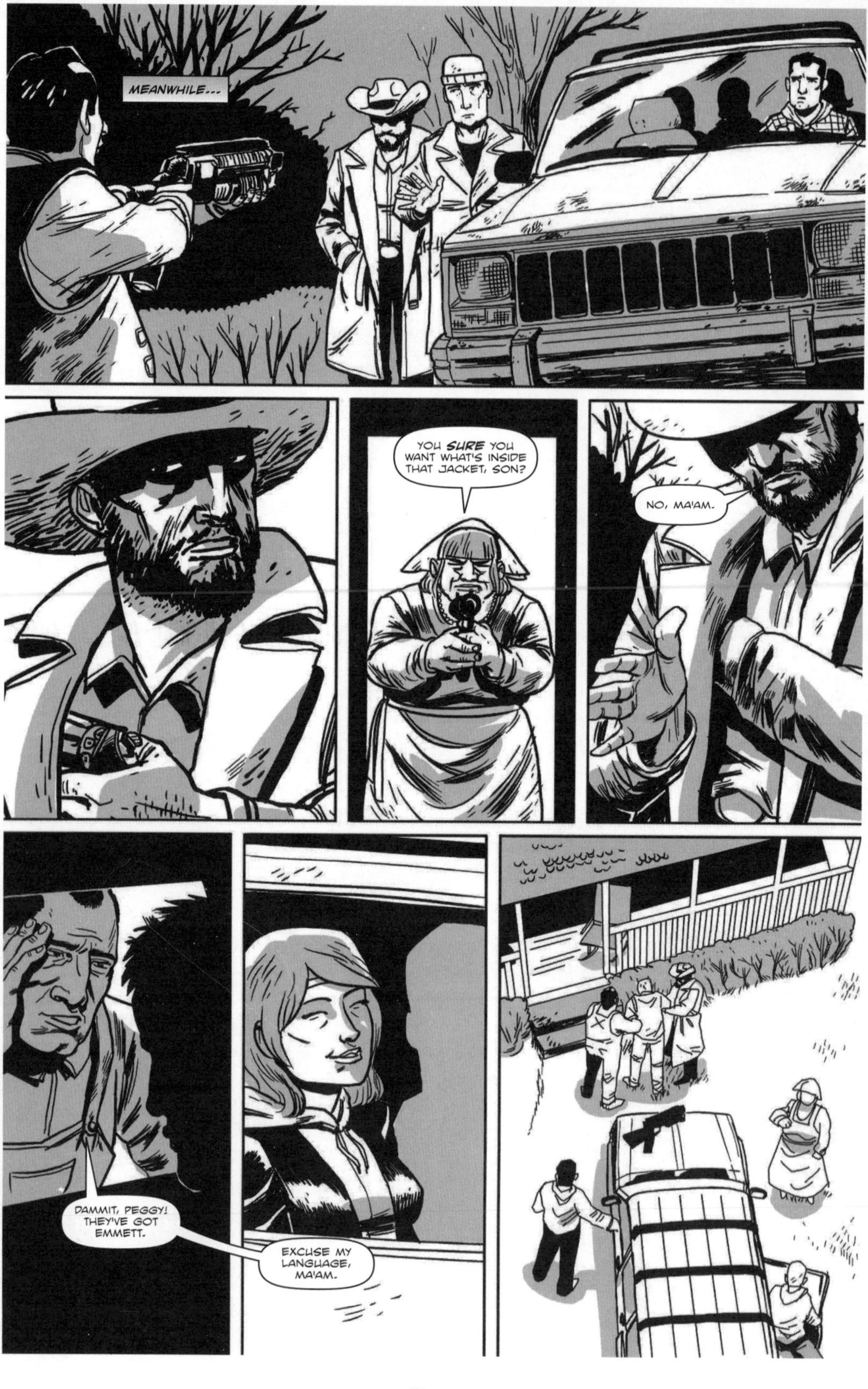
MEANWHILE...
YOU SURE YOU WANT WHAT'S INSIDE THAT JACKET, SON?
NO, MA'AM.
DAMMIT, PEGGY! THEY'VE GOT EMMETT.
EXCUSE MY LANGUAGE, MA'AM.

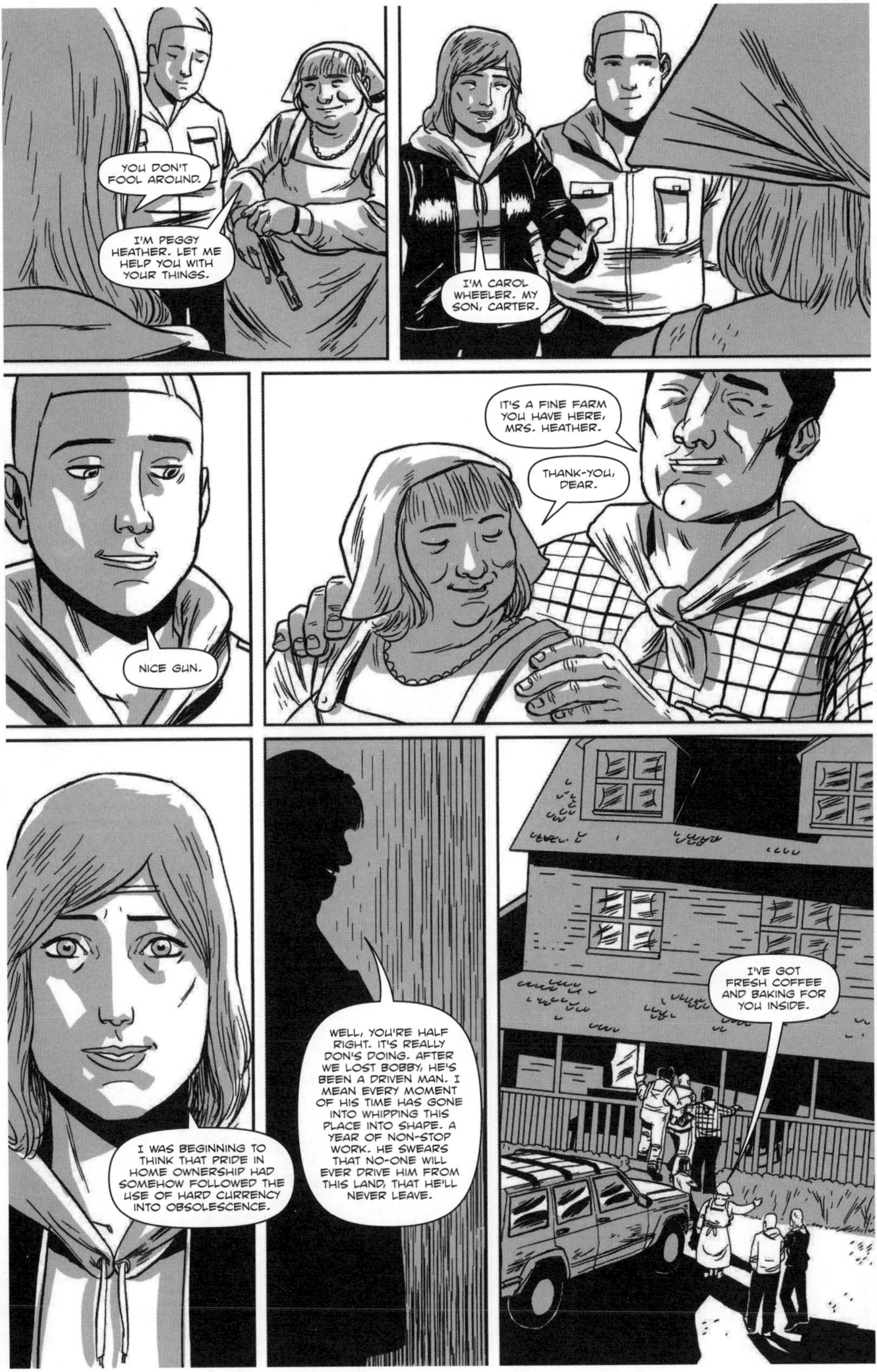
YOU DON'T FOOL AROUND.
I'M PEGGY HEATHER. LET ME HELP YOU WITH YOUR THINGS.
I'M CAROL WHEELER. MY SON, CARTER.
NICE GUN.
IT'S A FINE FARM YOU HAVE HERE, MRS. HEATHER.
THANK-YOU, DEAR.
I WAS BEGINNING TO THINK THAT PRIDE IN HOME OWNERSHIP HAD SOMEHOW FOLLOWED THE USE OF HARD CURRENCY INTO OBSOLESCENCE.
WELL, YOU'RE HALF RIGHT. IT'S REALLY DON'S DOING. AFTER WE LOST BOBBY, HE'S BEEN A DRIVEN MAN. I MEAN EVERY MOMENT OF HIS TIME HAS GONE INTO WHIPPING THIS PLACE INTO SHAPE. A YEAR OF NON-STOP WORK. HE SWEARS THAT NO-ONE WILL EVER DRIVE HIM FROM THIS LAND, THAT HE'LL NEVER LEAVE.
I'VE GOT FRESH COFFEE AND BAKING FOR YOU INSIDE.

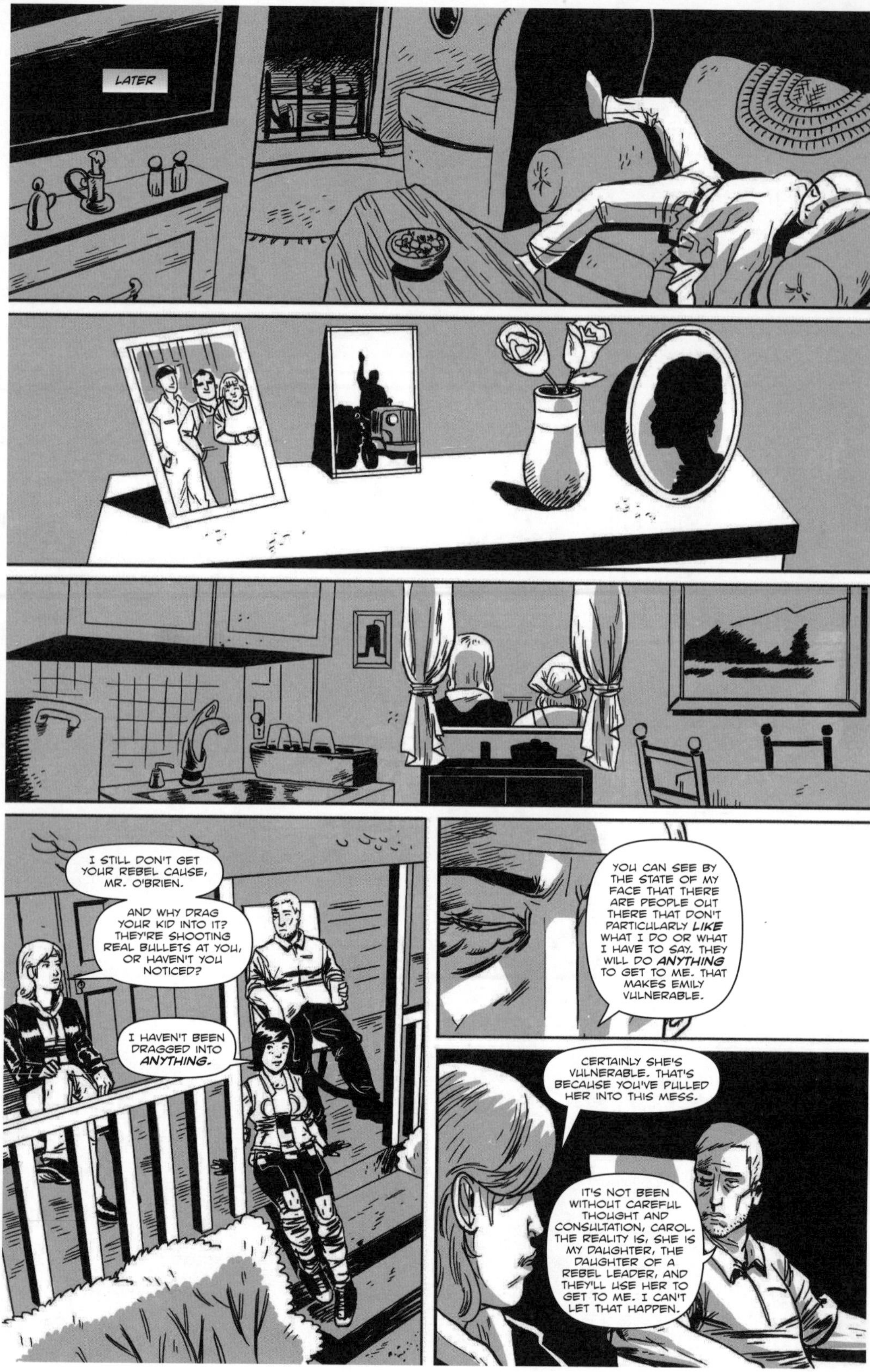
LATER
I STILL DON'T GET YOUR REBEL CAUSE, MR. O'BRIEN.
AND WHY DRAG YOUR KID INTO IT? THEY'RE SHOOTING REAL BULLETS AT YOU, OR HAVEN'T YOU NOTICED?
I HAVEN'T BEEN DRAGGED INTO ANYTHING.
YOU CAN SEE BY THE STATE OF MY FACE THAT THERE ARE PEOPLE OUT THERE THAT DON'T PARTICULARLY LIKE WHAT I DO OR WHAT I HAVE TO SAY. THEY WILL DO ANYTHING TO GET TO ME. THAT MAKES EMILY VULNERABLE.
CERTAINLY SHE'S VULNERABLE. THAT'S BECAUSE YOU'VE PULLED HER INTO THIS MESS.
IT'S NOT BEEN WITHOUT CAREFUL THOUGHT AND CONSULTATION, CAROL. THE REALITY IS, SHE IS MY DAUGHTER, THE DAUGHTER OF A REBEL LEADER, AND THEY'LL USE HER TO GET TO ME. I CAN'T LET THAT HAPPEN.

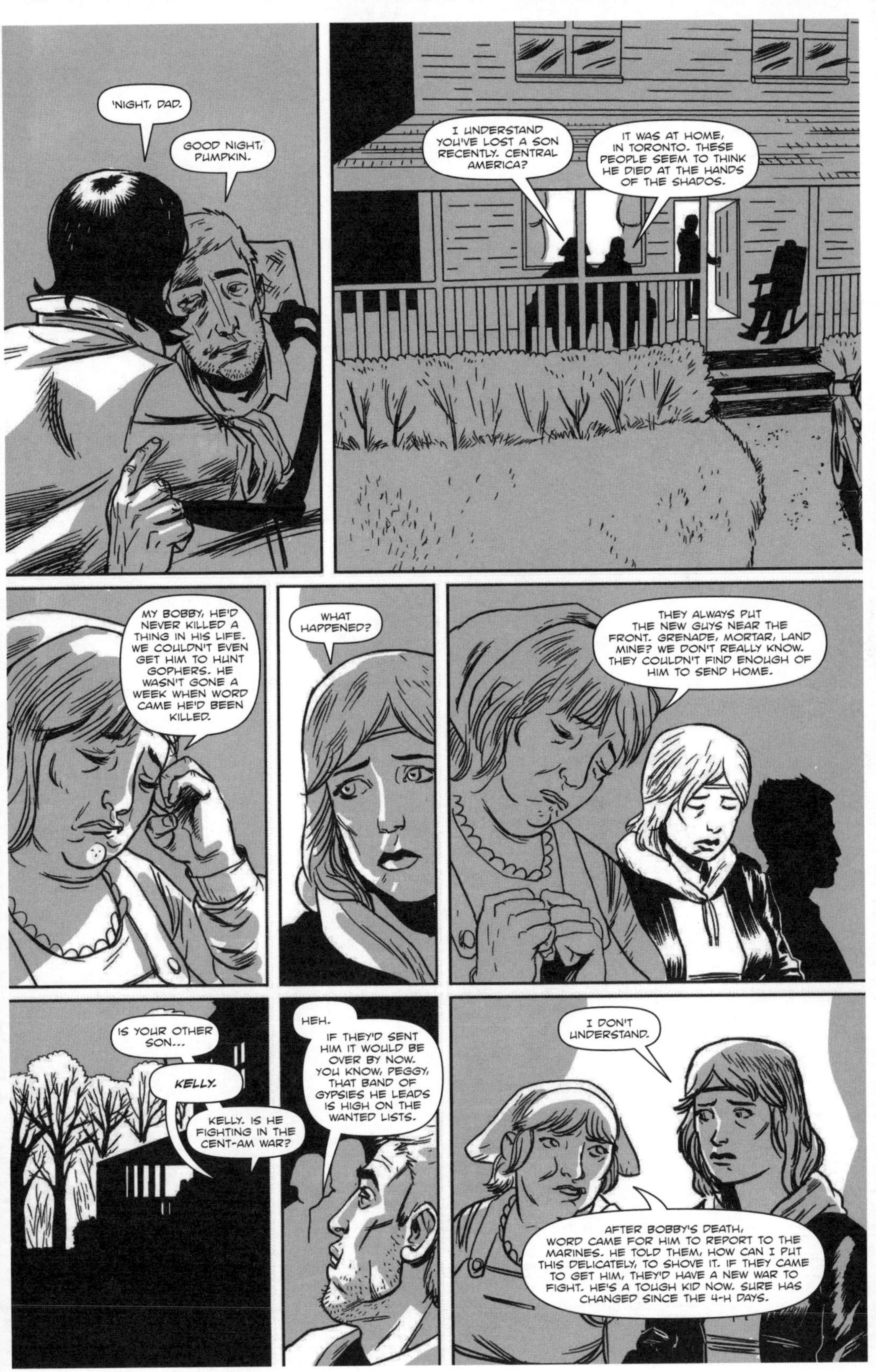
'NIGHT, DAD.
GOOD NIGHT, PUMPKIN.
I UNDERSTAND YOU'VE LOST A SON RECENTLY. CENTRAL AMERICA?
IT WAS AT HOME, IN TORONTO. THESE PEOPLE SEEM TO THINK HE DIED AT THE HANDS OF THE SHADOS.
MY BOBBY, HE'D NEVER KILLED A THING IN HIS LIFE. WE COULDN'T EVEN GET HIM TO HUNT GOPHERS. HE WASN'T GONE A WEEK WHEN WORD CAME HE'D BEEN KILLED.
WHAT HAPPENED?
THEY ALWAYS PUT THE NEW GUYS NEAR THE FRONT. GRENADE, MORTAR, LAND MINE? WE DON'T REALLY KNOW. THEY COULDN'T FIND ENOUGH OF HIM TO SEND HOME.
IS YOUR OTHER SON...
KELLY.
KELLY. IS HE FIGHTING IN THE CENT-AM WAR?
HEH.
IF THEY'D SENT HIM IT WOULD BE OVER BY NOW. YOU KNOW, PEGGY, THAT BAND OF GYPSIES HE LEADS IS HIGH ON THE WANTED LISTS.
I DON'T UNDERSTAND.
AFTER BOBBY'S DEATH, WORD CAME FOR HIM TO REPORT TO THE MARINES. HE TOLD THEM, HOW CAN I PUT THIS DELICATELY, TO SHOVE IT. IF THEY CAME TO GET HIM, THEY'D HAVE A NEW WAR TO FIGHT. HE'S A TOUGH KID NOW. SURE HAS CHANGED SINCE THE 4-H DAYS.

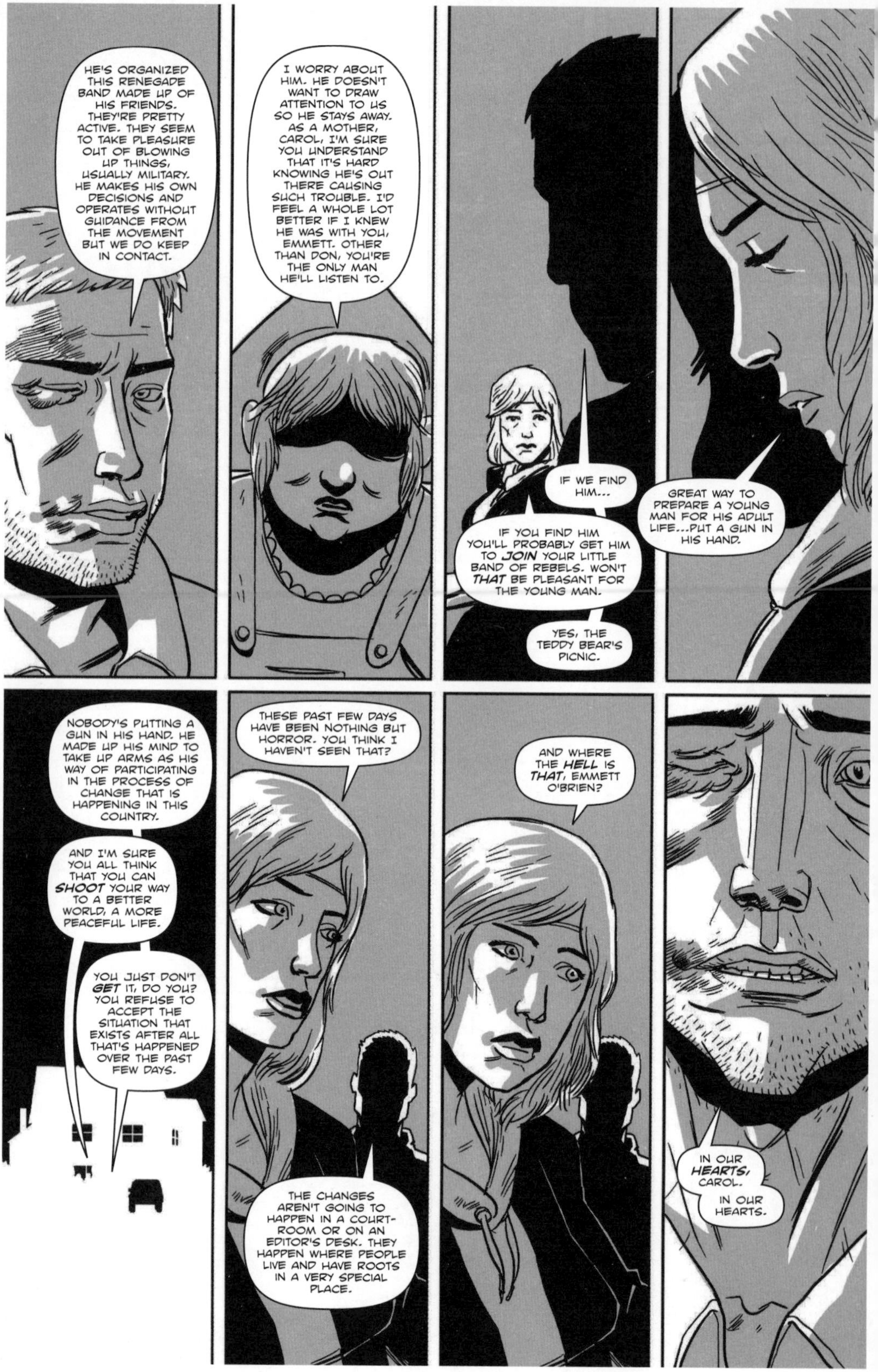
HE'S ORGANIZED THIS RENEGADE BAND MADE UP OF HIS FRIENDS. THEY'RE PRETTY ACTIVE. THEY SEEM TO TAKE PLEASURE OUT OF BLOWING UP THINGS, USUALLY MILITARY. HE MAKES HIS OWN DECISIONS AND OPERATES WITHOUT GUIDANCE FROM THE MOVEMENT BUT WE DO KEEP IN CONTACT.
I WORRY ABOUT HIM. HE DOESN'T WANT TO DRAW ATTENTION TO US SO HE STAYS AWAY. AS A MOTHER, CAROL, I'M SURE YOU UNDERSTAND THAT IT'S HARD KNOWING HE'S OUT THERE CAUSING SUCH TROUBLE. I'D FEEL A WHOLE LOT BETTER IF I KNEW HE WAS WITH YOU, EMMETT. OTHER THAN DON, YOU'RE THE ONLY MAN HE'LL LISTEN TO.
IF WE FIND HIM...
IF YOU FIND HIM YOU'LL PROBABLY GET HIM TO JOIN YOUR LITTLE BAND OF REBELS. WON'T THAT BE PLEASANT FOR THE YOUNG MAN.
YES, THE TEDDY BEAR'S PICNIC.
GREAT WAY TO PREPARE A YOUNG MAN FOR HIS ADULT LIFE...PUT A GUN IN HIS HAND.
NOBODY'S PUTTING A GUN IN HIS HAND. HE MADE UP HIS MIND TO TAKE UP ARMS AS HIS WAY OF PARTICIPATING IN THE PROCESS OF CHANGE THAT IS HAPPENING IN THIS COUNTRY.
AND I'M SURE YOU ALL THINK THAT YOU CAN SHOOT YOUR WAY TO A BETTER WORLD, A MORE PEACEFUL LIFE.
YOU JUST DON'T GET IT, DO YOU? YOU REFUSE TO ACCEPT THE SITUATION THAT EXISTS AFTER ALL THAT'S HAPPENED OVER THE PAST FEW DAYS.
THESE PAST FEW DAYS HAVE BEEN NOTHING BUT HORROR. YOU THINK I HAVEN'T SEEN THAT?
THE CHANGES AREN'T GOING TO HAPPEN IN A COURT-ROOM OR ON AN EDITOR'S DESK. THEY HAPPEN WHERE PEOPLE LIVE AND HAVE ROOTS IN A VERY SPECIAL PLACE.
AND WHERE THE HELL IS THAT, EMMETT O'BRIEN?
IN OUR HEARTS, CAROL.
IN OUR HEARTS.

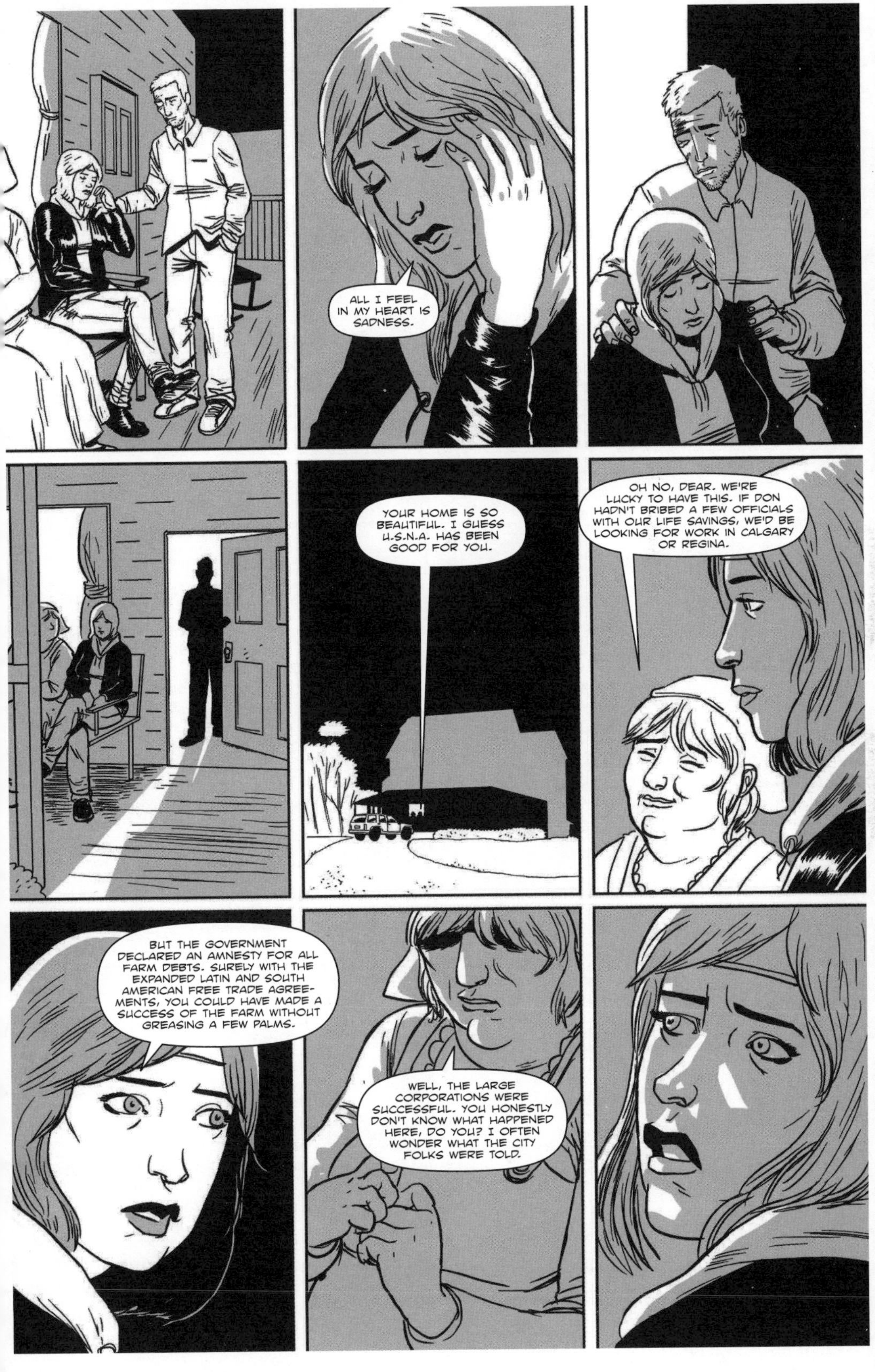
ALL I FEEL IN MY HEART IS SADNESS.
YOUR HOME IS SO BEAUTIFUL. I GUESS U.S.N.A. HAS BEEN GOOD FOR YOU.
OH NO, DEAR. WE'RE LUCKY TO HAVE THIS. IF DON HADN'T BRIBED A FEW OFFICIALS WITH OUR LIFE SAVINGS, WE'D BE LOOKING FOR WORK IN CALGARY OR REGINA.
BUT THE GOVERNMENT DECLARED AN AMNESTY FOR ALL FARM DEBTS. SURELY WITH THE EXPANDED LATIN AND SOUTH AMERICAN FREE TRADE AGREE-MENTS, YOU COULD HAVE MADE A SUCCESS OF THE FARM WITHOUT GREASING A FEW PALMS.
WELL, THE LARGE CORPORATIONS WERE SUCCESSFUL. YOU HONESTLY DON'T KNOW WHAT HAPPENED HERE, DO YOU? I OFTEN WONDER WHAT THE CITY FOLKS WERE TOLD.

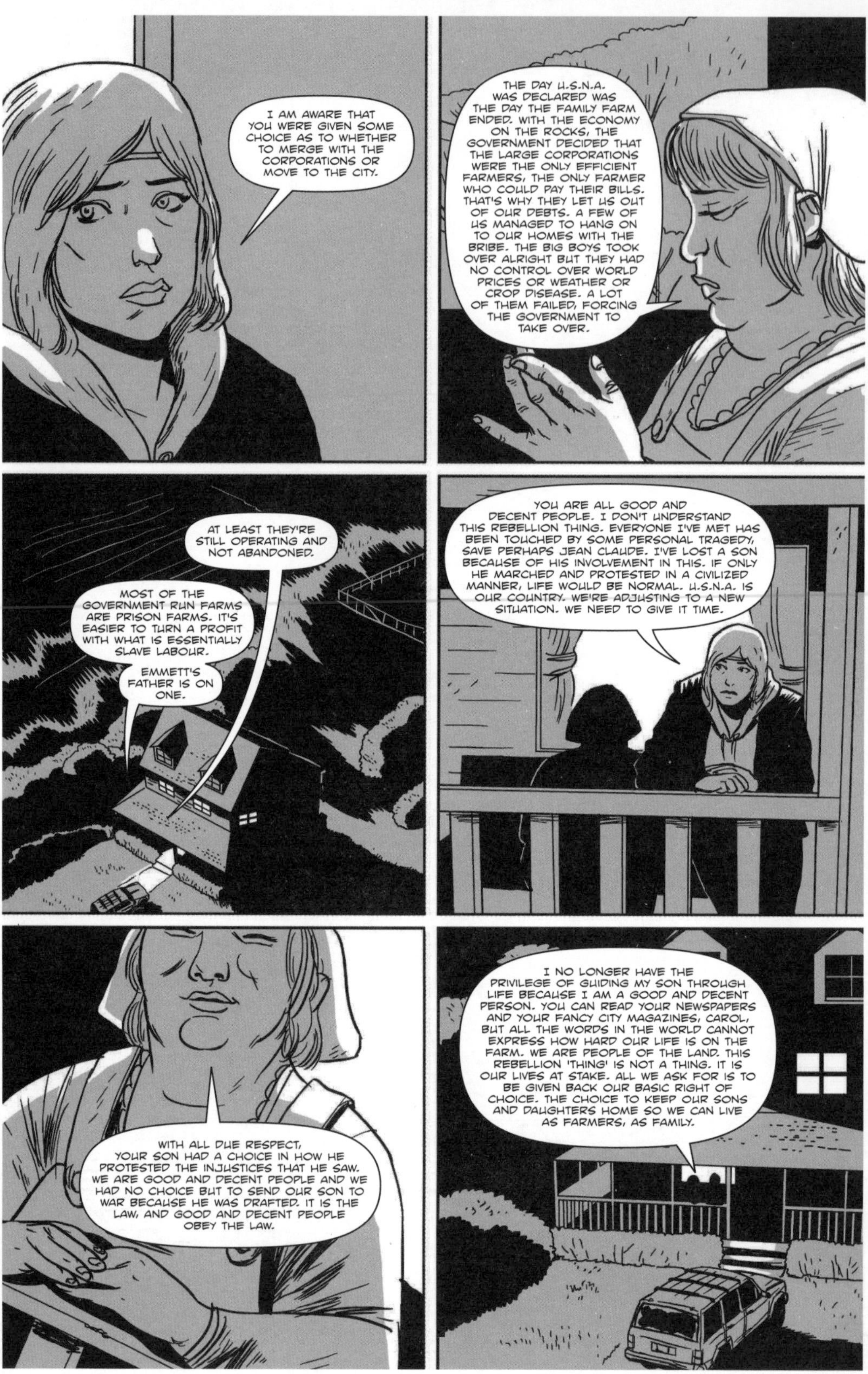
I AM AWARE THAT YOU WERE GIVEN SOME CHOICE AS TO WHETHER TO MERGE WITH THE CORPORATIONS OR MOVE TO THE CITY.
THE DAY U.S.N.A. WAS DECLARED WAS THE DAY THE FAMILY FARM ENDED. WITH THE ECONOMY ON THE ROCKS, THE GOVERNMENT DECIDED THAT THE LARGE CORPORATIONS WERE THE ONLY EFFICIENT FARMERS, THE ONLY FARMER WHO COULD PAY THEIR BILLS. THAT'S WHY THEY LET US OUT OF OUR DEBTS. A FEW OF US MANAGED TO HANG ON TO OUR HOMES WITH THE BRIBE. THE BIG BOYS TOOK OVER ALRIGHT BUT THEY HAD NO CONTROL OVER WORLD PRICES OR WEATHER OR CROP DISEASE. A LOT OF THEM FAILED, FORCING THE GOVERNMENT TO TAKE OVER.
MOST OF THE GOVERNMENT RUN FARMS ARE PRISON FARMS. IT'S EASIER TO TURN A PROFIT WITH WHAT IS ESSENTIALLY SLAVE LABOUR.
EMMETT'S FATHER IS ON ONE.
AT LEAST THEY'RE STILL OPERATING AND NOT ABANDONED.
YOU ARE ALL GOOD AND DECENT PEOPLE. I DON'T UNDERSTAND THIS REBELLION THING. EVERYONE I'VE MET HAS BEEN TOUCHED BY SOME PERSONAL TRAGEDY, SAVE PERHAPS JEAN CLAUDE. I'VE LOST A SON BECAUSE OF HIS INVOLVEMENT IN THIS. IF ONLY HE MARCHED AND PROTESTED IN A CIVILIZED MANNER, LIFE WOULD BE NORMAL. U.S.N.A. IS OUR COUNTRY. WE'RE ADJUSTING TO A NEW SITUATION. WE NEED TO GIVE IT TIME.
WITH ALL DUE RESPECT, YOUR SON HAD A CHOICE IN HOW HE PROTESTED THE INJUSTICES THAT HE SAW. WE ARE GOOD AND DECENT PEOPLE AND WE HAD NO CHOICE BUT TO SEND OUR SON TO WAR BECAUSE HE WAS DRAFTED. IT IS THE LAW, AND GOOD AND DECENT PEOPLE OBEY THE LAW.
I NO LONGER HAVE THE PRIVILEGE OF GUIDING MY SON THROUGH LIFE BECAUSE I AM A GOOD AND DECENT PERSON. YOU CAN READ YOUR NEWSPAPERS AND YOUR FANCY CITY MAGAZINES, CAROL, BUT ALL THE WORDS IN THE WORLD CANNOT EXPRESS HOW HARD OUR LIFE IS ON THE FARM. WE ARE PEOPLE OF THE LAND. THIS REBELLION 'THING' IS NOT A THING. IT IS OUR LIVES AT STAKE. ALL WE ASK FOR IS TO BE GIVEN BACK OUR BASIC RIGHT OF CHOICE. THE CHOICE TO KEEP OUR SONS AND DAUGHTERS HOME SO WE CAN LIVE AS FARMERS, AS FAMILY.

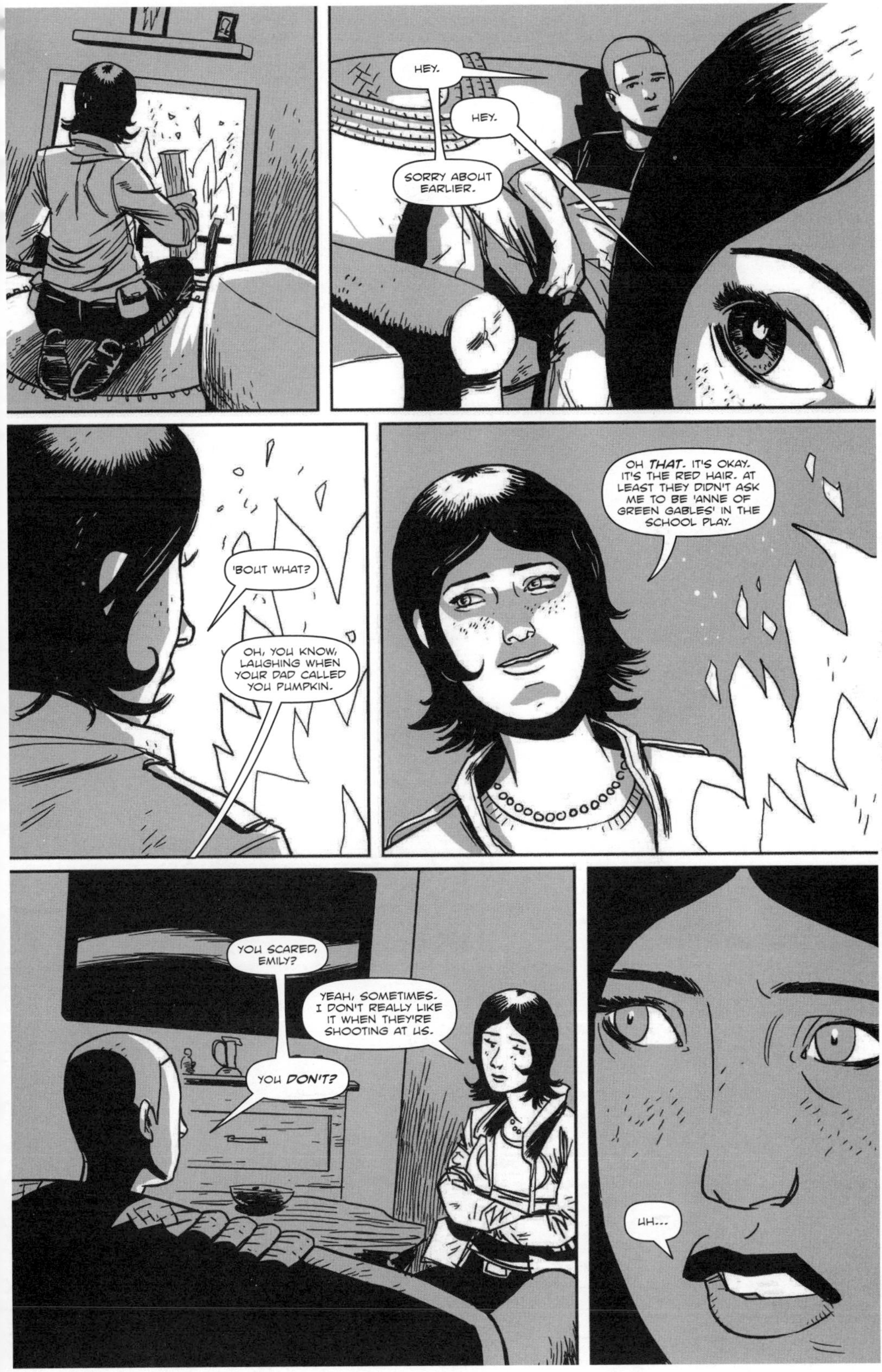
HEY.
HEY.
SORRY ABOUT EARLIER.
'BOUT WHAT?
OH, YOU KNOW, LAUGHING WHEN YOUR DAD CALLED YOU PUMPKIN.
OH *THAT*. IT'S OKAY. IT'S THE RED HAIR. AT LEAST THEY DIDN'T ASK ME TO BE 'ANNE OF GREEN GABLES' IN THE SCHOOL PLAY.
YOU SCARED, EMILY?
YEAH, SOMETIMES. I DON'T REALLY LIKE IT WHEN THEY'RE SHOOTING AT US.
YOU *DON'T?*
UH...

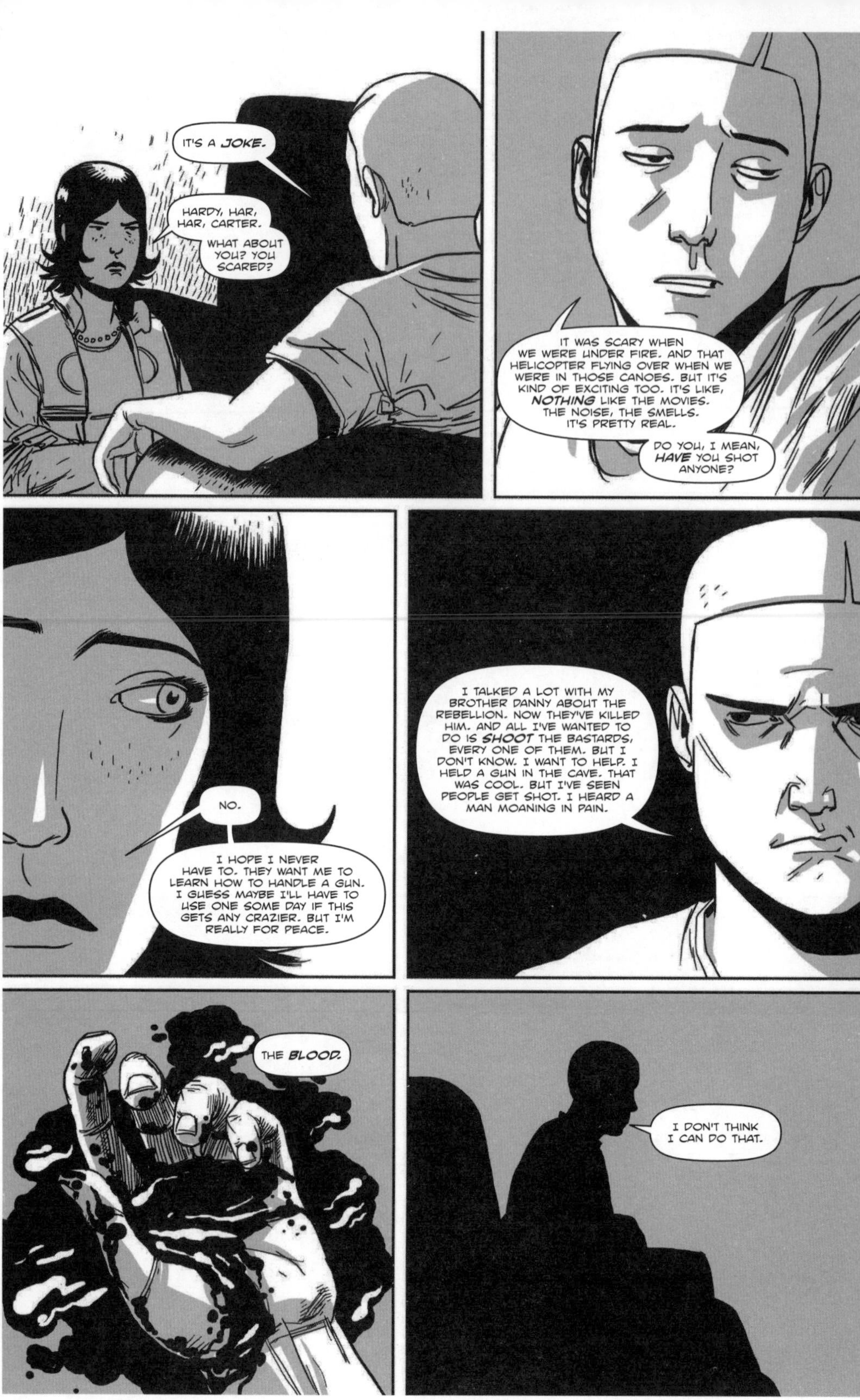

IT'S A JOKE.
HARDY, HAR, HAR, CARTER.
WHAT ABOUT YOU? YOU SCARED?
IT WAS SCARY WHEN WE WERE UNDER FIRE. AND THAT HELICOPTER FLYING OVER WHEN WE WERE IN THOSE CANOES. BUT IT'S KIND OF EXCITING TOO. IT'S LIKE, NOTHING LIKE THE MOVIES. THE NOISE, THE SMELLS. IT'S PRETTY REAL.
DO YOU, I MEAN, HAVE YOU SHOT ANYONE?
NO.
I HOPE I NEVER HAVE TO. THEY WANT ME TO LEARN HOW TO HANDLE A GUN. I GUESS MAYBE I'LL HAVE TO USE ONE SOME DAY IF THIS GETS ANY CRAZIER. BUT I'M REALLY FOR PEACE.
I TALKED A LOT WITH MY BROTHER DANNY ABOUT THE REBELLION. NOW THEY'VE KILLED HIM. AND ALL I'VE WANTED TO DO IS SHOOT THE BASTARDS, EVERY ONE OF THEM. BUT I DON'T KNOW. I WANT TO HELP. I HELD A GUN IN THE CAVE. THAT WAS COOL. BUT I'VE SEEN PEOPLE GET SHOT. I HEARD A MAN MOANING IN PAIN.
THE BLOOD.
I DON'T THINK I CAN DO THAT.

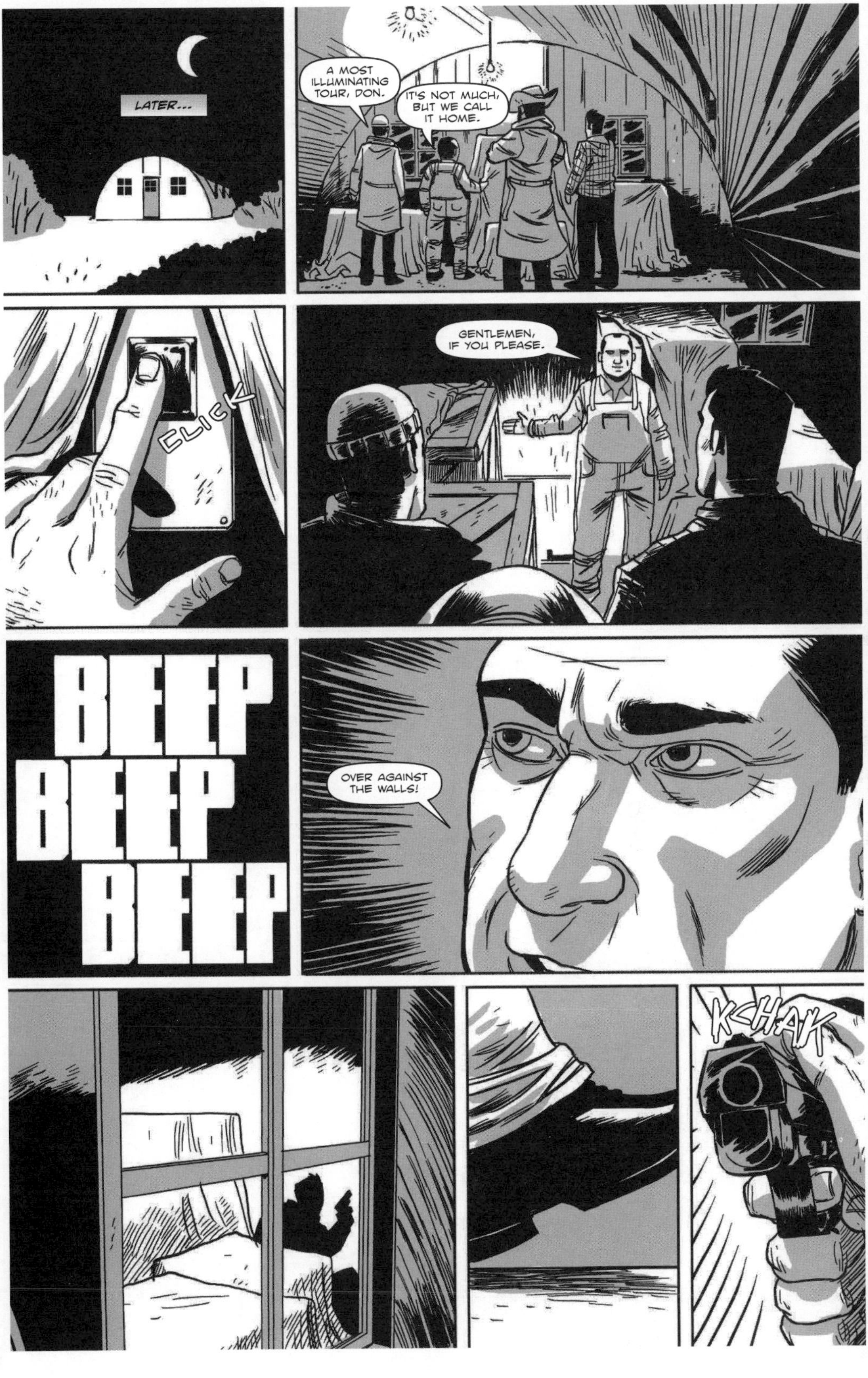
LATER...
A MOST ILLUMINATING TOUR, DON.
IT'S NOT MUCH, BUT WE CALL IT HOME.
CLICK
GENTLEMEN, IF YOU PLEASE.
BEEP BEEP BEEP
OVER AGAINST THE WALLS!
KCHAK

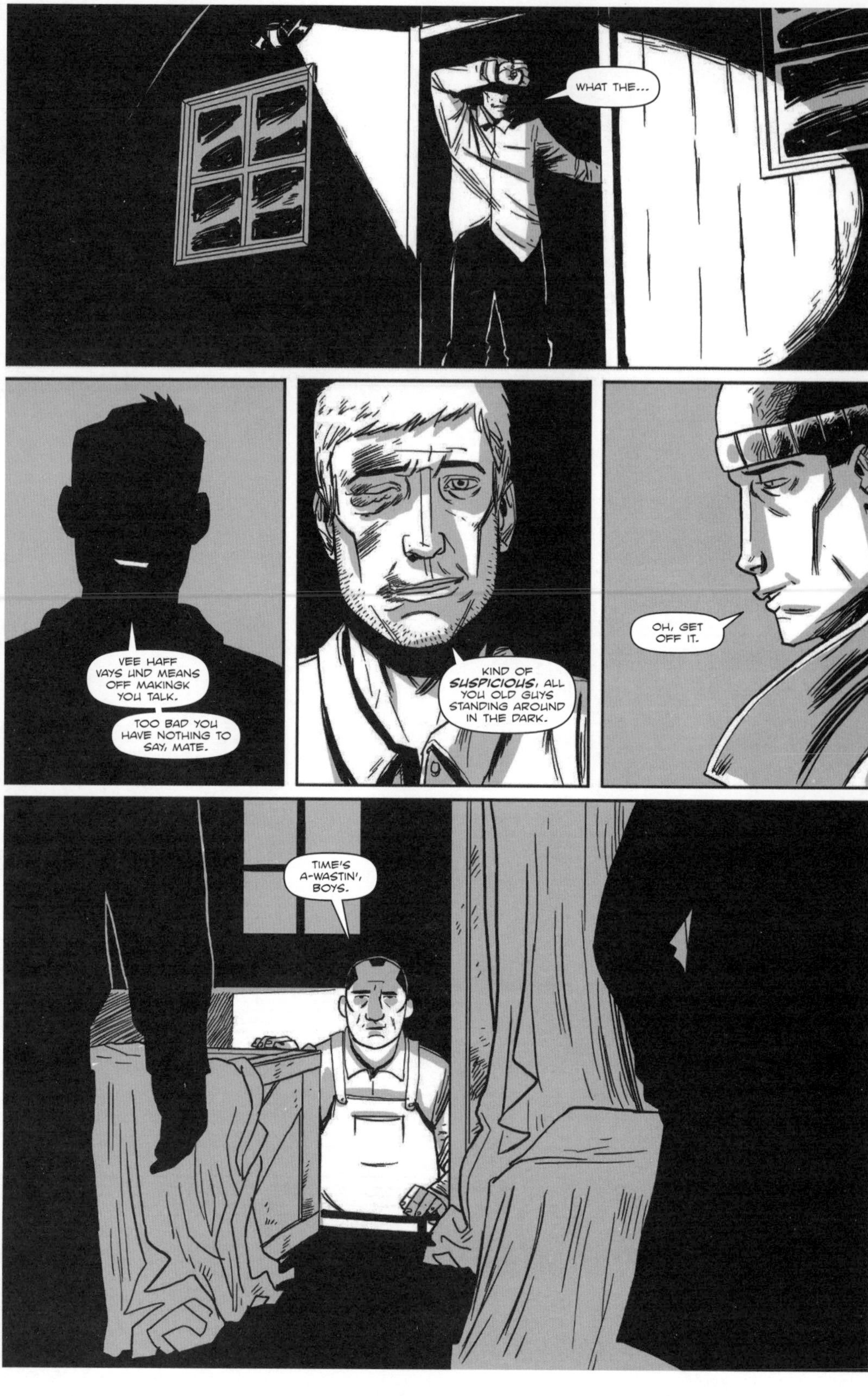
WHAT THE...
VEE HAFF VAYS UND MEANS OFF MAKINGK YOU TALK.
TOO BAD YOU HAVE NOTHING TO SAY, MATE.
KIND OF SUSPICIOUS, ALL YOU OLD GUYS STANDING AROUND IN THE DARK.
OH, GET OFF IT.
TIME'S A-WASTIN', BOYS.

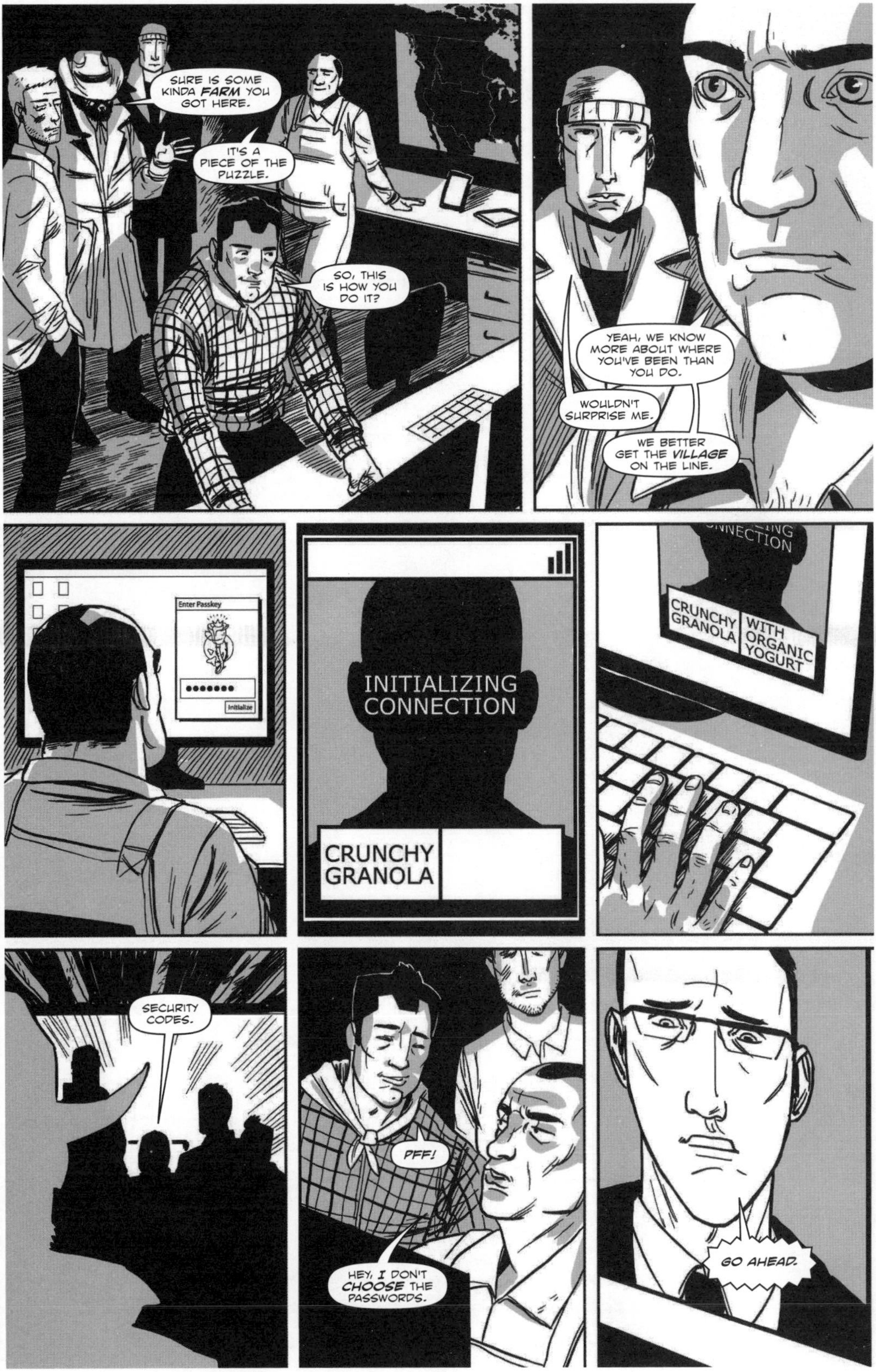
SURE IS SOME KINDA FARM YOU GOT HERE.
IT'S A PIECE OF THE PUZZLE.
SO, THIS IS HOW YOU DO IT?
YEAH, WE KNOW MORE ABOUT WHERE YOU'VE BEEN THAN YOU DO.
WOULDN'T SURPRISE ME.
WE BETTER GET THE VILLAGE ON THE LINE.
Enter Passkey
Initialize
INITIALIZING CONNECTION
CRUNCHY GRANOLA
CRUNCHY GRANOLA
WITH ORGANIC YOGURT
SECURITY CODES.
PFF!
HEY, I DON'T CHOOSE THE PASSWORDS.
GO AHEAD.

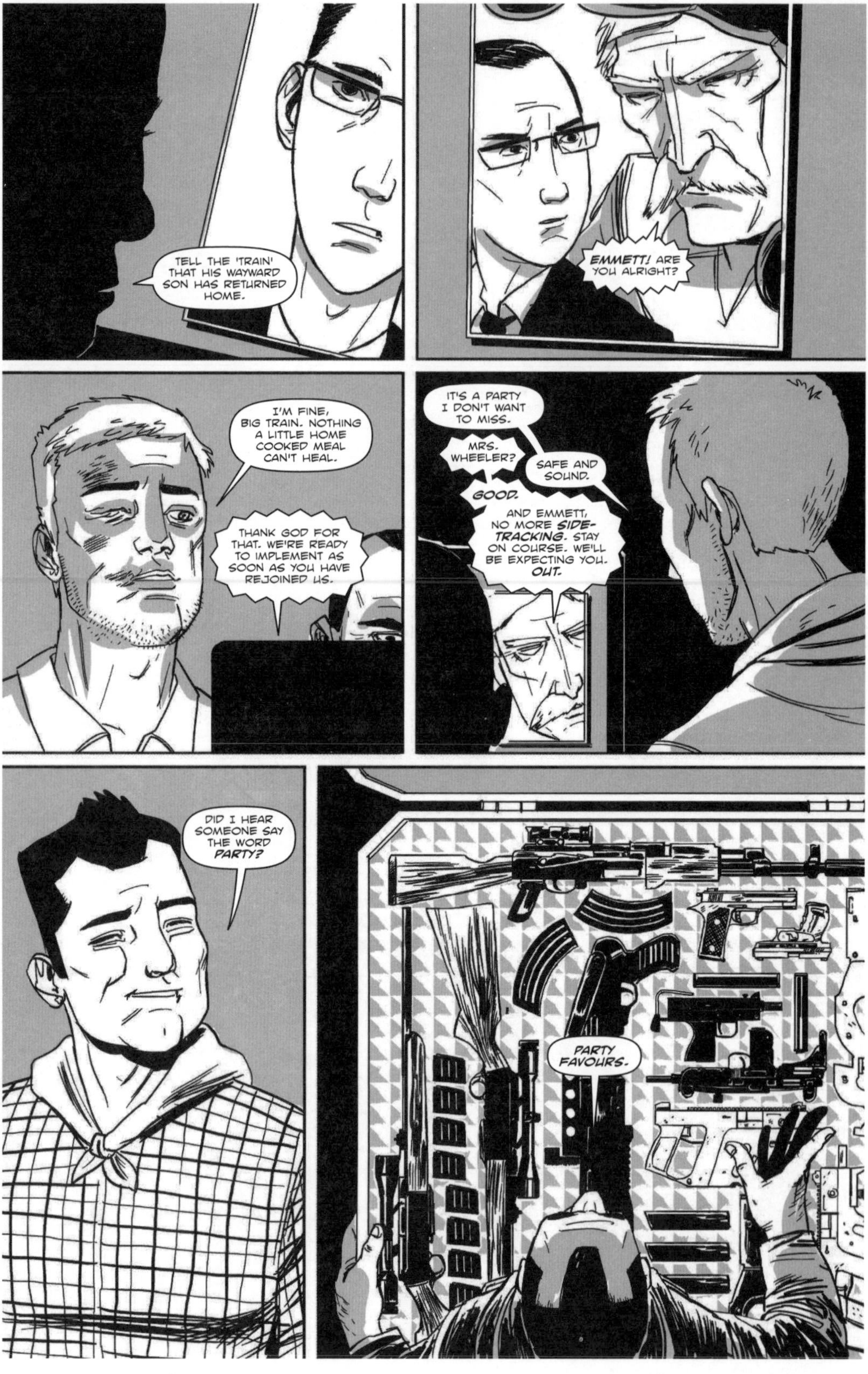
TELL THE 'TRAIN' THAT HIS WAYWARD SON HAS RETURNED HOME.
EMMETT! ARE YOU ALRIGHT?
I'M FINE, BIG TRAIN. NOTHING A LITTLE HOME COOKED MEAL CAN'T HEAL.
THANK GOD FOR THAT. WE'RE READY TO IMPLEMENT AS SOON AS YOU HAVE REJOINED US.
IT'S A PARTY I DON'T WANT TO MISS.
MRS. WHEELER?
SAFE AND SOUND.
GOOD.
AND EMMETT, NO MORE SIDE-TRACKING. STAY ON COURSE. WE'LL BE EXPECTING YOU. OUT.
DID I HEAR SOMEONE SAY THE WORD PARTY?
PARTY FAVOURS.

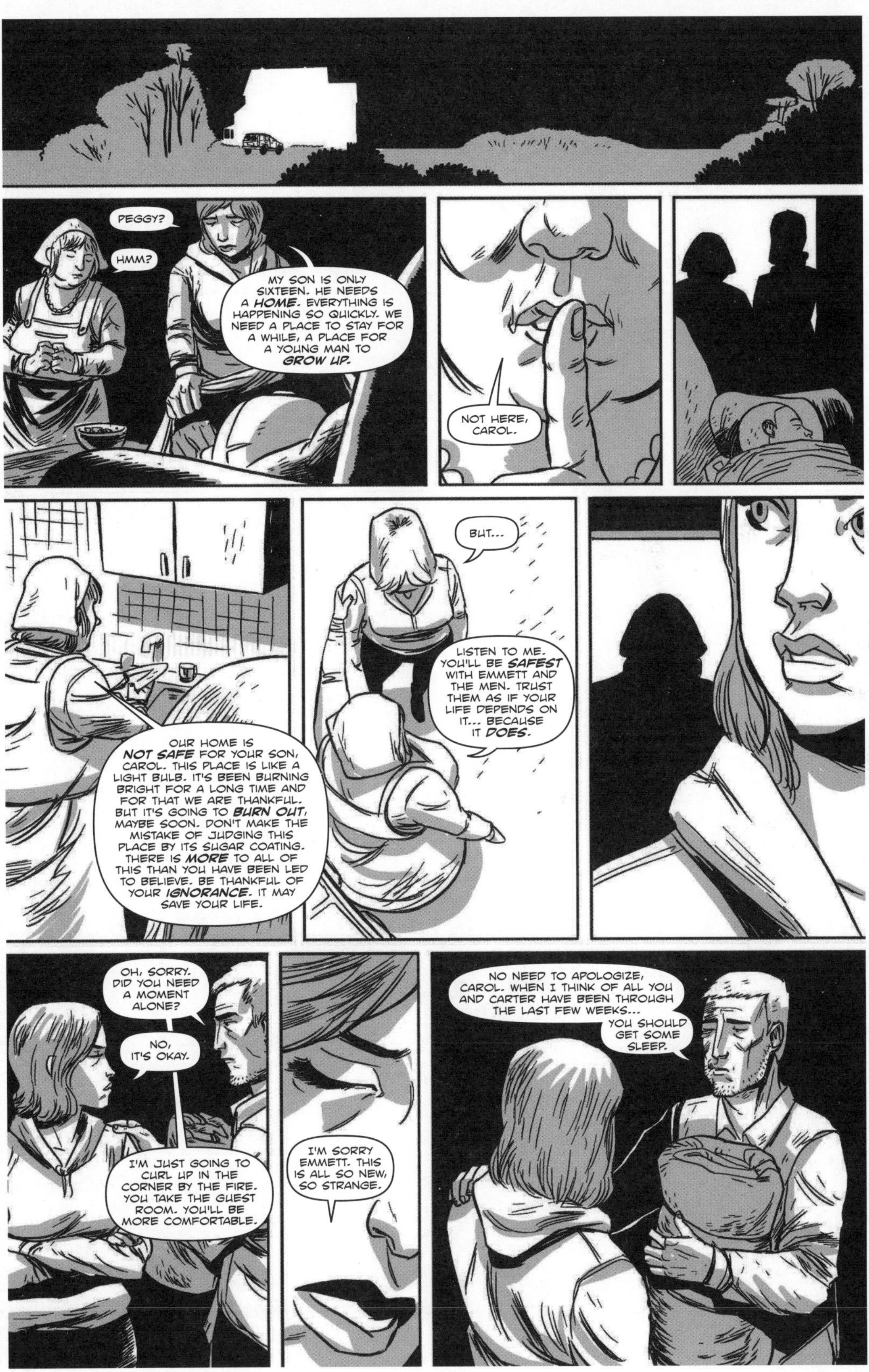
PEGGY?
HMM?
MY SON IS ONLY SIXTEEN. HE NEEDS A HOME. EVERYTHING IS HAPPENING SO QUICKLY. WE NEED A PLACE TO STAY FOR A WHILE, A PLACE FOR A YOUNG MAN TO GROW UP.
NOT HERE, CAROL.
OUR HOME IS NOT SAFE FOR YOUR SON, CAROL. THIS PLACE IS LIKE A LIGHT BULB. IT'S BEEN BURNING BRIGHT FOR A LONG TIME AND FOR THAT WE ARE THANKFUL. BUT IT'S GOING TO BURN OUT, MAYBE SOON. DON'T MAKE THE MISTAKE OF JUDGING THIS PLACE BY ITS SUGAR COATING. THERE IS MORE TO ALL OF THIS THAN YOU HAVE BEEN LED TO BELIEVE. BE THANKFUL OF YOUR IGNORANCE. IT MAY SAVE YOUR LIFE.
BUT...
LISTEN TO ME. YOU'LL BE SAFEST WITH EMMETT AND THE MEN. TRUST THEM AS IF YOUR LIFE DEPENDS ON IT... BECAUSE IT DOES.
OH, SORRY. DID YOU NEED A MOMENT ALONE?
NO, IT'S OKAY.
I'M JUST GOING TO CURL UP IN THE CORNER BY THE FIRE. YOU TAKE THE GUEST ROOM. YOU'LL BE MORE COMFORTABLE.
I'M SORRY EMMETT. THIS IS ALL SO NEW, SO STRANGE.
NO NEED TO APOLOGIZE, CAROL. WHEN I THINK OF ALL YOU AND CARTER HAVE BEEN THROUGH THE LAST FEW WEEKS...
YOU SHOULD GET SOME SLEEP.

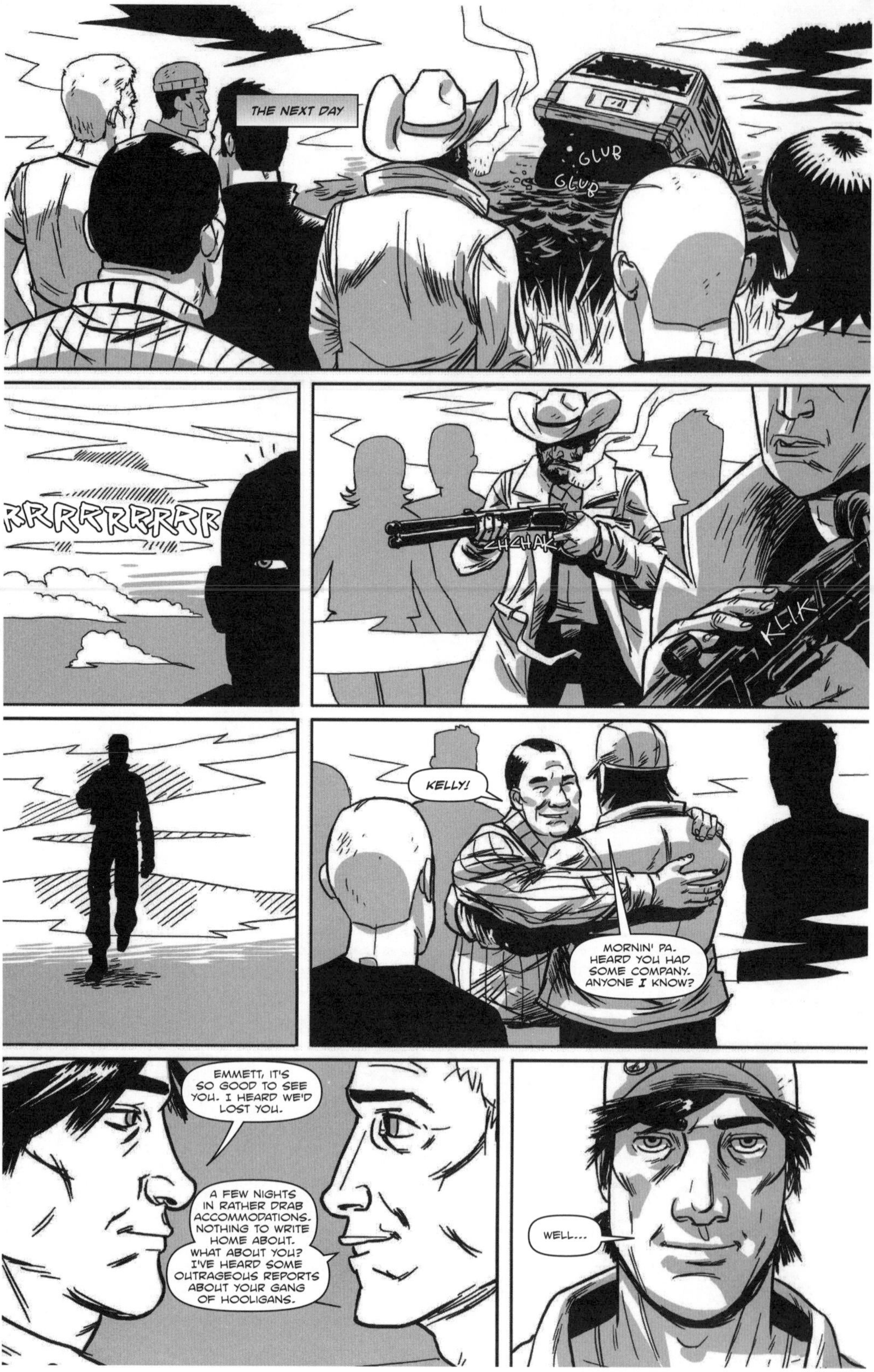
THE NEXT DAY
GLUB
GLUB
RRRRRRRRRR
CHCHAK
KLIK
KELLY!
MORNIN' PA. HEARD YOU HAD SOME COMPANY. ANYONE I KNOW?
EMMETT, IT'S SO GOOD TO SEE YOU. I HEARD WE'D LOST YOU.
A FEW NIGHTS IN RATHER DRAB ACCOMMODATIONS. NOTHING TO WRITE HOME ABOUT. WHAT ABOUT YOU? I'VE HEARD SOME OUTRAGEOUS REPORTS ABOUT YOUR GANG OF HOOLIGANS.
WELL...

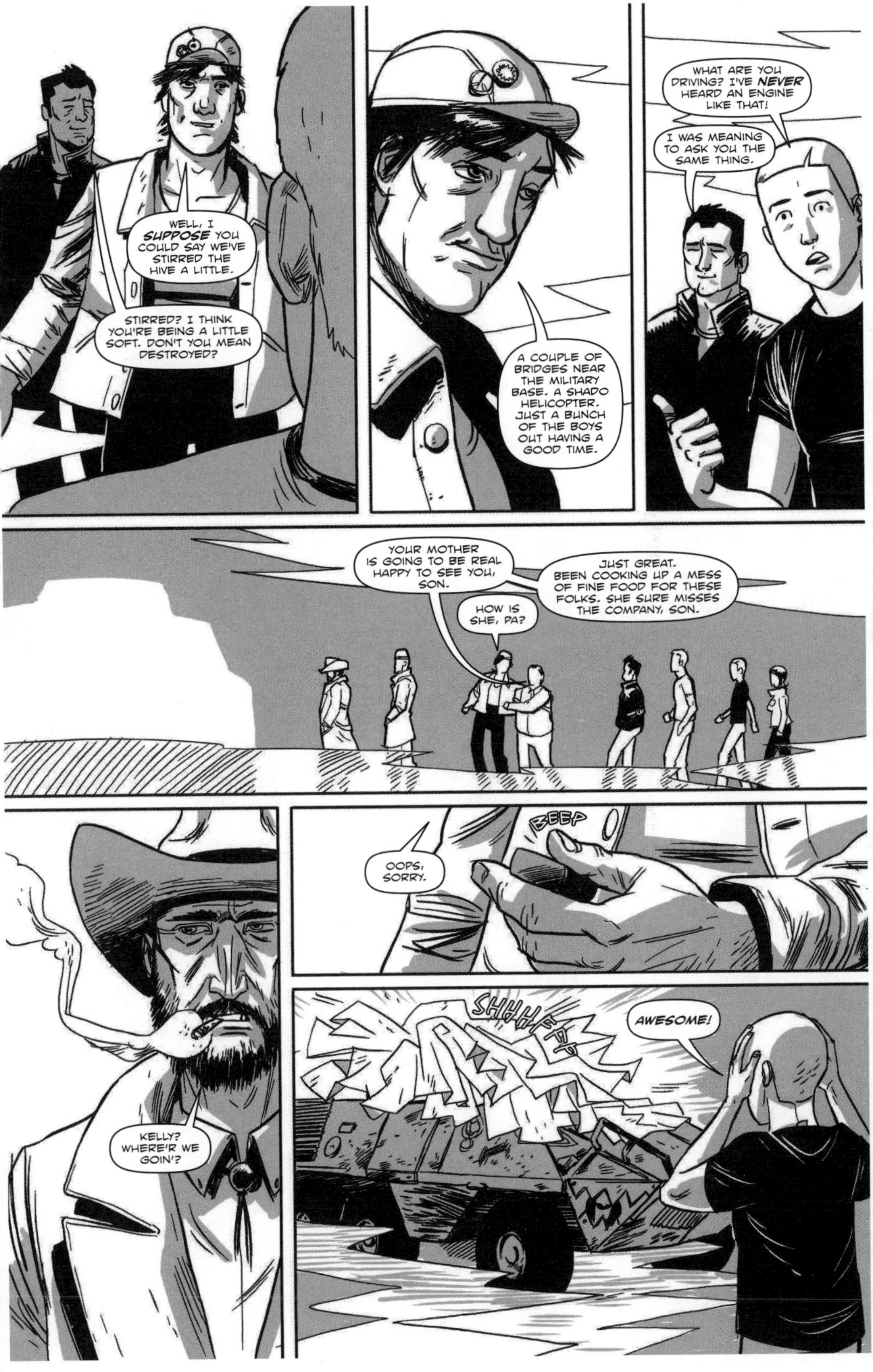
WELL, I *SUPPOSE* YOU COULD SAY WE'VE STIRRED THE HIVE A LITTLE.
STIRRED? I THINK YOU'RE BEING A LITTLE SOFT. DON'T YOU MEAN DESTROYED?
A COUPLE OF BRIDGES NEAR THE MILITARY BASE. A SHADO HELICOPTER. JUST A BUNCH OF THE BOYS OUT HAVING A GOOD TIME.
WHAT ARE YOU DRIVING? I'VE *NEVER* HEARD AN ENGINE LIKE THAT!
I WAS MEANING TO ASK YOU THE SAME THING.
YOUR MOTHER IS GOING TO BE REAL HAPPY TO SEE YOU, SON.
HOW IS SHE, PA?
JUST GREAT. BEEN COOKING UP A MESS OF FINE FOOD FOR THESE FOLKS. SHE SURE MISSES THE COMPANY, SON.
KELLY? WHERE'R WE GOIN'?
BEEP
OOPS, SORRY.
SHHHFFT
AWESOME!

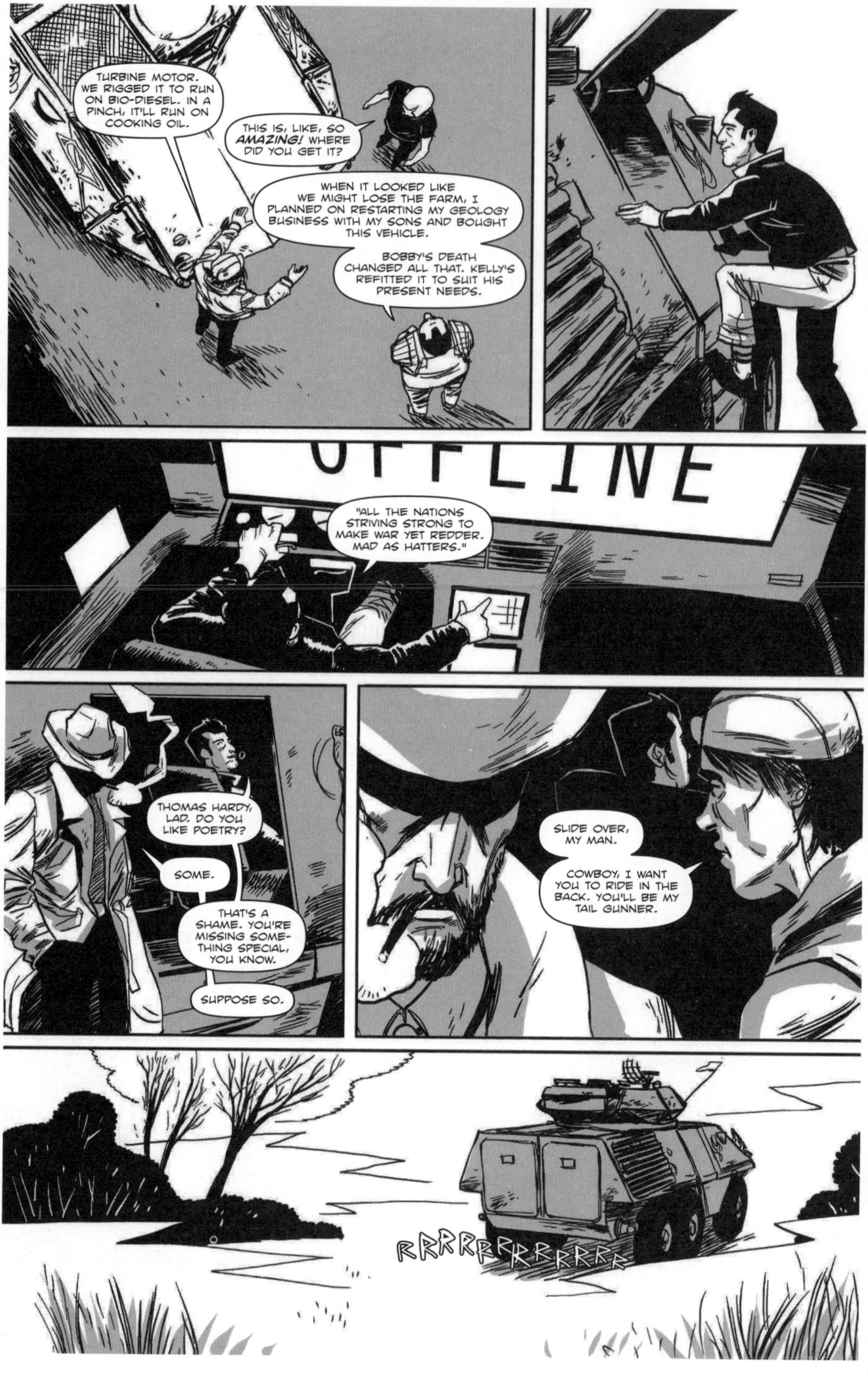
TURBINE MOTOR. WE RIGGED IT TO RUN ON BIO-DIESEL. IN A PINCH, IT'LL RUN ON COOKING OIL.
THIS IS, LIKE, SO AMAZING! WHERE DID YOU GET IT?
WHEN IT LOOKED LIKE WE MIGHT LOSE THE FARM, I PLANNED ON RESTARTING MY GEOLOGY BUSINESS WITH MY SONS AND BOUGHT THIS VEHICLE.
BOBBY'S DEATH CHANGED ALL THAT. KELLY'S REFITTED IT TO SUIT HIS PRESENT NEEDS.
OFFLINE
"ALL THE NATIONS STRIVING STRONG TO MAKE WAR YET REDDER. MAD AS HATTERS."
THOMAS HARDY, LAD. DO YOU LIKE POETRY?
SOME.
THAT'S A SHAME. YOU'RE MISSING SOMETHING SPECIAL, YOU KNOW.
SUPPOSE SO.
SLIDE OVER, MY MAN.
COWBOY, I WANT YOU TO RIDE IN THE BACK. YOU'LL BE MY TAIL GUNNER.
RRRRRRRRRRRR

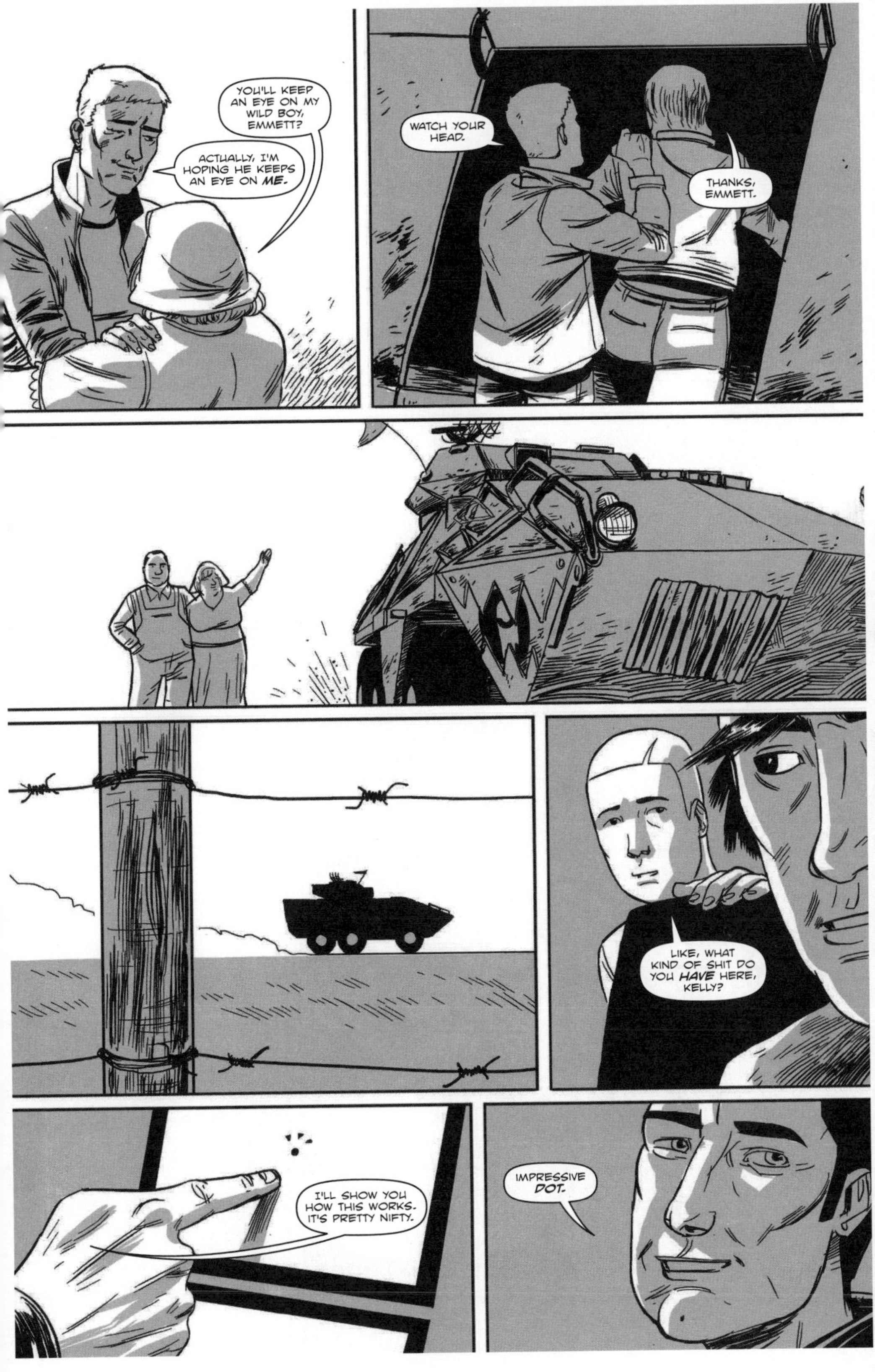
YOU'LL KEEP AN EYE ON MY WILD BOY, EMMETT?
ACTUALLY, I'M HOPING HE KEEPS AN EYE ON ME.
WATCH YOUR HEAD.
THANKS, EMMETT.
LIKE, WHAT KIND OF SHIT DO YOU HAVE HERE, KELLY?
I'LL SHOW YOU HOW THIS WORKS. IT'S PRETTY NIFTY.
IMPRESSIVE DOT.

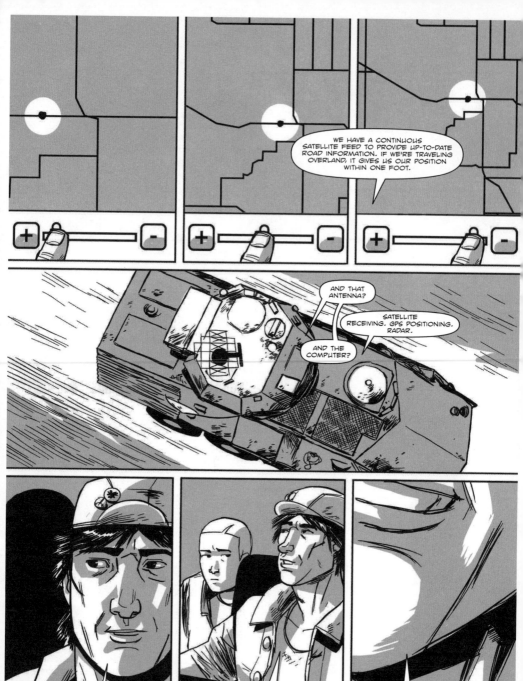

WE HAVE A CONTINUOUS SATELLITE FEED TO PROVIDE UP-TO-DATE ROAD INFORMATION. IF WE'RE TRAVELING OVERLAND, IT GIVES US OUR POSITION WITHIN ONE FOOT.

AND THAT ANTENNA?

SATELLITE RECEIVING. GPS POSITIONING. RADAR.

AND THE COMPUTER?

STATE OF THE ART HACKING. IT PROVIDES COMPLETELY ENCRYPTED DATA TRANSFER, POSITIONAL MASKING AND PROVIDES A FALSE I.P. LOCATION WHENEVER WE GO SEARCHING ON THE NET. THE SYSTEM HAS ENOUGH BACK-UP POWER TO RUN FOR 48 HOURS AND SOLAR PANELS PROVIDE CONTINUAL CHARGE.

WE GET REGULAR UPDATES ON WEATHER, SHADO MOVEMENT, TROOPERS, THAT SORT OF THING. WE ALSO HAVE TRAVEL INFO SUCH AS DISTANCE TO DESTINATION, FUEL ON BOARD, NEAREST FUEL DEPOT. IT'S ALSO HOOKED TO WEAPONS SYSTEM CONTROL.

THE COMPUTERS HAVE DOUBLE REDUNDANT BACK-UP.

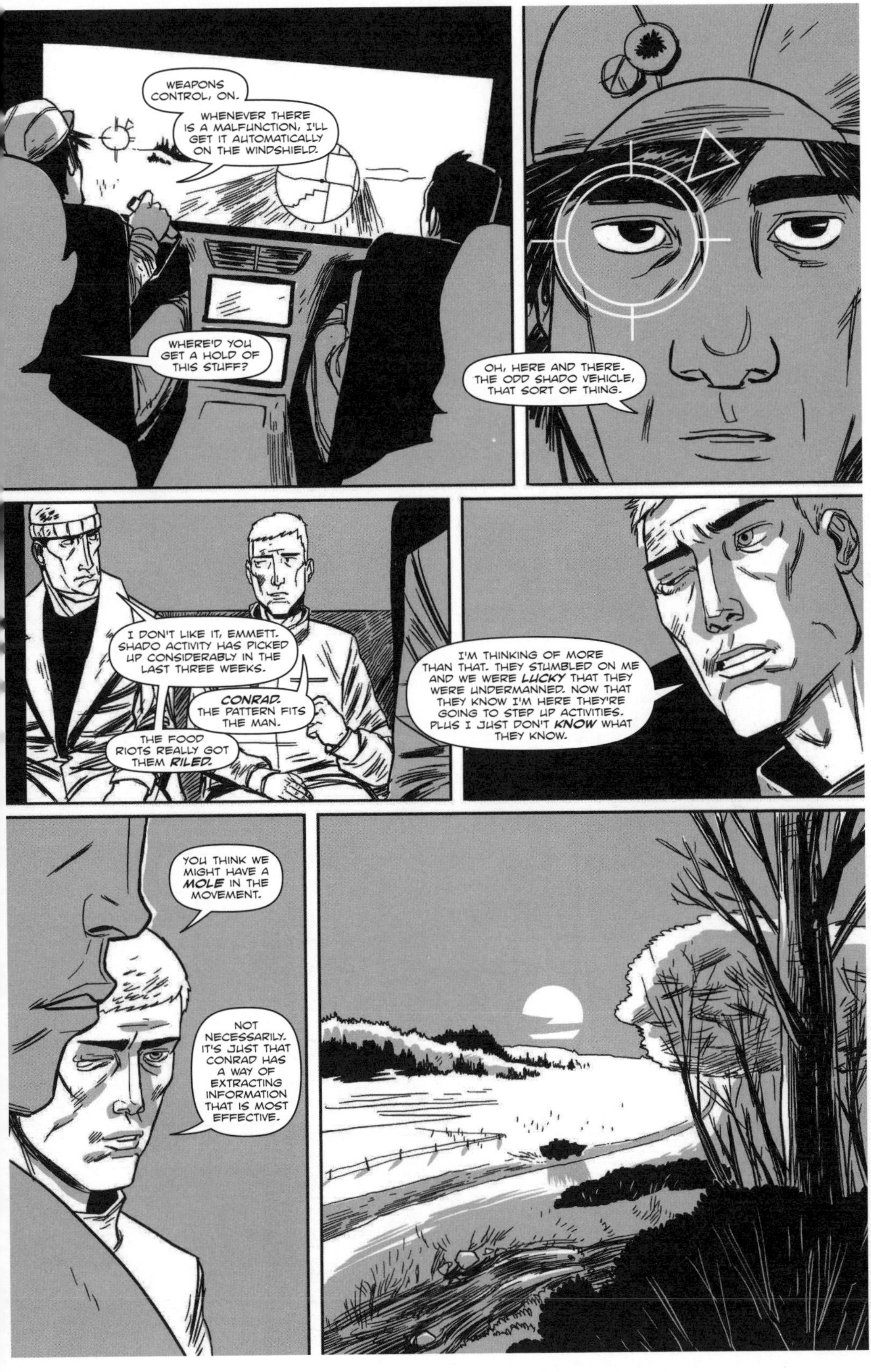
WEAPONS CONTROL, ON.
WHENEVER THERE IS A MALFUNCTION, I'LL GET IT AUTOMATICALLY ON THE WINDSHIELD.
WHERE'D YOU GET A HOLD OF THIS STUFF?
OH, HERE AND THERE. THE ODD SHADO VEHICLE, THAT SORT OF THING.
I DON'T LIKE IT, EMMETT. SHADO ACTIVITY HAS PICKED UP CONSIDERABLY IN THE LAST THREE WEEKS.
CONRAD. THE PATTERN FITS THE MAN.
THE FOOD RIOTS REALLY GOT THEM RILED.
I'M THINKING OF MORE THAN THAT. THEY STUMBLED ON ME AND WE WERE LUCKY THAT THEY WERE UNDERMANNED. NOW THAT THEY KNOW I'M HERE THEY'RE GOING TO STEP UP ACTIVITIES. PLUS I JUST DON'T KNOW WHAT THEY KNOW.
YOU THINK WE MIGHT HAVE A MOLE IN THE MOVEMENT.
NOT NECESSARILY. IT'S JUST THAT CONRAD HAS A WAY OF EXTRACTING INFORMATION THAT IS MOST EFFECTIVE.

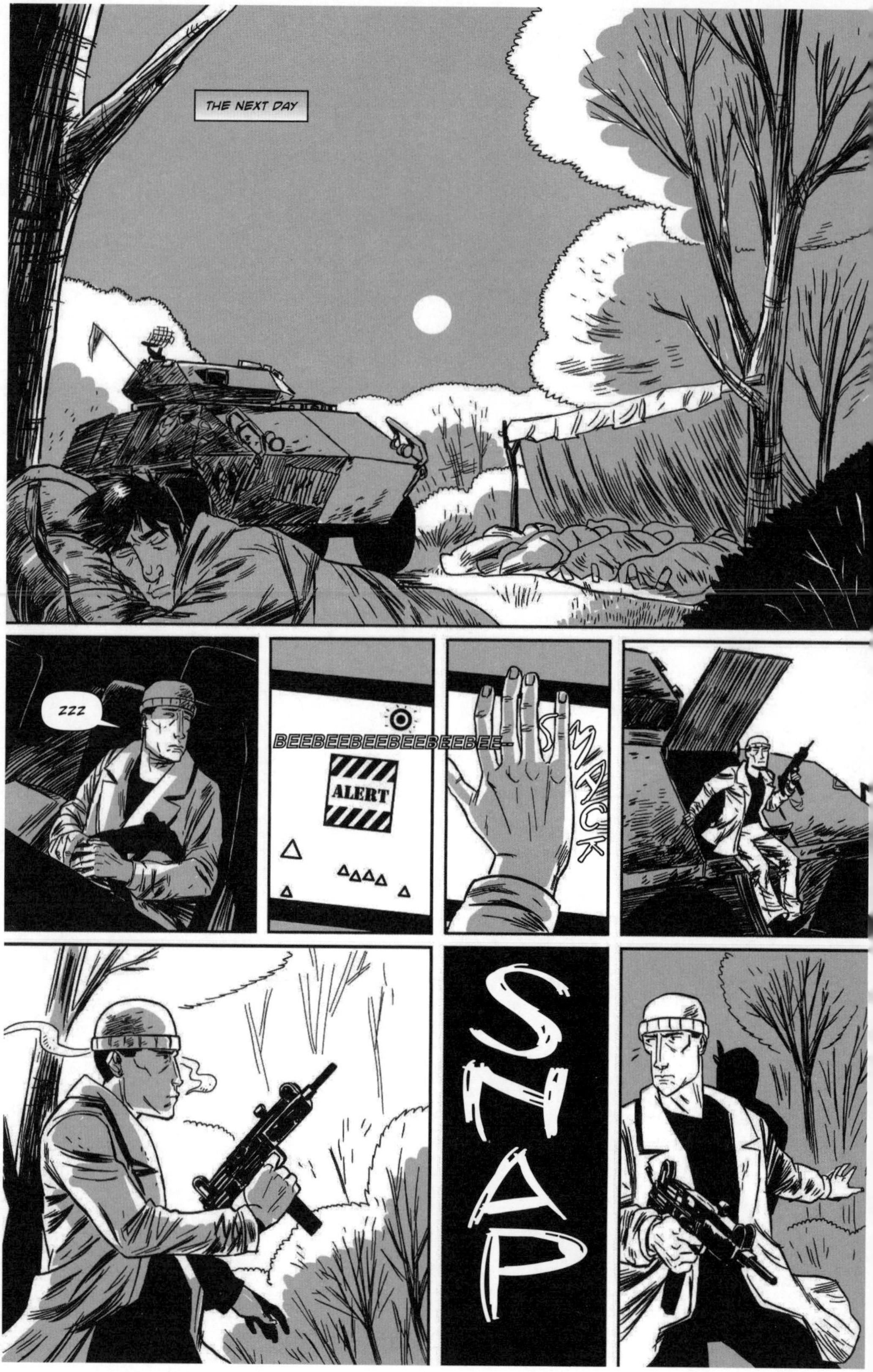
THE NEXT DAY
ZZZ
BEEBEEBEEBEEBEEBEEBEE–
ALERT
SMACK
SNAP

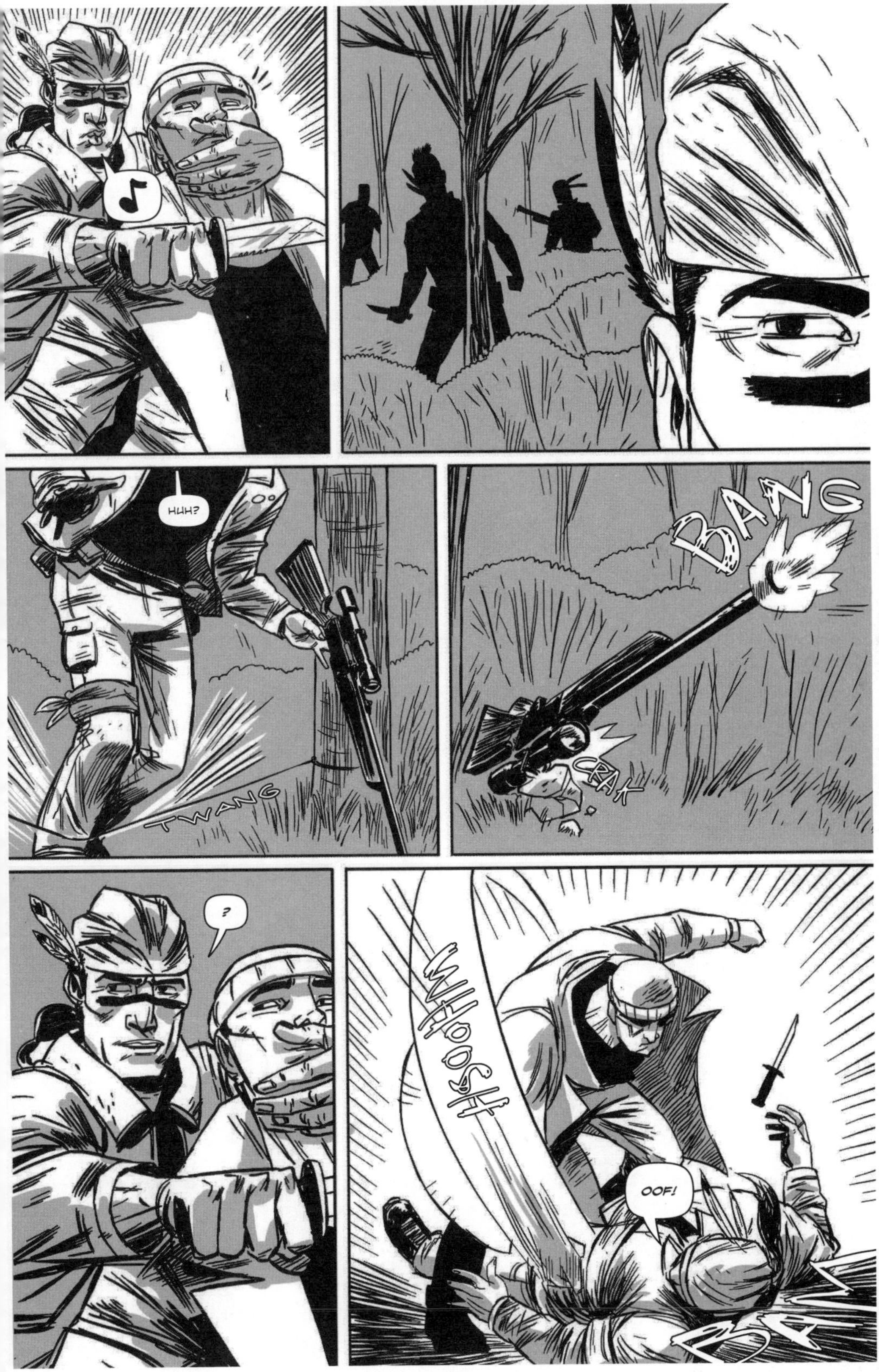
♪
HUH?
TWANG
BANG
CRAK
?
WHOOSH
OOF!

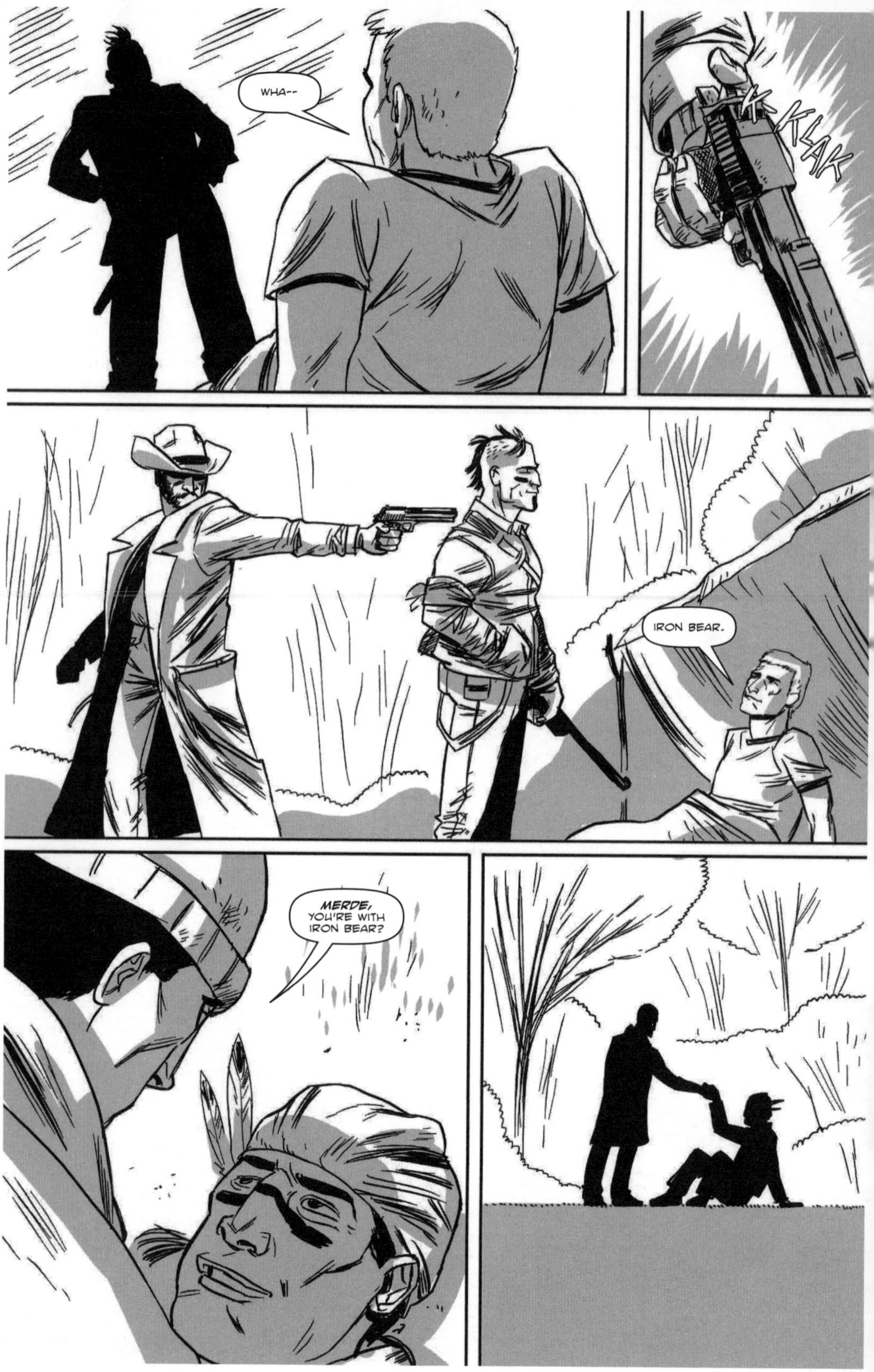
WHA--
K-KLAK
IRON BEAR.
MERDE, YOU'RE WITH IRON BEAR?

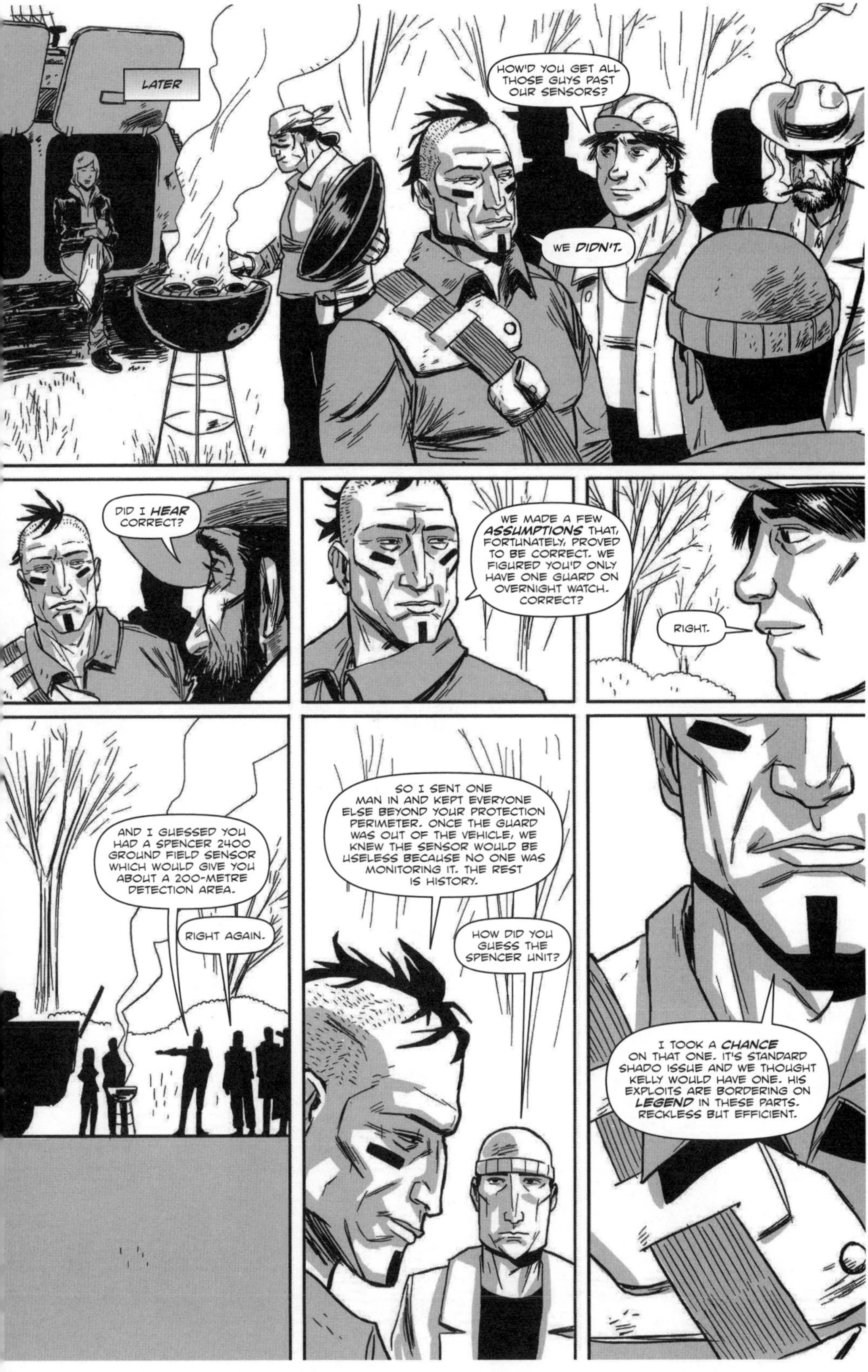
LATER
HOW'D YOU GET ALL THOSE GUYS PAST OUR SENSORS?
WE DIDN'T.
DID I HEAR CORRECT?
WE MADE A FEW ASSUMPTIONS THAT, FORTUNATELY, PROVED TO BE CORRECT. WE FIGURED YOU'D ONLY HAVE ONE GUARD ON OVERNIGHT WATCH. CORRECT?
RIGHT.
AND I GUESSED YOU HAD A SPENCER 2400 GROUND FIELD SENSOR WHICH WOULD GIVE YOU ABOUT A 200-METRE DETECTION AREA.
RIGHT AGAIN.
SO I SENT ONE MAN IN AND KEPT EVERYONE ELSE BEYOND YOUR PROTECTION PERIMETER. ONCE THE GUARD WAS OUT OF THE VEHICLE, WE KNEW THE SENSOR WOULD BE USELESS BECAUSE NO ONE WAS MONITORING IT. THE REST IS HISTORY.
HOW DID YOU GUESS THE SPENCER UNIT?
I TOOK A CHANCE ON THAT ONE. IT'S STANDARD SHADO ISSUE AND WE THOUGHT KELLY WOULD HAVE ONE. HIS EXPLOITS ARE BORDERING ON LEGEND IN THESE PARTS. RECKLESS BUT EFFICIENT.

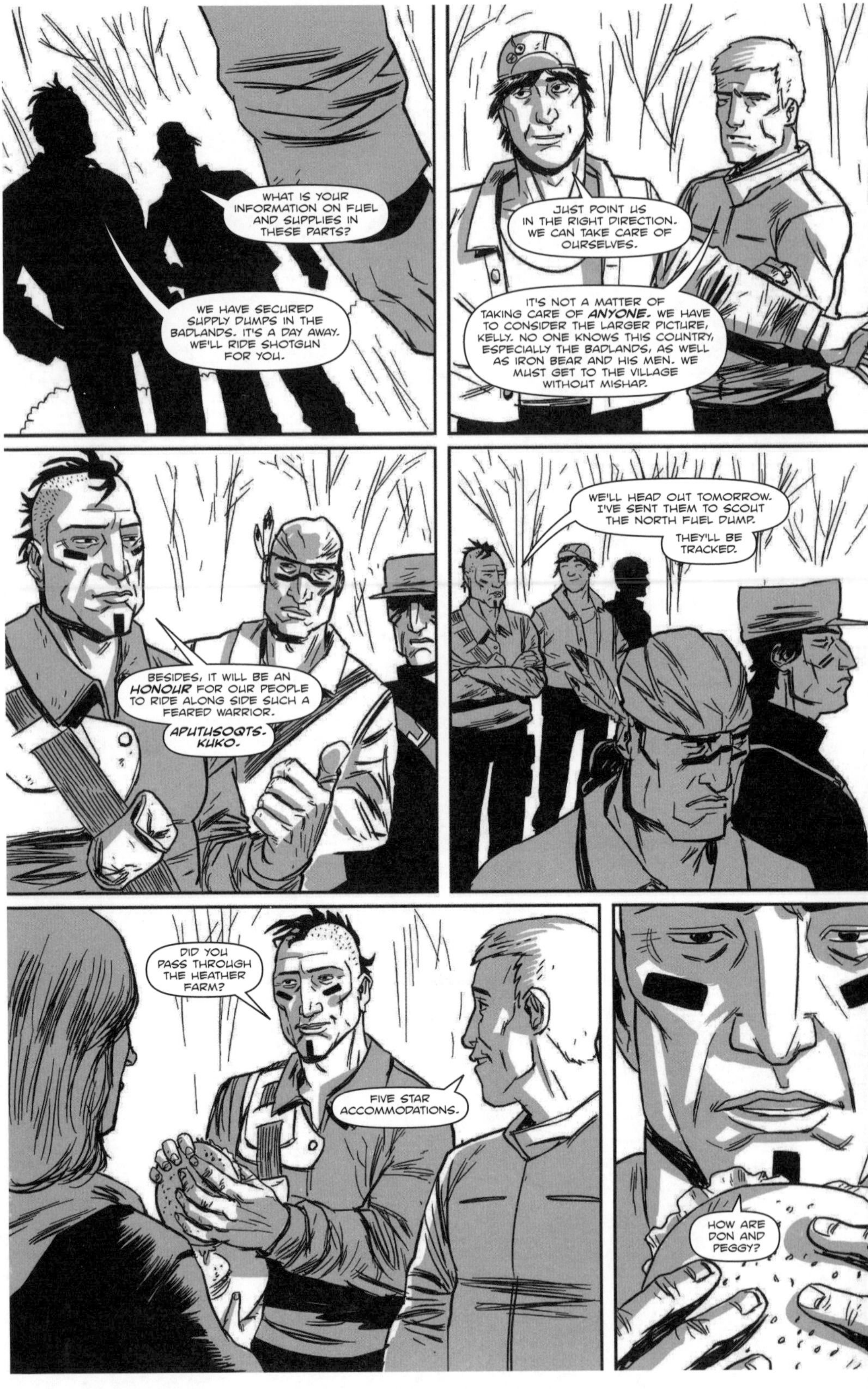
WHAT IS YOUR INFORMATION ON FUEL AND SUPPLIES IN THESE PARTS?
WE HAVE SECURED SUPPLY DUMPS IN THE BADLANDS. IT'S A DAY AWAY. WE'LL RIDE SHOTGUN FOR YOU.
JUST POINT US IN THE RIGHT DIRECTION. WE CAN TAKE CARE OF OURSELVES.
IT'S NOT A MATTER OF TAKING CARE OF ANYONE. WE HAVE TO CONSIDER THE LARGER PICTURE, KELLY. NO ONE KNOWS THIS COUNTRY, ESPECIALLY THE BADLANDS, AS WELL AS IRON BEAR AND HIS MEN. WE MUST GET TO THE VILLAGE WITHOUT MISHAP.
BESIDES, IT WILL BE AN HONOUR FOR OUR PEOPLE TO RIDE ALONG SIDE SUCH A FEARED WARRIOR.
APUTUSOQTS. KUKO.
WE'LL HEAD OUT TOMORROW. I'VE SENT THEM TO SCOUT THE NORTH FUEL DUMP.
THEY'LL BE TRACKED.
DID YOU PASS THROUGH THE HEATHER FARM?
FIVE STAR ACCOMMODATIONS.
HOW ARE DON AND PEGGY?

MEANWHILE...

BE STRONG, PEGGY

LUHUPLUHUPLUHUPLUHUPLUHUPI

LATER

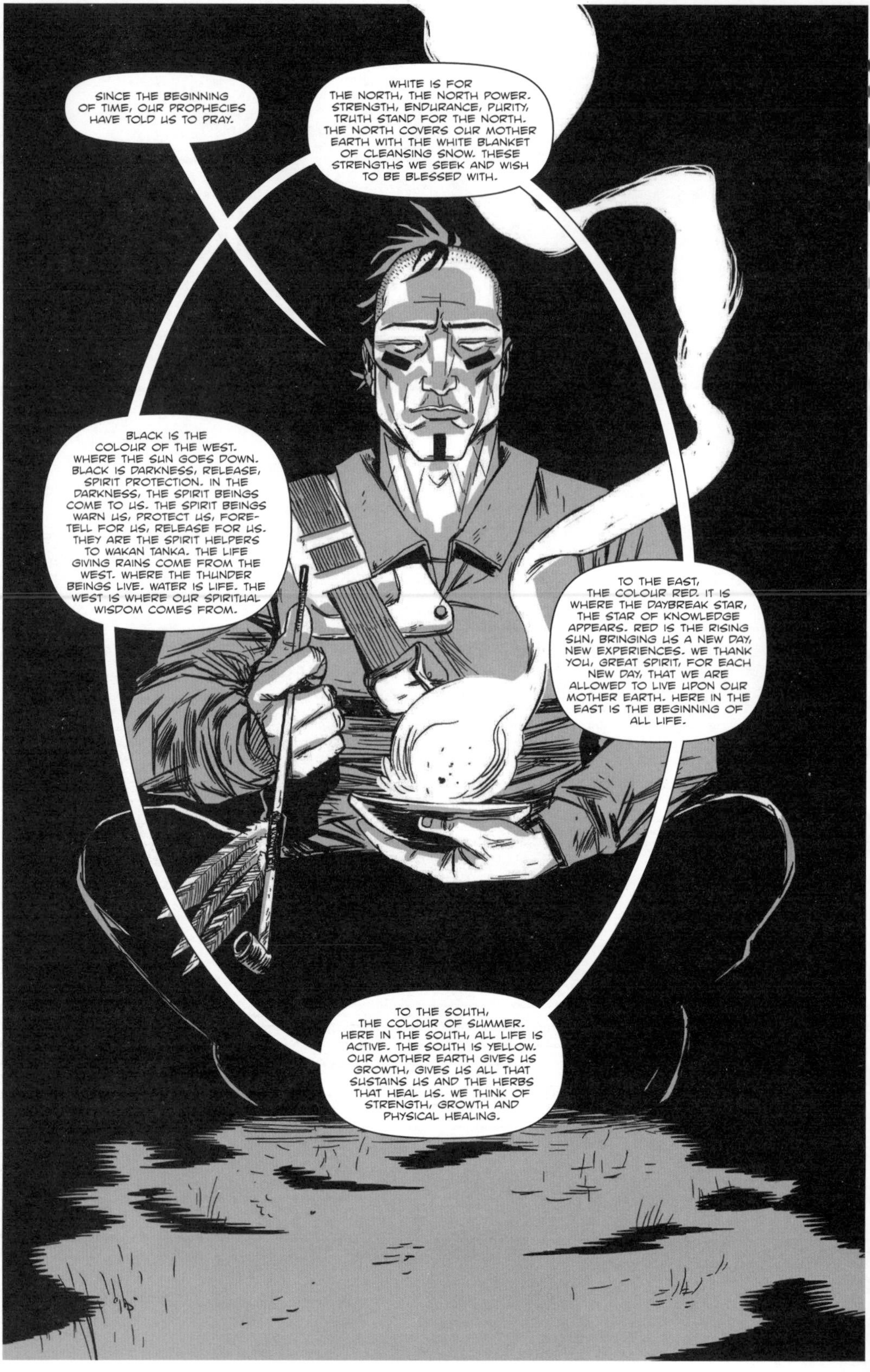
SINCE THE BEGINNING OF TIME, OUR PROPHECIES HAVE TOLD US TO PRAY.
WHITE IS FOR THE NORTH, THE NORTH POWER. STRENGTH, ENDURANCE, PURITY, TRUTH STAND FOR THE NORTH. THE NORTH COVERS OUR MOTHER EARTH WITH THE WHITE BLANKET OF CLEANSING SNOW. THESE STRENGTHS WE SEEK AND WISH TO BE BLESSED WITH.
BLACK IS THE COLOUR OF THE WEST. WHERE THE SUN GOES DOWN. BLACK IS DARKNESS, RELEASE, SPIRIT PROTECTION. IN THE DARKNESS, THE SPIRIT BEINGS COME TO US. THE SPIRIT BEINGS WARN US, PROTECT US, FORETELL FOR US, RELEASE FOR US. THEY ARE THE SPIRIT HELPERS TO WAKAN TANKA. THE LIFE GIVING RAINS COME FROM THE WEST. WHERE THE THUNDER BEINGS LIVE. WATER IS LIFE. THE WEST IS WHERE OUR SPIRITUAL WISDOM COMES FROM.
TO THE EAST, THE COLOUR RED. IT IS WHERE THE DAYBREAK STAR, THE STAR OF KNOWLEDGE APPEARS. RED IS THE RISING SUN, BRINGING US A NEW DAY, NEW EXPERIENCES. WE THANK YOU, GREAT SPIRIT, FOR EACH NEW DAY, THAT WE ARE ALLOWED TO LIVE UPON OUR MOTHER EARTH. HERE IN THE EAST IS THE BEGINNING OF ALL LIFE.
TO THE SOUTH, THE COLOUR OF SUMMER. HERE IN THE SOUTH, ALL LIFE IS ACTIVE. THE SOUTH IS YELLOW. OUR MOTHER EARTH GIVES US GROWTH, GIVES US ALL THAT SUSTAINS US AND THE HERBS THAT HEAL US. WE THINK OF STRENGTH, GROWTH AND PHYSICAL HEALING.

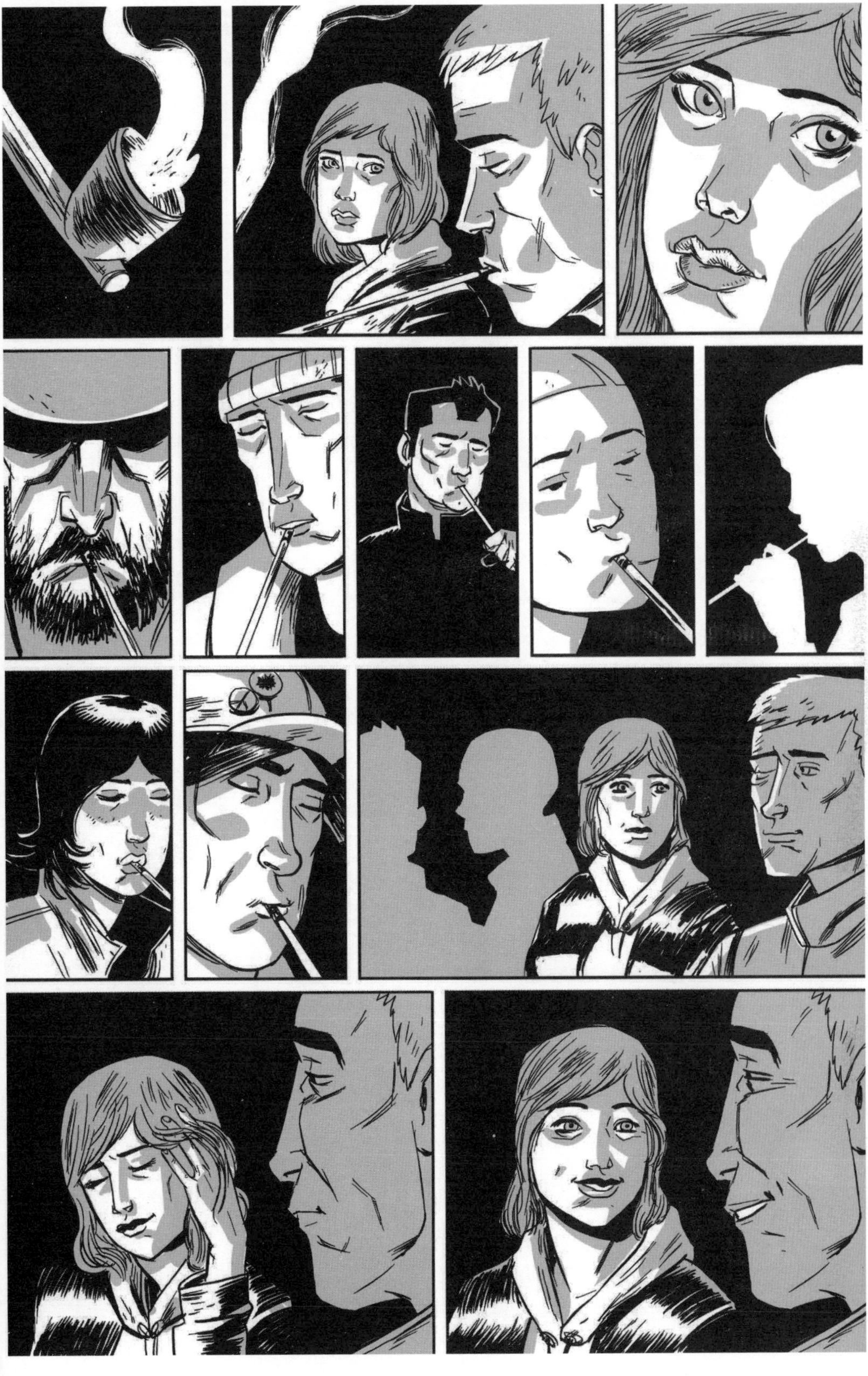

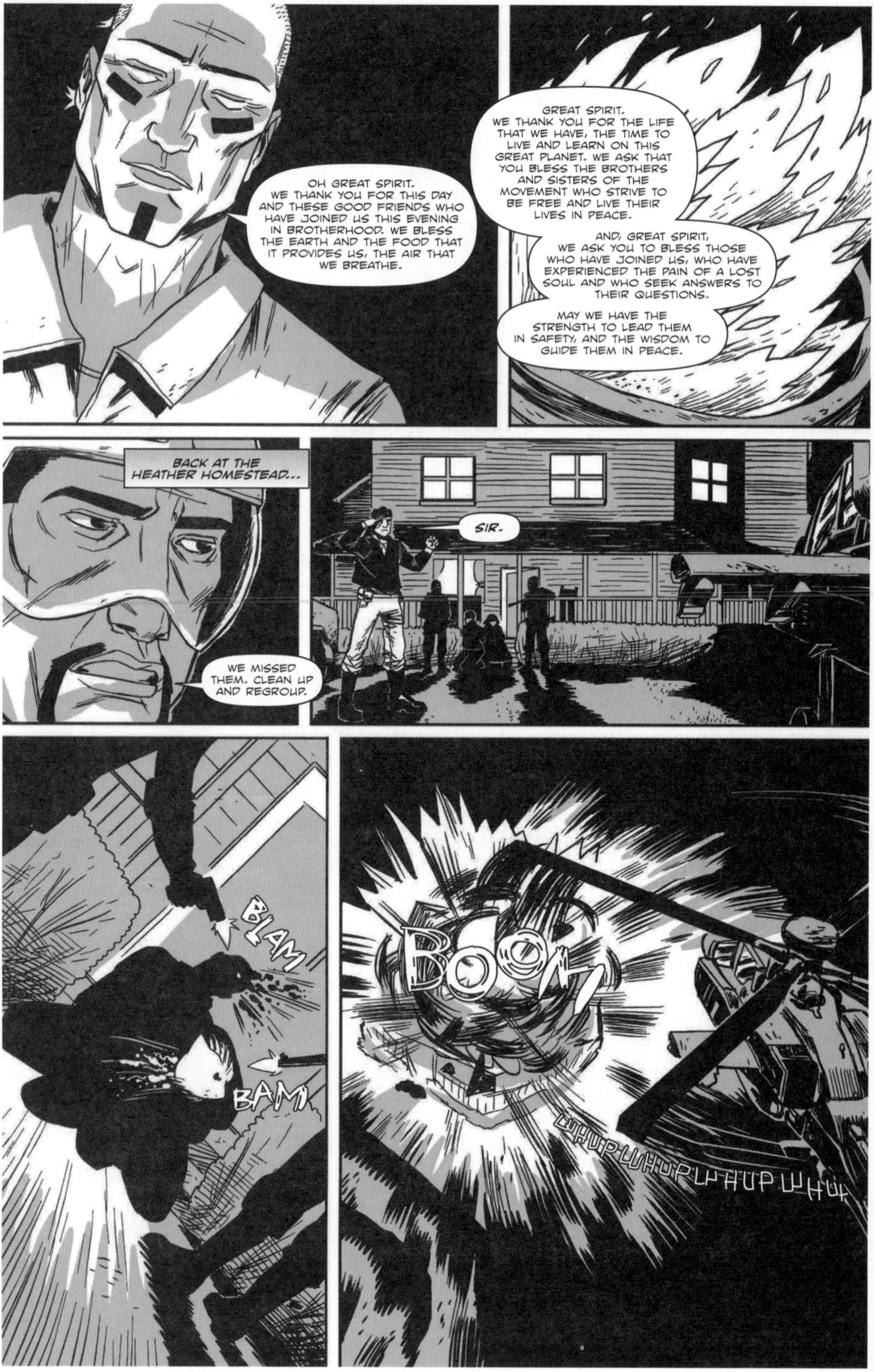
OH GREAT SPIRIT. WE THANK YOU FOR THIS DAY AND THESE GOOD FRIENDS WHO HAVE JOINED US THIS EVENING IN BROTHERHOOD. WE BLESS THE EARTH AND THE FOOD THAT IT PROVIDES US, THE AIR THAT WE BREATHE.
GREAT SPIRIT. WE THANK YOU FOR THE LIFE THAT WE HAVE, THE TIME TO LIVE AND LEARN ON THIS GREAT PLANET. WE ASK THAT YOU BLESS THE BROTHERS AND SISTERS OF THE MOVEMENT WHO STRIVE TO BE FREE AND LIVE THEIR LIVES IN PEACE.
AND, GREAT SPIRIT, WE ASK YOU TO BLESS THOSE WHO HAVE JOINED US, WHO HAVE EXPERIENCED THE PAIN OF A LOST SOUL AND WHO SEEK ANSWERS TO THEIR QUESTIONS.
MAY WE HAVE THE STRENGTH TO LEAD THEM IN SAFETY, AND THE WISDOM TO GUIDE THEM IN PEACE.
BACK AT THE HEATHER HOMESTEAD...
WE MISSED THEM. CLEAN UP AND REGROUP.
SIR.
BLAM
BAM
BOOM
WHUPWHUPWHUP WHUP WHUP

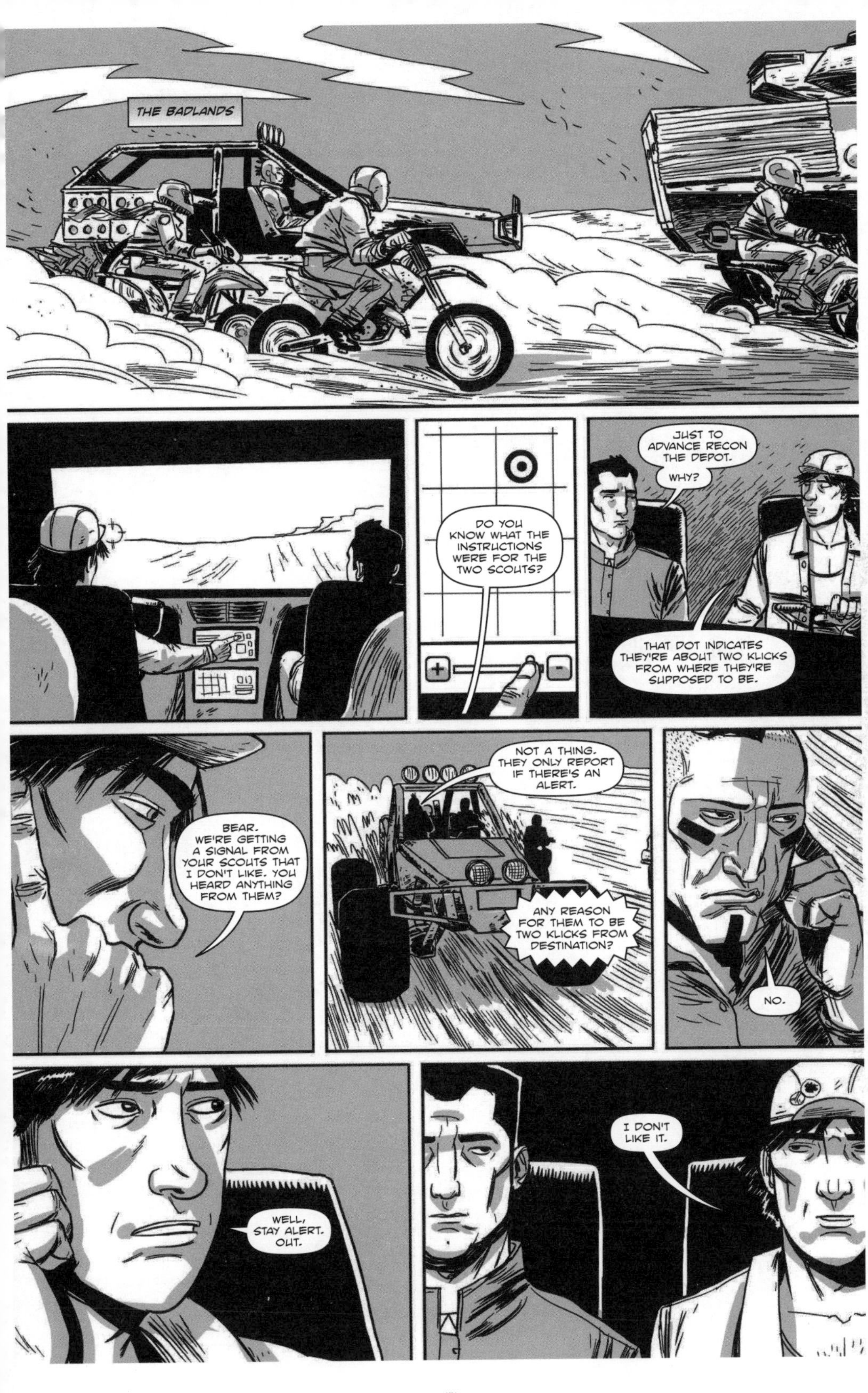
THE BADLANDS
DO YOU KNOW WHAT THE INSTRUCTIONS WERE FOR THE TWO SCOUTS?
JUST TO ADVANCE RECON THE DEPOT.
WHY?
THAT DOT INDICATES THEY'RE ABOUT TWO KLICKS FROM WHERE THEY'RE SUPPOSED TO BE.
BEAR. WE'RE GETTING A SIGNAL FROM YOUR SCOUTS THAT I DON'T LIKE. YOU HEARD ANYTHING FROM THEM?
NOT A THING. THEY ONLY REPORT IF THERE'S AN ALERT.
ANY REASON FOR THEM TO BE TWO KLICKS FROM DESTINATION?
NO.
WELL, STAY ALERT. OUT.
I DON'T LIKE IT.

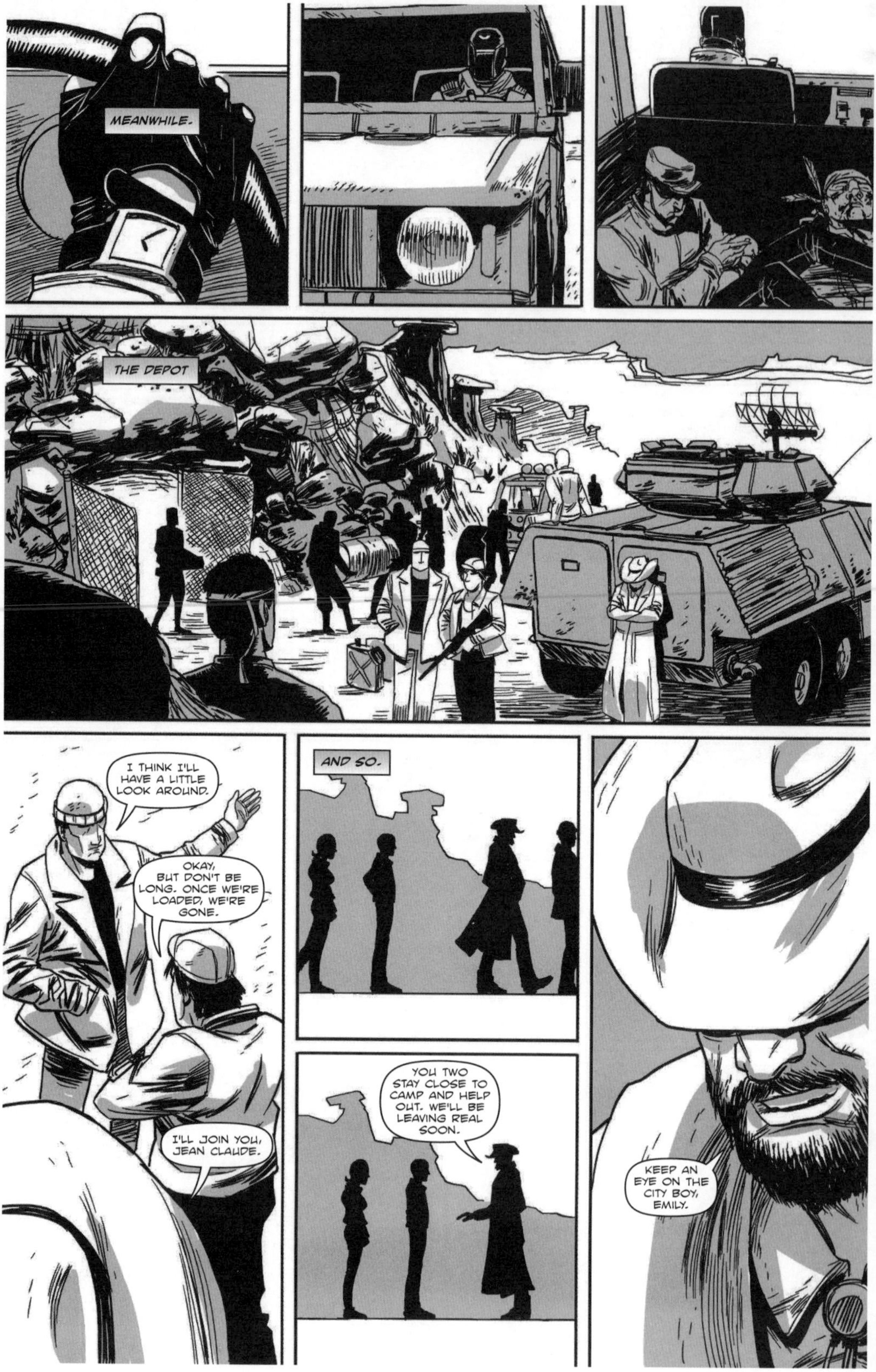
MEANWHILE.
THE DEPOT
I THINK I'LL HAVE A LITTLE LOOK AROUND.
OKAY, BUT DON'T BE LONG. ONCE WE'RE LOADED, WE'RE GONE.
I'LL JOIN YOU, JEAN CLAUDE.
AND SO.
YOU TWO STAY CLOSE TO CAMP AND HELP OUT. WE'LL BE LEAVING REAL SOON.
KEEP AN EYE ON THE CITY BOY, EMILY.

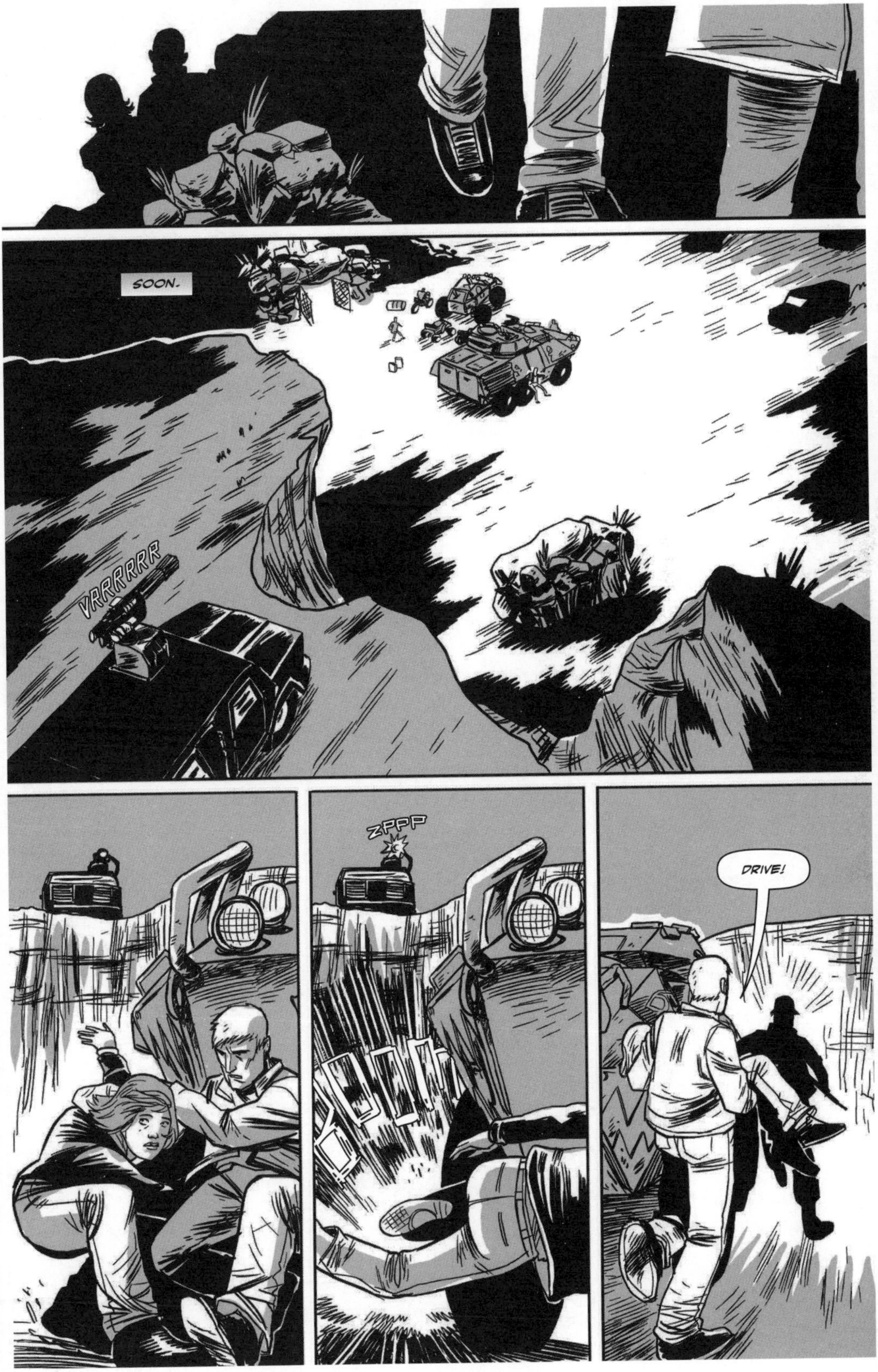
SOON.
VRRRRRR
ZPPP
DRIVE!

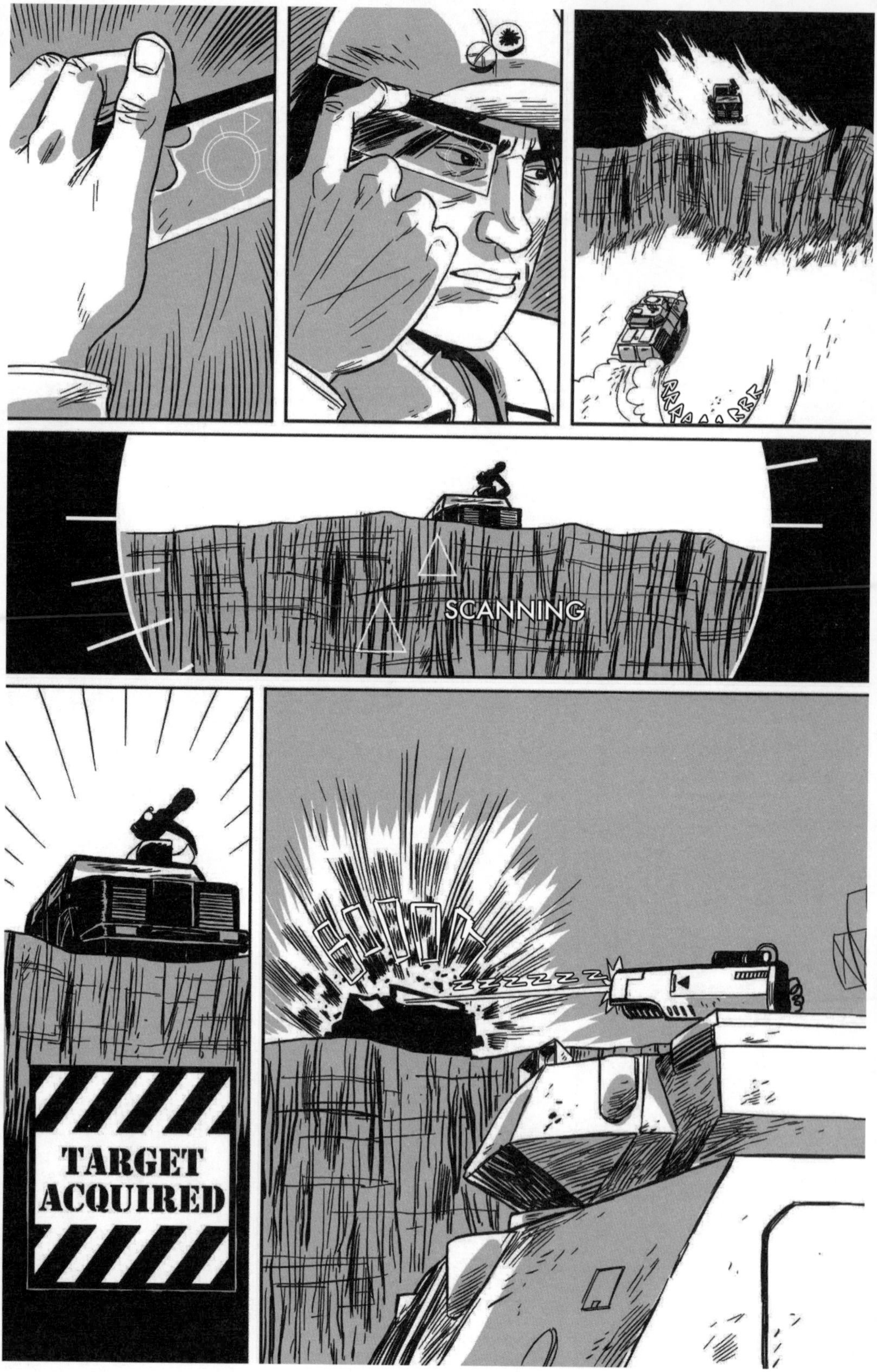
RRAAARRK
SCANNING
TARGET ACQUIRED
ZZZZZZZ

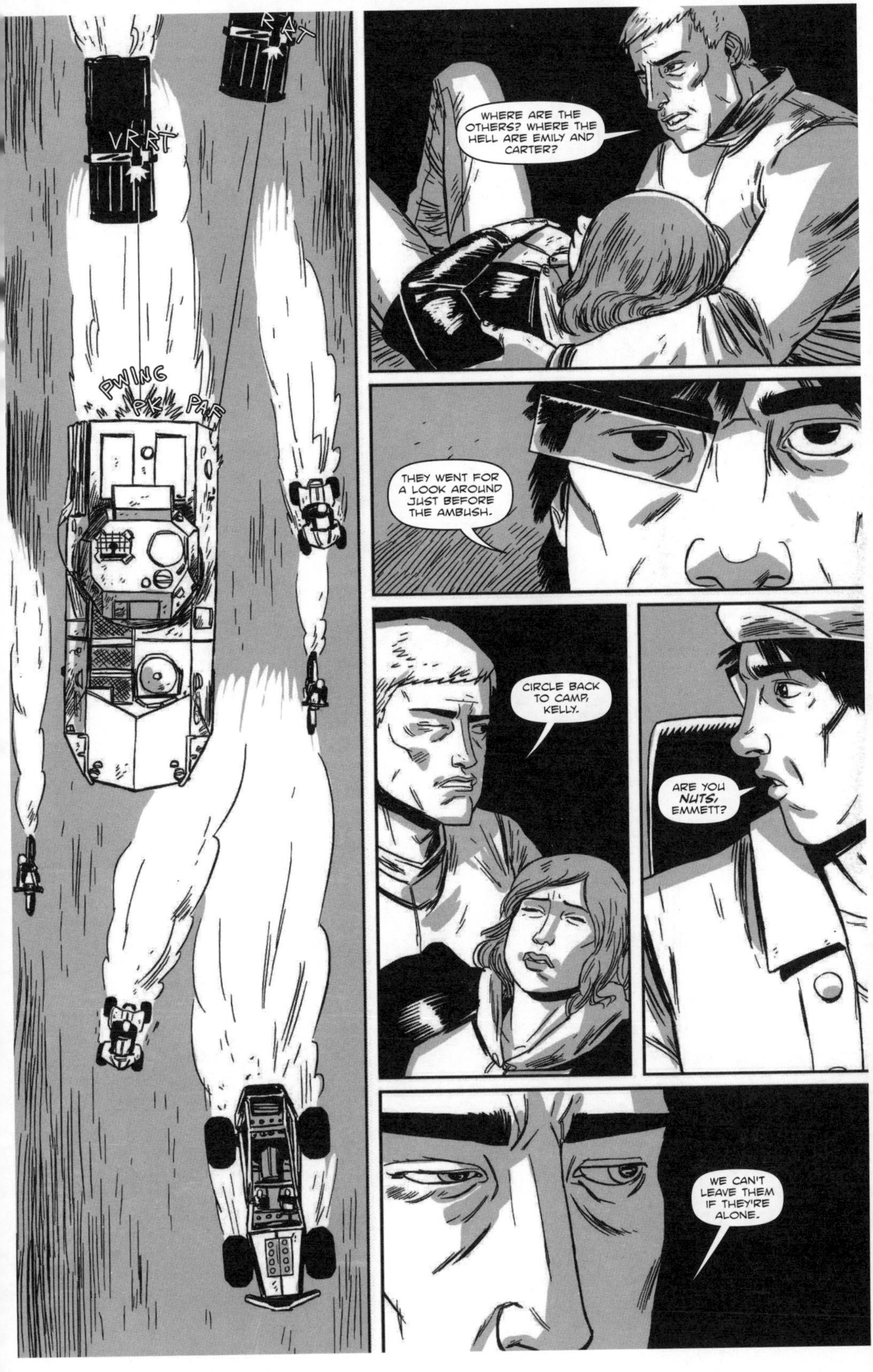

VRRT
RRRT
PWING
PK
PAF
WHERE ARE THE OTHERS? WHERE THE HELL ARE EMILY AND CARTER?
THEY WENT FOR A LOOK AROUND JUST BEFORE THE AMBUSH.
CIRCLE BACK TO CAMP, KELLY.
ARE YOU NUTS, EMMETT?
WE CAN'T LEAVE THEM IF THEY'RE ALONE.

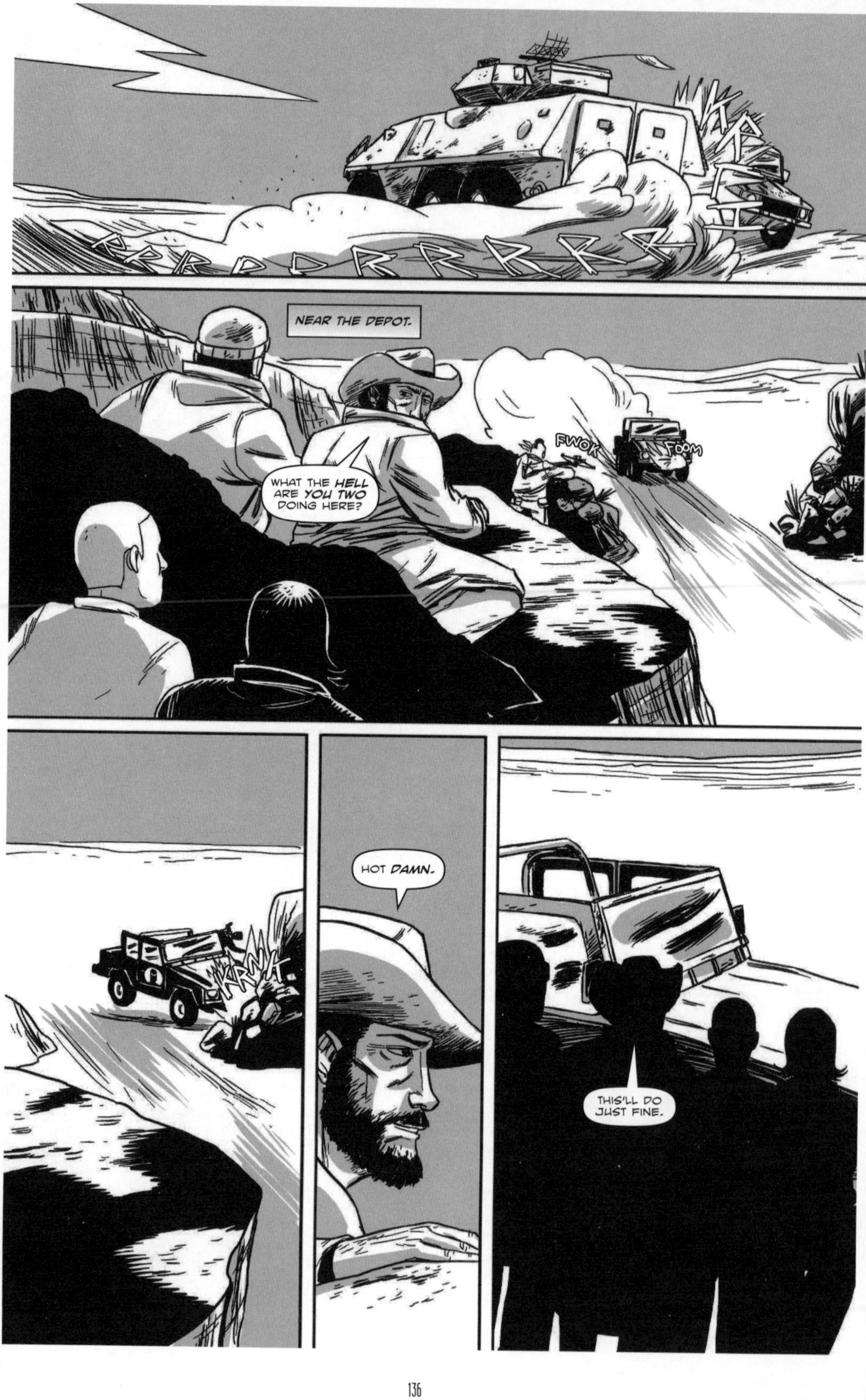
KRRR
RRRRRRRRRR
NEAR THE DEPOT.
WHAT THE HELL ARE YOU TWO DOING HERE?
FWOK
FOOM
KRNCH
HOT DAMN.
THIS'LL DO JUST FINE.

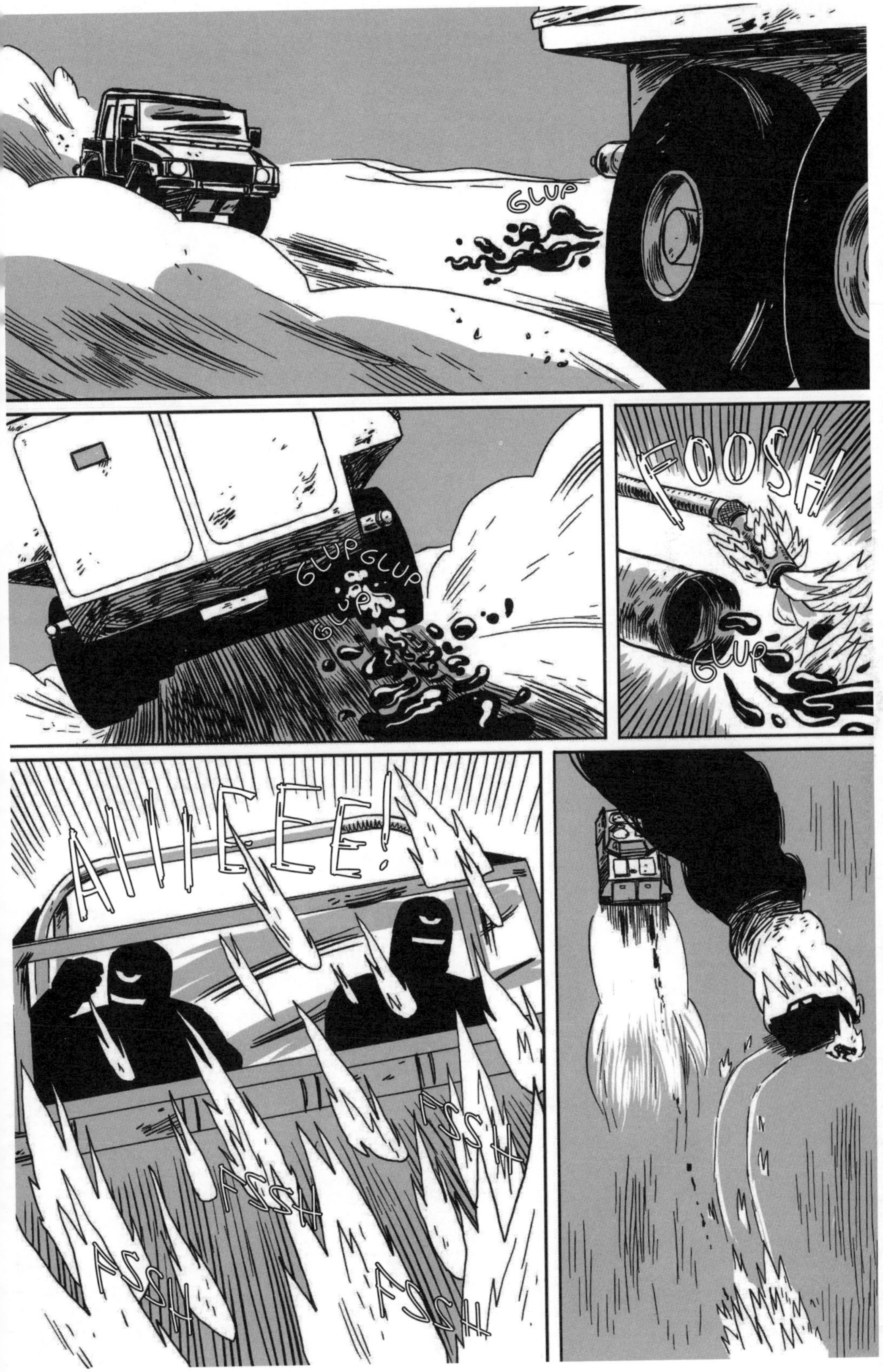
GLUP
GLUP GLUP
GLUP
GLUP
FOOSH
GLUP
AIIEEE!
FSSH
FSSH
FSSH
FSSH

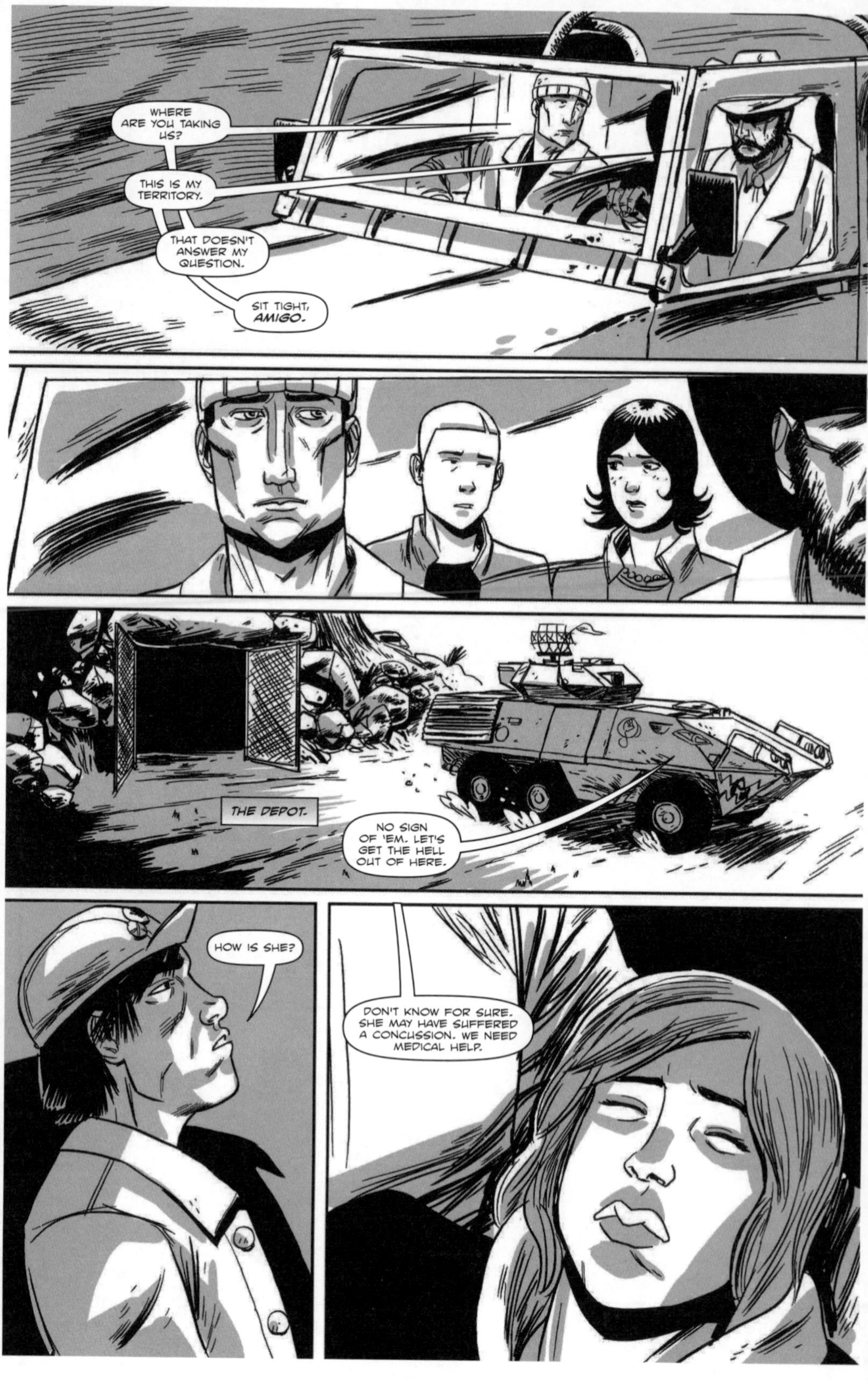
WHERE ARE YOU TAKING US?
THIS IS MY TERRITORY.
THAT DOESN'T ANSWER MY QUESTION.
SIT TIGHT, AMIGO.
THE DEPOT.
NO SIGN OF 'EM. LET'S GET THE HELL OUT OF HERE.
HOW IS SHE?
DON'T KNOW FOR SURE. SHE MAY HAVE SUFFERED A CONCUSSION. WE NEED MEDICAL HELP.

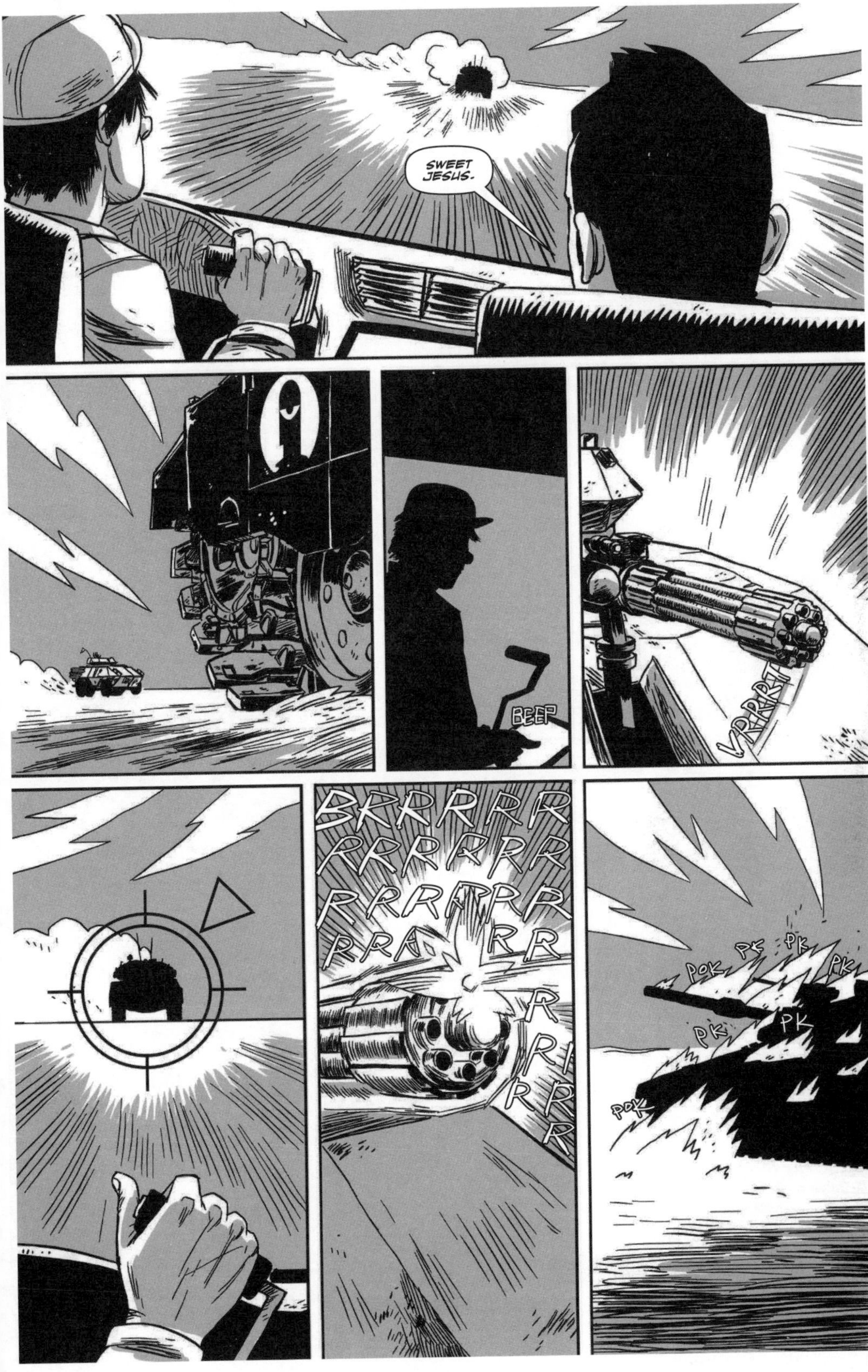
SWEET JESUS.
BEEP
VRRRRT
BRRRRRR
RRRRRRR
RRRRRRR
RRA RR
R
R
R
R
POK
PK
PK
PK
PK
PK
POK

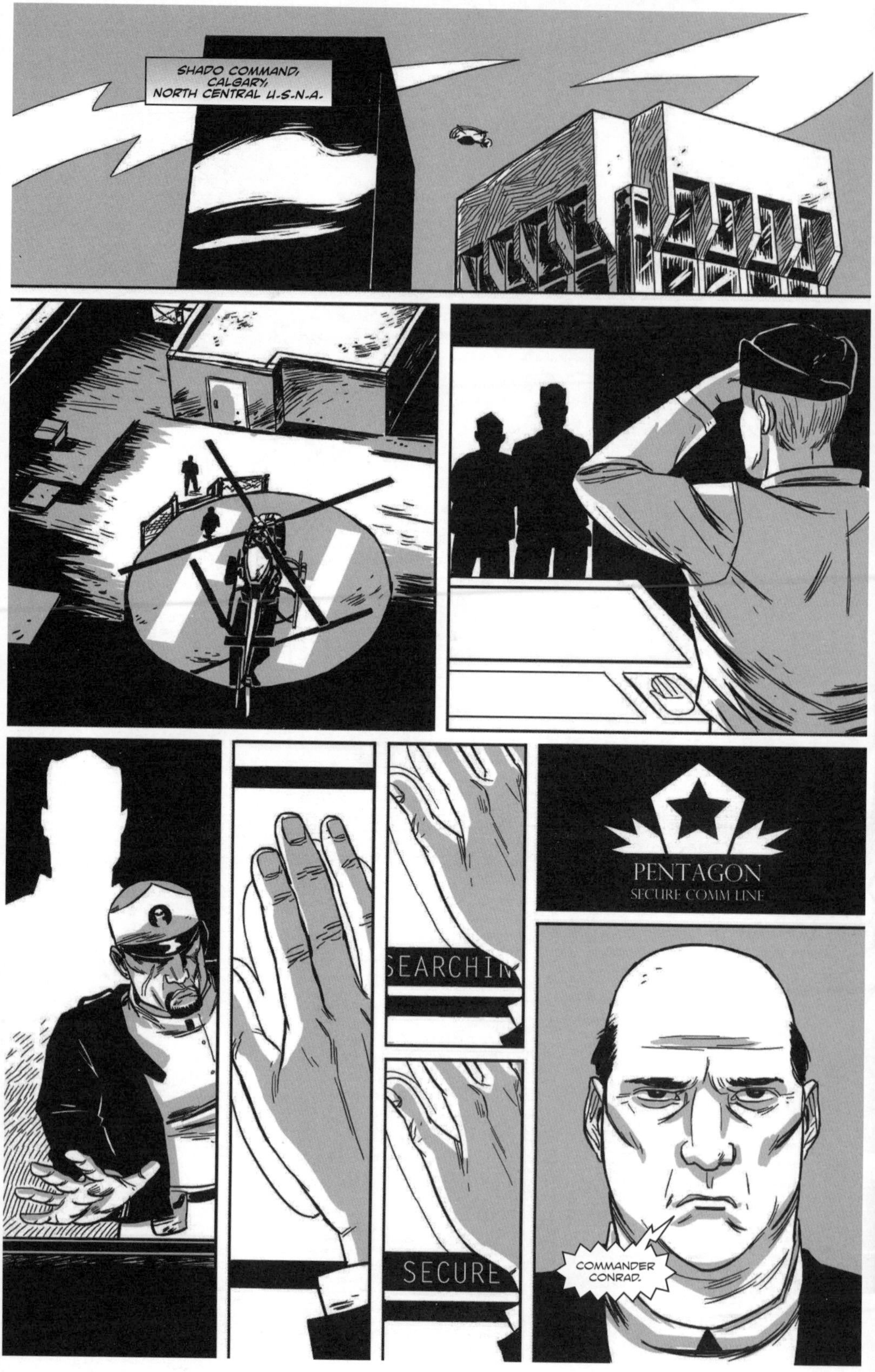
SHADO COMMAND, CALGARY, NORTH CENTRAL U-S-N-A-
PENTAGON
SECURE COMM LINE
SEARCHIN
SECURE
COMMANDER CONRAD.

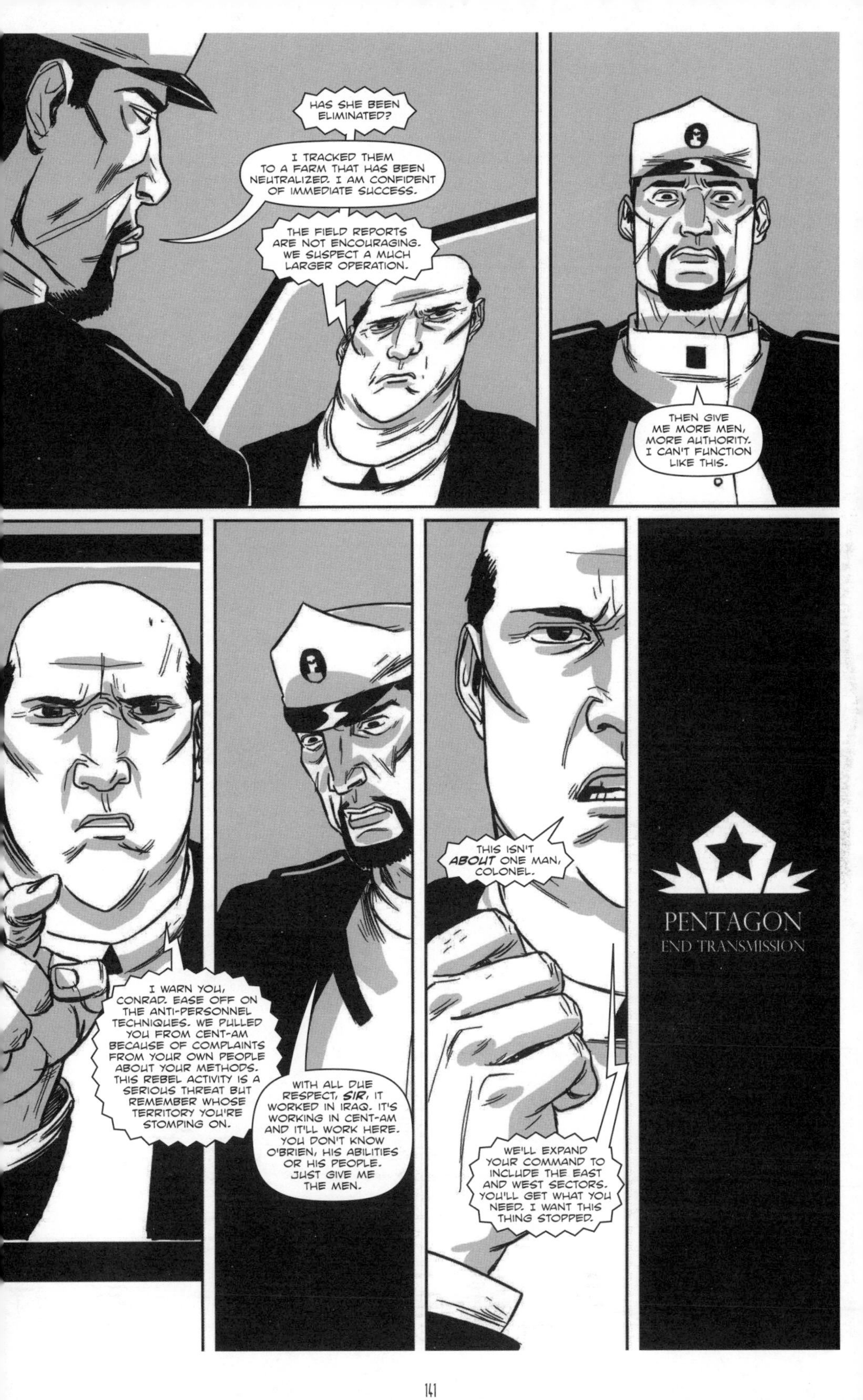
HAS SHE BEEN ELIMINATED?
I TRACKED THEM TO A FARM THAT HAS BEEN NEUTRALIZED. I AM CONFIDENT OF IMMEDIATE SUCCESS.
THE FIELD REPORTS ARE NOT ENCOURAGING. WE SUSPECT A MUCH LARGER OPERATION.
THEN GIVE ME MORE MEN, MORE AUTHORITY. I CAN'T FUNCTION LIKE THIS.
I WARN YOU, CONRAD. EASE OFF ON THE ANTI-PERSONNEL TECHNIQUES. WE PULLED YOU FROM CENT-AM BECAUSE OF COMPLAINTS FROM YOUR OWN PEOPLE ABOUT YOUR METHODS. THIS REBEL ACTIVITY IS A SERIOUS THREAT BUT REMEMBER WHOSE TERRITORY YOU'RE STOMPING ON.
WITH ALL DUE RESPECT, SIR, IT WORKED IN IRAQ. IT'S WORKING IN CENT-AM AND IT'LL WORK HERE. YOU DON'T KNOW O'BRIEN, HIS ABILITIES OR HIS PEOPLE. JUST GIVE ME THE MEN.
THIS ISN'T ABOUT ONE MAN, COLONEL.
WE'LL EXPAND YOUR COMMAND TO INCLUDE THE EAST AND WEST SECTORS. YOU'LL GET WHAT YOU NEED. I WANT THIS THING STOPPED.
PENTAGON
END TRANSMISSION

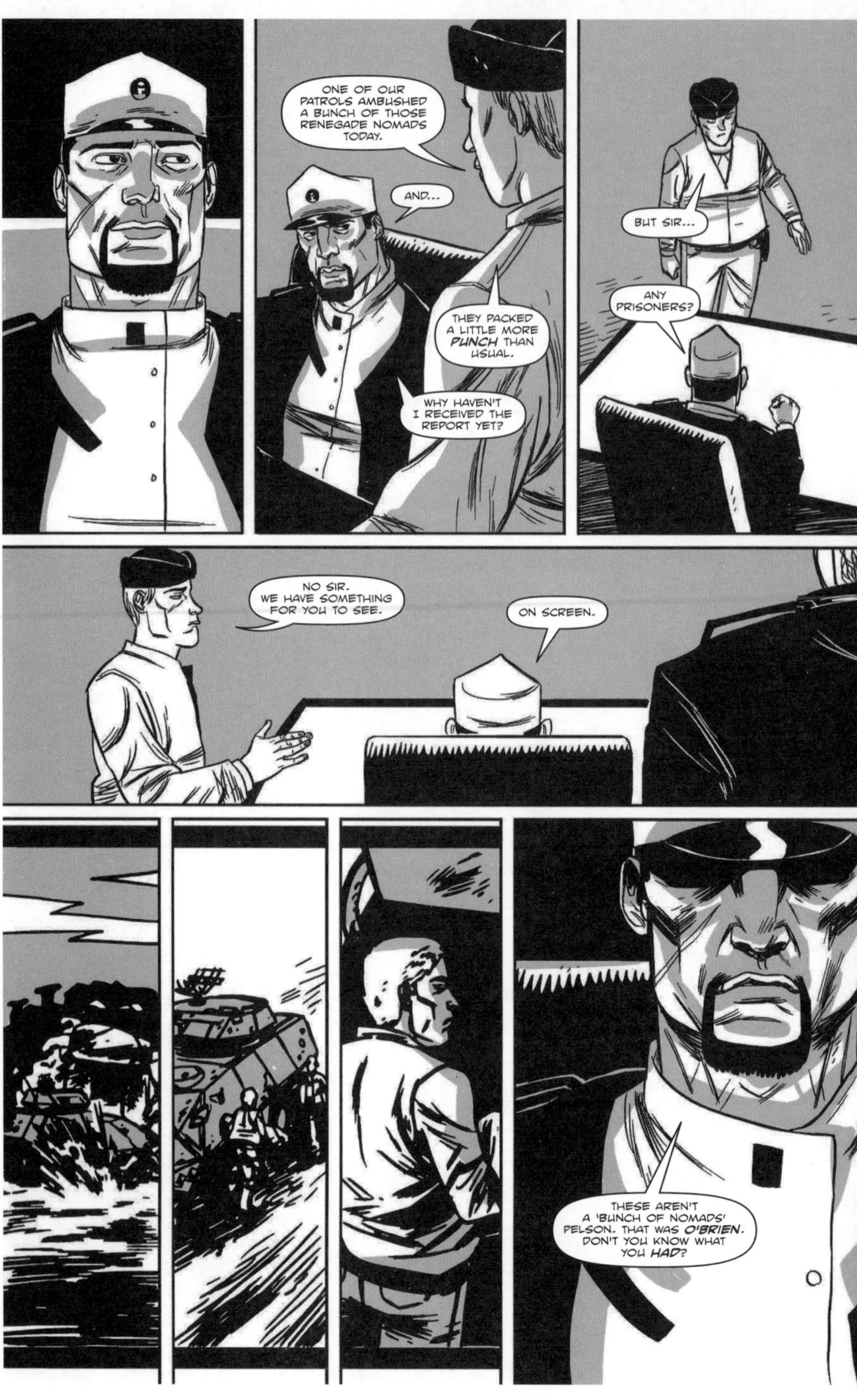

ONE OF OUR PATROLS AMBUSHED A BUNCH OF THOSE RENEGADE NOMADS TODAY.
AND...
THEY PACKED A LITTLE MORE PUNCH THAN USUAL.
WHY HAVEN'T I RECEIVED THE REPORT YET?
BUT SIR...
ANY PRISONERS?
NO SIR. WE HAVE SOMETHING FOR YOU TO SEE.
ON SCREEN.
THESE AREN'T A 'BUNCH OF NOMADS' PELSON. THAT WAS O'BRIEN. DON'T YOU KNOW WHAT YOU HAD?

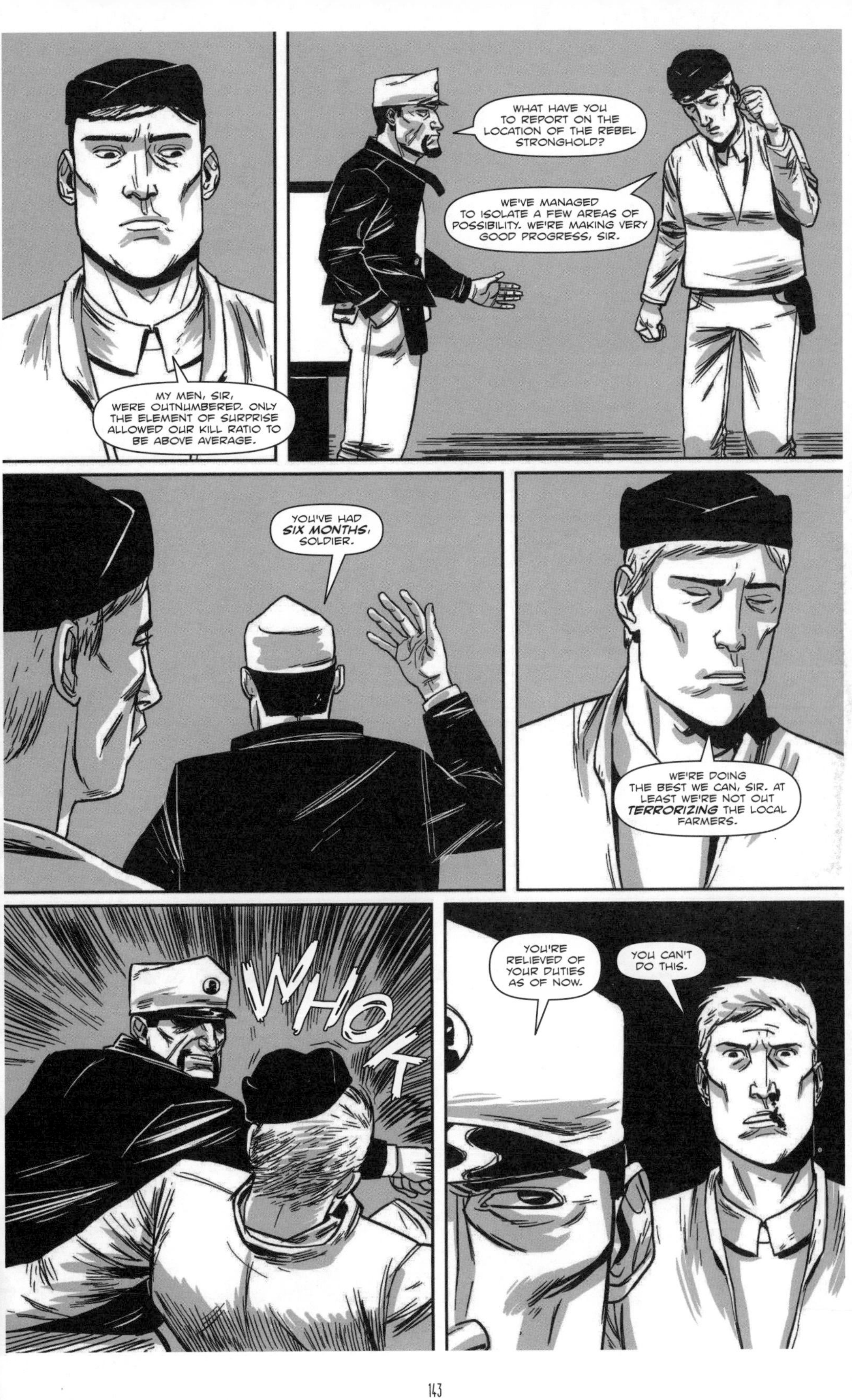
MY MEN, SIR, WERE OUTNUMBERED. ONLY THE ELEMENT OF SURPRISE ALLOWED OUR KILL RATIO TO BE ABOVE AVERAGE.
WHAT HAVE YOU TO REPORT ON THE LOCATION OF THE REBEL STRONGHOLD?
WE'VE MANAGED TO ISOLATE A FEW AREAS OF POSSIBILITY. WE'RE MAKING VERY GOOD PROGRESS, SIR.
YOU'VE HAD *SIX MONTHS*, SOLDIER.
WE'RE DOING THE BEST WE CAN, SIR. AT LEAST WE'RE NOT OUT *TERRORIZING* THE LOCAL FARMERS.
WHOK
YOU'RE RELIEVED OF YOUR DUTIES AS OF NOW.
YOU CAN'T DO THIS.

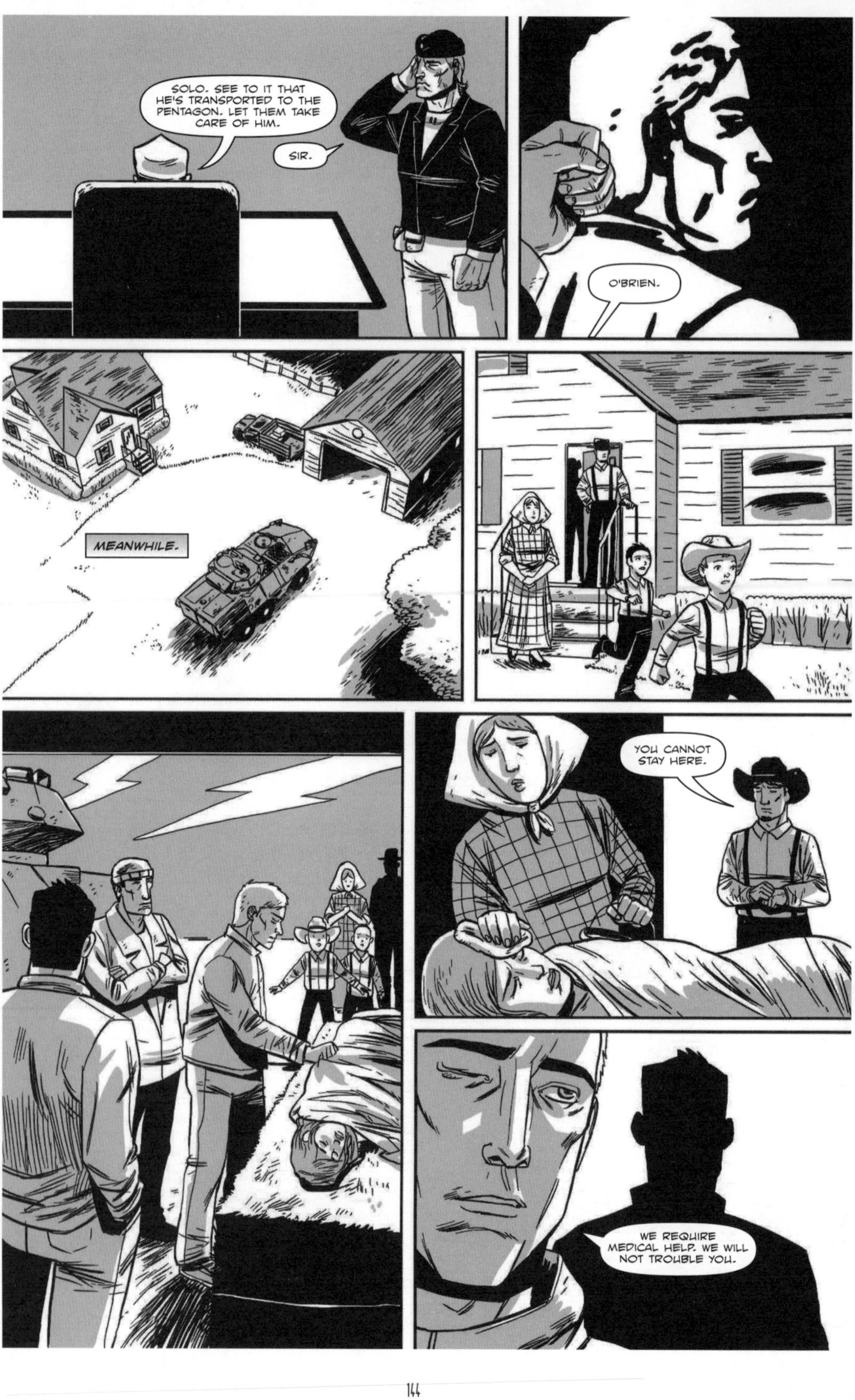
SOLO. SEE TO IT THAT HE'S TRANSPORTED TO THE PENTAGON. LET THEM TAKE CARE OF HIM.
SIR.
O'BRIEN.
MEANWHILE.
YOU CANNOT STAY HERE.
WE REQUIRE MEDICAL HELP. WE WILL NOT TROUBLE YOU.

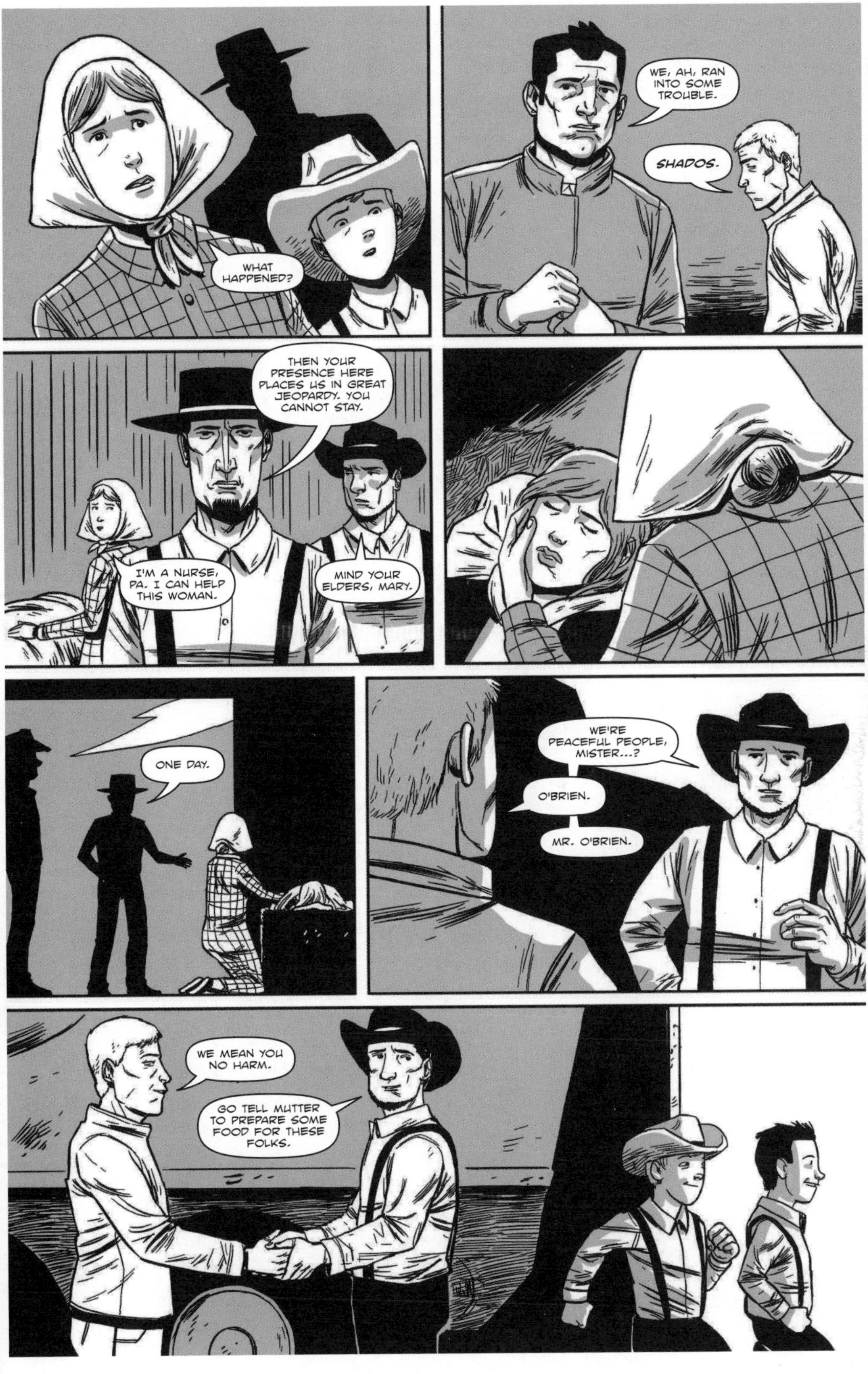
WHAT HAPPENED?
WE, AH, RAN INTO SOME TROUBLE.
SHADOS.
THEN YOUR PRESENCE HERE PLACES US IN GREAT JEOPARDY. YOU CANNOT STAY.
I'M A NURSE, PA. I CAN HELP THIS WOMAN.
MIND YOUR ELDERS, MARY.
ONE DAY.
WE'RE PEACEFUL PEOPLE, MISTER...?
O'BRIEN.
MR. O'BRIEN.
WE MEAN YOU NO HARM.
GO TELL MUTTER TO PREPARE SOME FOOD FOR THESE FOLKS.

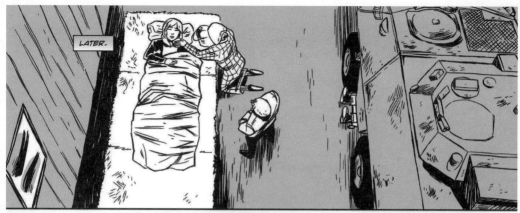

LATER.

THERE'S NOT MUCH MORE WE CAN DO RIGHT NOW. SHE NEEDS REST, MR. O'BRIEN.

THANK YOU, MARY.

GUESS I'M MORE TROUBLE THAN I'M WORTH?

I WAS GOING TO *ASK* YOU ABOUT YOUR NET WORTH...

DON'T SUPPOSE THERE'S AN APPRAISER AROUND?

NAH. THEY'RE ALWAYS INFLATING THE PRICES. I *HATE* TO PAY ABOVE MARKET VALUE.

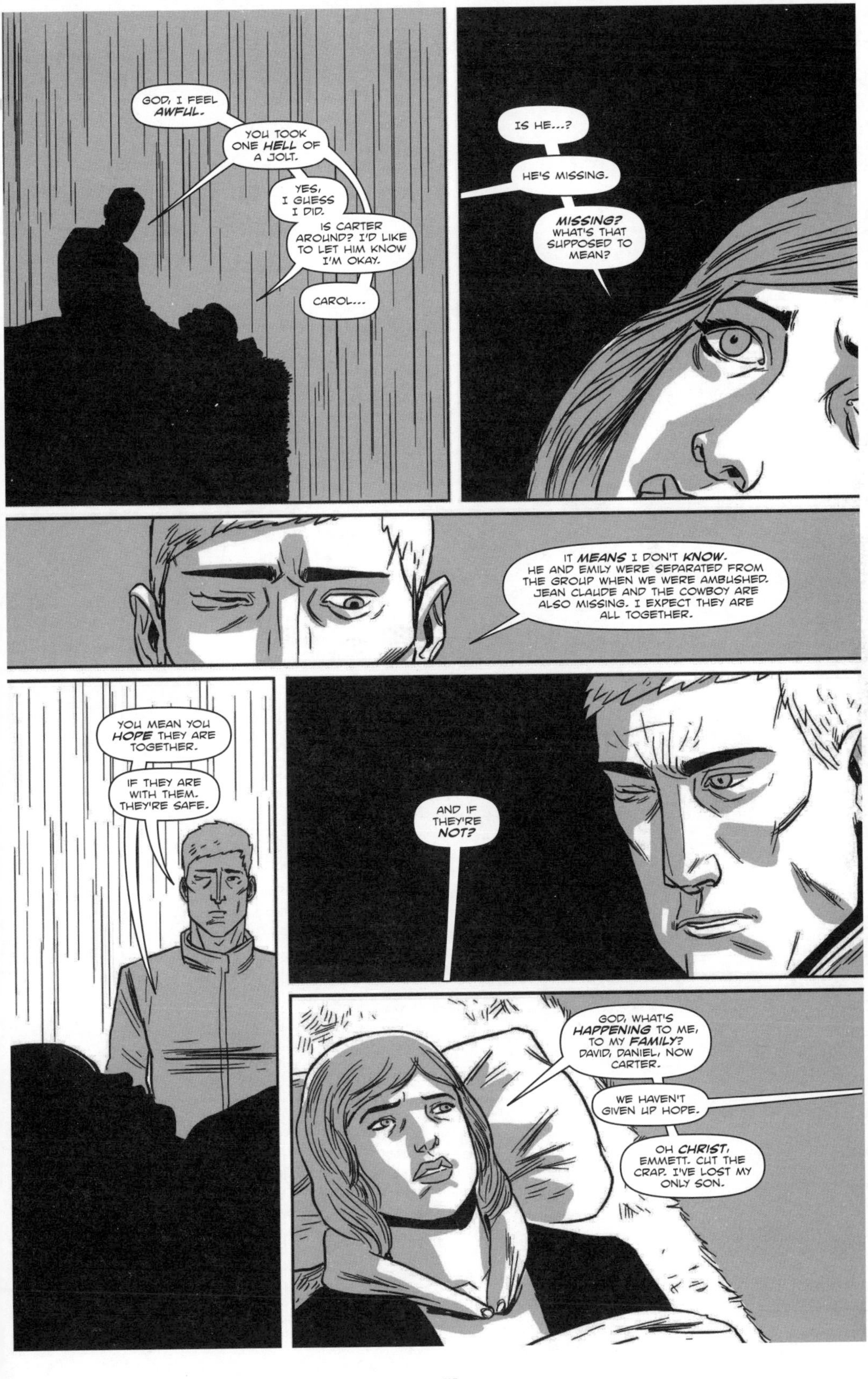
GOD, I FEEL AWFUL.
YOU TOOK ONE HELL OF A JOLT.
YES, I GUESS I DID.
IS CARTER AROUND? I'D LIKE TO LET HIM KNOW I'M OKAY.
CAROL...
IS HE...?
HE'S MISSING.
MISSING? WHAT'S THAT SUPPOSED TO MEAN?
IT MEANS I DON'T KNOW. HE AND EMILY WERE SEPARATED FROM THE GROUP WHEN WE WERE AMBUSHED. JEAN CLAUDE AND THE COWBOY ARE ALSO MISSING. I EXPECT THEY ARE ALL TOGETHER.
YOU MEAN YOU HOPE THEY ARE TOGETHER.
IF THEY ARE WITH THEM. THEY'RE SAFE.
AND IF THEY'RE NOT?
GOD, WHAT'S HAPPENING TO ME, TO MY FAMILY? DAVID, DANIEL, NOW CARTER.
WE HAVEN'T GIVEN UP HOPE.
OH CHRIST, EMMETT. CUT THE CRAP. I'VE LOST MY ONLY SON.

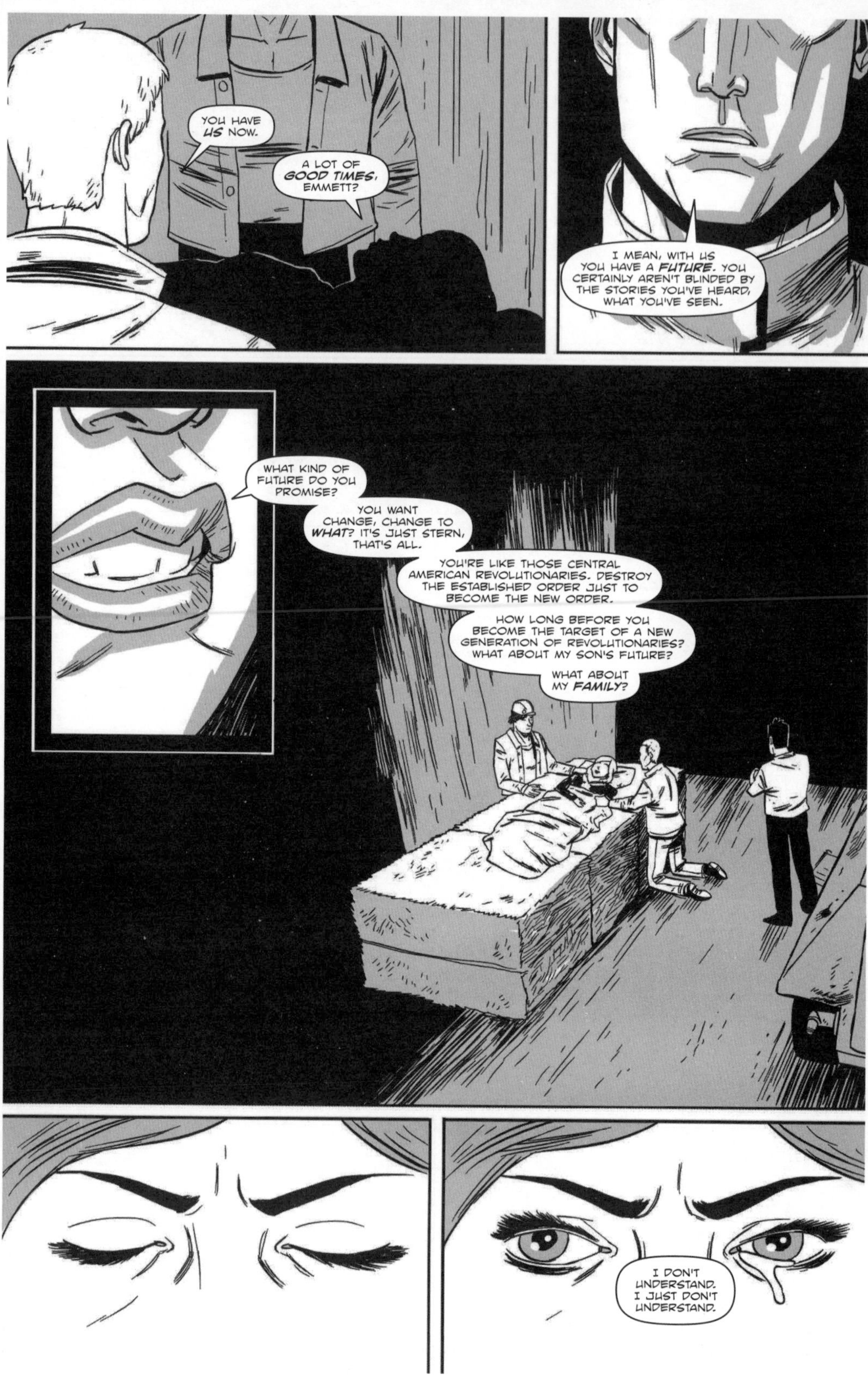
YOU HAVE US NOW.
A LOT OF GOOD TIMES, EMMETT?
I MEAN, WITH US YOU HAVE A FUTURE. YOU CERTAINLY AREN'T BLINDED BY THE STORIES YOU'VE HEARD, WHAT YOU'VE SEEN.
WHAT KIND OF FUTURE DO YOU PROMISE?
YOU WANT CHANGE, CHANGE TO WHAT? IT'S JUST STERN, THAT'S ALL.
YOU'RE LIKE THOSE CENTRAL AMERICAN REVOLUTIONARIES. DESTROY THE ESTABLISHED ORDER JUST TO BECOME THE NEW ORDER.
HOW LONG BEFORE YOU BECOME THE TARGET OF A NEW GENERATION OF REVOLUTIONARIES? WHAT ABOUT MY SON'S FUTURE?
WHAT ABOUT MY FAMILY?
I DON'T UNDERSTAND. I JUST DON'T UNDERSTAND.

THE NEXT DAY.

IT'S AN OLD TRADING ROUTE. I DON'T EXPECT YOU'LL HAVE ANY TROUBLE.

I'VE GOT IT LOGGED IN. THANKS.

NO SUDDEN BUMPS OR STOPS NOW. SHE'S NOT OUT OF THE WOODS YET. GOD BE WITH YOU.

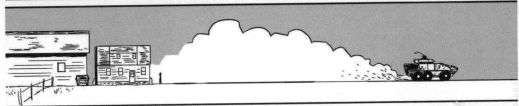

MEANWHILE.

ROGER. WE'RE TEN NORTH OF THE CITY. WE'LL BE HEADING UP ANOTHER 20 BEFORE RETURNING TO BASE. OVER.

GOOD THING THESE SHADO COMMUNICATIONS ARE SCRAMBLED. WE'D NEVER KNOW WHERE THEY ARE.

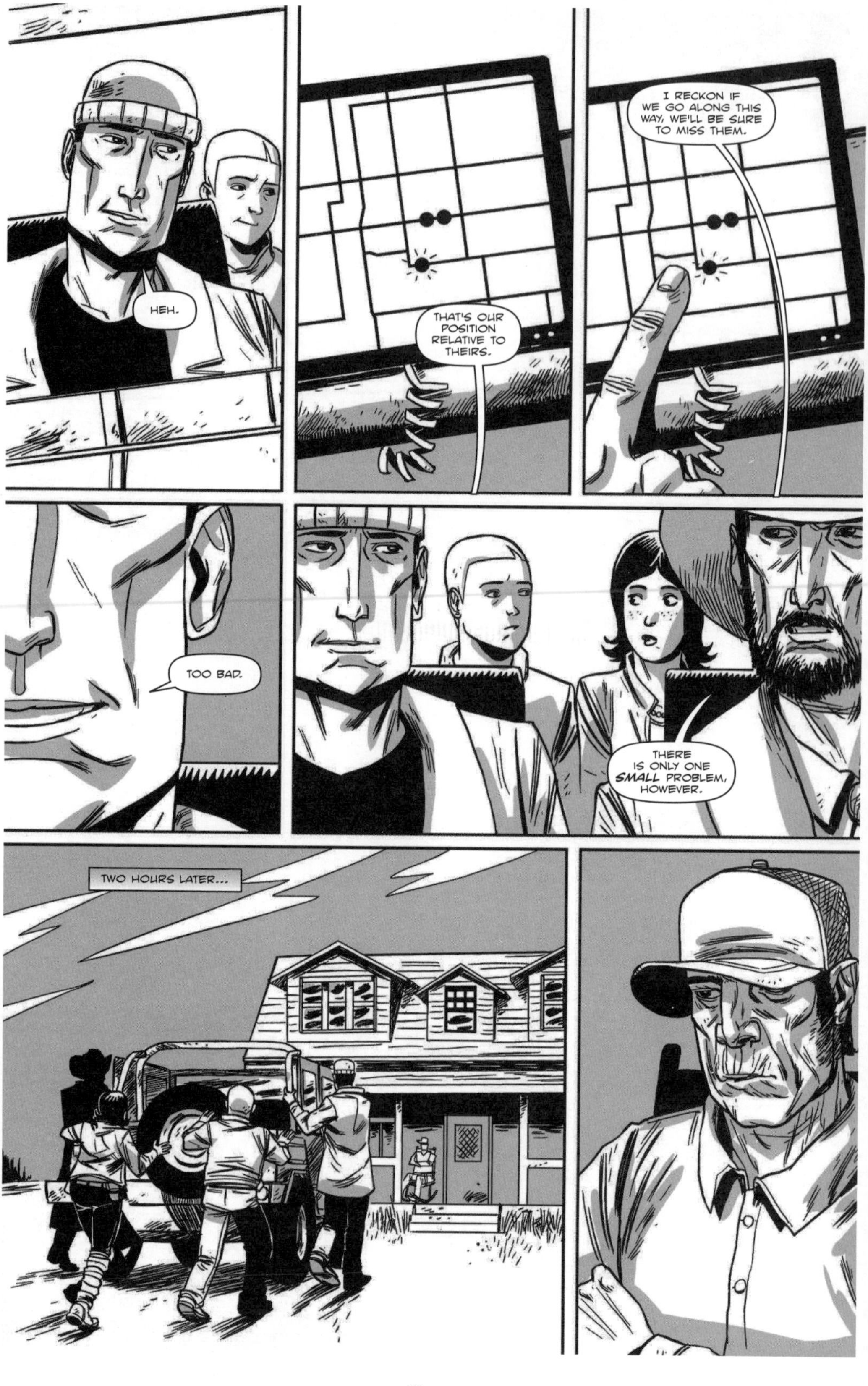
HEH.
THAT'S OUR POSITION RELATIVE TO THEIRS.
I RECKON IF WE GO ALONG THIS WAY, WE'LL BE SURE TO MISS THEM.
TOO BAD.
THERE IS ONLY ONE SMALL PROBLEM, HOWEVER.
TWO HOURS LATER...

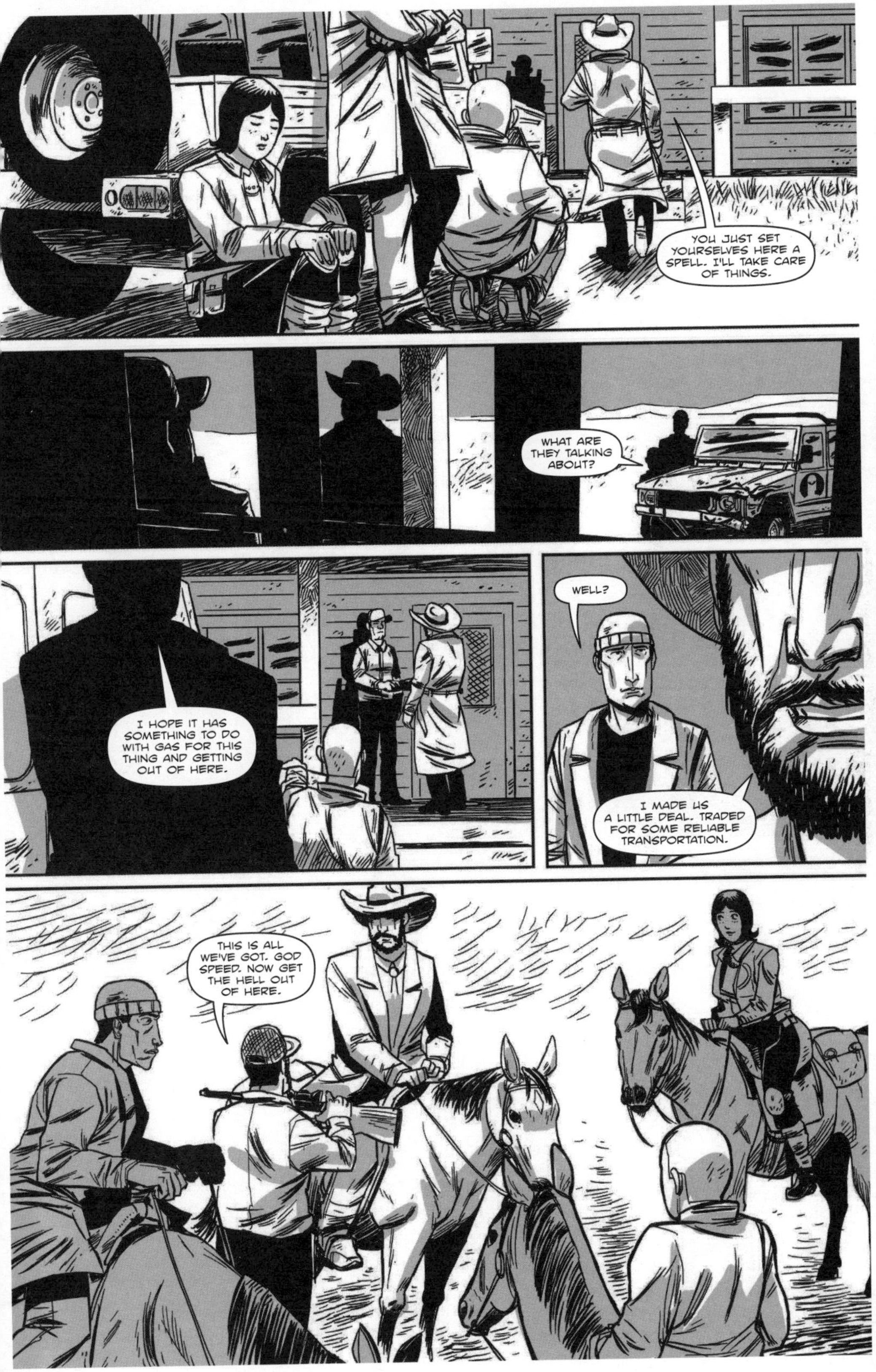
YOU JUST SET YOURSELVES HERE A SPELL. I'LL TAKE CARE OF THINGS.
WHAT ARE THEY TALKING ABOUT?
I HOPE IT HAS SOMETHING TO DO WITH GAS FOR THIS THING AND GETTING OUT OF HERE.
WELL?
I MADE US A LITTLE DEAL. TRADED FOR SOME RELIABLE TRANSPORTATION.
THIS IS ALL WE'VE GOT. GOD SPEED. NOW GET THE HELL OUT OF HERE.

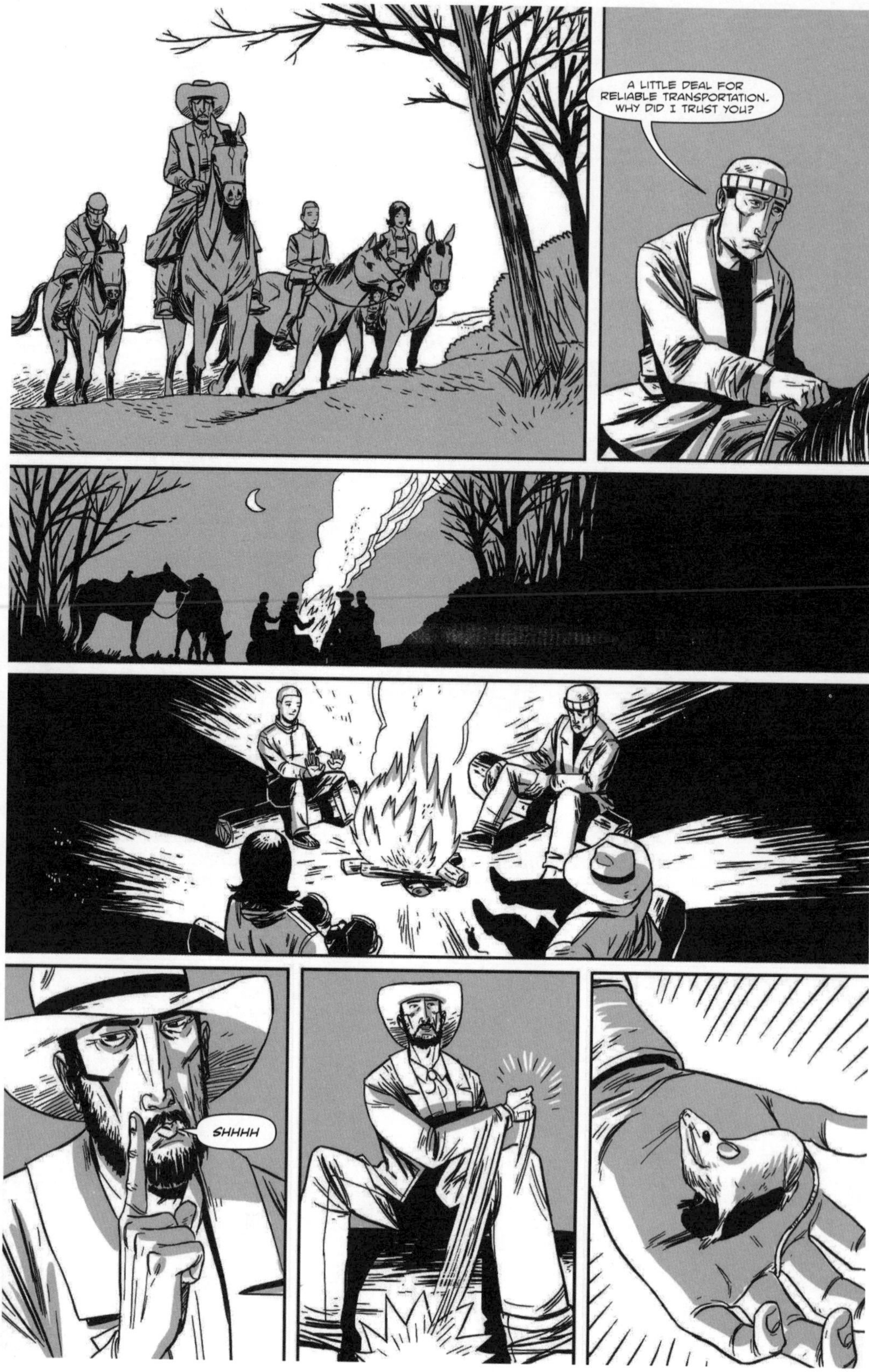
A LITTLE DEAL FOR RELIABLE TRANSPORTATION. WHY DID I TRUST YOU?
SHHHH

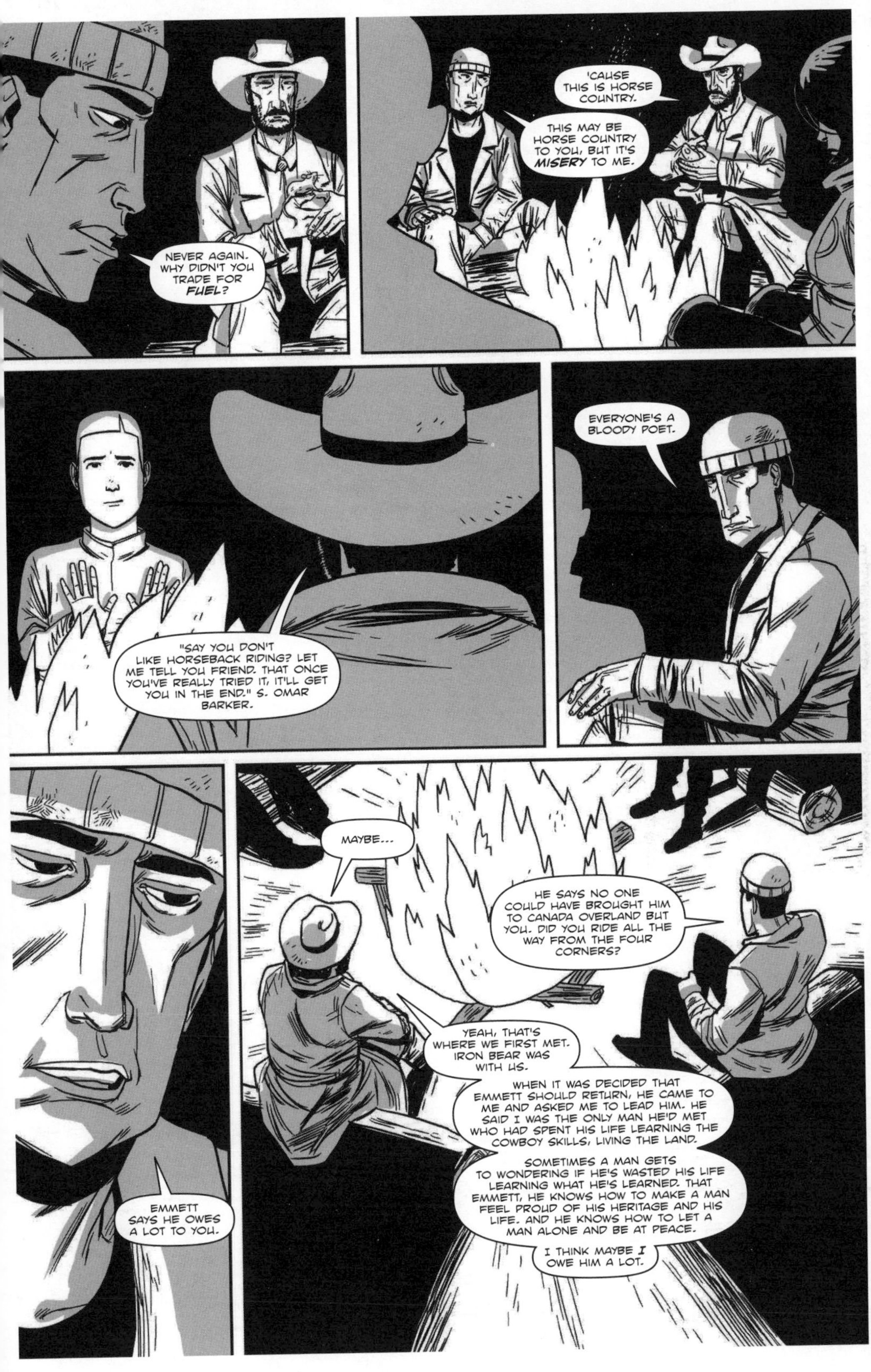
NEVER AGAIN. WHY DIDN'T YOU TRADE FOR FUEL?
'CAUSE THIS IS HORSE COUNTRY.
THIS MAY BE HORSE COUNTRY TO YOU, BUT IT'S MISERY TO ME.
"SAY YOU DON'T LIKE HORSEBACK RIDING? LET ME TELL YOU FRIEND. THAT ONCE YOU'VE REALLY TRIED IT, IT'LL GET YOU IN THE END." S. OMAR BARKER.
EVERYONE'S A BLOODY POET.
EMMETT SAYS HE OWES A LOT TO YOU.
MAYBE...
HE SAYS NO ONE COULD HAVE BROUGHT HIM TO CANADA OVERLAND BUT YOU. DID YOU RIDE ALL THE WAY FROM THE FOUR CORNERS?
YEAH, THAT'S WHERE WE FIRST MET. IRON BEAR WAS WITH US.
WHEN IT WAS DECIDED THAT EMMETT SHOULD RETURN, HE CAME TO ME AND ASKED ME TO LEAD HIM. HE SAID I WAS THE ONLY MAN HE'D MET WHO HAD SPENT HIS LIFE LEARNING THE COWBOY SKILLS, LIVING THE LAND.
SOMETIMES A MAN GETS TO WONDERING IF HE'S WASTED HIS LIFE LEARNING WHAT HE'S LEARNED. THAT EMMETT, HE KNOWS HOW TO MAKE A MAN FEEL PROUD OF HIS HERITAGE AND HIS LIFE. AND HE KNOWS HOW TO LET A MAN ALONE AND BE AT PEACE.
I THINK MAYBE I OWE HIM A LOT.

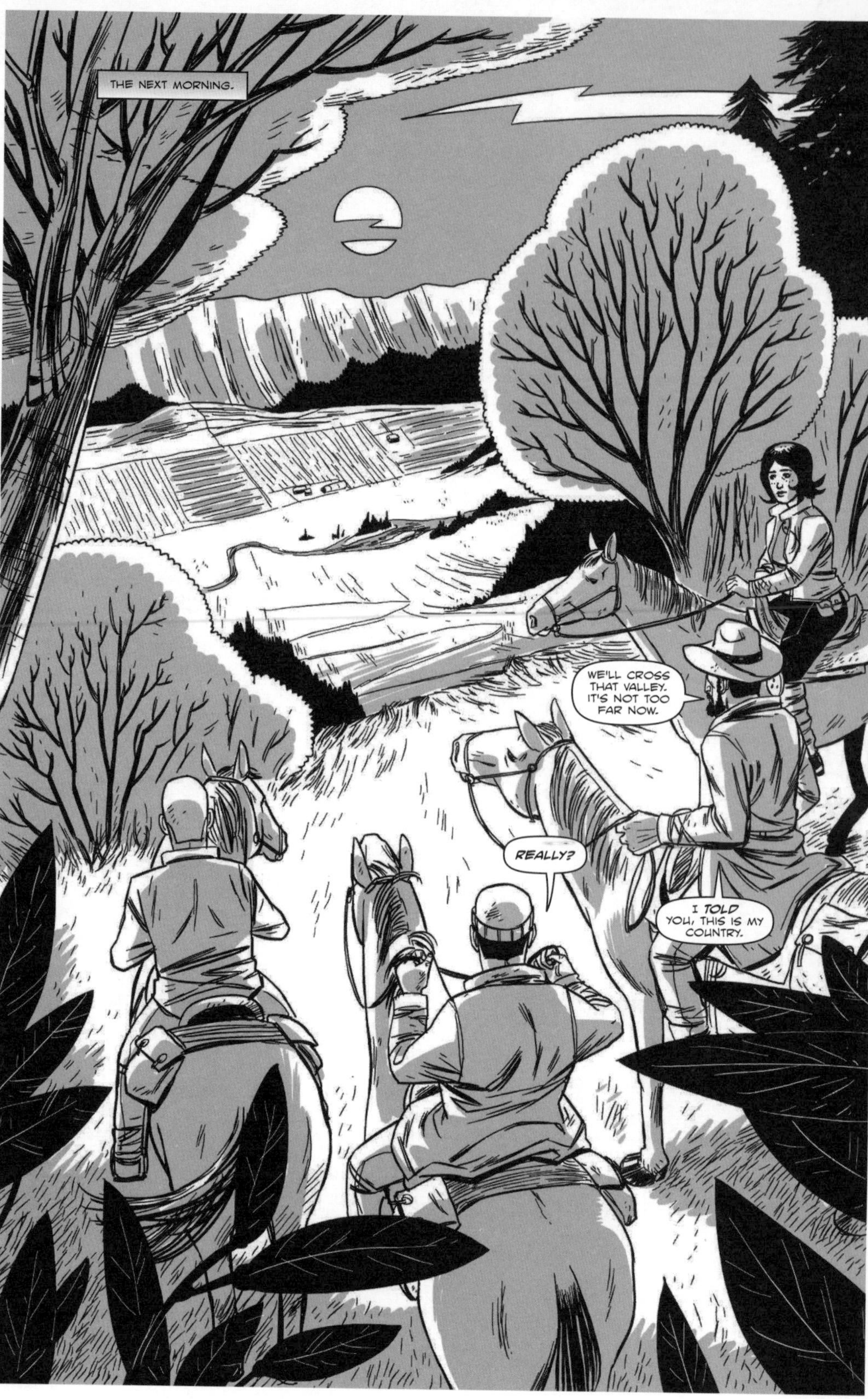
THE NEXT MORNING.
WE'LL CROSS THAT VALLEY. IT'S NOT TOO FAR NOW.
REALLY?
I TOLD YOU, THIS IS MY COUNTRY.

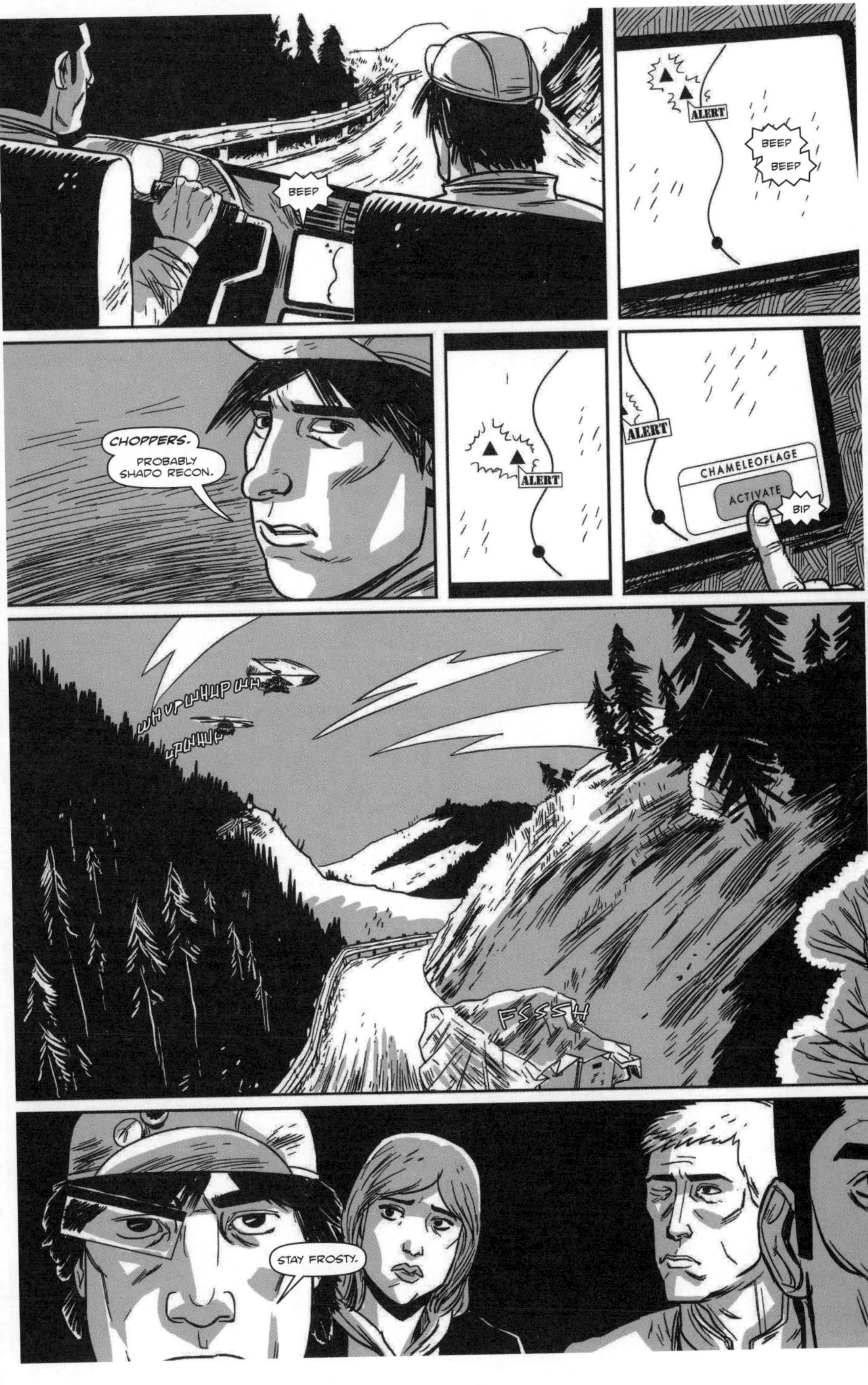
BEEP
ALERT
BEEP
BEEP
CHOPPERS.
PROBABLY SHADO RECON.
ALERT
ALERT
CHAMELEOFLAGE
ACTIVATE
BIP
FSSSH
STAY FROSTY.

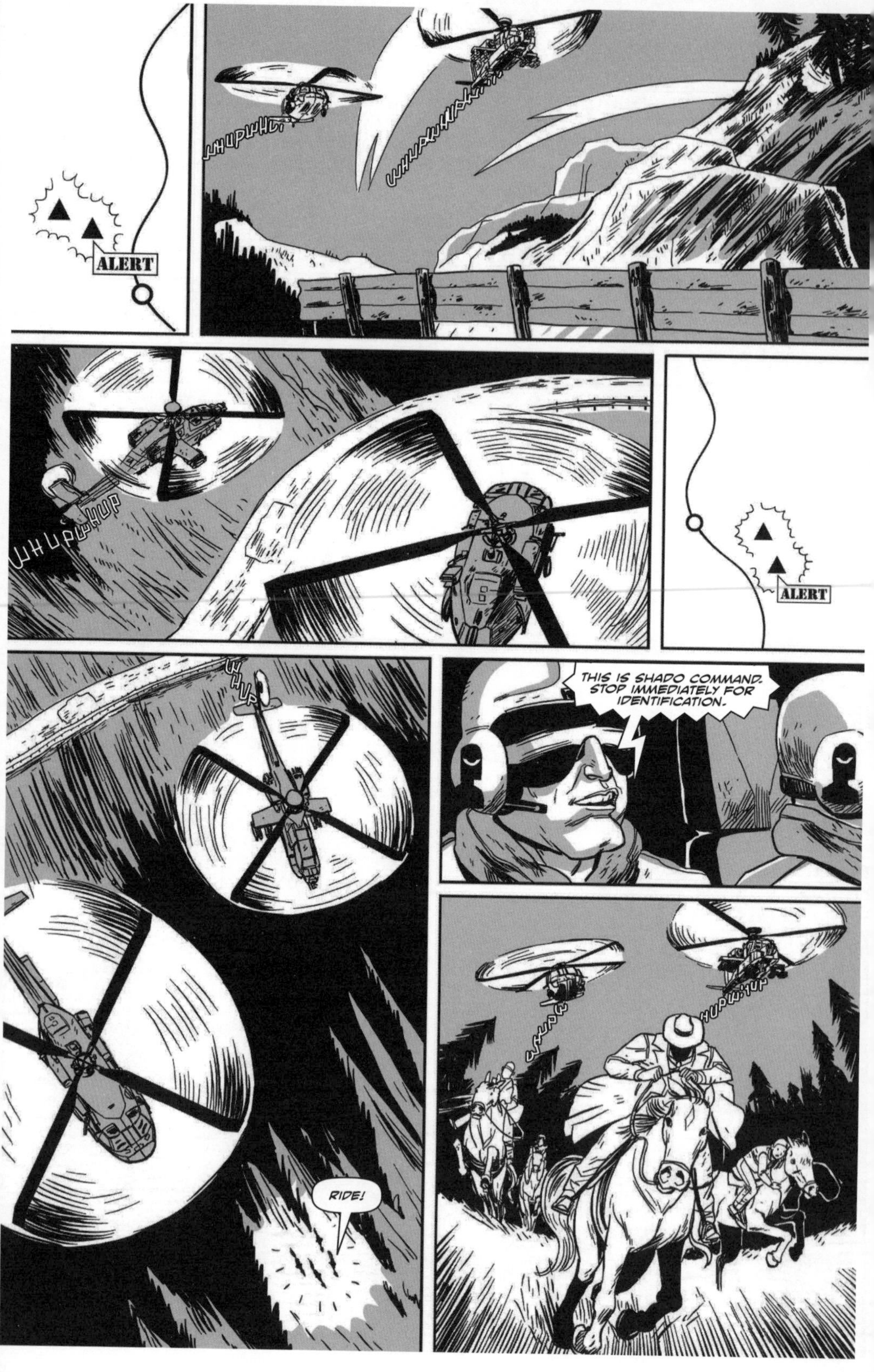
ALERT
ALERT
THIS IS SHADO COMMAND. STOP IMMEDIATELY FOR IDENTIFICATION.
RIDE!

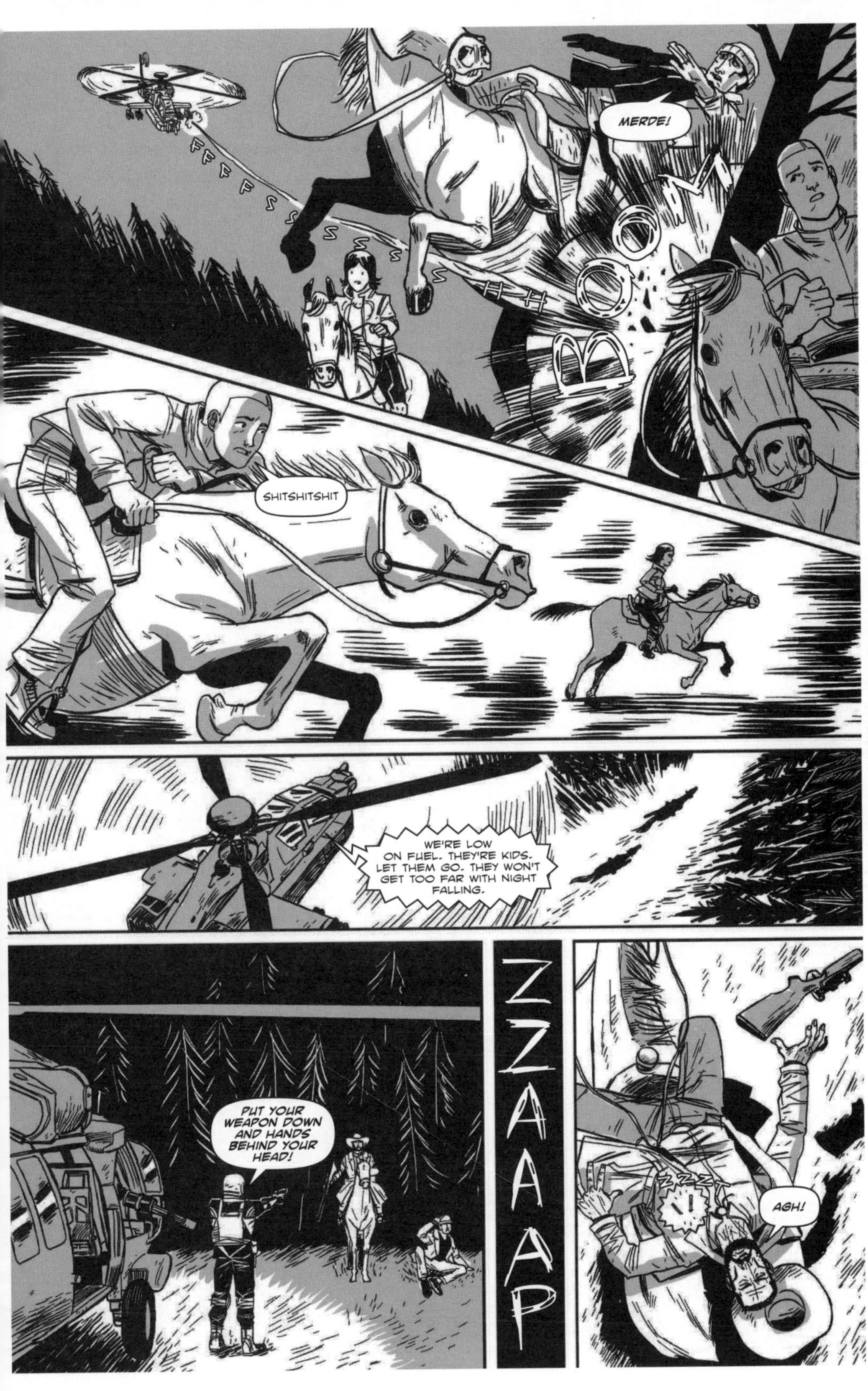
MERDE!
BOOOM
SHITSHITSHIT
WE'RE LOW ON FUEL. THEY'RE KIDS. LET THEM GO. THEY WON'T GET TOO FAR WITH NIGHT FALLING.
PUT YOUR WEAPON DOWN AND HANDS BEHIND YOUR HEAD!
ZZAAAP
ZZZT
!
AGH!

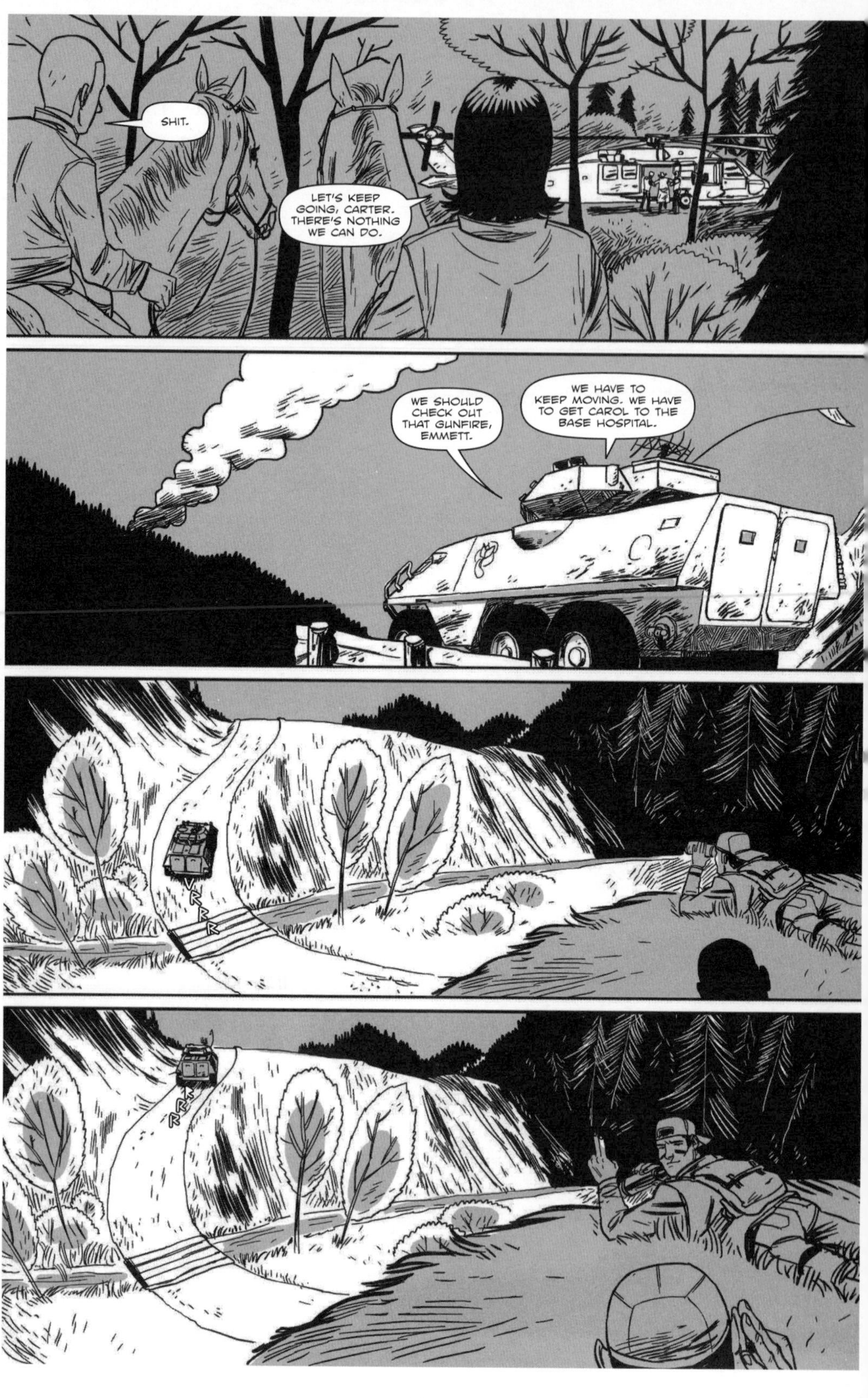
SHIT.
LET'S KEEP GOING, CARTER. THERE'S NOTHING WE CAN DO.
WE SHOULD CHECK OUT THAT GUNFIRE, EMMETT.
WE HAVE TO KEEP MOVING. WE HAVE TO GET CAROL TO THE BASE HOSPITAL.
VRRR
RRR

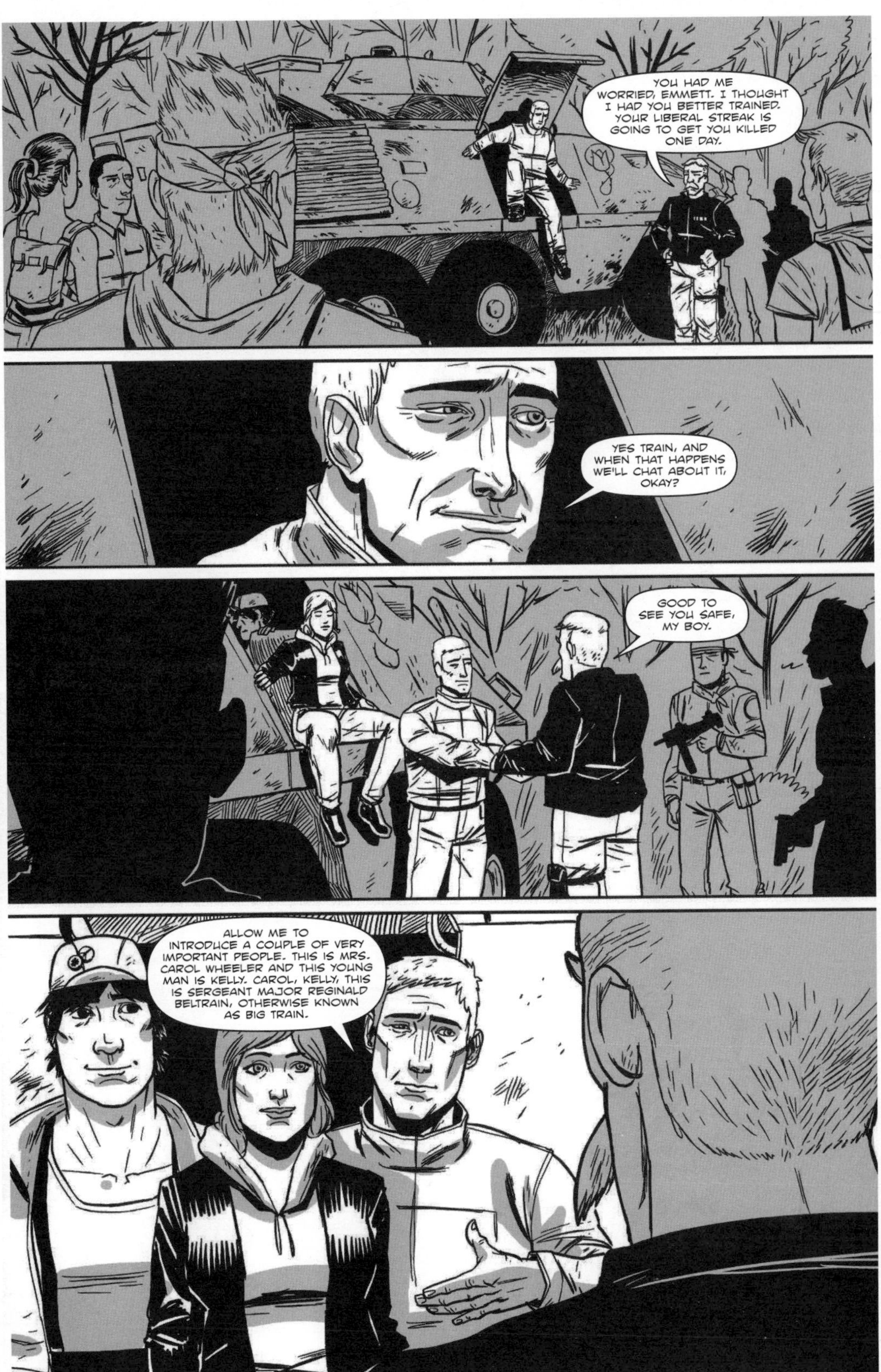
YOU HAD ME WORRIED, EMMETT. I THOUGHT I HAD YOU BETTER TRAINED. YOUR LIBERAL STREAK IS GOING TO GET YOU KILLED ONE DAY.
YES TRAIN, AND WHEN THAT HAPPENS WE'LL CHAT ABOUT IT, OKAY?
GOOD TO SEE YOU SAFE, MY BOY.
ALLOW ME TO INTRODUCE A COUPLE OF VERY IMPORTANT PEOPLE. THIS IS MRS. CAROL WHEELER AND THIS YOUNG MAN IS KELLY. CAROL, KELLY, THIS IS SERGEANT MAJOR REGINALD BELTRAIN, OTHERWISE KNOWN AS BIG TRAIN.

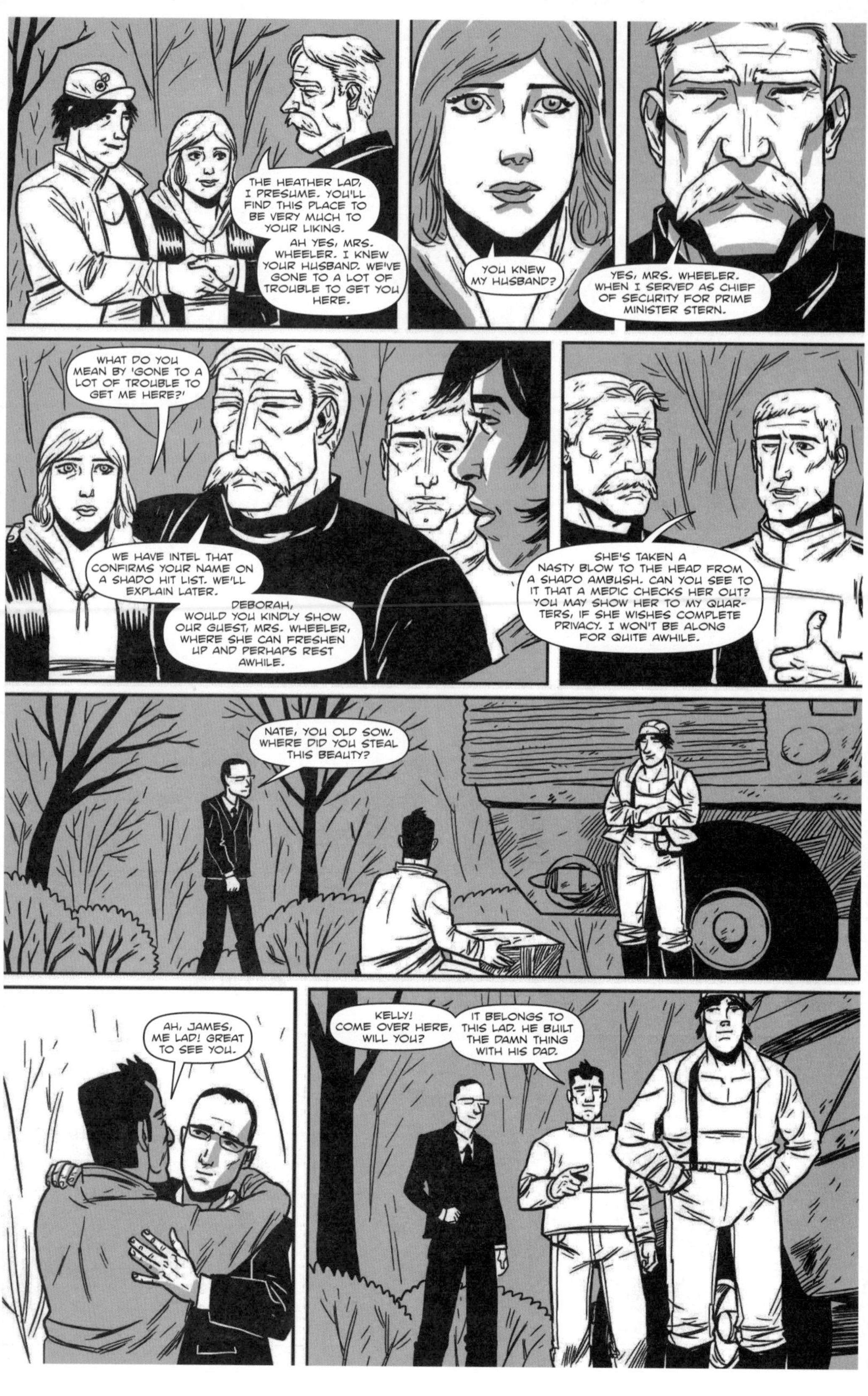
THE HEATHER LAD, I PRESUME. YOU'LL FIND THIS PLACE TO BE VERY MUCH TO YOUR LIKING.
AH YES, MRS. WHEELER. I KNEW YOUR HUSBAND. WE'VE GONE TO A LOT OF TROUBLE TO GET YOU HERE.
YOU KNEW MY HUSBAND?
YES, MRS. WHEELER. WHEN I SERVED AS CHIEF OF SECURITY FOR PRIME MINISTER STERN.
WHAT DO YOU MEAN BY 'GONE TO A LOT OF TROUBLE TO GET ME HERE?'
WE HAVE INTEL THAT CONFIRMS YOUR NAME ON A SHADO HIT LIST. WE'LL EXPLAIN LATER.
DEBORAH, WOULD YOU KINDLY SHOW OUR GUEST, MRS. WHEELER, WHERE SHE CAN FRESHEN UP AND PERHAPS REST AWHILE.
SHE'S TAKEN A NASTY BLOW TO THE HEAD FROM A SHADO AMBUSH. CAN YOU SEE TO IT THAT A MEDIC CHECKS HER OUT? YOU MAY SHOW HER TO MY QUARTERS, IF SHE WISHES COMPLETE PRIVACY. I WON'T BE ALONG FOR QUITE AWHILE.
NATE, YOU OLD SOW. WHERE DID YOU STEAL THIS BEAUTY?
AH, JAMES, ME LAD! GREAT TO SEE YOU.
KELLY! COME OVER HERE, WILL YOU?
IT BELONGS TO THIS LAD. HE BUILT THE DAMN THING WITH HIS DAD.

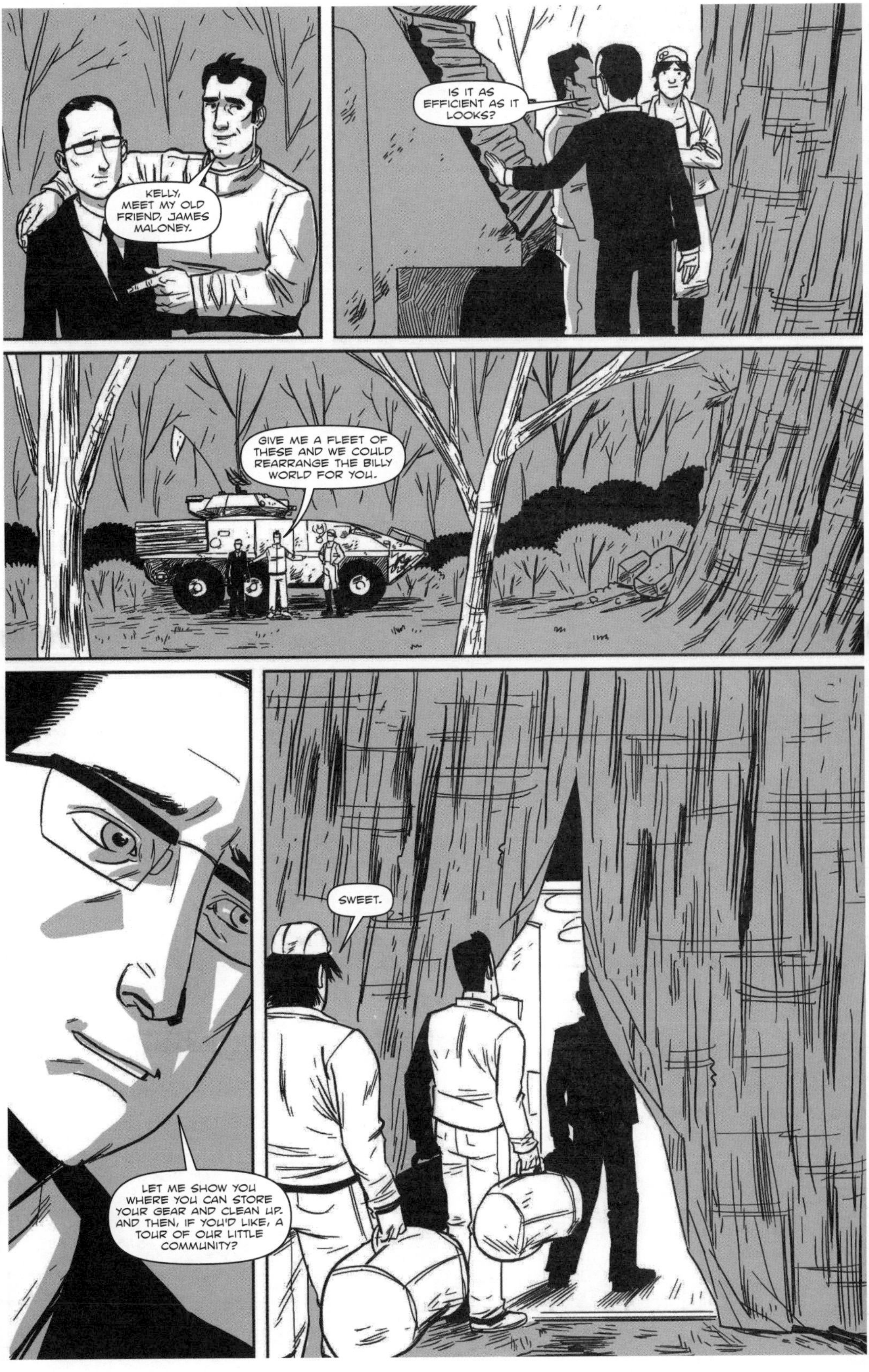
KELLY, MEET MY OLD FRIEND, JAMES MALONEY.
IS IT AS EFFICIENT AS IT LOOKS?
GIVE ME A FLEET OF THESE AND WE COULD REARRANGE THE BILLY WORLD FOR YOU.
LET ME SHOW YOU WHERE YOU CAN STORE YOUR GEAR AND CLEAN UP. AND THEN, IF YOU'D LIKE, A TOUR OF OUR LITTLE COMMUNITY?
SWEET.

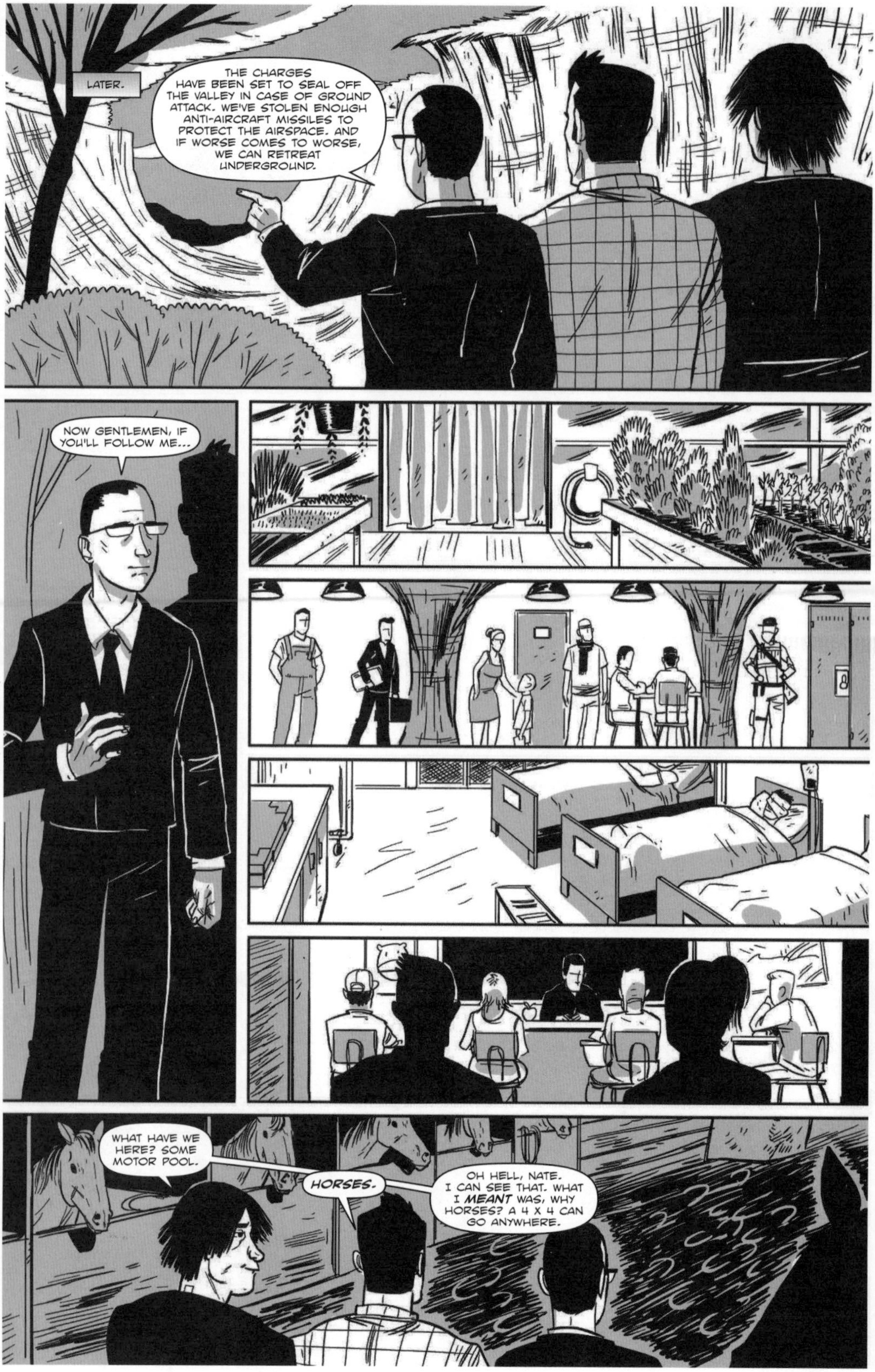
LATER.
THE CHARGES HAVE BEEN SET TO SEAL OFF THE VALLEY IN CASE OF GROUND ATTACK. WE'VE STOLEN ENOUGH ANTI-AIRCRAFT MISSILES TO PROTECT THE AIRSPACE. AND IF WORSE COMES TO WORSE, WE CAN RETREAT UNDERGROUND.
NOW GENTLEMEN, IF YOU'LL FOLLOW ME...
WHAT HAVE WE HERE? SOME MOTOR POOL.
HORSES.
OH HELL, NATE. I CAN SEE THAT. WHAT I MEANT WAS, WHY HORSES? A 4 X 4 CAN GO ANYWHERE.

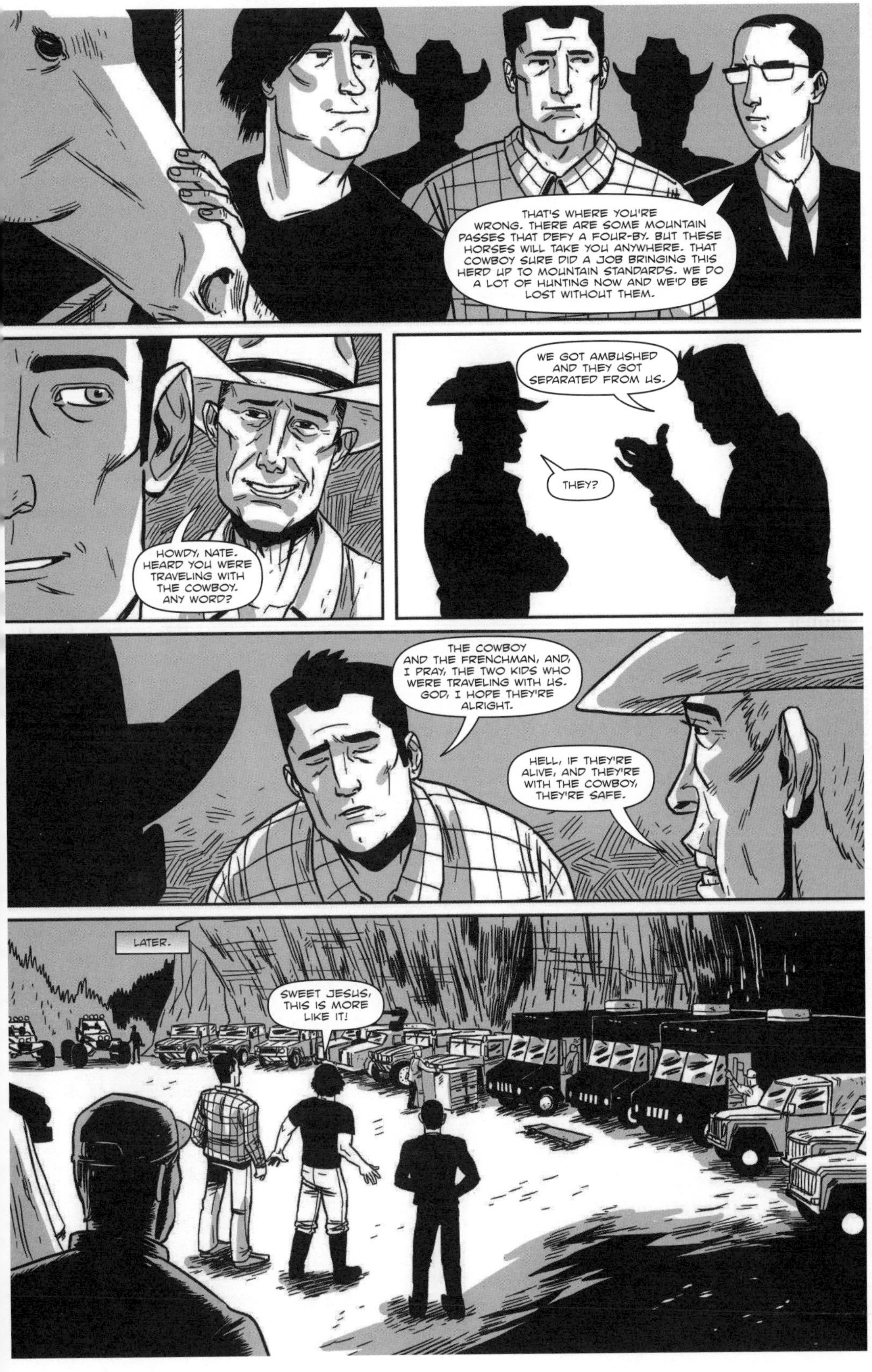
THAT'S WHERE YOU'RE WRONG. THERE ARE SOME MOUNTAIN PASSES THAT DEFY A FOUR-BY. BUT THESE HORSES WILL TAKE YOU ANYWHERE. THAT COWBOY SURE DID A JOB BRINGING THIS HERD UP TO MOUNTAIN STANDARDS. WE DO A LOT OF HUNTING NOW AND WE'D BE LOST WITHOUT THEM.
HOWDY, NATE. HEARD YOU WERE TRAVELING WITH THE COWBOY. ANY WORD?
WE GOT AMBUSHED AND THEY GOT SEPARATED FROM US.
THEY?
THE COWBOY AND THE FRENCHMAN, AND, I PRAY, THE TWO KIDS WHO WERE TRAVELING WITH US. GOD, I HOPE THEY'RE ALRIGHT.
HELL, IF THEY'RE ALIVE, AND THEY'RE WITH THE COWBOY, THEY'RE SAFE.
LATER.
SWEET JESUS, THIS IS MORE LIKE IT!

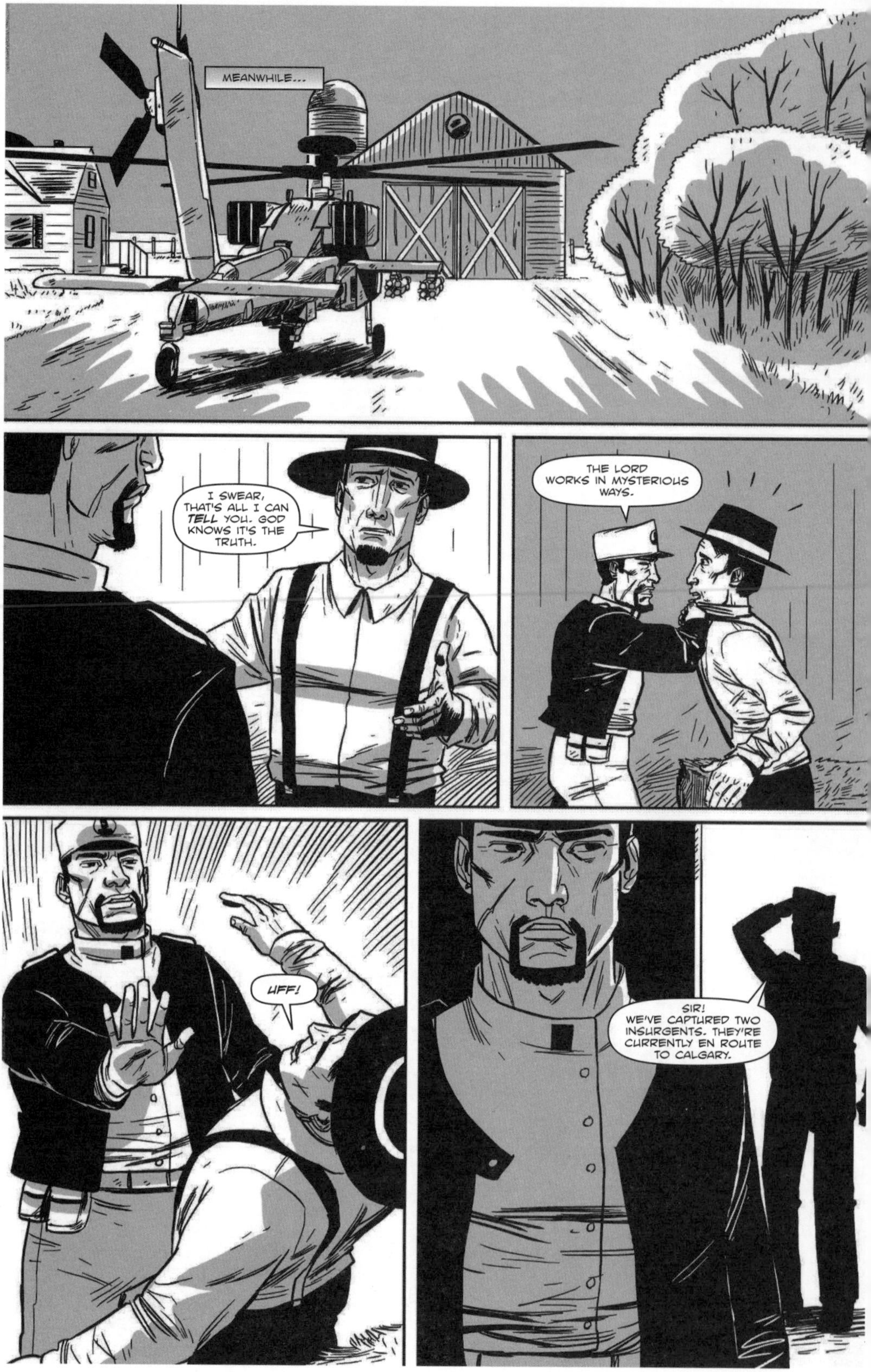
MEANWHILE...
I SWEAR, THAT'S ALL I CAN TELL YOU. GOD KNOWS IT'S THE TRUTH.
THE LORD WORKS IN MYSTERIOUS WAYS.
UFF!
SIR! WE'VE CAPTURED TWO INSURGENTS. THEY'RE CURRENTLY EN ROUTE TO CALGARY.

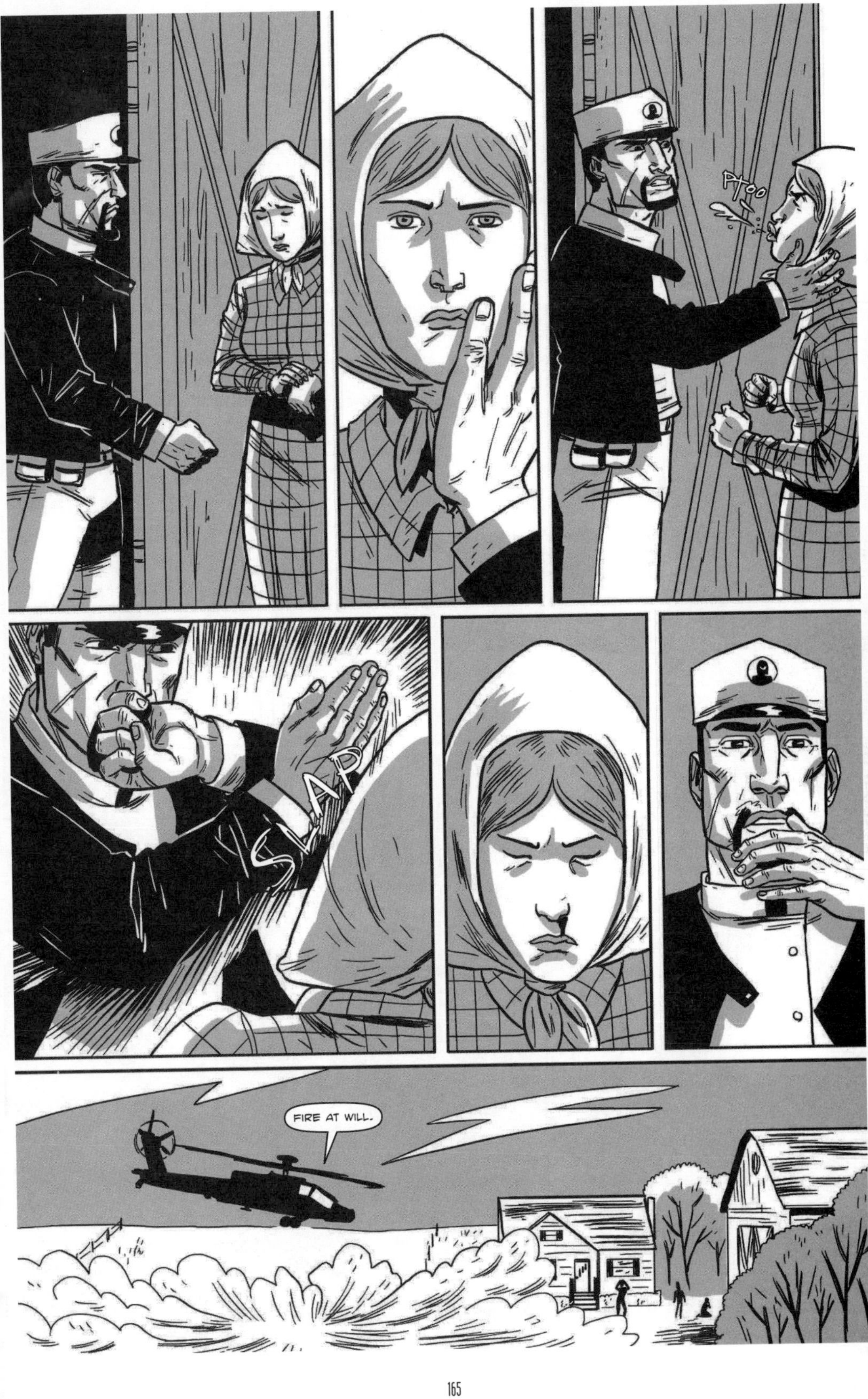
PTOO
SLAP
FIRE AT WILL.

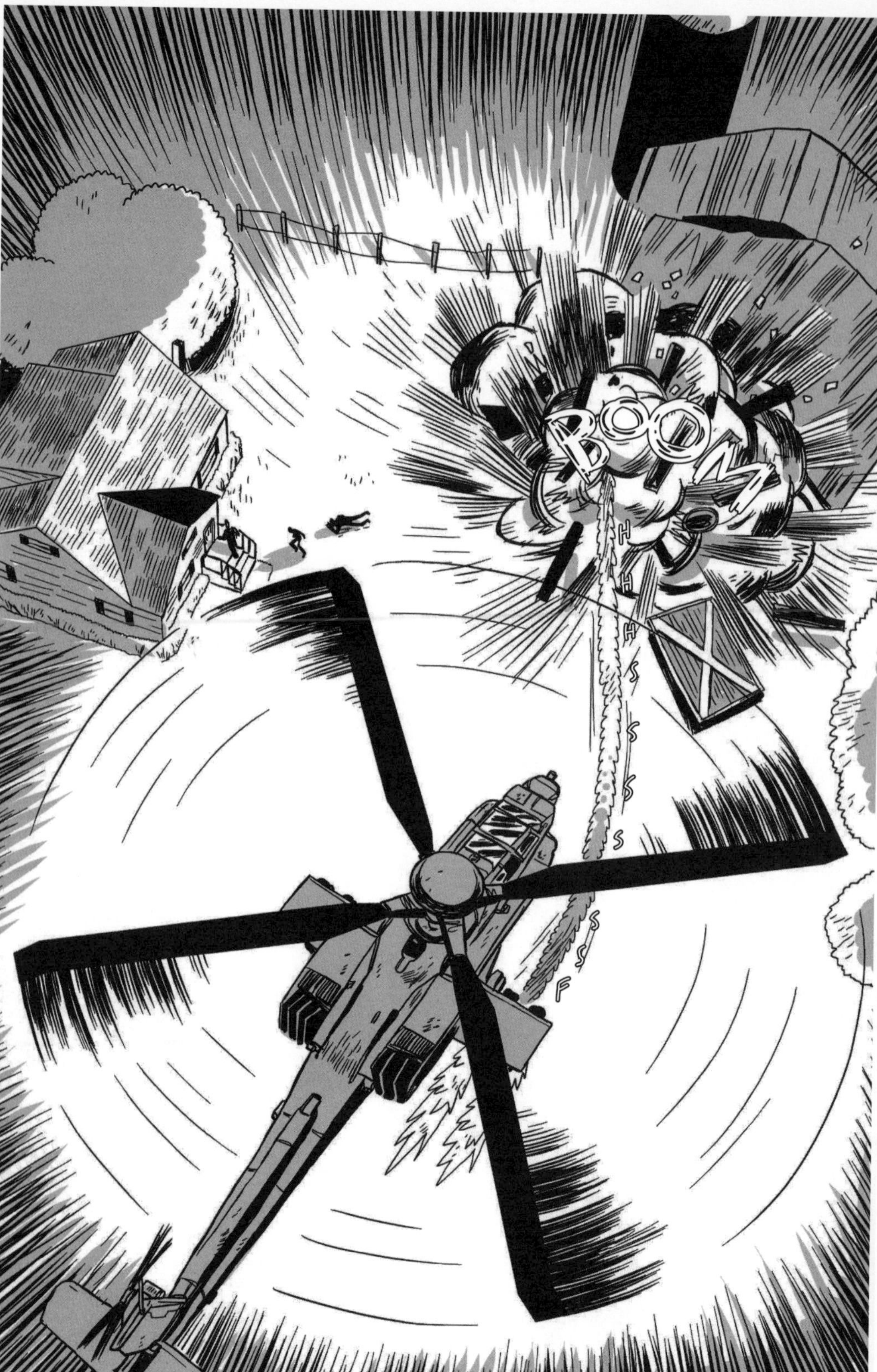
BOOM
FSSSSSSHHH

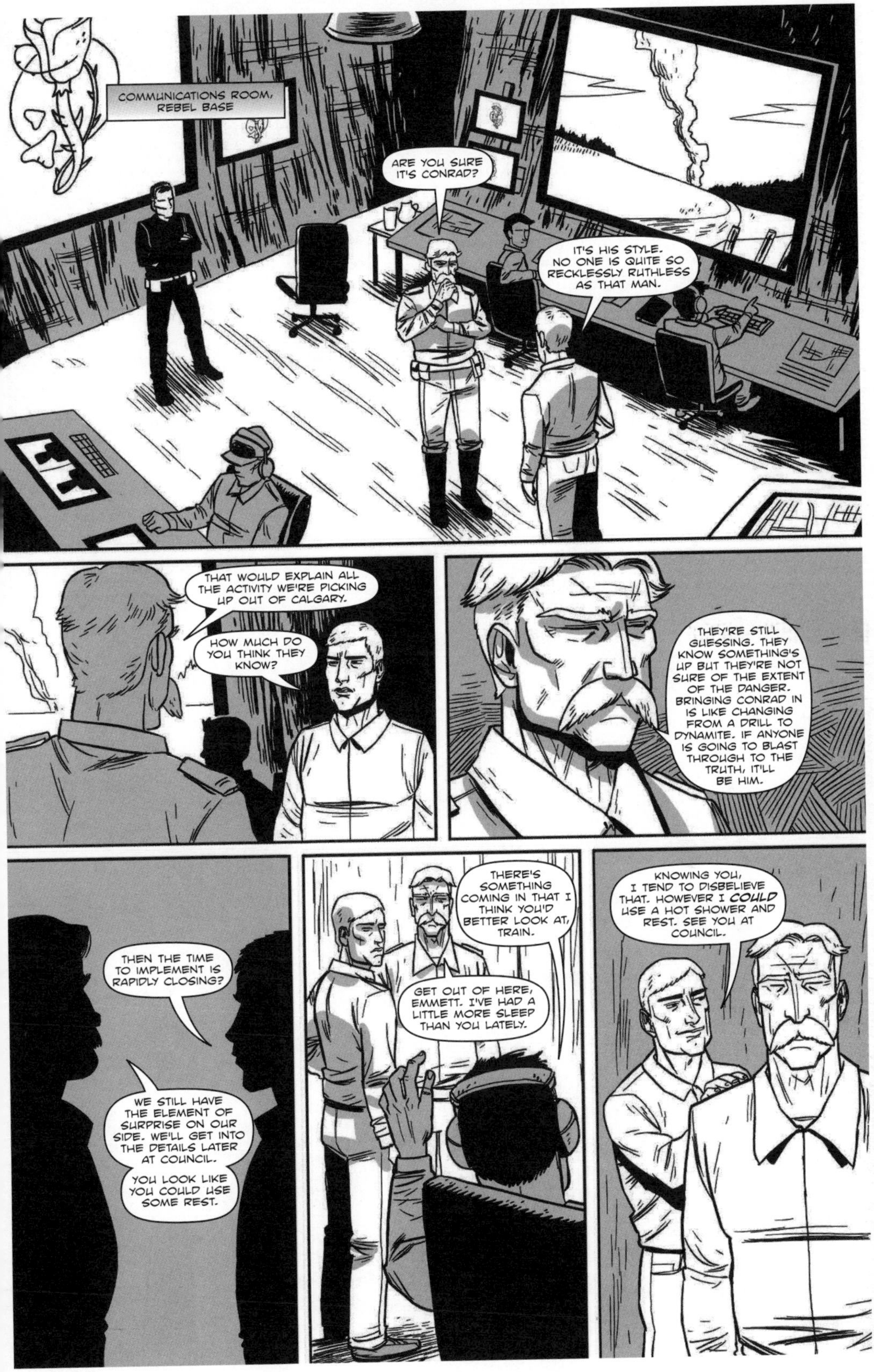
COMMUNICATIONS ROOM, REBEL BASE
ARE YOU SURE IT'S CONRAD?
IT'S HIS STYLE. NO ONE IS QUITE SO RECKLESSLY RUTHLESS AS THAT MAN.
THAT WOULD EXPLAIN ALL THE ACTIVITY WE'RE PICKING UP OUT OF CALGARY.
HOW MUCH DO YOU THINK THEY KNOW?
THEY'RE STILL GUESSING. THEY KNOW SOMETHING'S UP BUT THEY'RE NOT SURE OF THE EXTENT OF THE DANGER. BRINGING CONRAD IN IS LIKE CHANGING FROM A DRILL TO DYNAMITE. IF ANYONE IS GOING TO BLAST THROUGH TO THE TRUTH, IT'LL BE HIM.
THEN THE TIME TO IMPLEMENT IS RAPIDLY CLOSING?
WE STILL HAVE THE ELEMENT OF SURPRISE ON OUR SIDE. WE'LL GET INTO THE DETAILS LATER AT COUNCIL.
YOU LOOK LIKE YOU COULD USE SOME REST.
THERE'S SOMETHING COMING IN THAT I THINK YOU'D BETTER LOOK AT, TRAIN.
GET OUT OF HERE, EMMETT. I'VE HAD A LITTLE MORE SLEEP THAN YOU LATELY.
KNOWING YOU, I TEND TO DISBELIEVE THAT. HOWEVER I *COULD* USE A HOT SHOWER AND REST. SEE YOU AT COUNCIL.

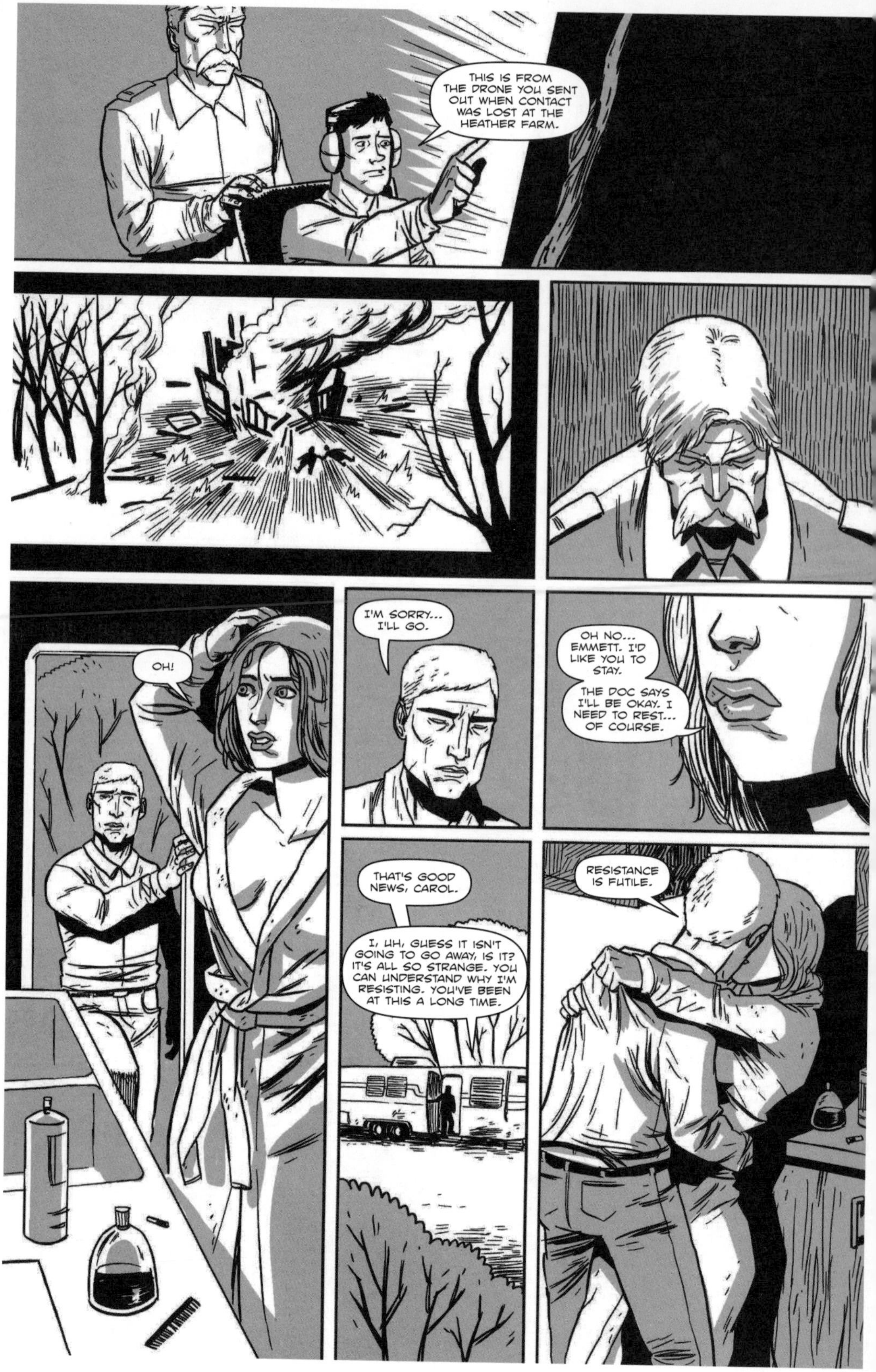
THIS IS FROM THE DRONE YOU SENT OUT WHEN CONTACT WAS LOST AT THE HEATHER FARM.
OH!
I'M SORRY... I'LL GO.
OH NO... EMMETT. I'D LIKE YOU TO STAY.
THE DOC SAYS I'LL BE OKAY. I NEED TO REST... OF COURSE.
THAT'S GOOD NEWS, CAROL.
I, UH, GUESS IT ISN'T GOING TO GO AWAY, IS IT? IT'S ALL SO STRANGE. YOU CAN UNDERSTAND WHY I'M RESISTING. YOU'VE BEEN AT THIS A LONG TIME.
RESISTANCE IS FUTILE.

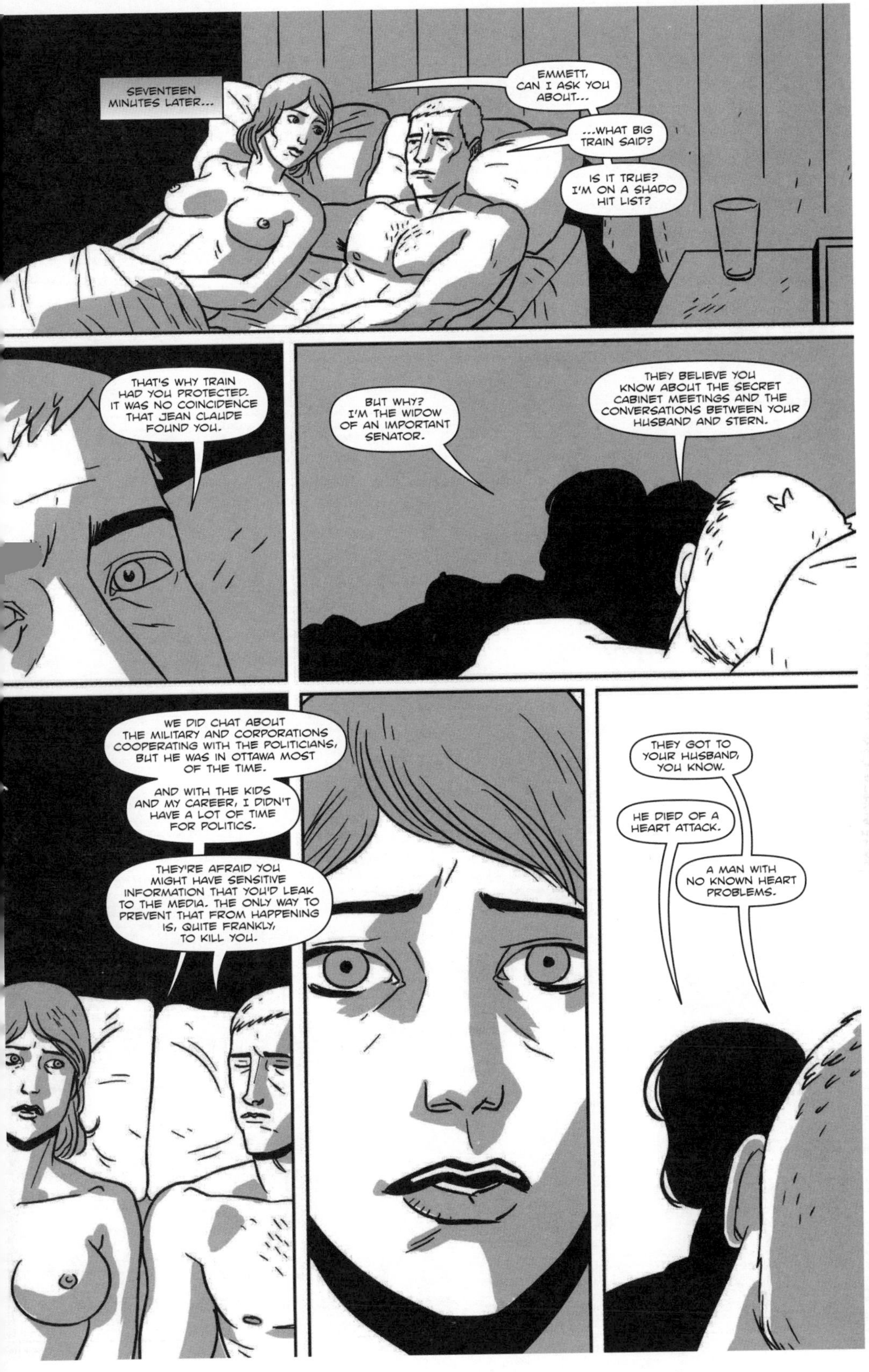
SEVENTEEN MINUTES LATER...
EMMETT, CAN I ASK YOU ABOUT...
...WHAT BIG TRAIN SAID?
IS IT TRUE? I'M ON A SHADO HIT LIST?
THAT'S WHY TRAIN HAD YOU PROTECTED. IT WAS NO COINCIDENCE THAT JEAN CLAUDE FOUND YOU.
BUT WHY? I'M THE WIDOW OF AN IMPORTANT SENATOR.
THEY BELIEVE YOU KNOW ABOUT THE SECRET CABINET MEETINGS AND THE CONVERSATIONS BETWEEN YOUR HUSBAND AND STERN.
WE DID CHAT ABOUT THE MILITARY AND CORPORATIONS COOPERATING WITH THE POLITICIANS, BUT HE WAS IN OTTAWA MOST OF THE TIME.
AND WITH THE KIDS AND MY CAREER, I DIDN'T HAVE A LOT OF TIME FOR POLITICS.
THEY'RE AFRAID YOU MIGHT HAVE SENSITIVE INFORMATION THAT YOU'D LEAK TO THE MEDIA. THE ONLY WAY TO PREVENT THAT FROM HAPPENING IS, QUITE FRANKLY, TO KILL YOU.
THEY GOT TO YOUR HUSBAND, YOU KNOW.
HE DIED OF A HEART ATTACK.
A MAN WITH NO KNOWN HEART PROBLEMS.

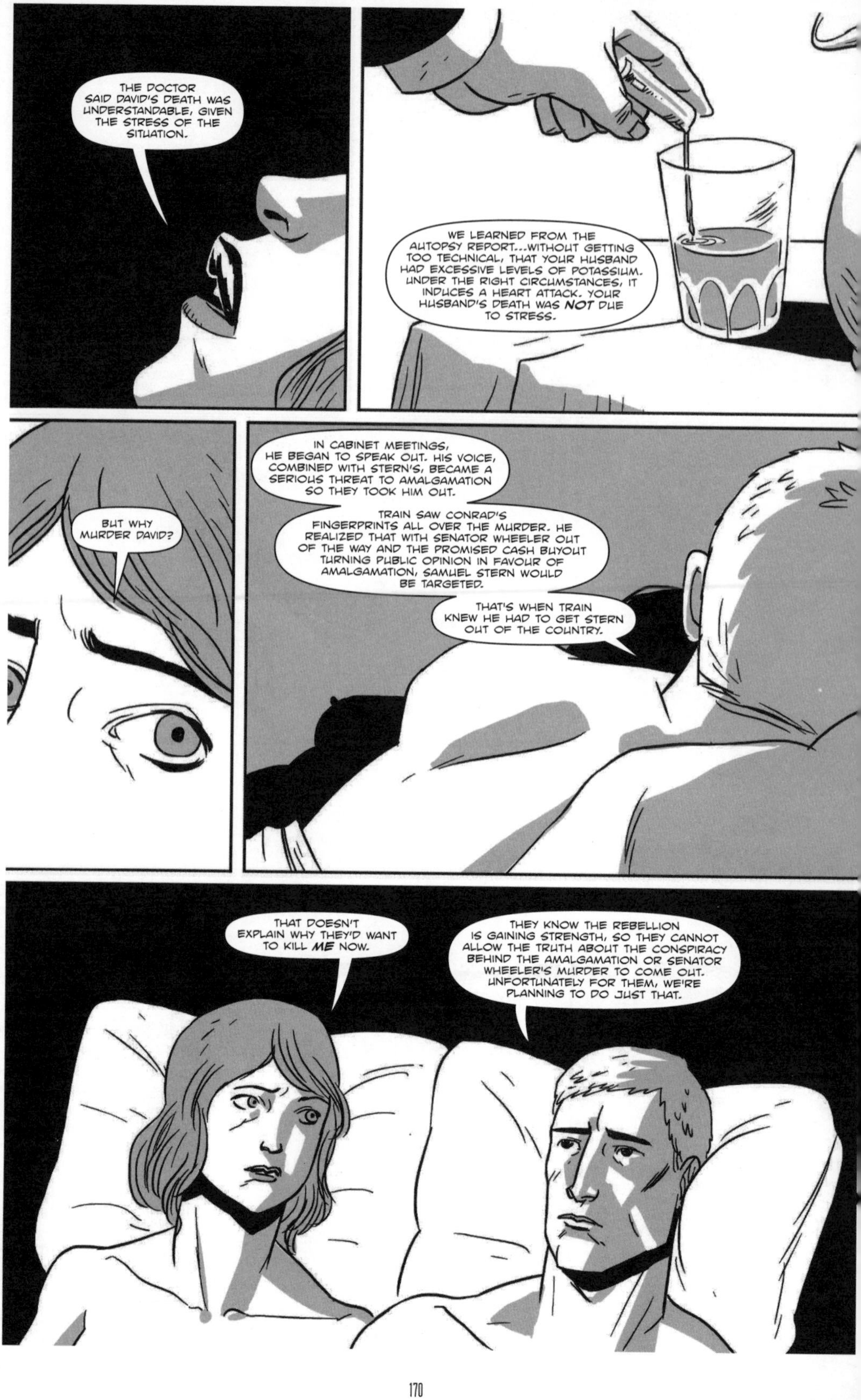
THE DOCTOR SAID DAVID'S DEATH WAS UNDERSTANDABLE, GIVEN THE STRESS OF THE SITUATION.
WE LEARNED FROM THE AUTOPSY REPORT...WITHOUT GETTING TOO TECHNICAL, THAT YOUR HUSBAND HAD EXCESSIVE LEVELS OF POTASSIUM. UNDER THE RIGHT CIRCUMSTANCES, IT INDUCES A HEART ATTACK. YOUR HUSBAND'S DEATH WAS *NOT* DUE TO STRESS.
BUT WHY MURDER DAVID?
IN CABINET MEETINGS, HE BEGAN TO SPEAK OUT. HIS VOICE, COMBINED WITH STERN'S, BECAME A SERIOUS THREAT TO AMALGAMATION SO THEY TOOK HIM OUT.
TRAIN SAW CONRAD'S FINGERPRINTS ALL OVER THE MURDER. HE REALIZED THAT WITH SENATOR WHEELER OUT OF THE WAY AND THE PROMISED CASH BUYOUT TURNING PUBLIC OPINION IN FAVOUR OF AMALGAMATION, SAMUEL STERN WOULD BE TARGETED.
THAT'S WHEN TRAIN KNEW HE HAD TO GET STERN OUT OF THE COUNTRY.
THAT DOESN'T EXPLAIN WHY THEY'D WANT TO KILL *ME* NOW.
THEY KNOW THE REBELLION IS GAINING STRENGTH, SO THEY CANNOT ALLOW THE TRUTH ABOUT THE CONSPIRACY BEHIND THE AMALGAMATION OR SENATOR WHEELER'S MURDER TO COME OUT. UNFORTUNATELY FOR THEM, WE'RE PLANNING TO DO JUST THAT.

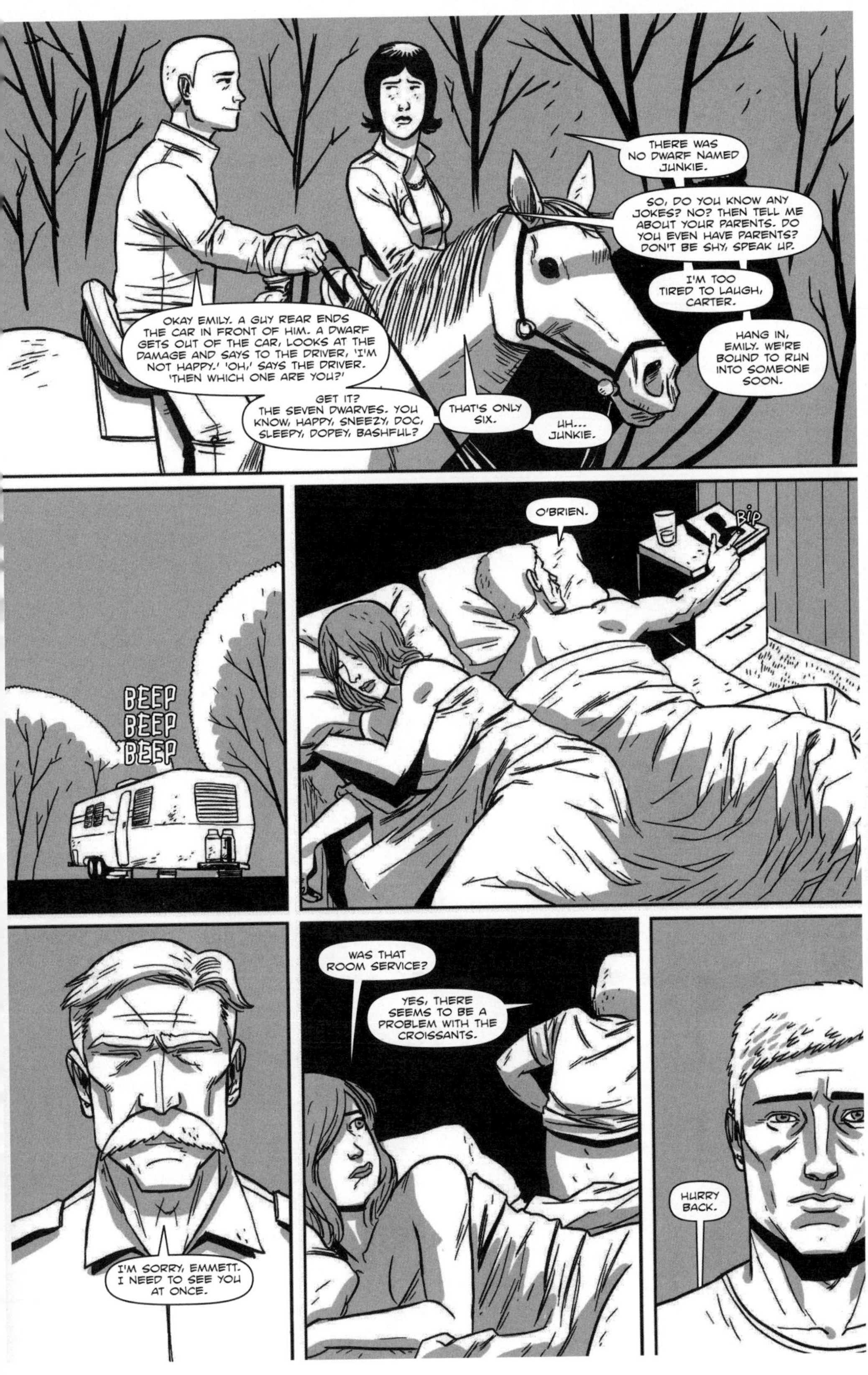
OKAY EMILY. A GUY REAR ENDS THE CAR IN FRONT OF HIM. A DWARF GETS OUT OF THE CAR, LOOKS AT THE DAMAGE AND SAYS TO THE DRIVER, 'I'M NOT HAPPY.' 'OH,' SAYS THE DRIVER. 'THEN WHICH ONE ARE YOU?'
GET IT? THE SEVEN DWARVES. YOU KNOW, HAPPY, SNEEZY, DOC, SLEEPY, DOPEY, BASHFUL?
THAT'S ONLY SIX.
UH... JUNKIE.
THERE WAS NO DWARF NAMED JUNKIE.
SO, DO YOU KNOW ANY JOKES? NO? THEN TELL ME ABOUT YOUR PARENTS. DO YOU EVEN HAVE PARENTS? DON'T BE SHY, SPEAK UP.
I'M TOO TIRED TO LAUGH, CARTER.
HANG IN, EMILY. WE'RE BOUND TO RUN INTO SOMEONE SOON.
BEEP BEEP BEEP
O'BRIEN.
BIP
I'M SORRY, EMMETT. I NEED TO SEE YOU AT ONCE.
WAS THAT ROOM SERVICE?
YES, THERE SEEMS TO BE A PROBLEM WITH THE CROISSANTS.
HURRY BACK.

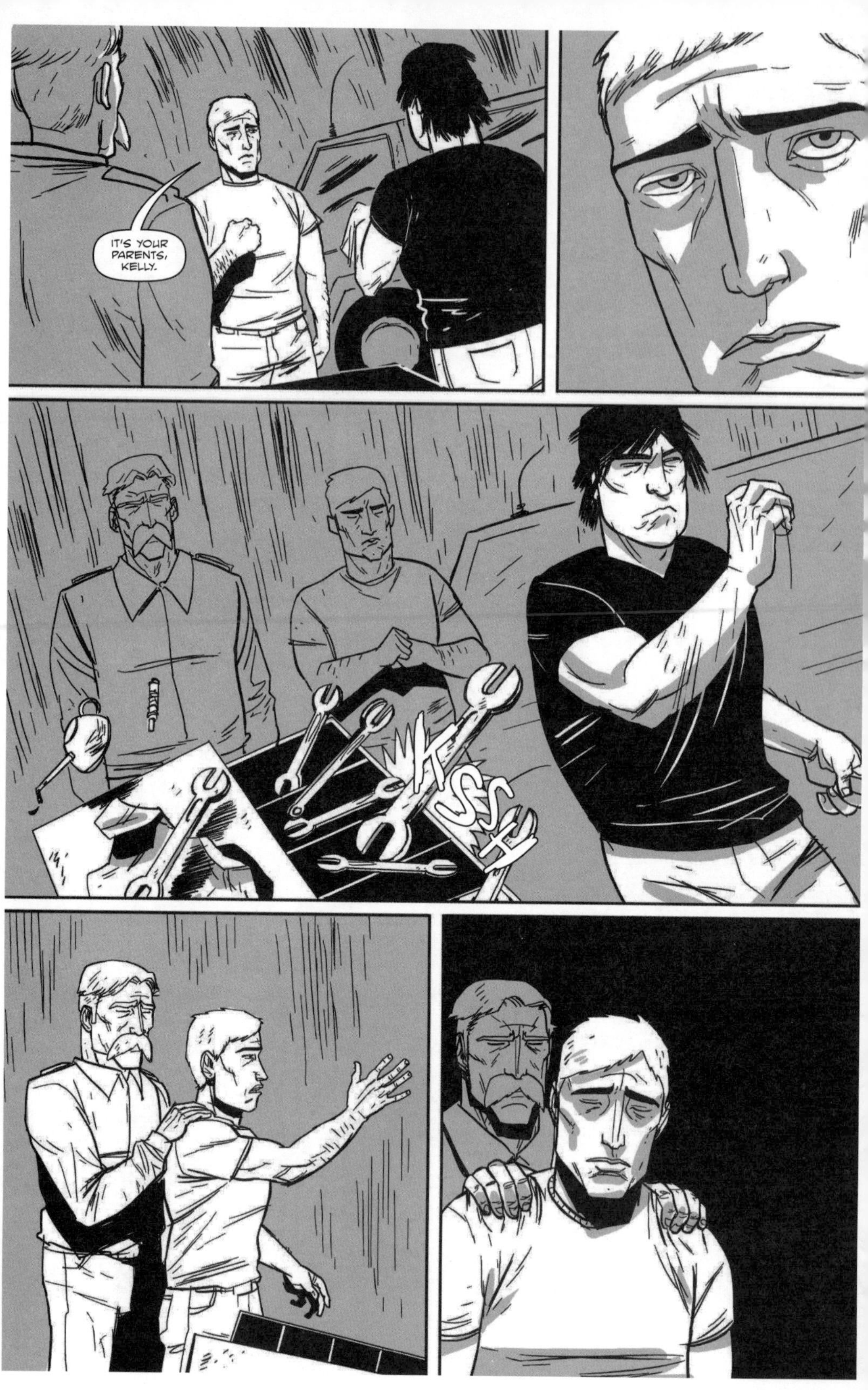
IT'S YOUR PARENTS, KELLY.
KSSH

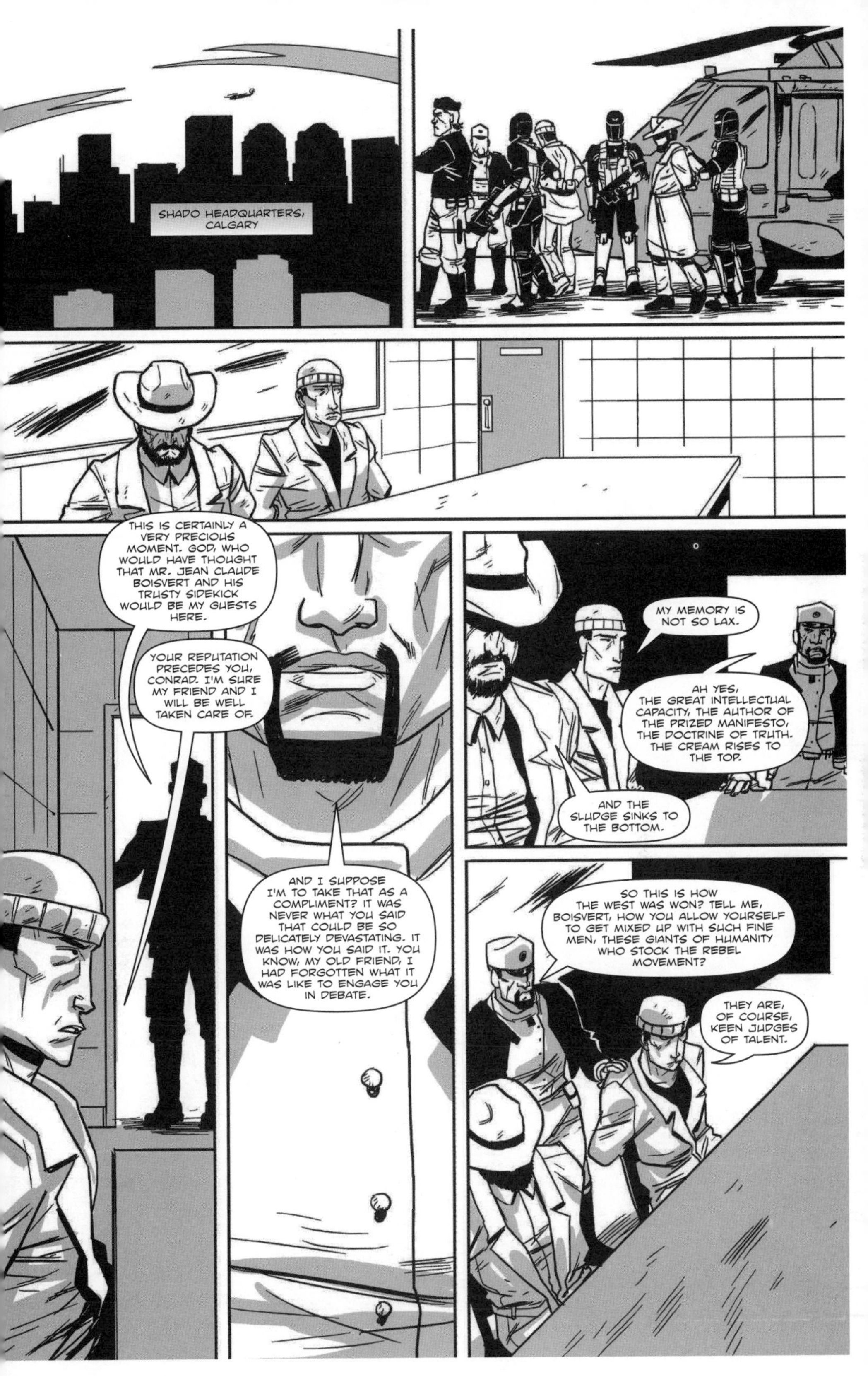
SHADO HEADQUARTERS, CALGARY
THIS IS CERTAINLY A VERY PRECIOUS MOMENT. GOD, WHO WOULD HAVE THOUGHT THAT MR. JEAN CLAUDE BOISVERT AND HIS TRUSTY SIDEKICK WOULD BE MY GUESTS HERE.
YOUR REPUTATION PRECEDES YOU, CONRAD. I'M SURE MY FRIEND AND I WILL BE WELL TAKEN CARE OF.
AND I SUPPOSE I'M TO TAKE THAT AS A COMPLIMENT? IT WAS NEVER WHAT YOU SAID THAT COULD BE SO DELICATELY DEVASTATING. IT WAS HOW YOU SAID IT. YOU KNOW, MY OLD FRIEND, I HAD FORGOTTEN WHAT IT WAS LIKE TO ENGAGE YOU IN DEBATE.
MY MEMORY IS NOT SO LAX.
AH YES, THE GREAT INTELLECTUAL CAPACITY, THE AUTHOR OF THE PRIZED MANIFESTO, THE DOCTRINE OF TRUTH. THE CREAM RISES TO THE TOP.
AND THE SLUDGE SINKS TO THE BOTTOM.
SO THIS IS HOW THE WEST WAS WON? TELL ME, BOISVERT, HOW YOU ALLOW YOURSELF TO GET MIXED UP WITH SUCH FINE MEN, THESE GIANTS OF HUMANITY WHO STOCK THE REBEL MOVEMENT?
THEY ARE, OF COURSE, KEEN JUDGES OF TALENT.

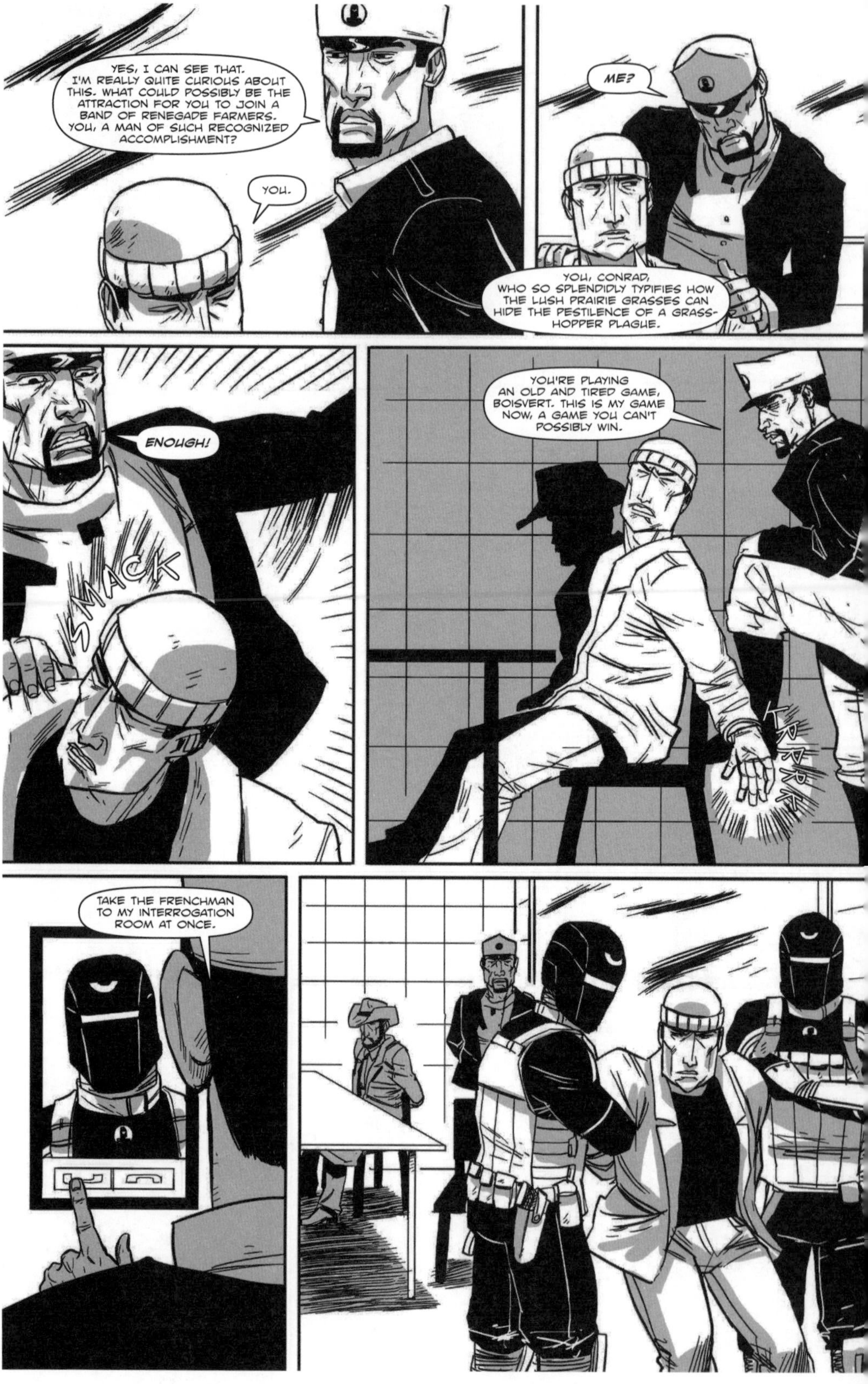
YES, I CAN SEE THAT. I'M REALLY QUITE CURIOUS ABOUT THIS. WHAT COULD POSSIBLY BE THE ATTRACTION FOR YOU TO JOIN A BAND OF RENEGADE FARMERS. YOU, A MAN OF SUCH RECOGNIZED ACCOMPLISHMENT?
YOU.
ME?
YOU, CONRAD, WHO SO SPLENDIDLY TYPIFIES HOW THE LUSH PRAIRIE GRASSES CAN HIDE THE PESTILENCE OF A GRASS-HOPPER PLAGUE.
ENOUGH!
SMACK
YOU'RE PLAYING AN OLD AND TIRED GAME, BOISVERT. THIS IS MY GAME NOW, A GAME YOU CAN'T POSSIBLY WIN.
KRRRK
TAKE THE FRENCHMAN TO MY INTERROGATION ROOM AT ONCE.

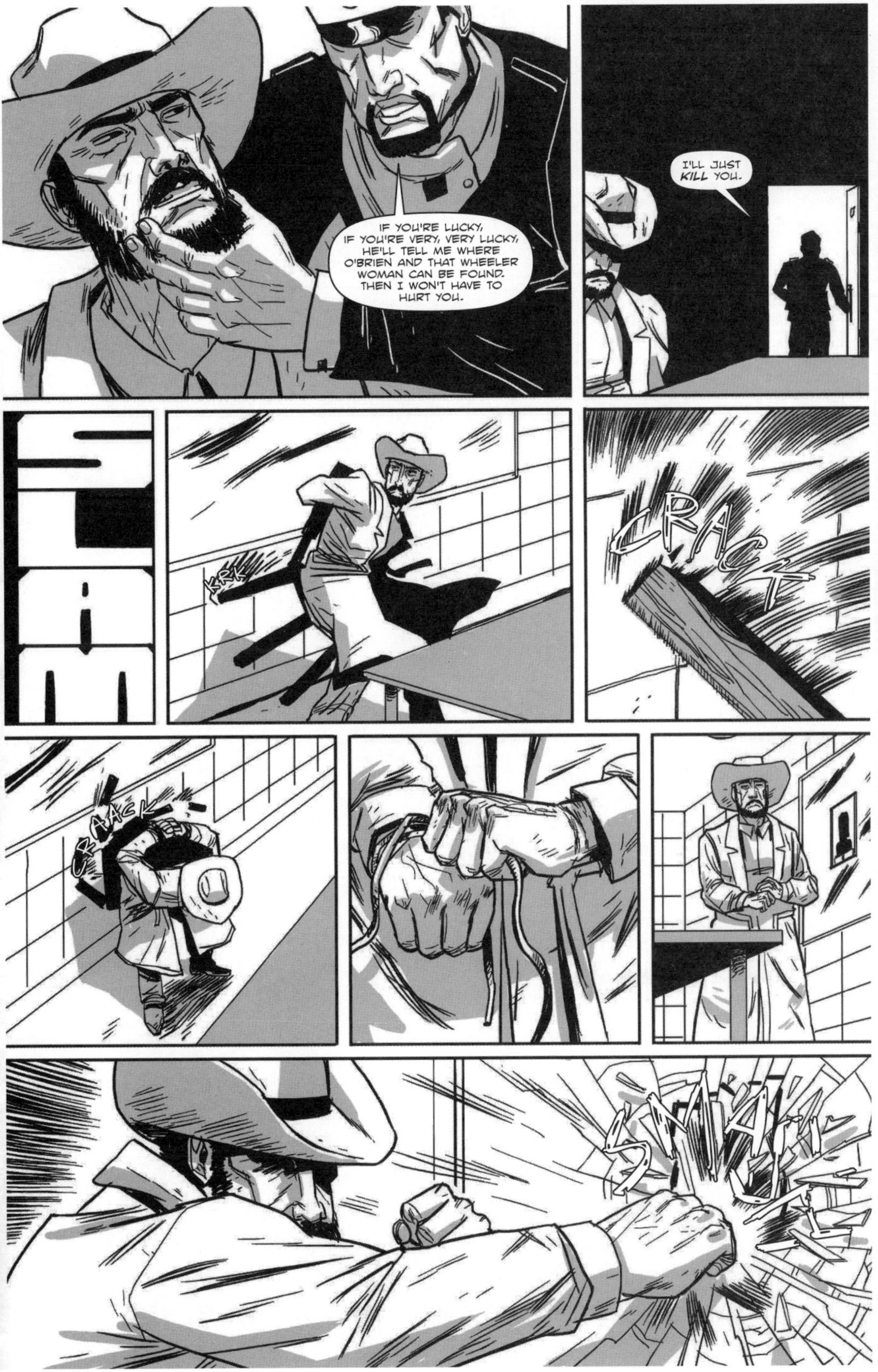
IF YOU'RE LUCKY, IF YOU'RE VERY, VERY LUCKY, HE'LL TELL ME WHERE O'BRIEN AND THAT WHEELER WOMAN CAN BE FOUND. THEN I WON'T HAVE TO HURT YOU.
I'LL JUST **KILL** YOU.
SLAM
KRK
CRACK
CRAACK

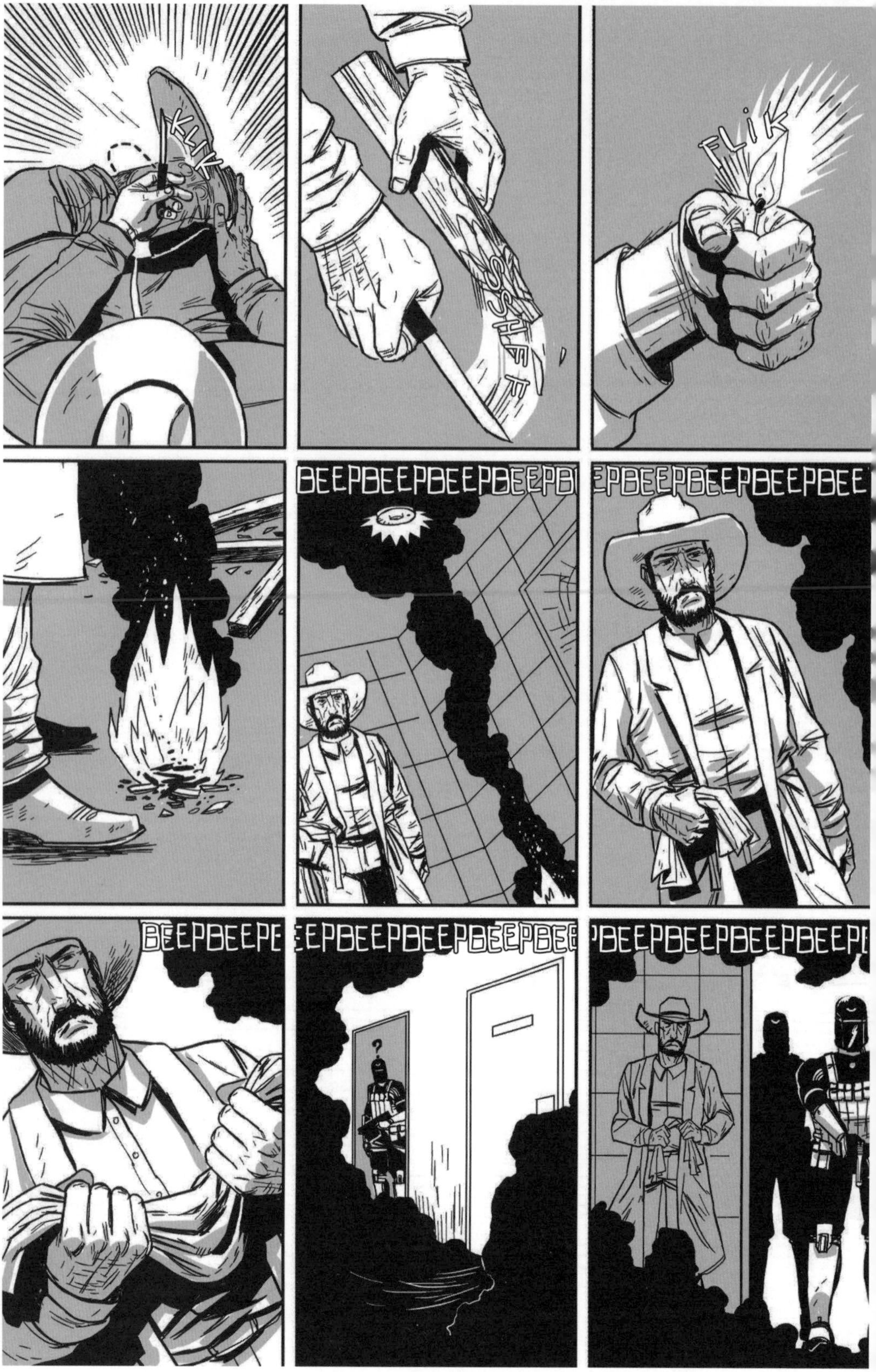
KLIK
SSHFF
FLIK
BEEPBEEPBEEPBEEPB
EPBEEPBEEPBEEPBEE
BEEPBEEPE
EEPBEEPBEEPBEEPBEE
PBEEPBEEPBEEPBEEPE

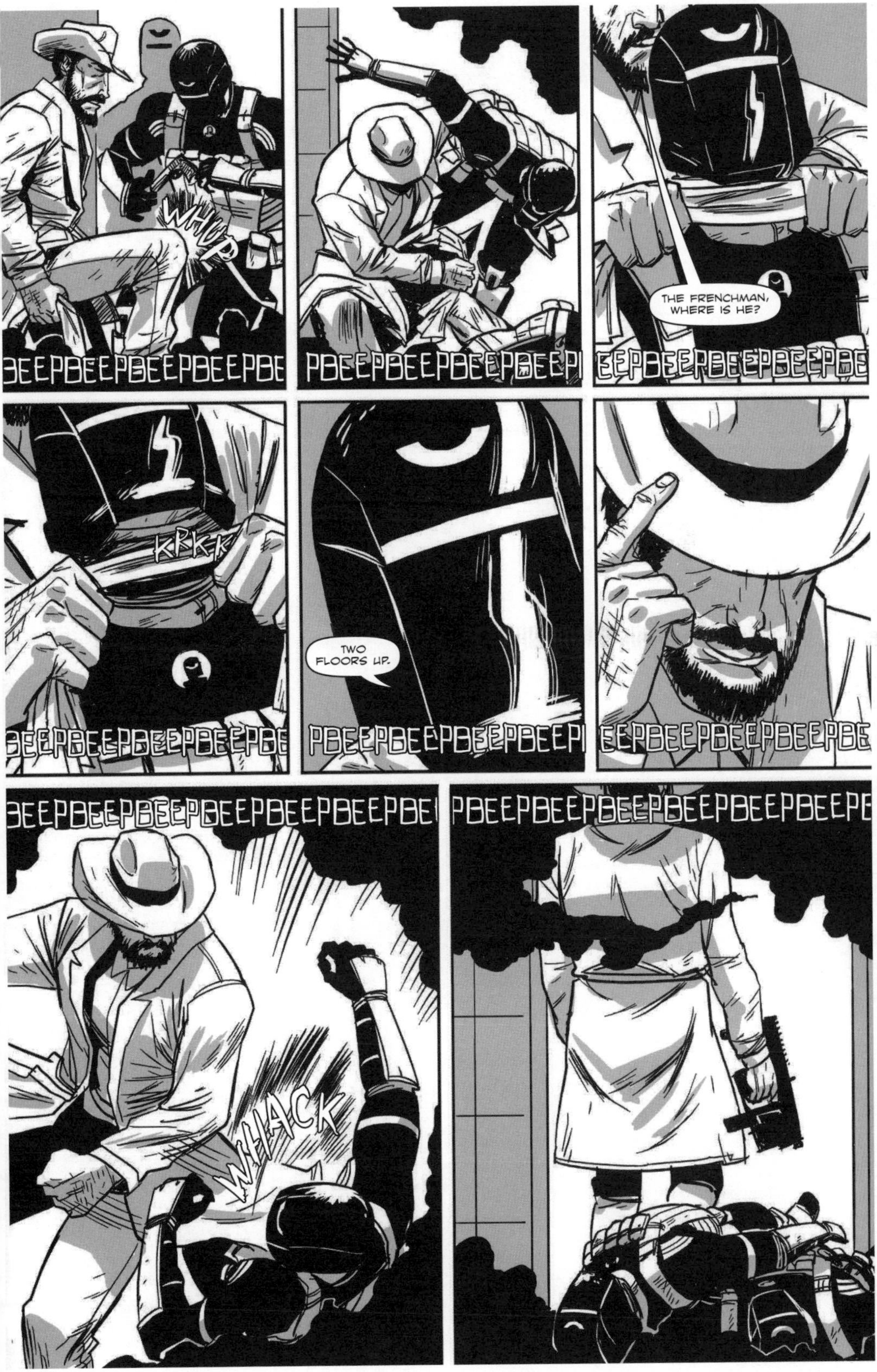
WHUP
BEEPBEEPBEEPBEEPBE
PBEEPBEEPBEEPBEEP
EEPBEEPBEEPBEEPBEE
THE FRENCHMAN, WHERE IS HE?
KRKK
BEEPBEEPBEEPBEEPBE
TWO FLOORS UP.
PBEEPBEEPBEEPBEEP
EEPBEEPBEEPBEEPBE
BEEPBEEPBEEPBEEPBEEPBEEPBE
PBEEPBEEPBEEPBEEPBEEPBEEPBEEPBE
WHACK

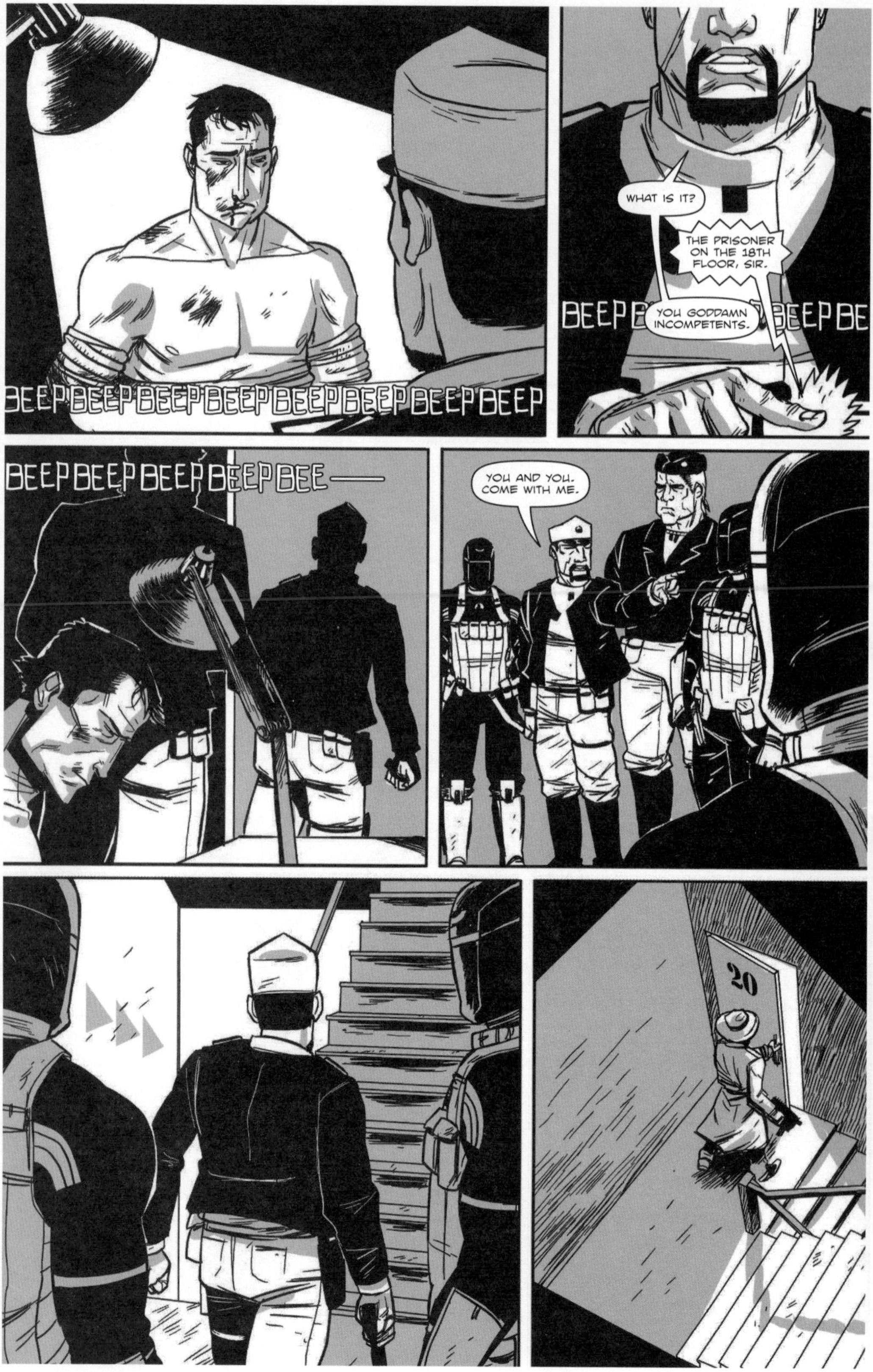
BEEP BEEP BEEP BEEP BEEP BEEP BEEP BEEP
WHAT IS IT?
THE PRISONER ON THE 18TH FLOOR, SIR.
YOU GODDAMN INCOMPETENTS.
BEEP BEEP BEEP BEEP BEEP BEEP BEE—
YOU AND YOU. COME WITH ME.
20

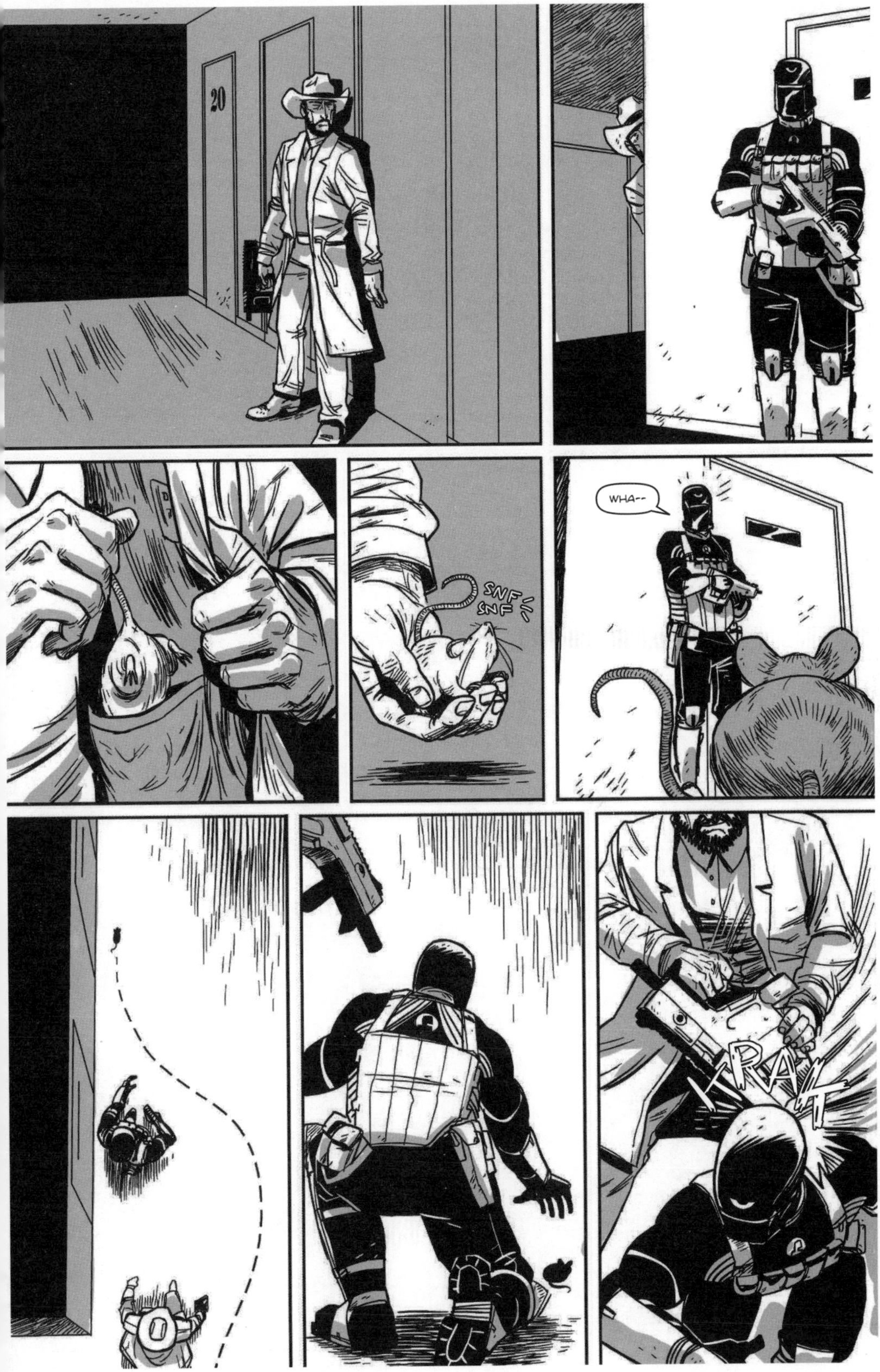
20
WHA--
SNF SNF
KRAK

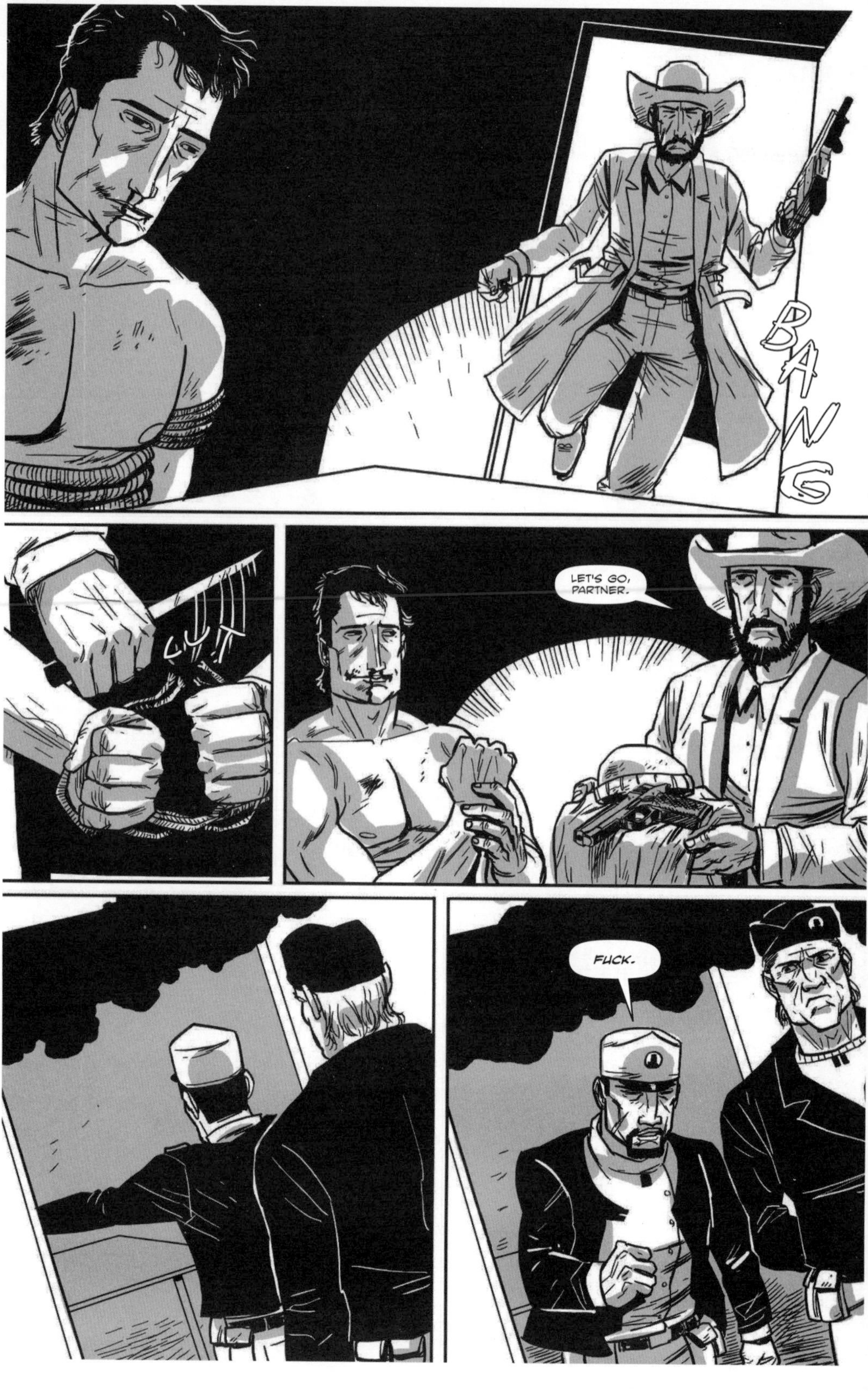
BANG
CUT
LET'S GO, PARTNER.
FUCK.

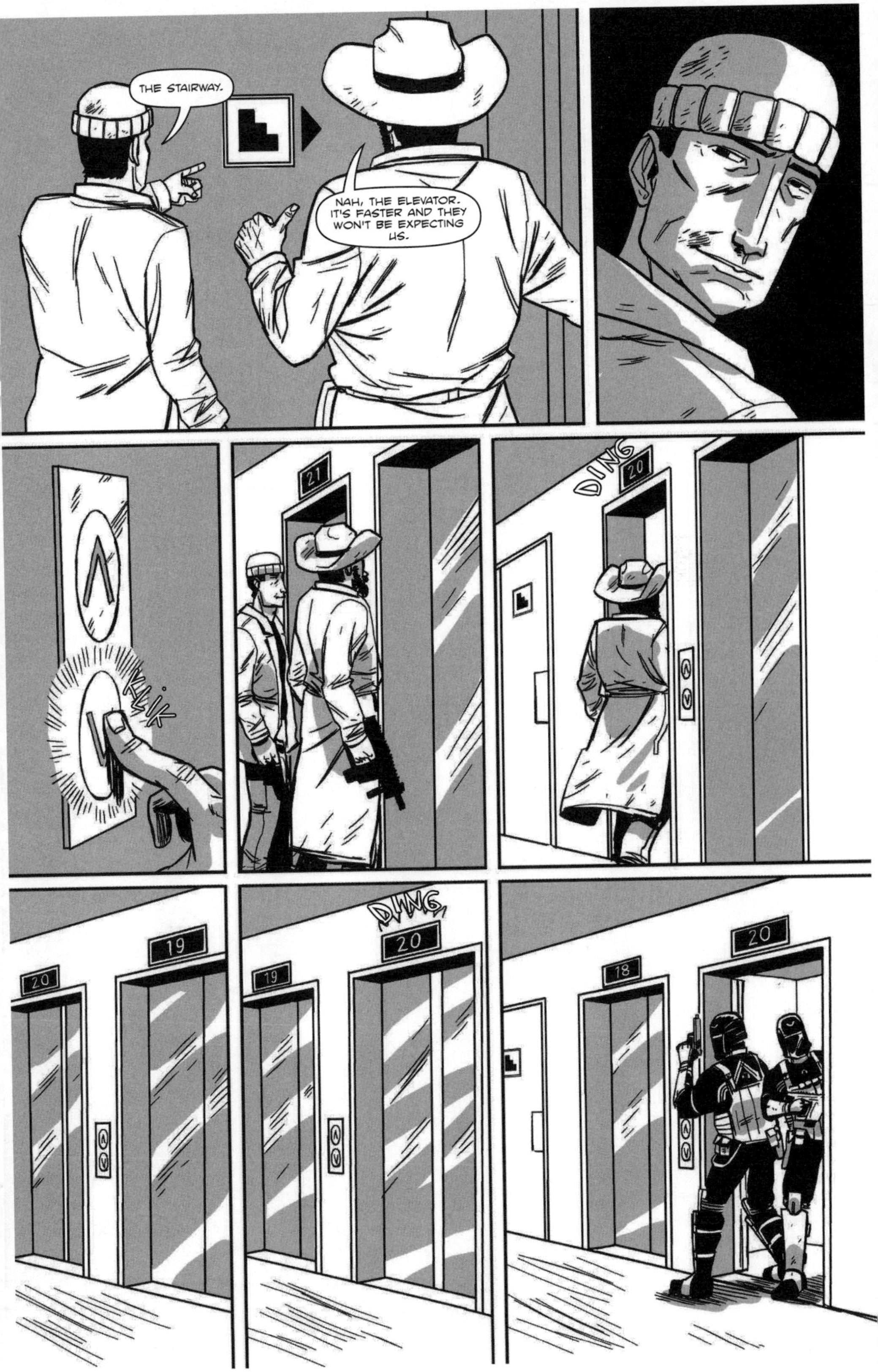

THE STAIRWAY.
NAH, THE ELEVATOR. IT'S FASTER AND THEY WON'T BE EXPECTING US.
KLIK
21
DING
20
20
19
DING
19
20
18
20

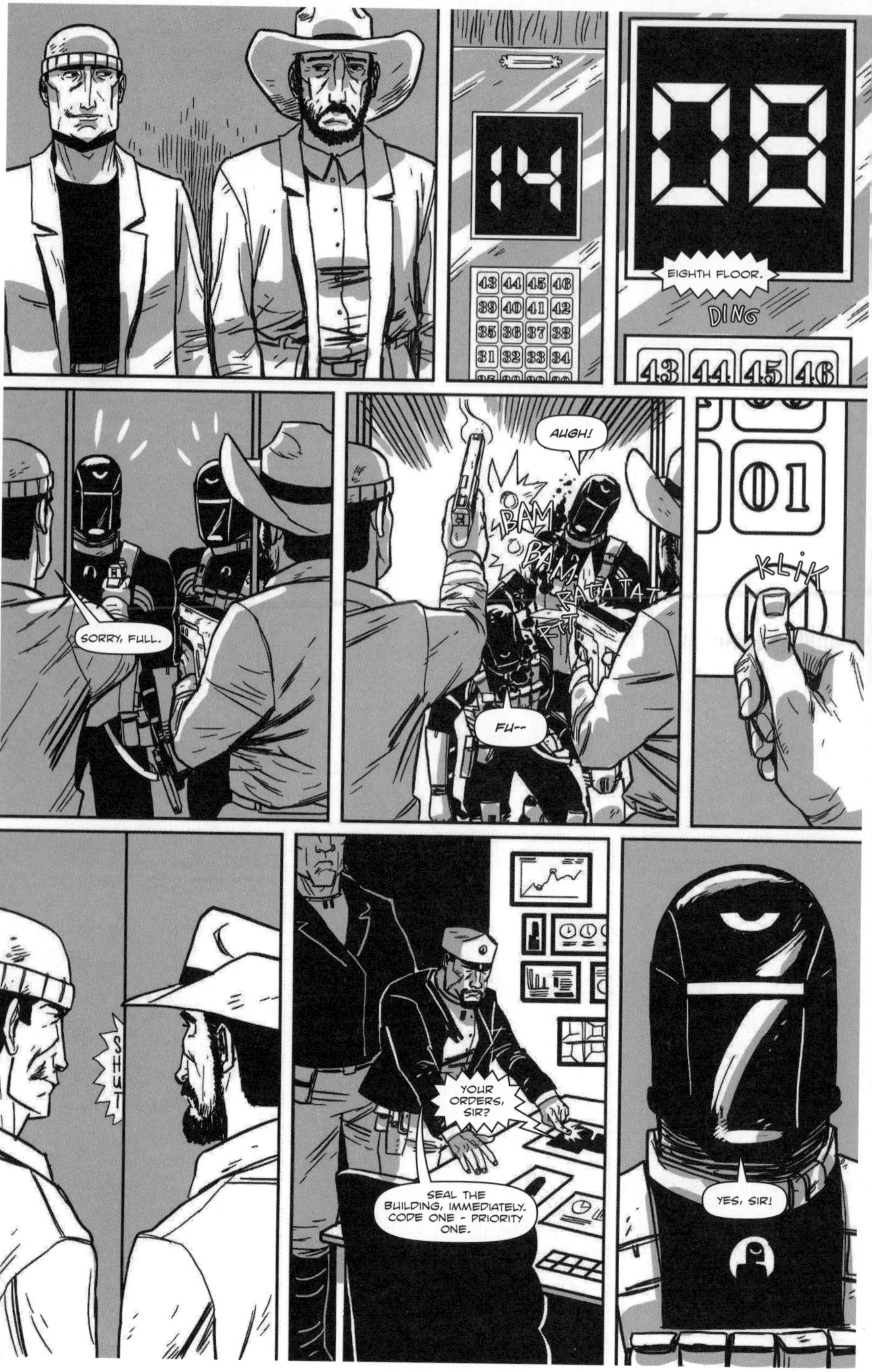
14
08
EIGHTH FLOOR.
DING
SORRY, FULL.
AUGH!
BAM
BAM
RATATAT
FU--
01
KLIK
SHUT
YOUR ORDERS, SIR?
SEAL THE BUILDING, IMMEDIATELY. CODE ONE - PRIORITY ONE.
YES, SIR!

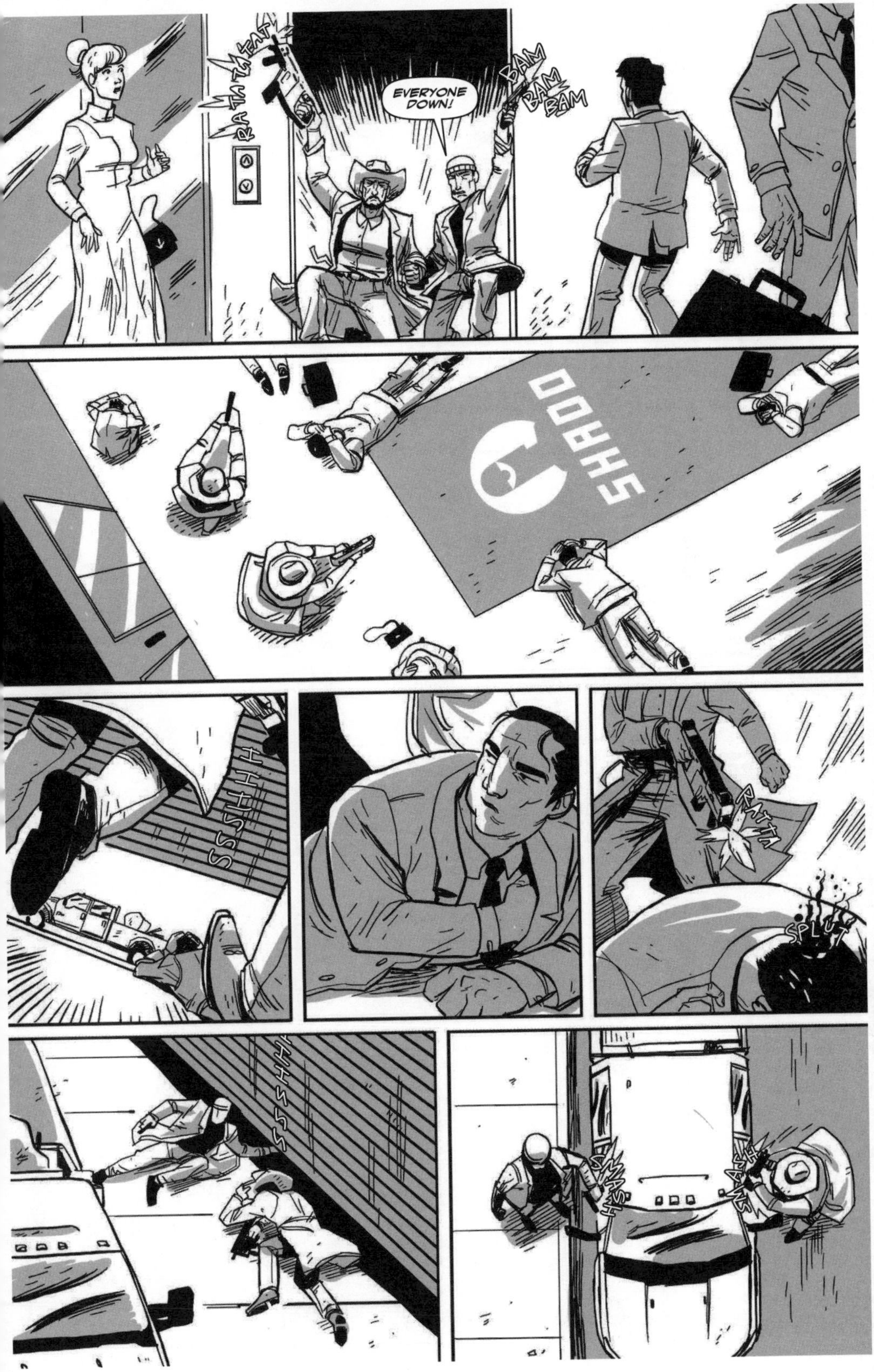
RA TA TA TAT
EVERYONE DOWN!
BAM BAM BAM
SHADO
SSSHHHH
RATTA
SPLUT
SSSHHH
SMASH
SMASH

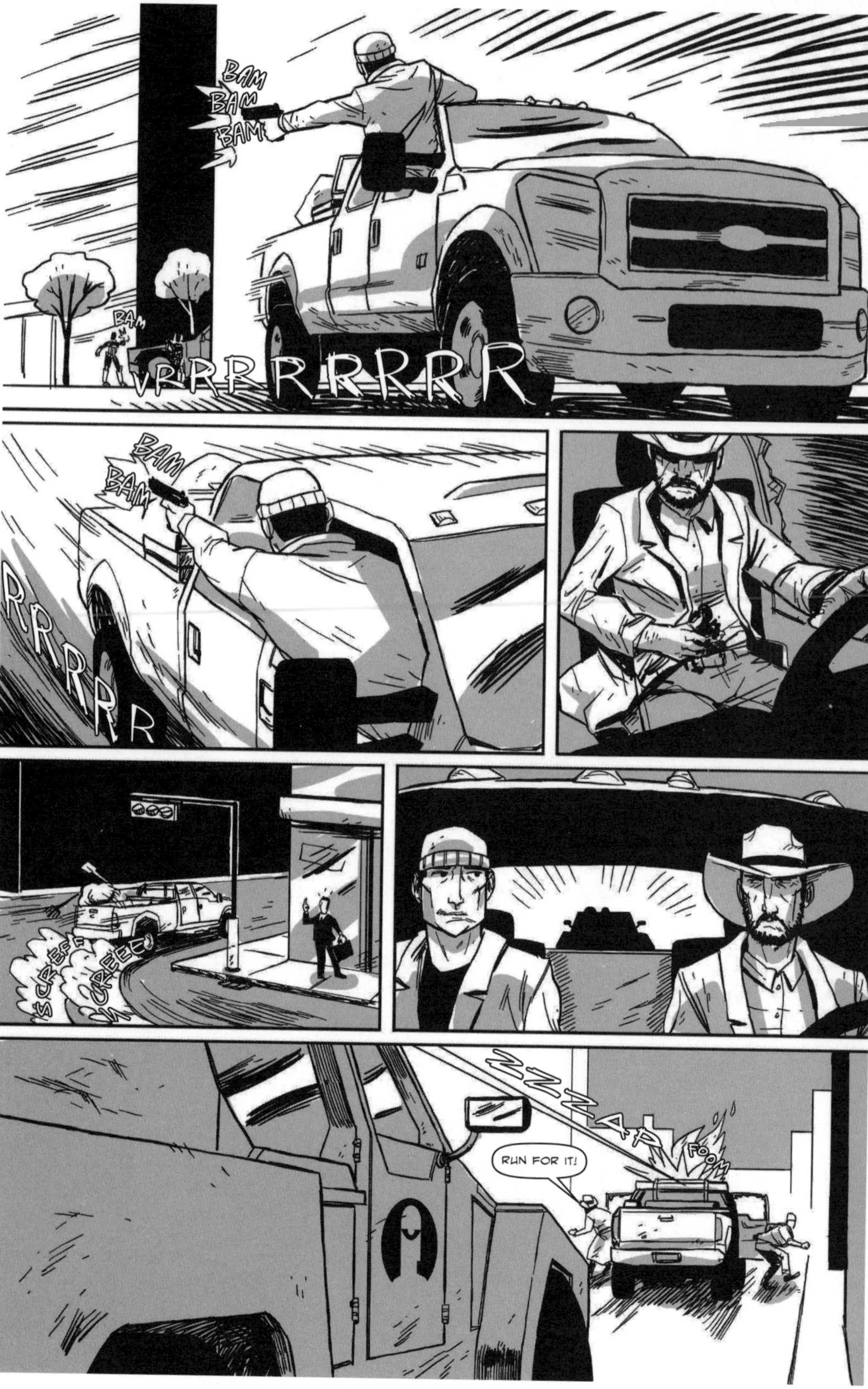
BAM
BAM
BAM
BAM
VRRRRRRRRR
BAM
BAM
RRRRRRR
SCREEE
SCREEE
ZZZZAP
FOOM
RUN FOR IT!

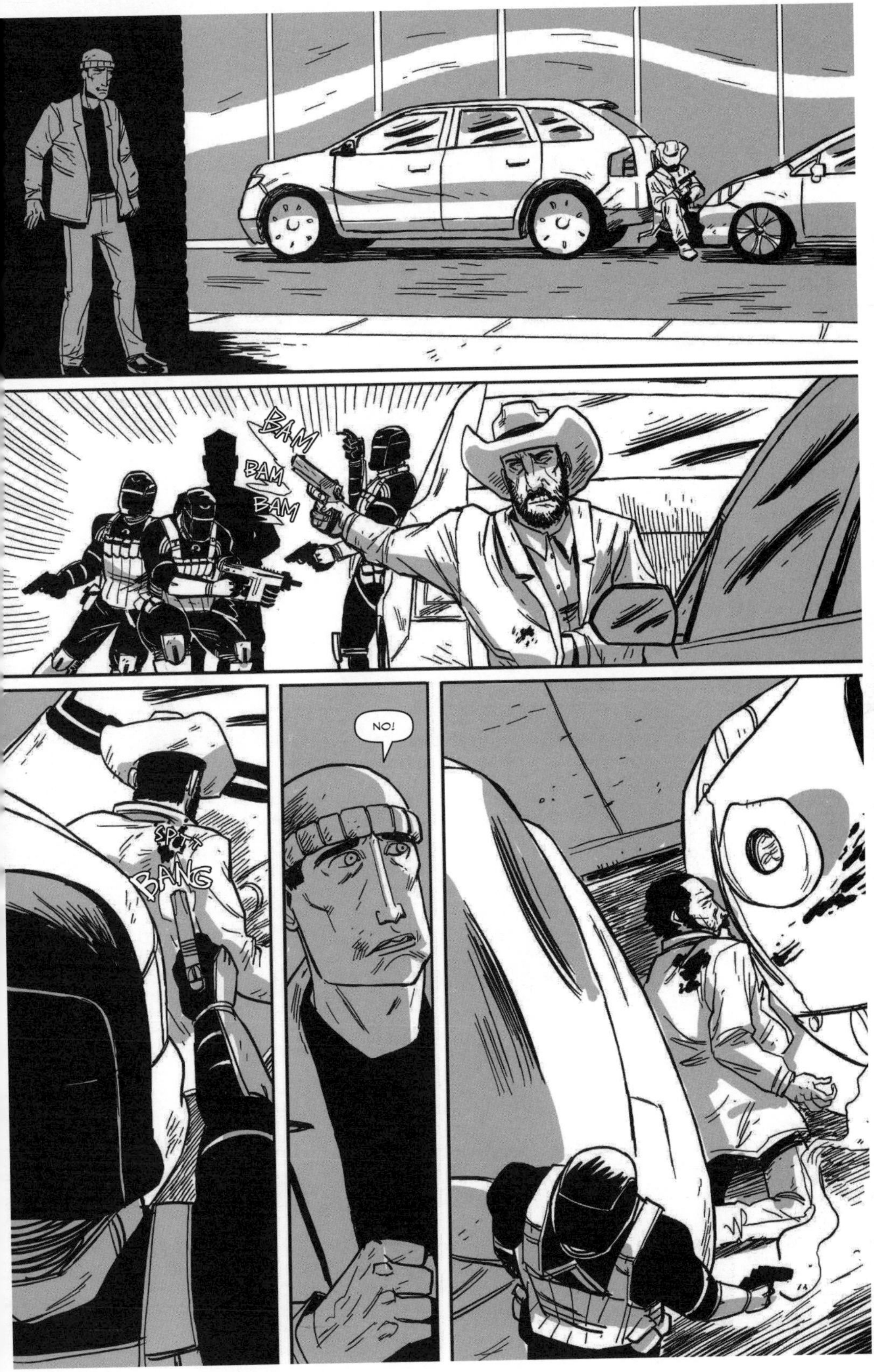
BAM
BAM
BAM
SPTT
BANG
NO!

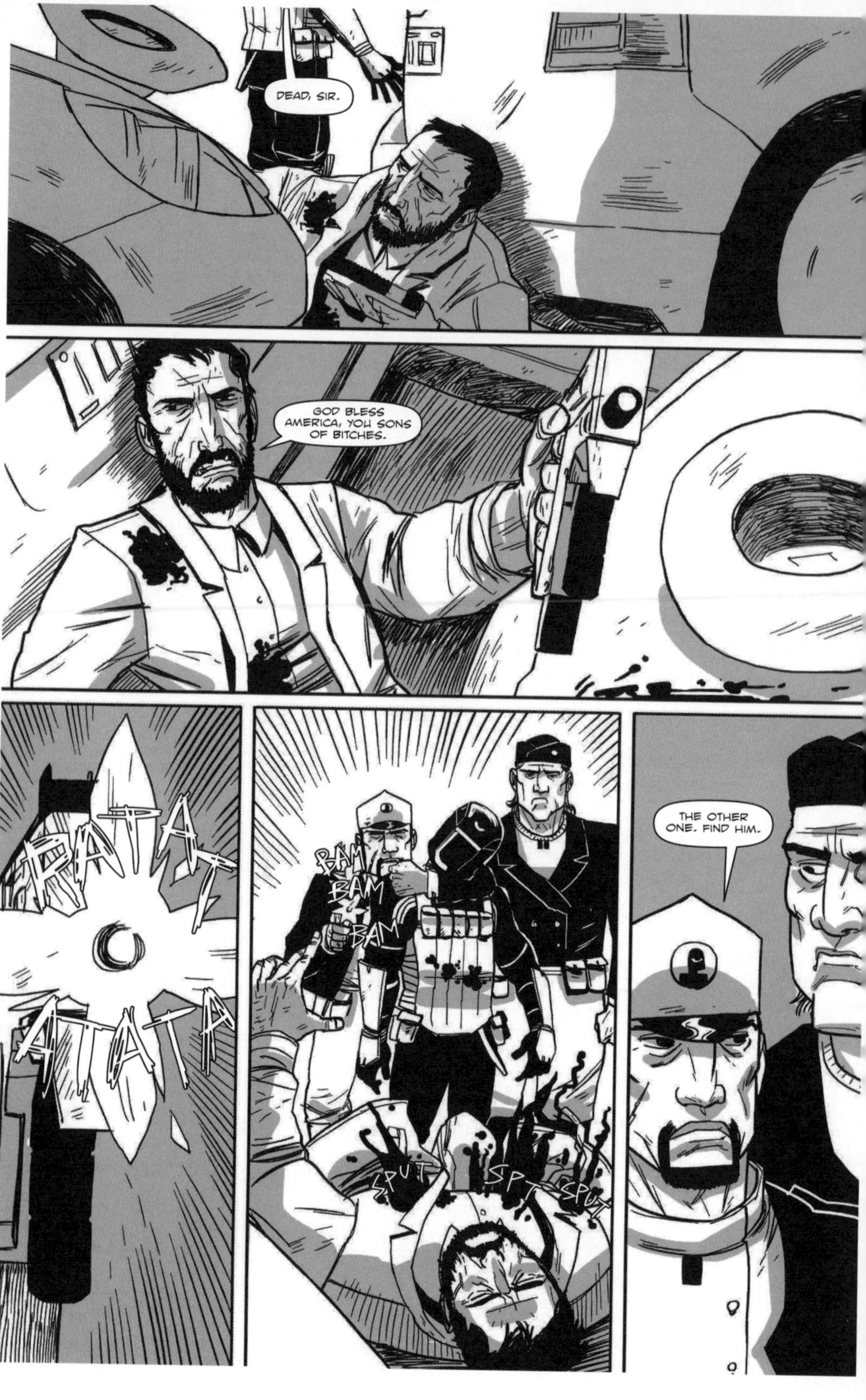
DEAD, SIR.
GOD BLESS AMERICA, YOU SONS OF BITCHES.
RATAT
ATATA
BAM
BAM
BAM
SPUT
SPT
SPUT
THE OTHER ONE. FIND HIM.

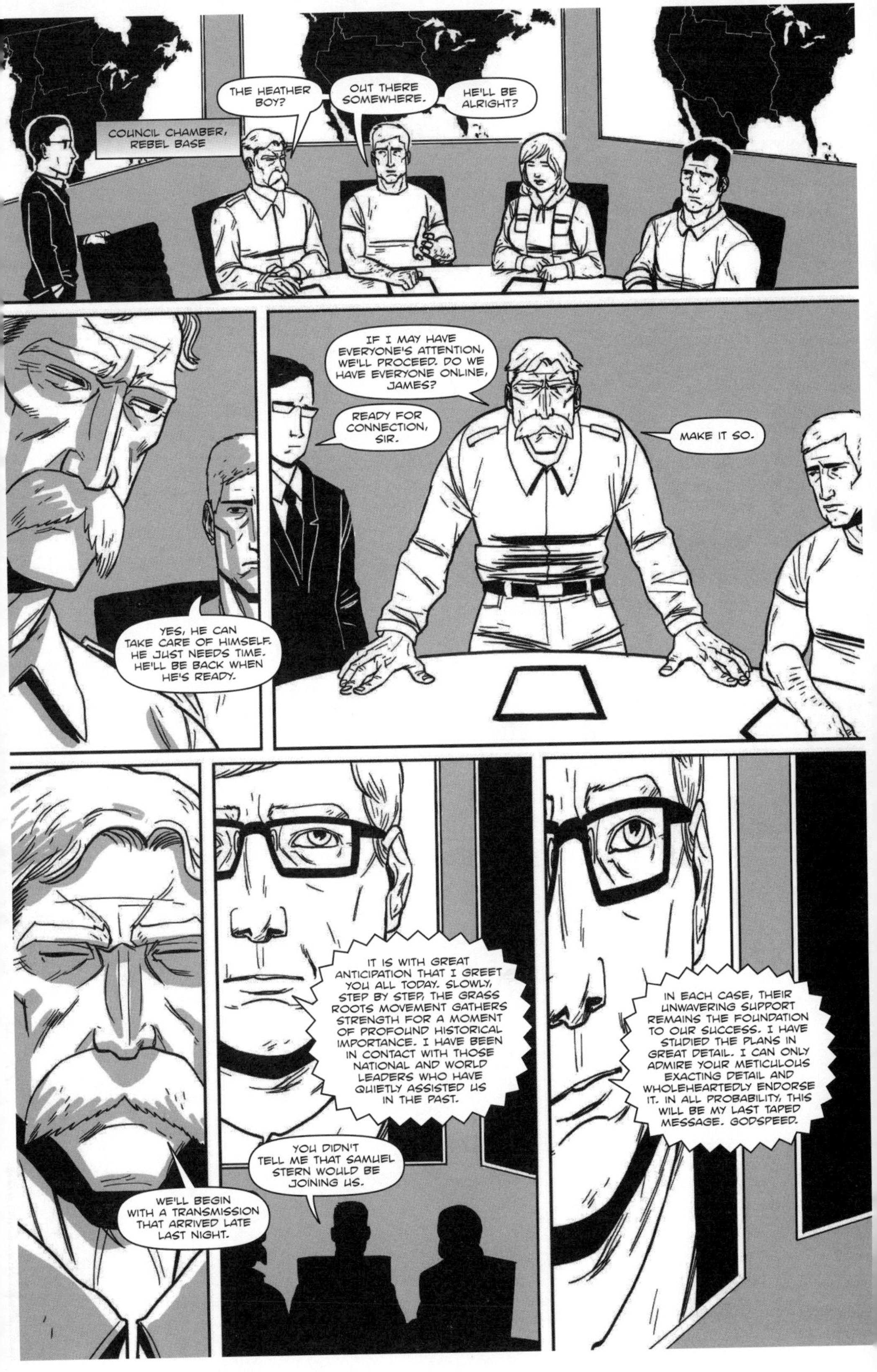
COUNCIL CHAMBER, REBEL BASE
THE HEATHER BOY?
OUT THERE SOMEWHERE.
HE'LL BE ALRIGHT?
YES, HE CAN TAKE CARE OF HIMSELF. HE JUST NEEDS TIME. HE'LL BE BACK WHEN HE'S READY.
IF I MAY HAVE EVERYONE'S ATTENTION, WE'LL PROCEED. DO WE HAVE EVERYONE ONLINE, JAMES?
READY FOR CONNECTION, SIR.
MAKE IT SO.
WE'LL BEGIN WITH A TRANSMISSION THAT ARRIVED LATE LAST NIGHT.
IT IS WITH GREAT ANTICIPATION THAT I GREET YOU ALL TODAY. SLOWLY, STEP BY STEP, THE GRASS ROOTS MOVEMENT GATHERS STRENGTH FOR A MOMENT OF PROFOUND HISTORICAL IMPORTANCE. I HAVE BEEN IN CONTACT WITH THOSE NATIONAL AND WORLD LEADERS WHO HAVE QUIETLY ASSISTED US IN THE PAST.
YOU DIDN'T TELL ME THAT SAMUEL STERN WOULD BE JOINING US.
IN EACH CASE, THEIR UNWAVERING SUPPORT REMAINS THE FOUNDATION TO OUR SUCCESS. I HAVE STUDIED THE PLANS IN GREAT DETAIL. I CAN ONLY ADMIRE YOUR METICULOUS EXACTING DETAIL AND WHOLEHEARTEDLY ENDORSE IT. IN ALL PROBABILITY, THIS WILL BE MY LAST TAPED MESSAGE. GODSPEED.

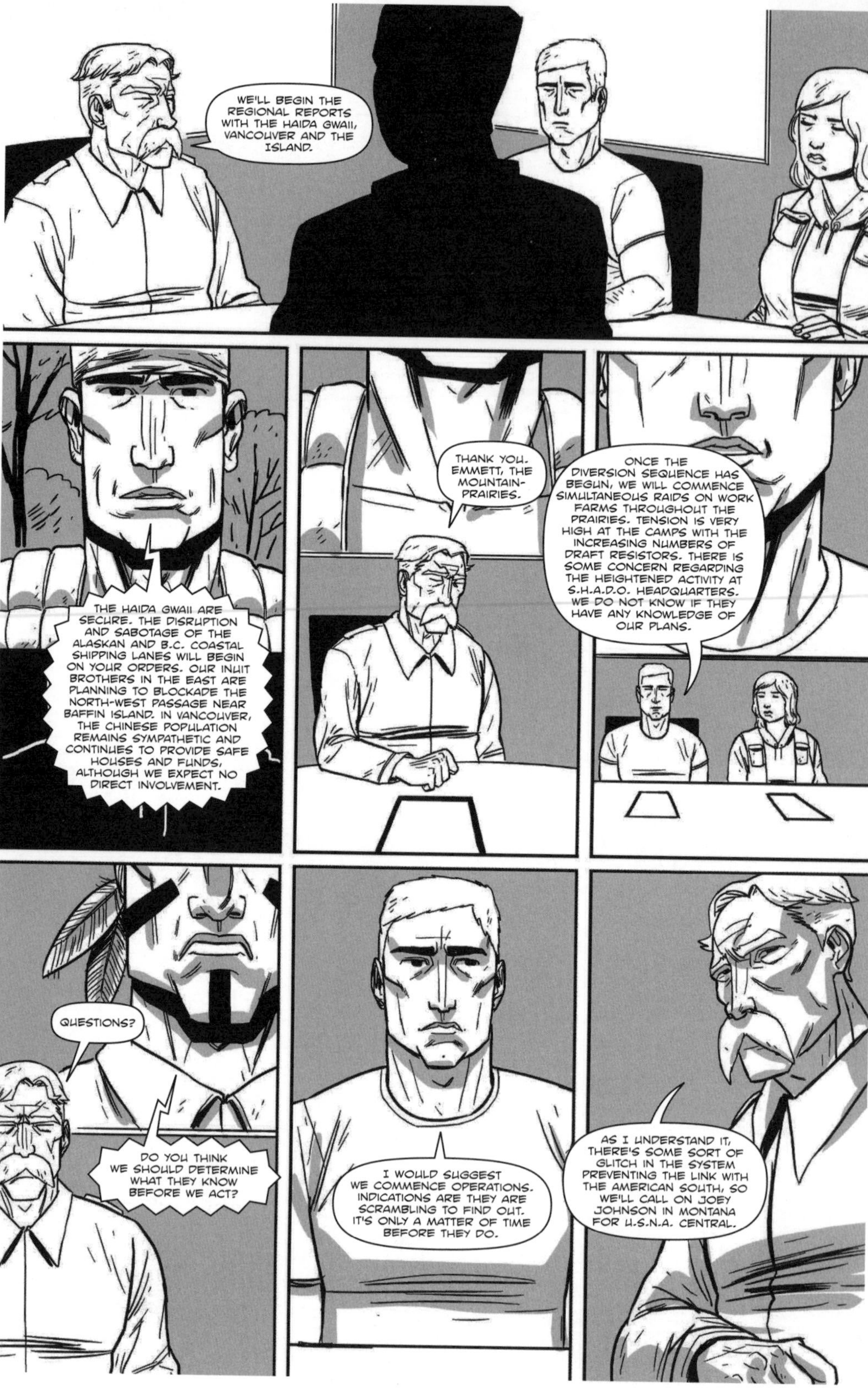

WE'LL BEGIN THE REGIONAL REPORTS WITH THE HAIDA GWAII, VANCOUVER AND THE ISLAND.
THE HAIDA GWAII ARE SECURE. THE DISRUPTION AND SABOTAGE OF THE ALASKAN AND B.C. COASTAL SHIPPING LANES WILL BEGIN ON YOUR ORDERS. OUR INUIT BROTHERS IN THE EAST ARE PLANNING TO BLOCKADE THE NORTH-WEST PASSAGE NEAR BAFFIN ISLAND. IN VANCOUVER, THE CHINESE POPULATION REMAINS SYMPATHETIC AND CONTINUES TO PROVIDE SAFE HOUSES AND FUNDS, ALTHOUGH WE EXPECT NO DIRECT INVOLVEMENT.
THANK YOU. EMMETT, THE MOUNTAIN-PRAIRIES.
ONCE THE DIVERSION SEQUENCE HAS BEGUN, WE WILL COMMENCE SIMULTANEOUS RAIDS ON WORK FARMS THROUGHOUT THE PRAIRIES. TENSION IS VERY HIGH AT THE CAMPS WITH THE INCREASING NUMBERS OF DRAFT RESISTORS. THERE IS SOME CONCERN REGARDING THE HEIGHTENED ACTIVITY AT S.H.A.D.O. HEADQUARTERS. WE DO NOT KNOW IF THEY HAVE ANY KNOWLEDGE OF OUR PLANS.
QUESTIONS?
DO YOU THINK WE SHOULD DETERMINE WHAT THEY KNOW BEFORE WE ACT?
I WOULD SUGGEST WE COMMENCE OPERATIONS. INDICATIONS ARE THEY ARE SCRAMBLING TO FIND OUT. IT'S ONLY A MATTER OF TIME BEFORE THEY DO.
AS I UNDERSTAND IT, THERE'S SOME SORT OF GLITCH IN THE SYSTEM PREVENTING THE LINK WITH THE AMERICAN SOUTH, SO WE'LL CALL ON JOEY JOHNSON IN MONTANA FOR U.S.N.A. CENTRAL.

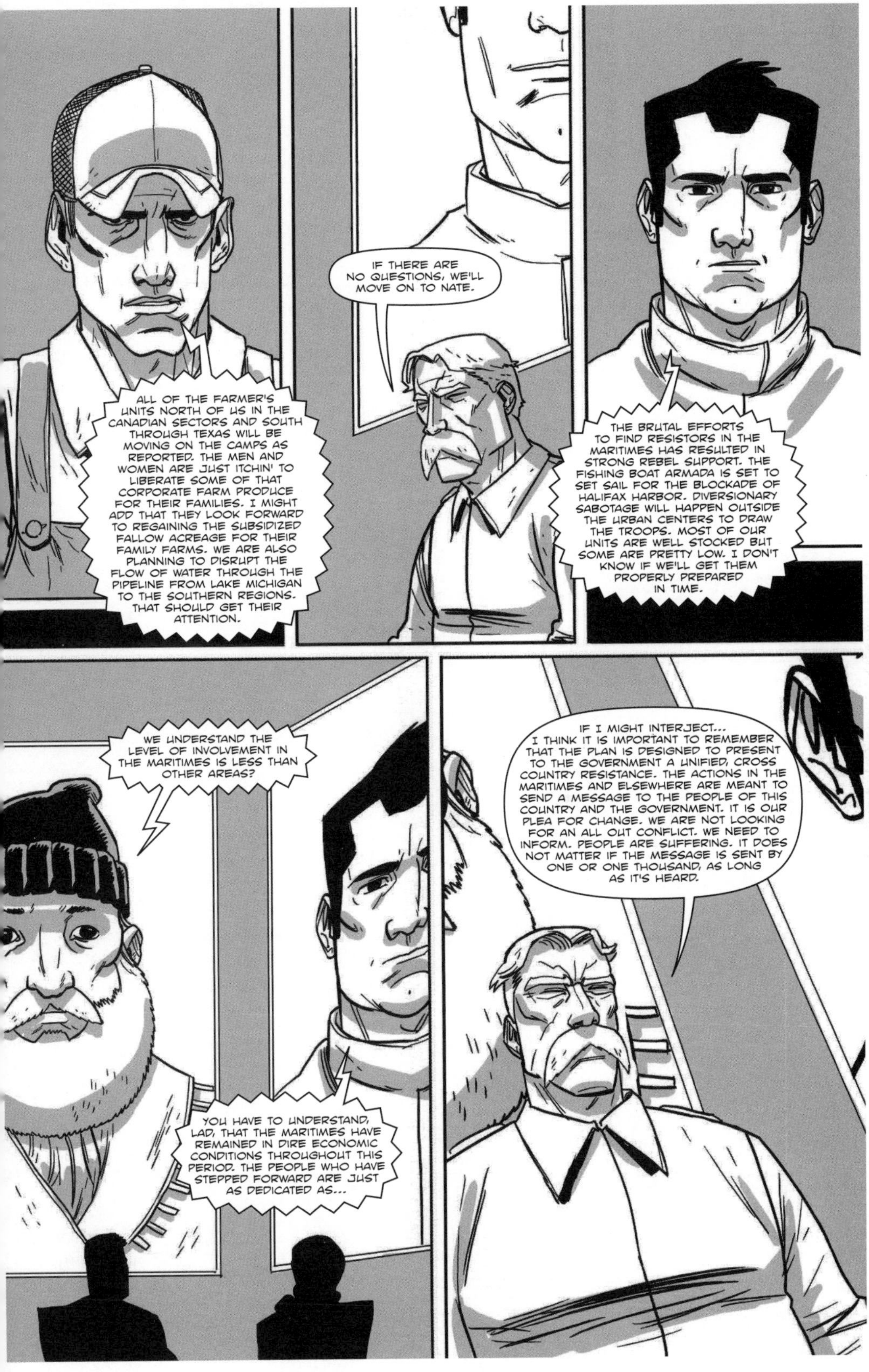
IF THERE ARE NO QUESTIONS, WE'LL MOVE ON TO NATE.
ALL OF THE FARMER'S UNITS NORTH OF US IN THE CANADIAN SECTORS AND SOUTH THROUGH TEXAS WILL BE MOVING ON THE CAMPS AS REPORTED. THE MEN AND WOMEN ARE JUST ITCHIN' TO LIBERATE SOME OF THAT CORPORATE FARM PRODUCE FOR THEIR FAMILIES. I MIGHT ADD THAT THEY LOOK FORWARD TO REGAINING THE SUBSIDIZED FALLOW ACREAGE FOR THEIR FAMILY FARMS. WE ARE ALSO PLANNING TO DISRUPT THE FLOW OF WATER THROUGH THE PIPELINE FROM LAKE MICHIGAN TO THE SOUTHERN REGIONS. THAT SHOULD GET THEIR ATTENTION.
THE BRUTAL EFFORTS TO FIND RESISTORS IN THE MARITIMES HAS RESULTED IN STRONG REBEL SUPPORT. THE FISHING BOAT ARMADA IS SET TO SET SAIL FOR THE BLOCKADE OF HALIFAX HARBOR. DIVERSIONARY SABOTAGE WILL HAPPEN OUTSIDE THE URBAN CENTERS TO DRAW THE TROOPS. MOST OF OUR UNITS ARE WELL STOCKED BUT SOME ARE PRETTY LOW. I DON'T KNOW IF WE'LL GET THEM PROPERLY PREPARED IN TIME.
WE UNDERSTAND THE LEVEL OF INVOLVEMENT IN THE MARITIMES IS LESS THAN OTHER AREAS?
YOU HAVE TO UNDERSTAND, LAD, THAT THE MARITIMES HAVE REMAINED IN DIRE ECONOMIC CONDITIONS THROUGHOUT THIS PERIOD. THE PEOPLE WHO HAVE STEPPED FORWARD ARE JUST AS DEDICATED AS...
IF I MIGHT INTERJECT... I THINK IT IS IMPORTANT TO REMEMBER THAT THE PLAN IS DESIGNED TO PRESENT TO THE GOVERNMENT A UNIFIED, CROSS COUNTRY RESISTANCE. THE ACTIONS IN THE MARITIMES AND ELSEWHERE ARE MEANT TO SEND A MESSAGE TO THE PEOPLE OF THIS COUNTRY AND THE GOVERNMENT. IT IS OUR PLEA FOR CHANGE. WE ARE NOT LOOKING FOR AN ALL OUT CONFLICT. WE NEED TO INFORM. PEOPLE ARE SUFFERING. IT DOES NOT MATTER IF THE MESSAGE IS SENT BY ONE OR ONE THOUSAND, AS LONG AS IT'S HEARD.

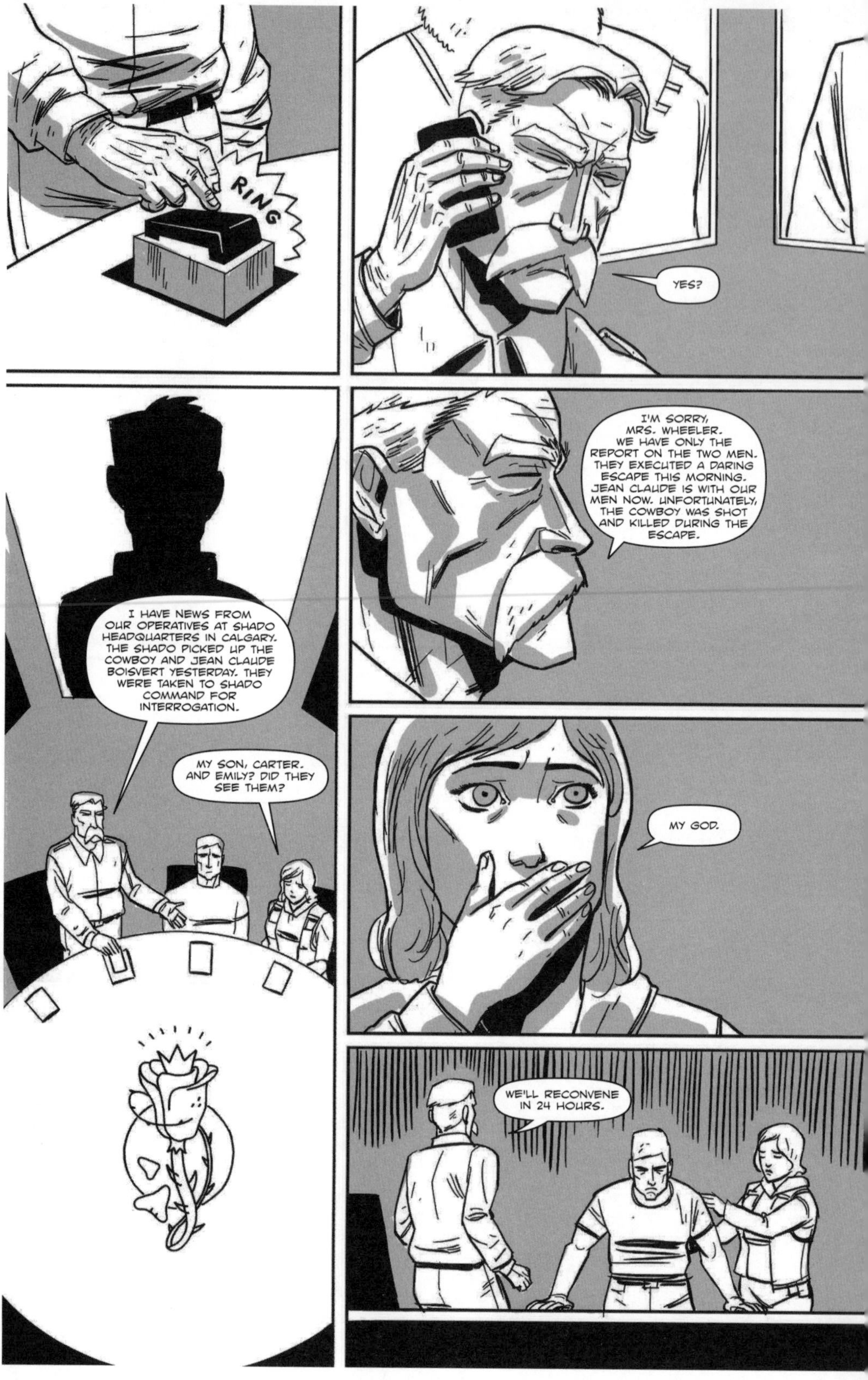
RING
YES?
I HAVE NEWS FROM OUR OPERATIVES AT SHADO HEADQUARTERS IN CALGARY. THE SHADO PICKED UP THE COWBOY AND JEAN CLAUDE BOISVERT YESTERDAY. THEY WERE TAKEN TO SHADO COMMAND FOR INTERROGATION.
MY SON, CARTER. AND EMILY? DID THEY SEE THEM?
I'M SORRY, MRS. WHEELER. WE HAVE ONLY THE REPORT ON THE TWO MEN. THEY EXECUTED A DARING ESCAPE THIS MORNING. JEAN CLAUDE IS WITH OUR MEN NOW. UNFORTUNATELY, THE COWBOY WAS SHOT AND KILLED DURING THE ESCAPE.
MY GOD.
WE'LL RECONVENE IN 24 HOURS.

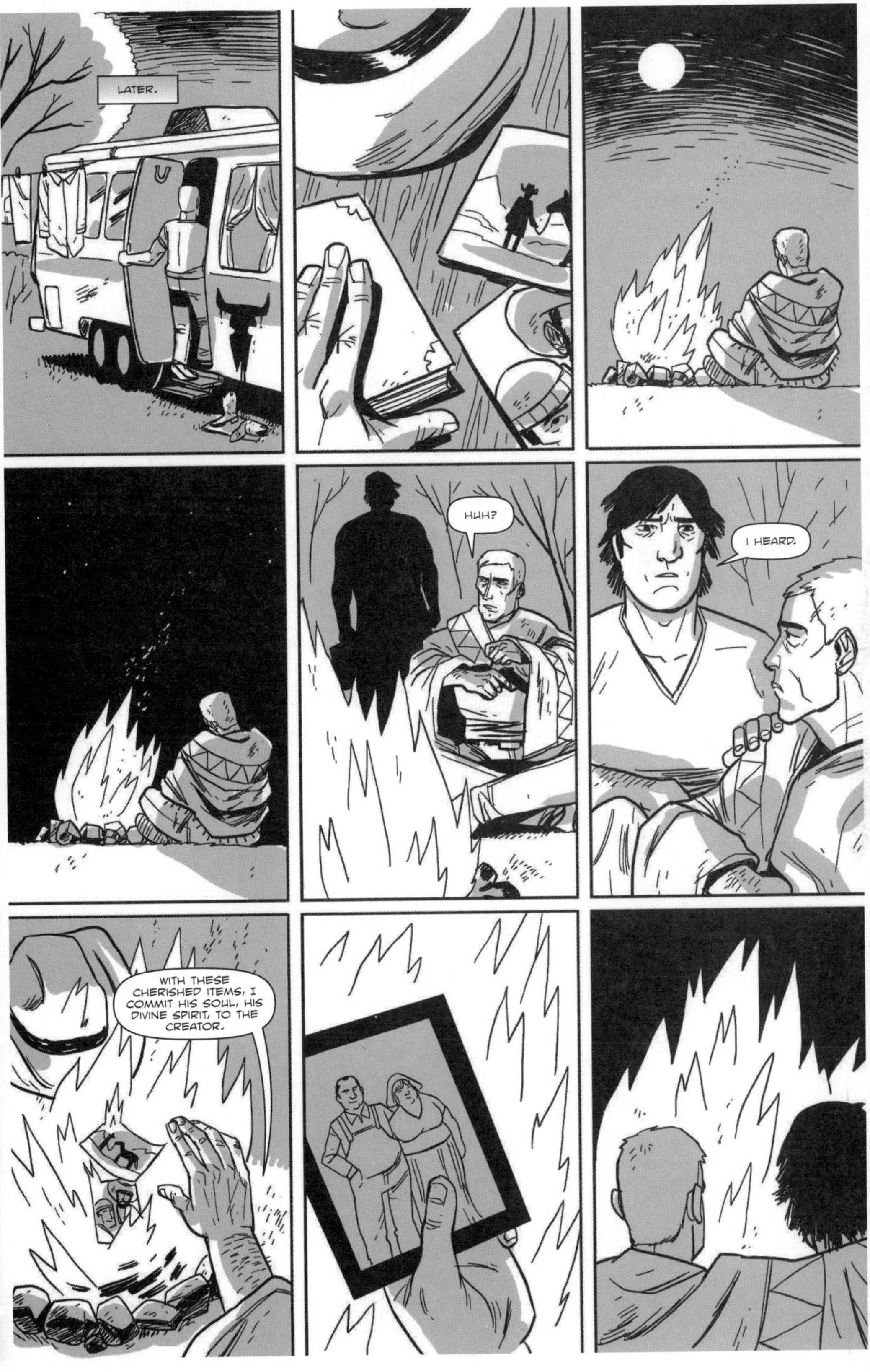
LATER.
HUH?
I HEARD.
WITH THESE CHERISHED ITEMS, I COMMIT HIS SOUL, HIS DIVINE SPIRIT, TO THE CREATOR.

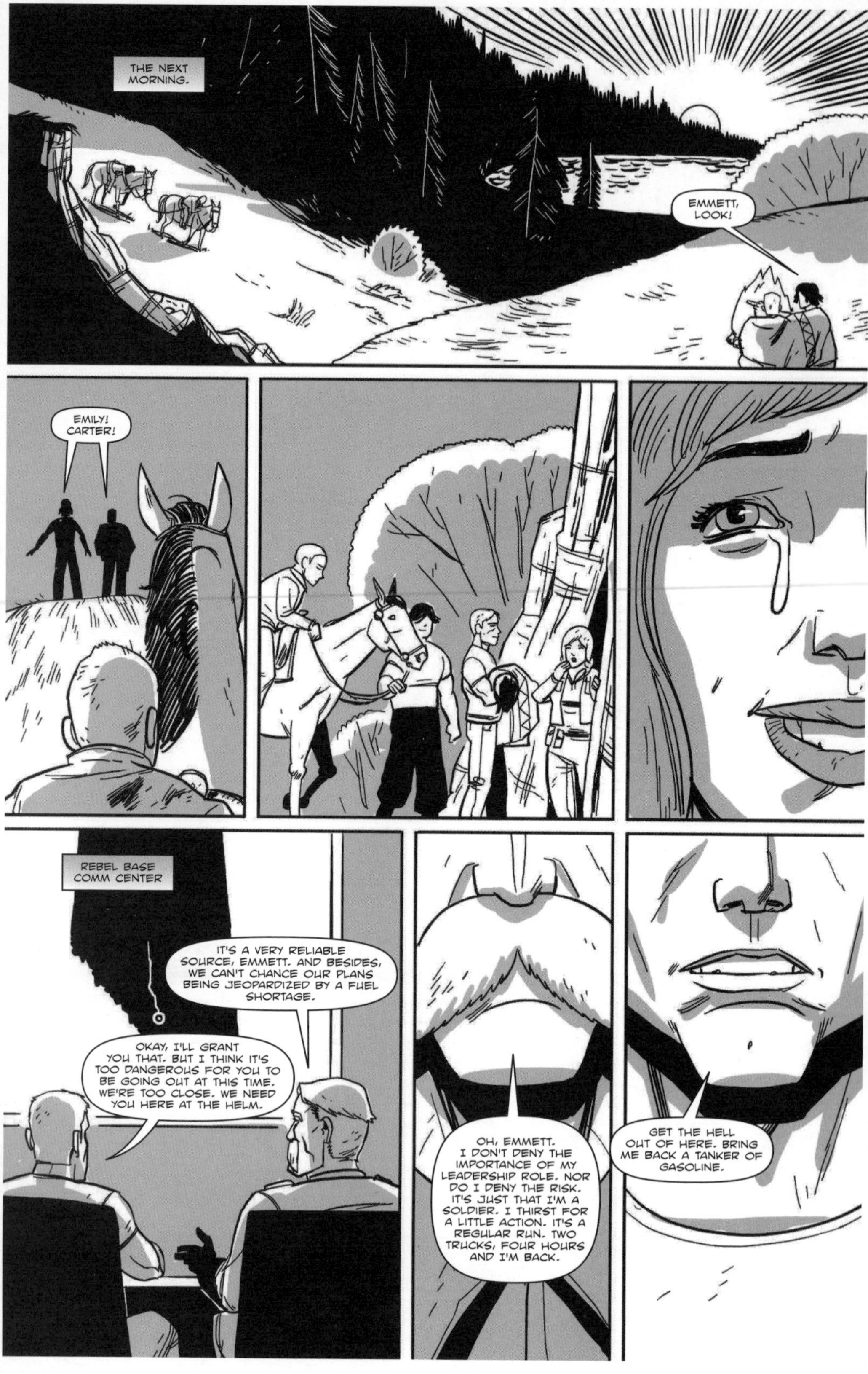
THE NEXT MORNING.
EMMETT, LOOK!
EMILY! CARTER!
REBEL BASE COMM CENTER
IT'S A VERY RELIABLE SOURCE, EMMETT. AND BESIDES, WE CAN'T CHANCE OUR PLANS BEING JEOPARDIZED BY A FUEL SHORTAGE.
OKAY, I'LL GRANT YOU THAT. BUT I THINK IT'S TOO DANGEROUS FOR YOU TO BE GOING OUT AT THIS TIME. WE'RE TOO CLOSE. WE NEED YOU HERE AT THE HELM.
OH, EMMETT. I DON'T DENY THE IMPORTANCE OF MY LEADERSHIP ROLE. NOR DO I DENY THE RISK. IT'S JUST THAT I'M A SOLDIER. I THIRST FOR A LITTLE ACTION. IT'S A REGULAR RUN. TWO TRUCKS, FOUR HOURS AND I'M BACK.
GET THE HELL OUT OF HERE. BRING ME BACK A TANKER OF GASOLINE.

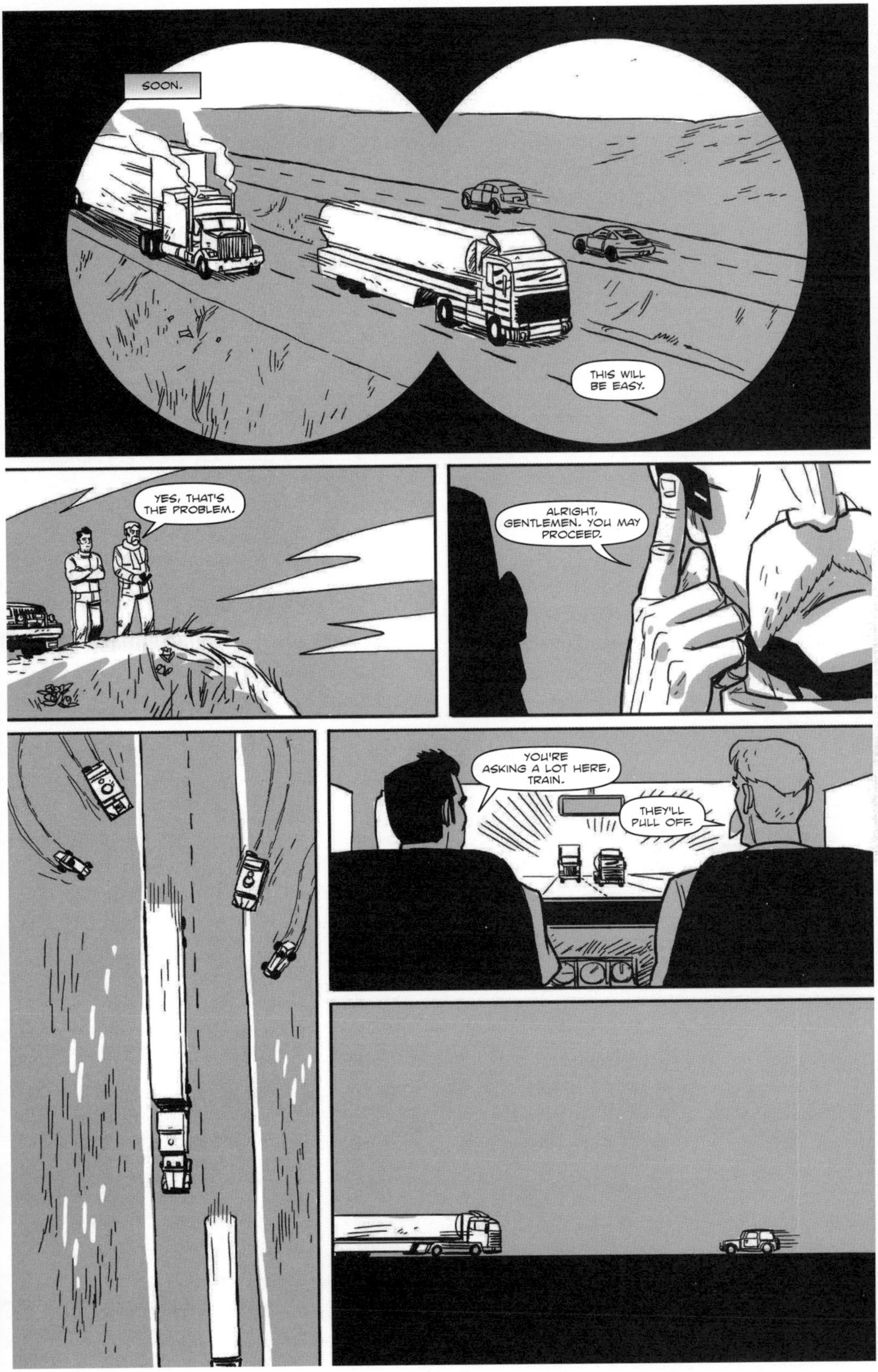
SOON.
THIS WILL BE EASY.
YES, THAT'S THE PROBLEM.
ALRIGHT, GENTLEMEN. YOU MAY PROCEED.
YOU'RE ASKING A LOT HERE, TRAIN.
THEY'LL PULL OFF.

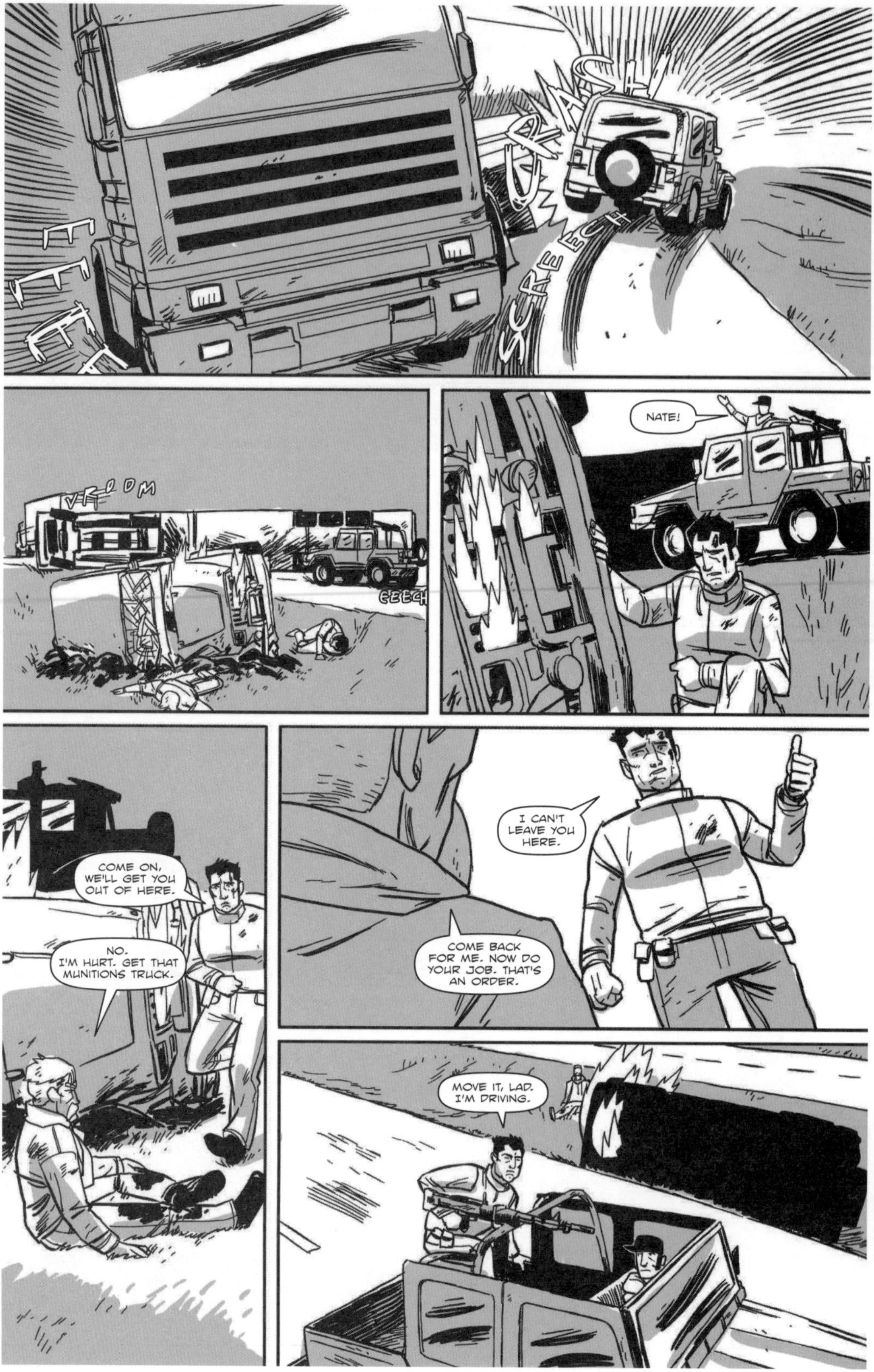
CRASH!
SCREECH
VROOM
EEECH
NATE!
COME ON, WE'LL GET YOU OUT OF HERE.
NO. I'M HURT. GET THAT MUNITIONS TRUCK.
I CAN'T LEAVE YOU HERE.
COME BACK FOR ME. NOW DO YOUR JOB. THAT'S AN ORDER.
MOVE IT, LAD. I'M DRIVING.

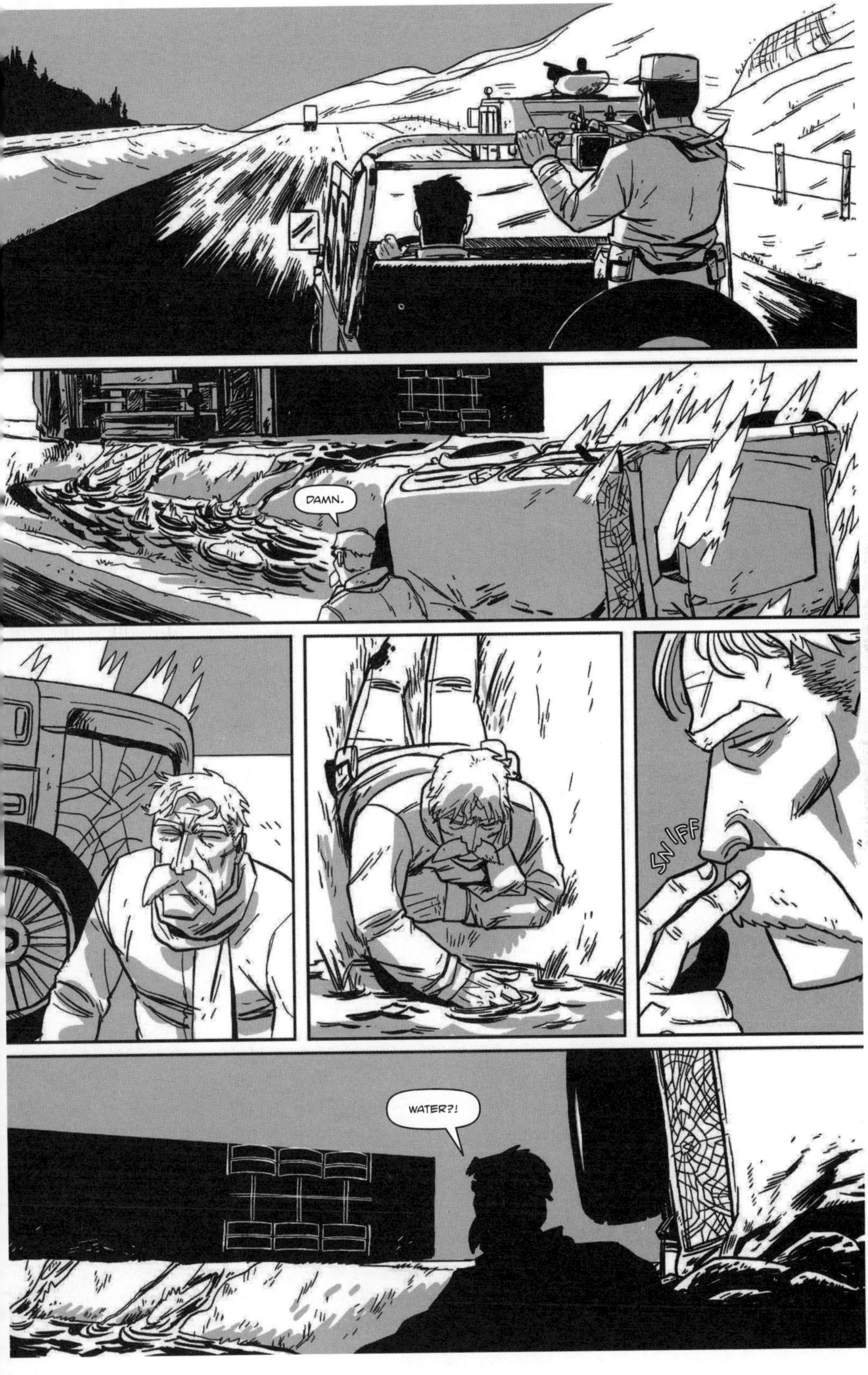
DAMN.
SNIFF
WATER?!

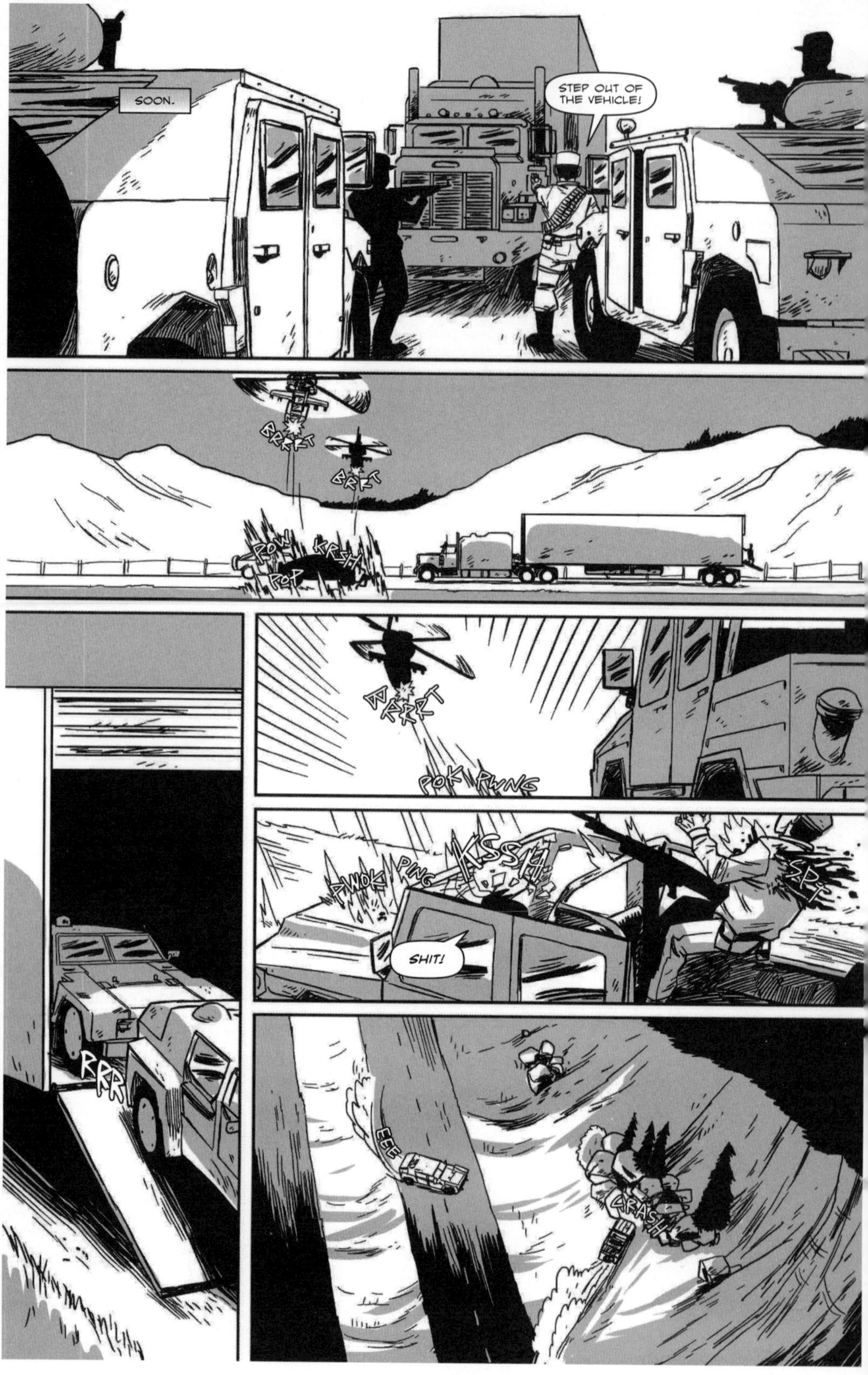
SOON.
STEP OUT OF THE VEHICLE!
BRRKT
BRRKT
POW
KRSH
POP
BRRKT
POK PWNG
RRR
PWOK
PING
KSSH
SPT
SHIT!
EEE
CRASH

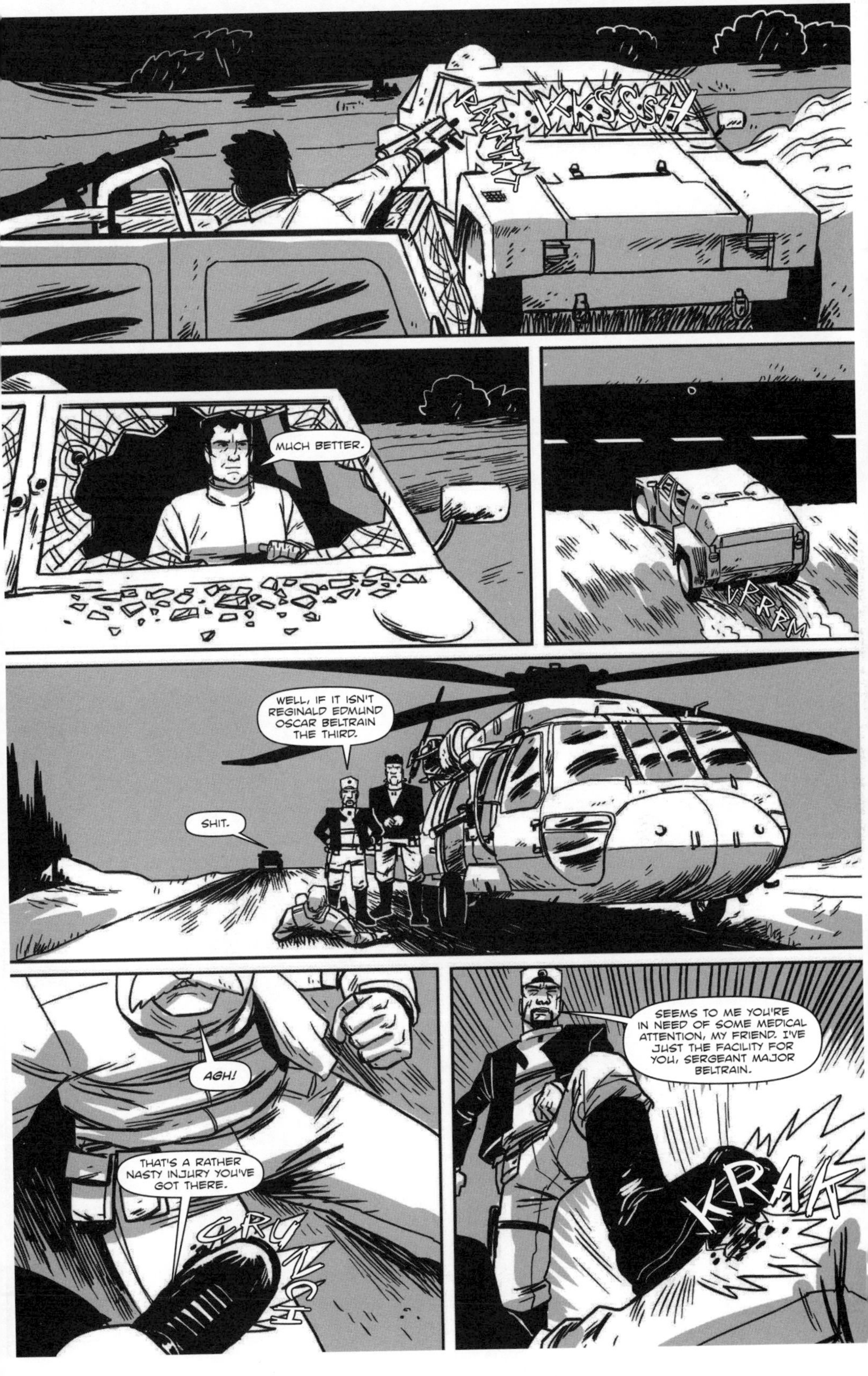
RAT-TAT-TAT
KKSSSH
MUCH BETTER.
VRRRM
WELL, IF IT ISN'T REGINALD EDMUND OSCAR BELTRAIN THE THIRD.
SHIT.
AGH!
THAT'S A RATHER NASTY INJURY YOU'VE GOT THERE.
CRUNCH
SEEMS TO ME YOU'RE IN NEED OF SOME MEDICAL ATTENTION, MY FRIEND. I'VE JUST THE FACILITY FOR YOU, SERGEANT MAJOR BELTRAIN.
KRAK

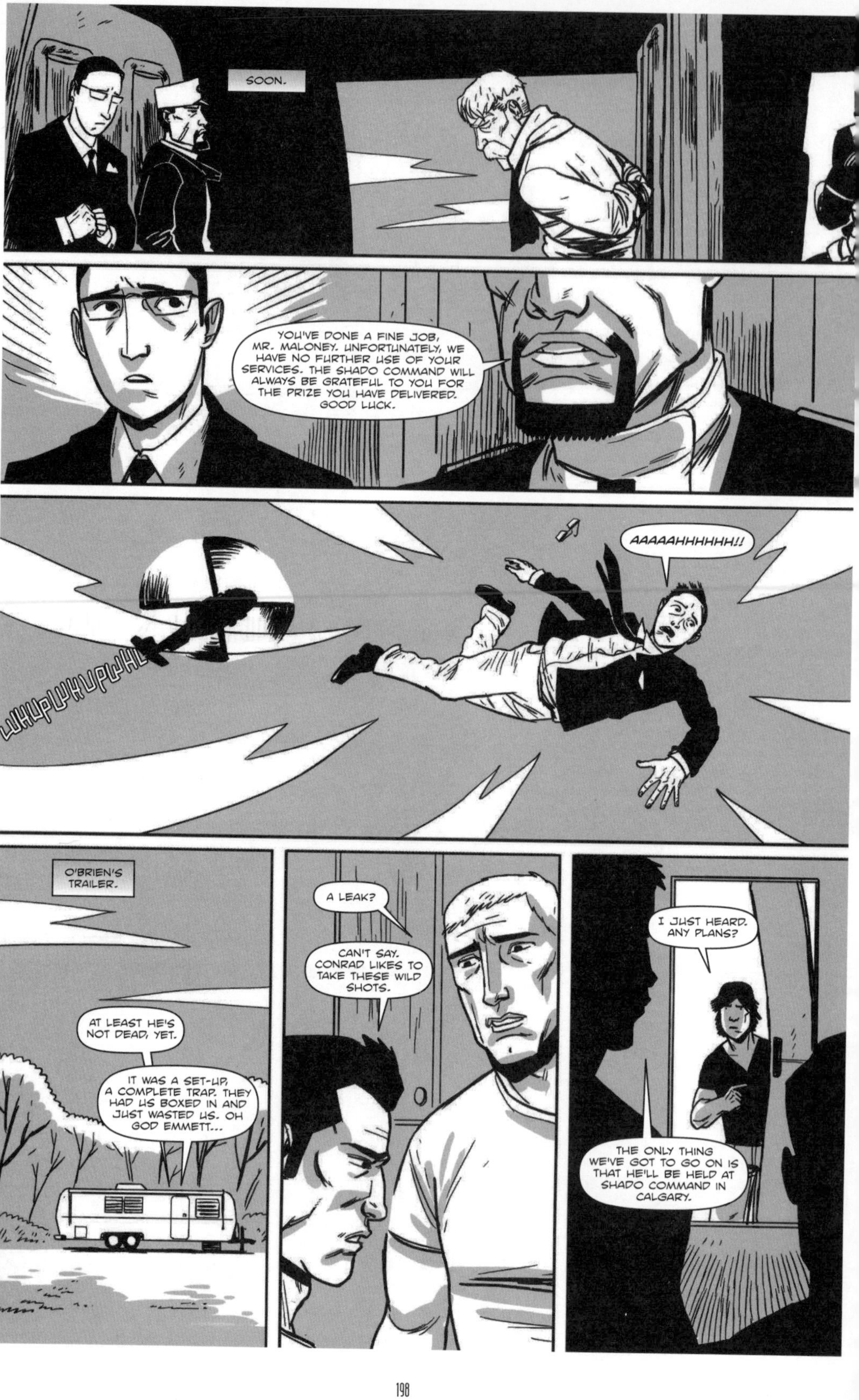
SOON.
YOU'VE DONE A FINE JOB, MR. MALONEY. UNFORTUNATELY, WE HAVE NO FURTHER USE OF YOUR SERVICES. THE SHADO COMMAND WILL ALWAYS BE GRATEFUL TO YOU FOR THE PRIZE YOU HAVE DELIVERED. GOOD LUCK.
AAAAAHHHHHH!!
WHUPWHUPWHL
O'BRIEN'S TRAILER.
AT LEAST HE'S NOT DEAD, YET.
IT WAS A SET-UP, A COMPLETE TRAP. THEY HAD US BOXED IN AND JUST WASTED US. OH GOD EMMETT...
A LEAK?
CAN'T SAY. CONRAD LIKES TO TAKE THESE WILD SHOTS.
I JUST HEARD. ANY PLANS?
THE ONLY THING WE'VE GOT TO GO ON IS THAT HE'LL BE HELD AT SHADO COMMAND IN CALGARY.

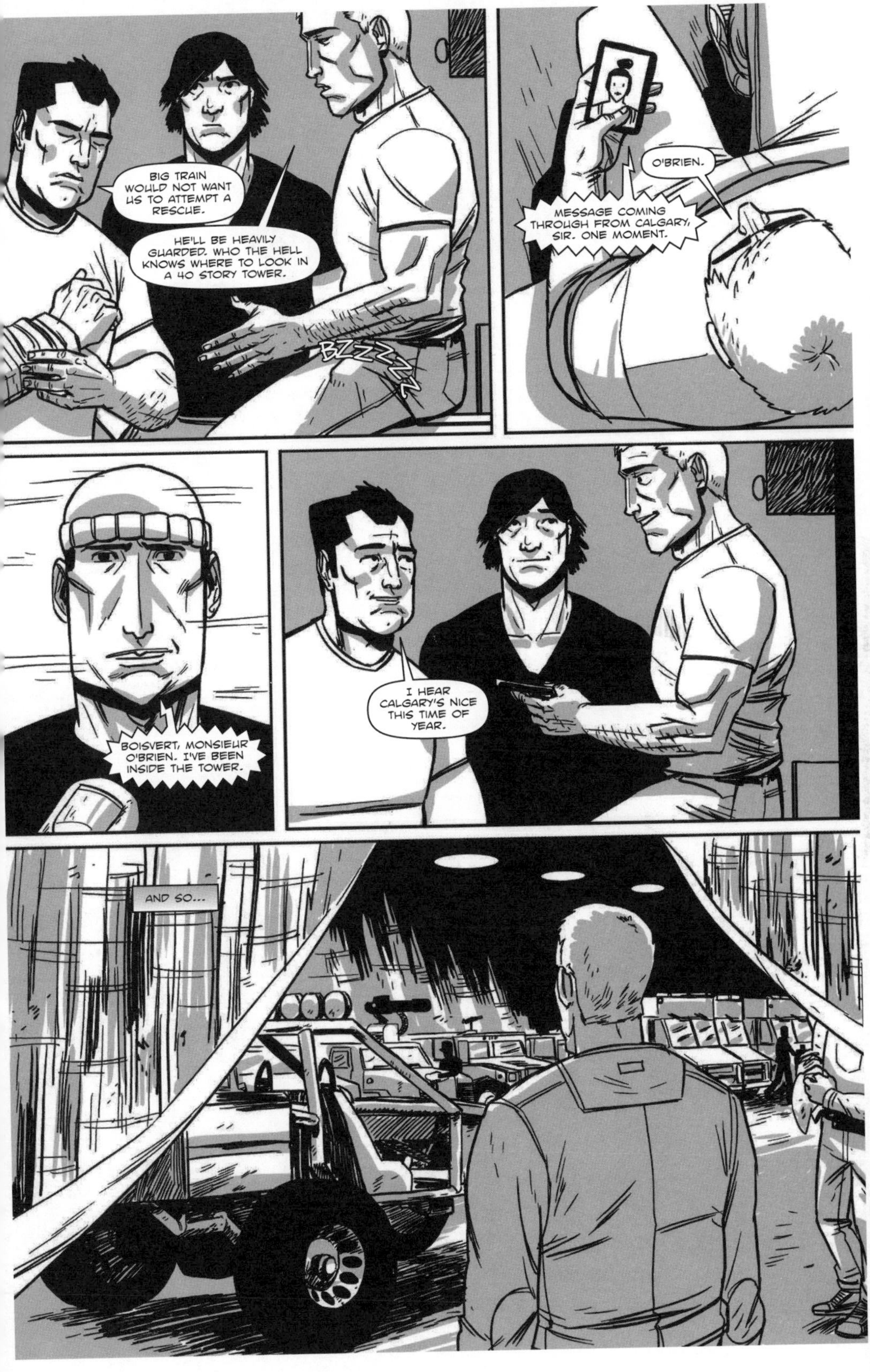
BIG TRAIN WOULD NOT WANT US TO ATTEMPT A RESCUE.
HE'LL BE HEAVILY GUARDED. WHO THE HELL KNOWS WHERE TO LOOK IN A 40 STORY TOWER.
BZZZZZZ
O'BRIEN.
MESSAGE COMING THROUGH FROM CALGARY, SIR. ONE MOMENT.
BOISVERT, MONSIEUR O'BRIEN. I'VE BEEN INSIDE THE TOWER.
I HEAR CALGARY'S NICE THIS TIME OF YEAR.
AND SO...

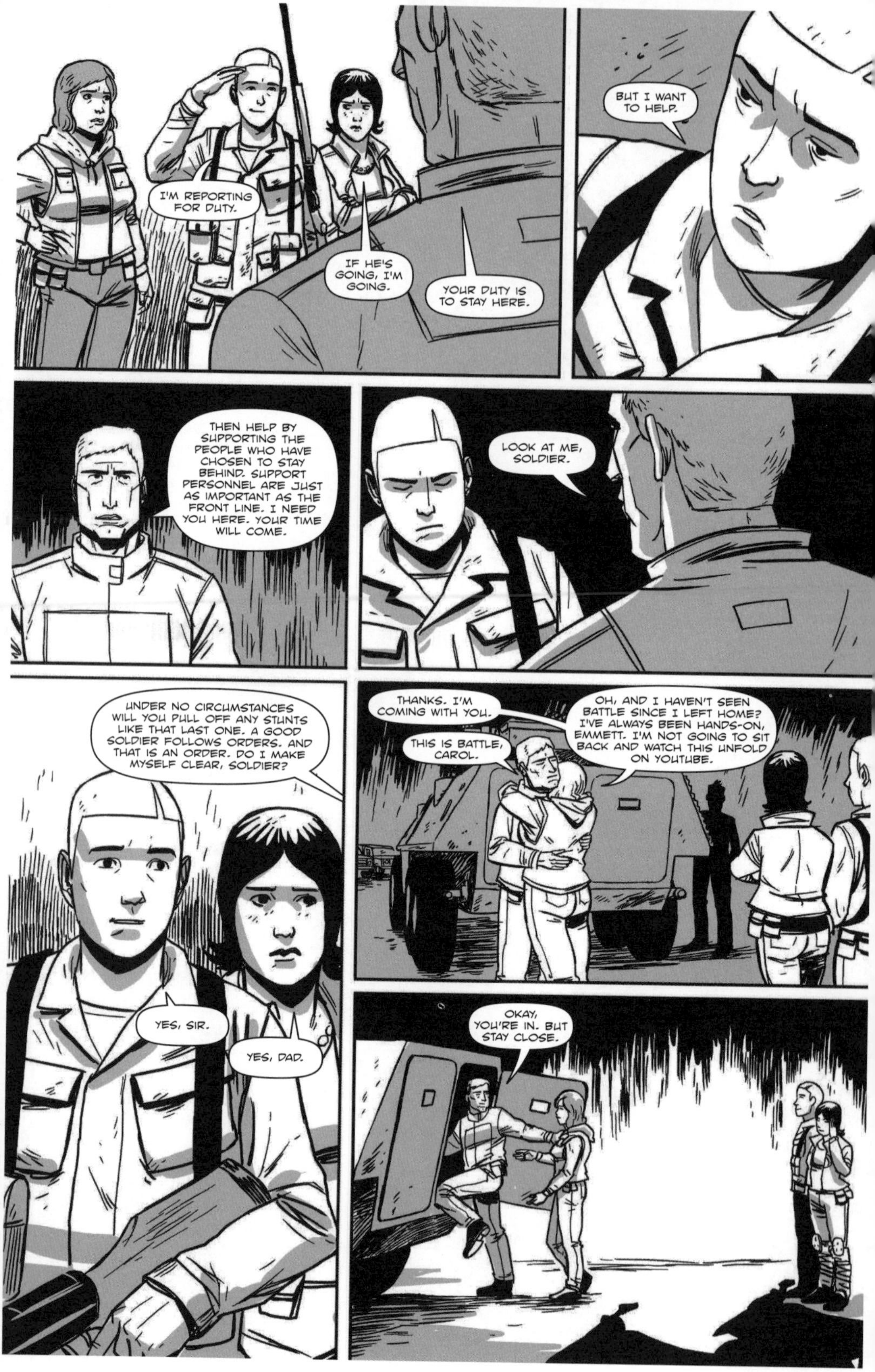
I'M REPORTING FOR DUTY.
IF HE'S GOING, I'M GOING.
YOUR DUTY IS TO STAY HERE.
BUT I WANT TO HELP.
THEN HELP BY SUPPORTING THE PEOPLE WHO HAVE CHOSEN TO STAY BEHIND. SUPPORT PERSONNEL ARE JUST AS IMPORTANT AS THE FRONT LINE. I NEED YOU HERE. YOUR TIME WILL COME.
LOOK AT ME, SOLDIER.
UNDER NO CIRCUMSTANCES WILL YOU PULL OFF ANY STUNTS LIKE THAT LAST ONE. A GOOD SOLDIER FOLLOWS ORDERS. AND THAT IS AN ORDER. DO I MAKE MYSELF CLEAR, SOLDIER?
YES, SIR.
YES, DAD.
THANKS. I'M COMING WITH YOU.
THIS IS BATTLE, CAROL.
OH, AND I HAVEN'T SEEN BATTLE SINCE I LEFT HOME? I'VE ALWAYS BEEN HANDS-ON, EMMETT. I'M NOT GOING TO SIT BACK AND WATCH THIS UNFOLD ON YOUTUBE.
OKAY, YOU'RE IN. BUT STAY CLOSE.

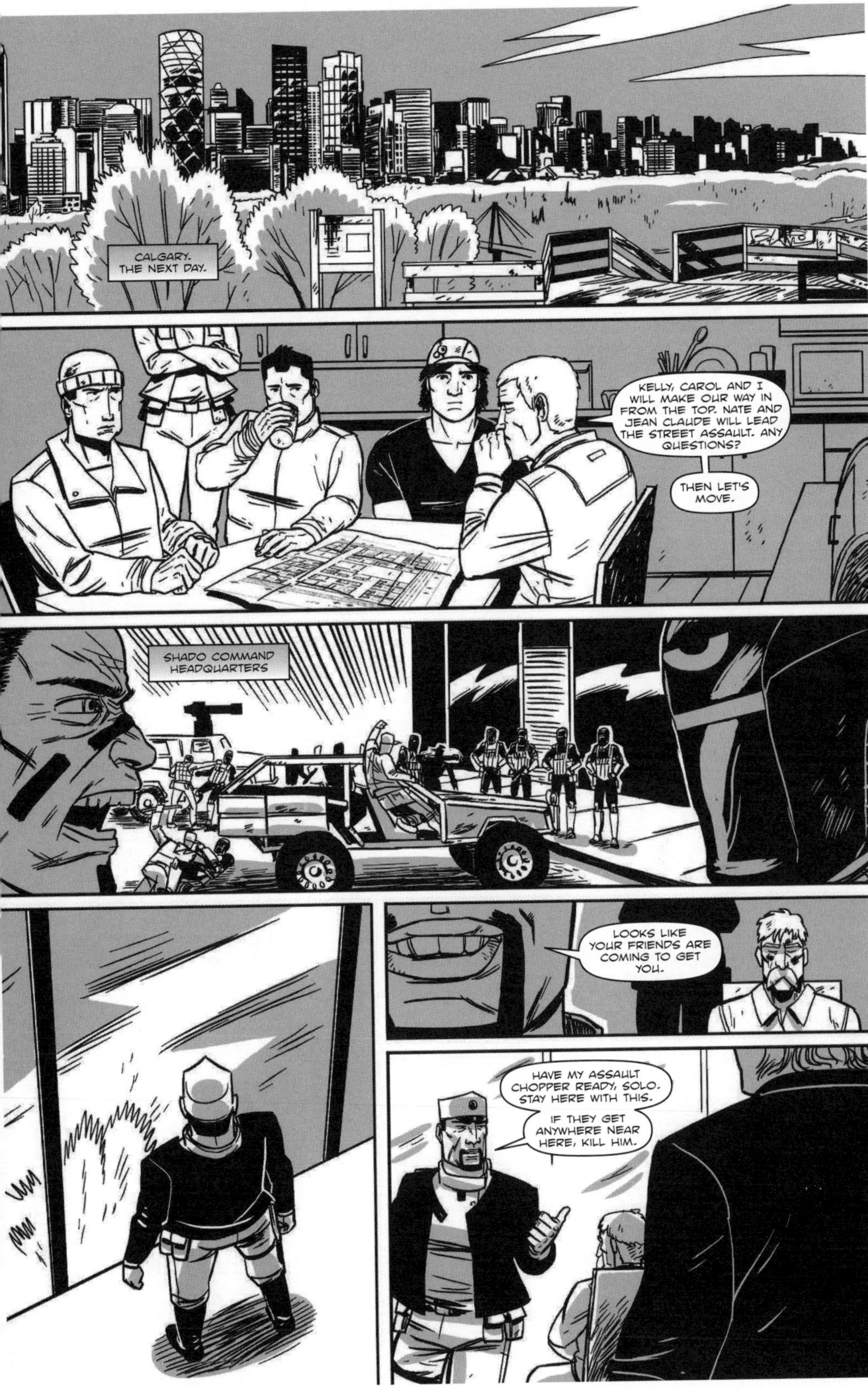
CALGARY. THE NEXT DAY.
KELLY, CAROL AND I WILL MAKE OUR WAY IN FROM THE TOP. NATE AND JEAN CLAUDE WILL LEAD THE STREET ASSAULT. ANY QUESTIONS?
THEN LET'S MOVE.
SHADO COMMAND HEADQUARTERS
LOOKS LIKE YOUR FRIENDS ARE COMING TO GET YOU.
HAVE MY ASSAULT CHOPPER READY, SOLO. STAY HERE WITH THIS.
IF THEY GET ANYWHERE NEAR HERE, KILL HIM.

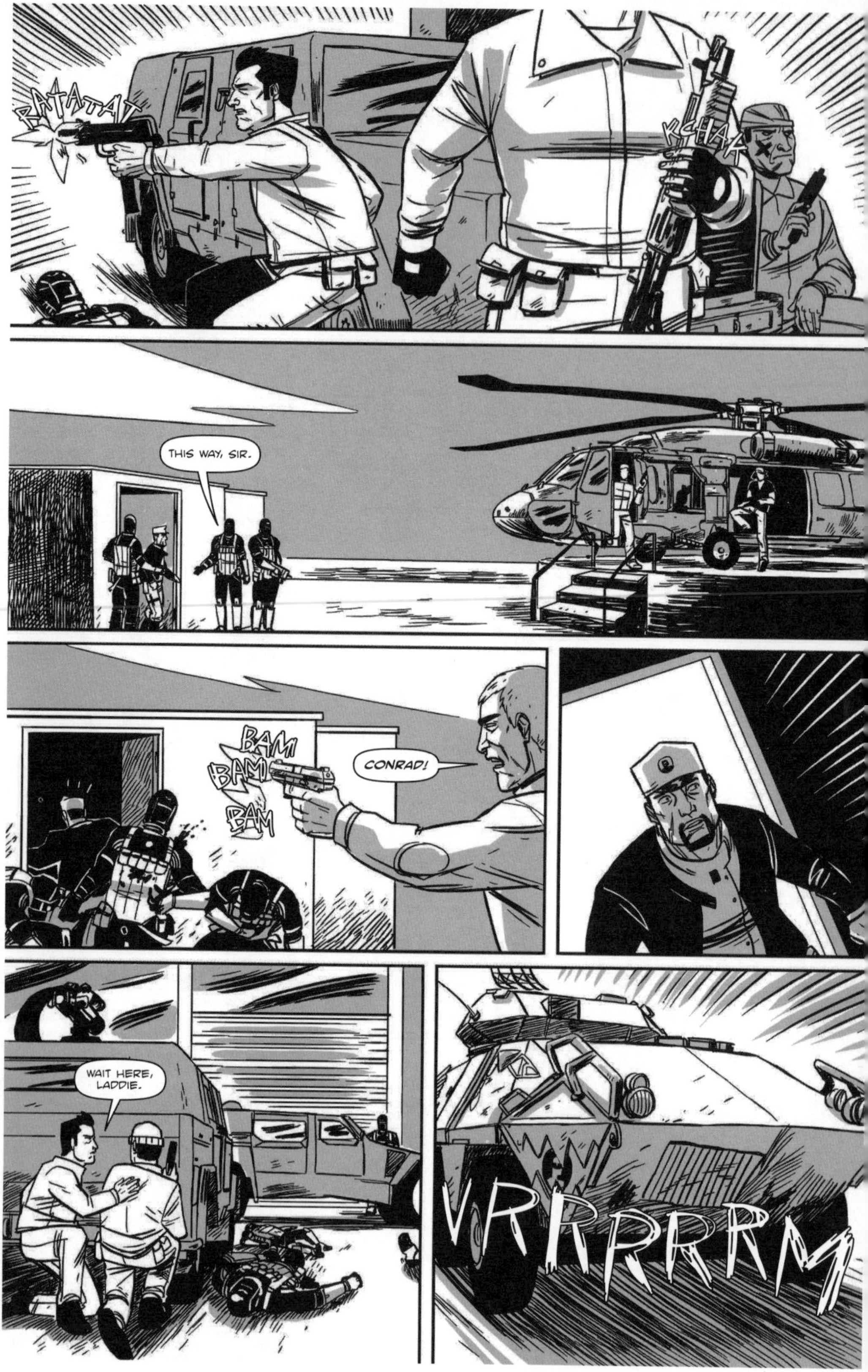
RATATAT
KCHAK
THIS WAY, SIR.
BAM
BAM
BAM
CONRAD!
WAIT HERE, LADDIE.
VRRRRRM

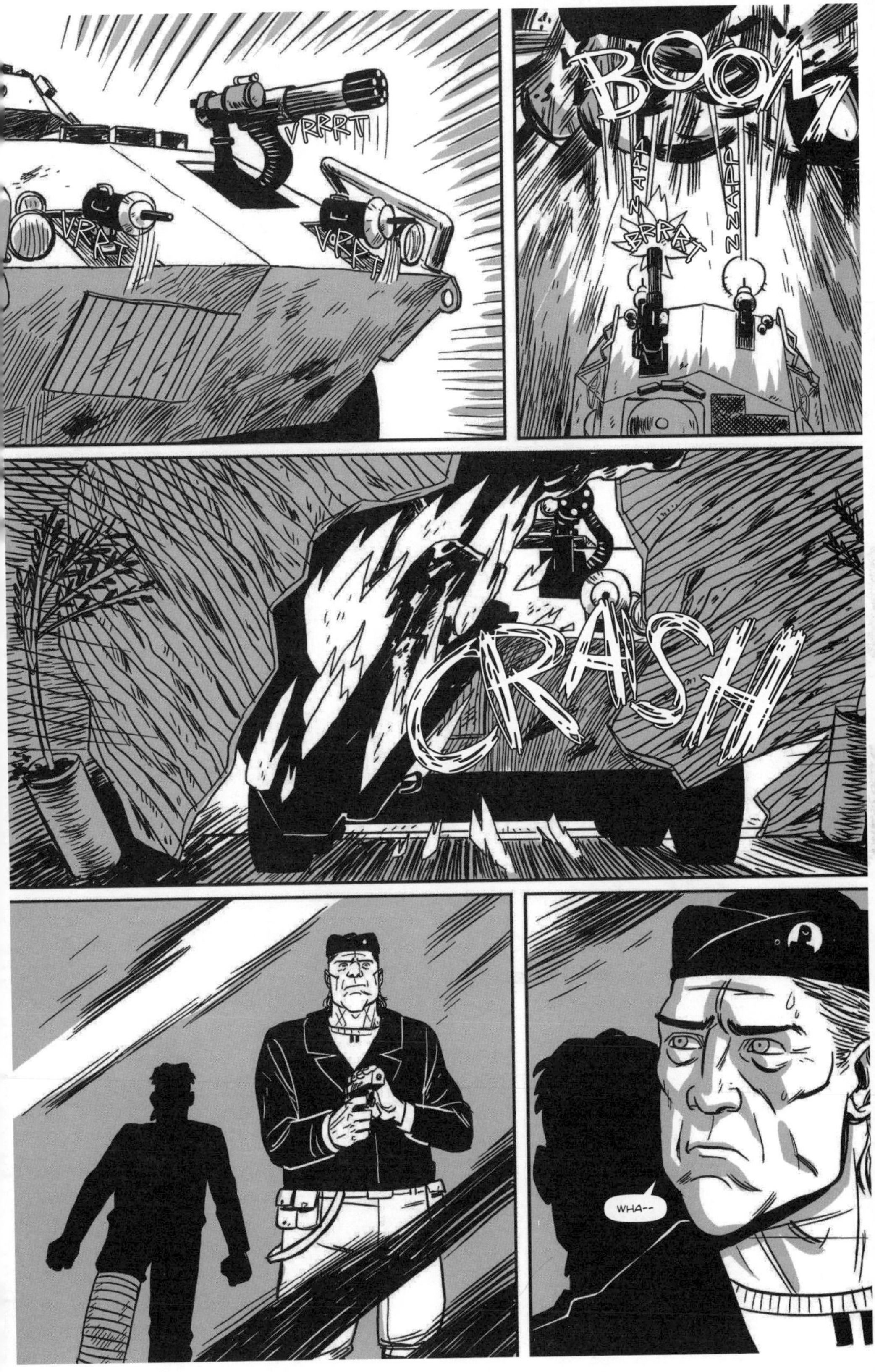
VRRRT
VRRT
VRRRT
BOOM
ZAPP
BRRAT
ZZAPP
CRASH
WHA--

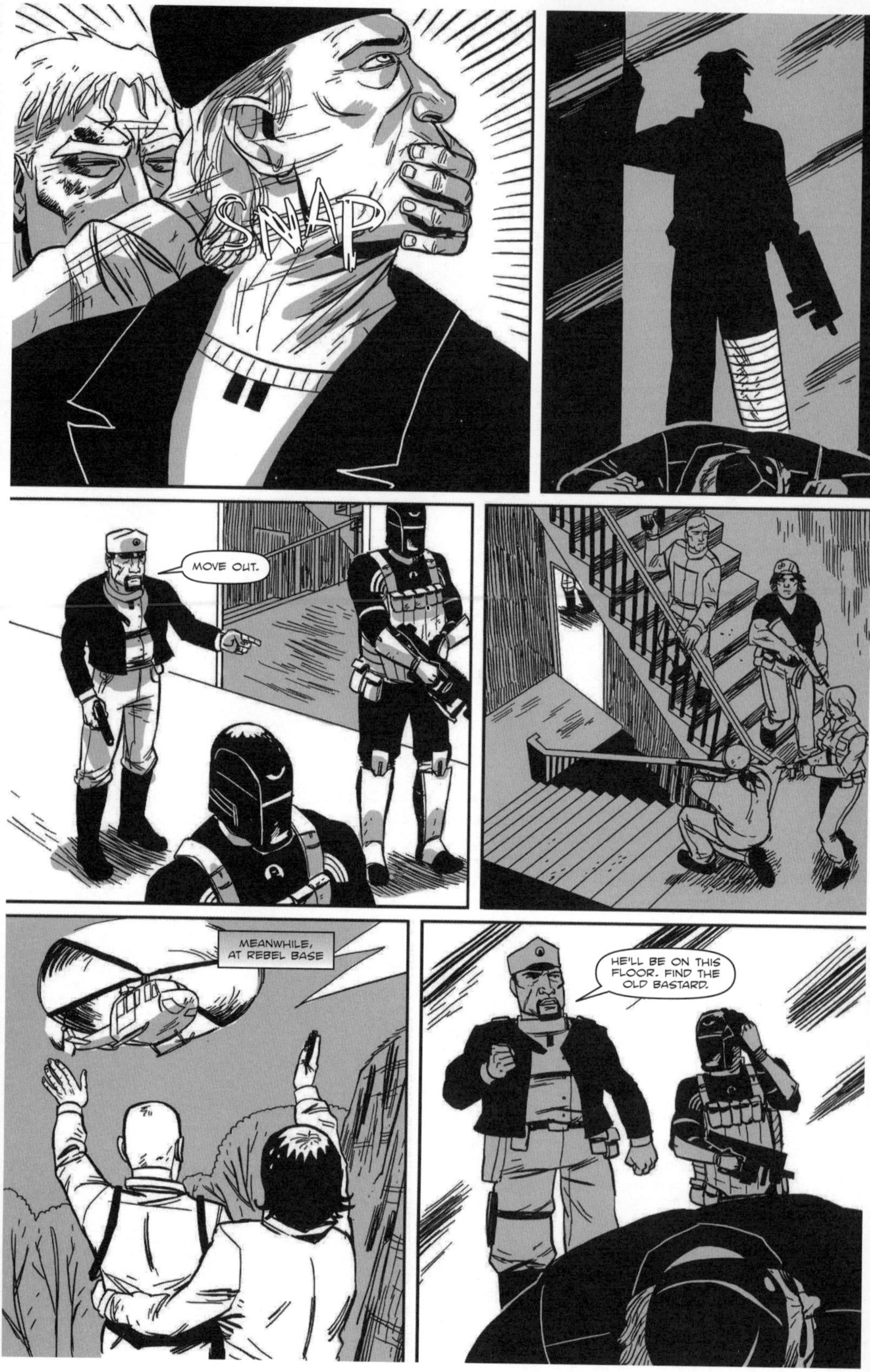
SNAP
MOVE OUT.
MEANWHILE, AT REBEL BASE
HE'LL BE ON THIS FLOOR. FIND THE OLD BASTARD.

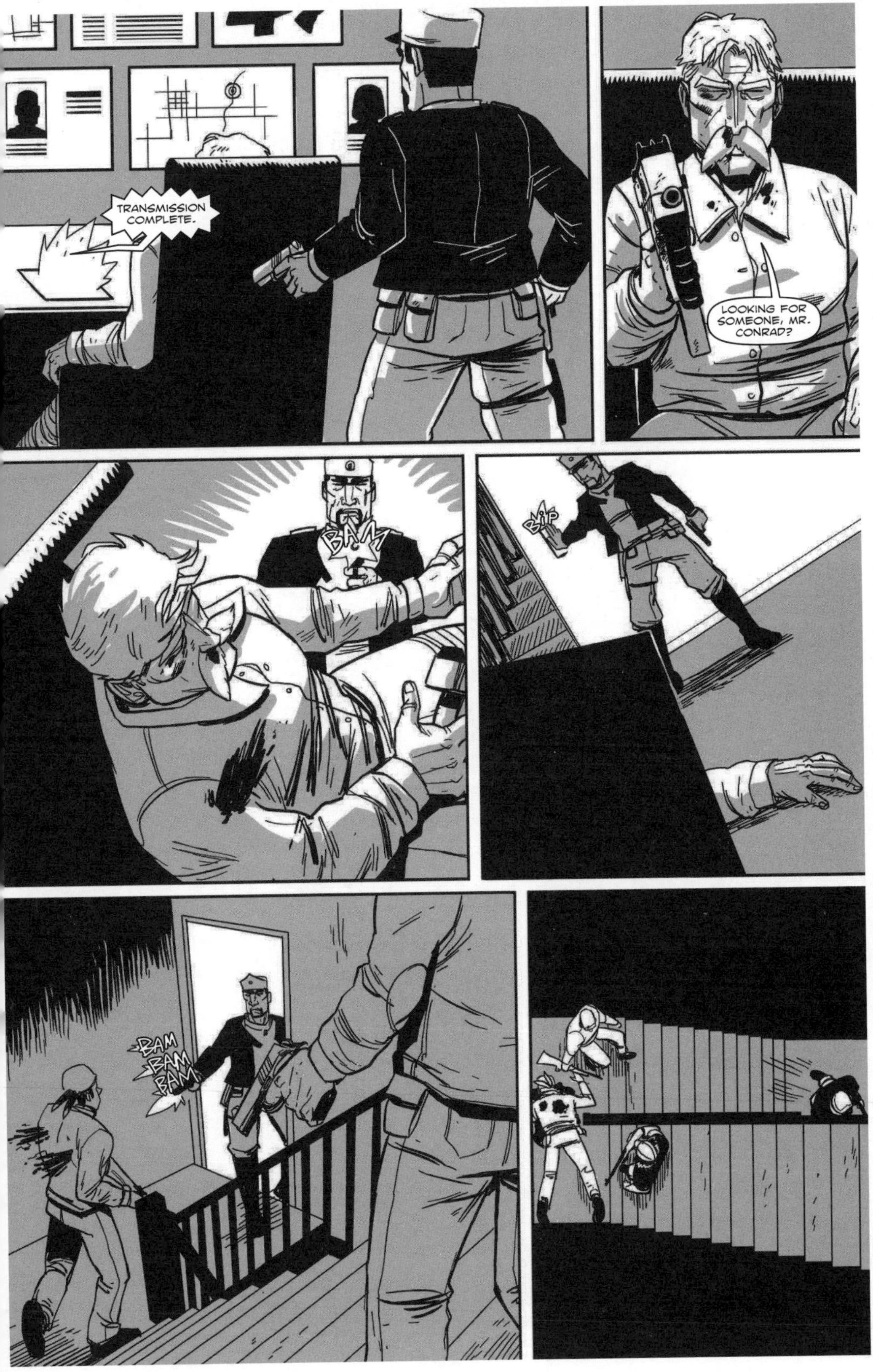
TRANSMISSION COMPLETE.
LOOKING FOR SOMEONE, MR. CONRAD?
BAM
BLIP
BAM BAM BAM

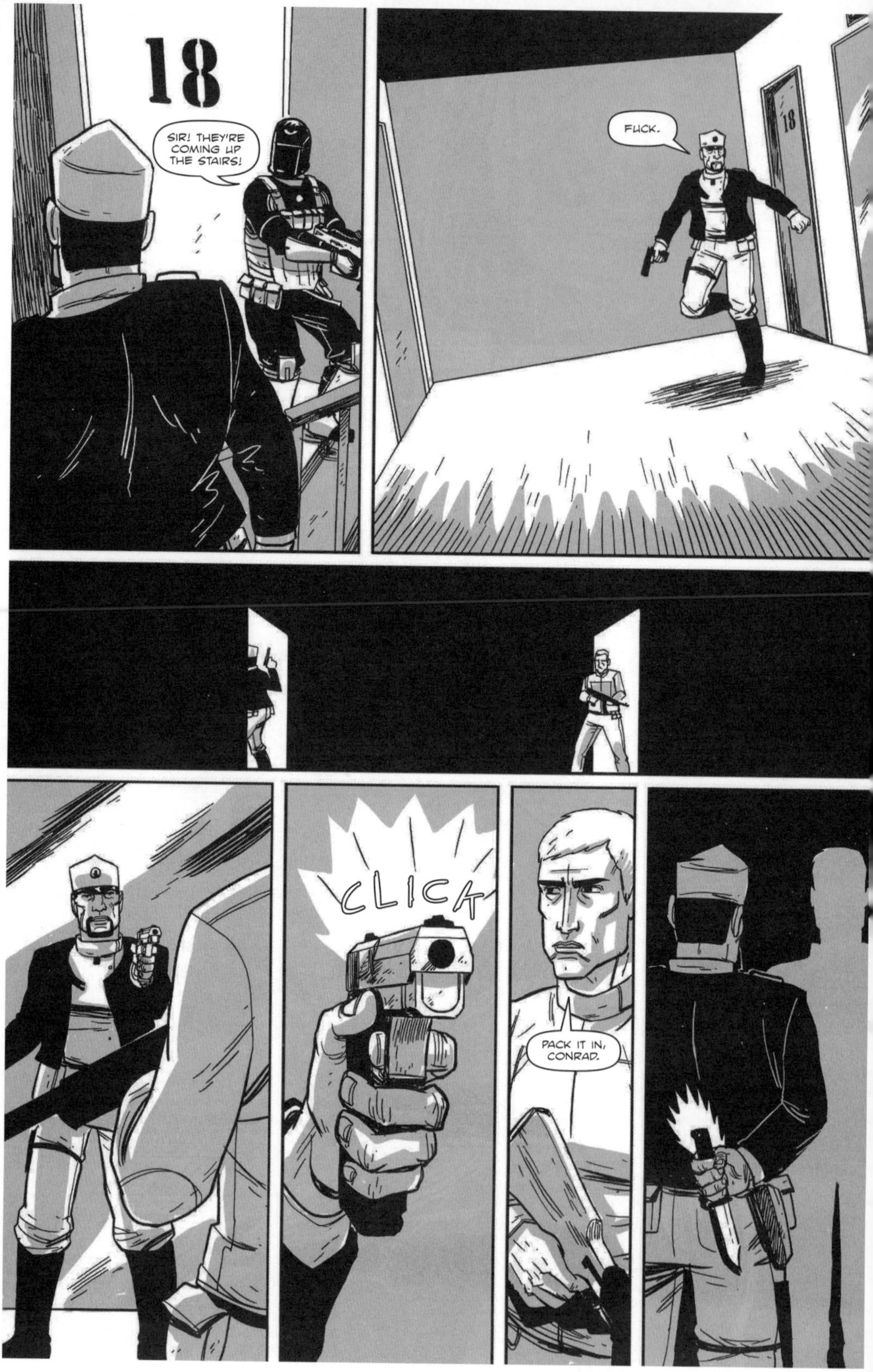
18
SIR! THEY'RE COMING UP THE STAIRS!
FUCK.
18
CLICK
PACK IT IN, CONRAD.

RRRRAAAAAHHH!

WHOK

UFF!

VSHAM

TONK

KAFF

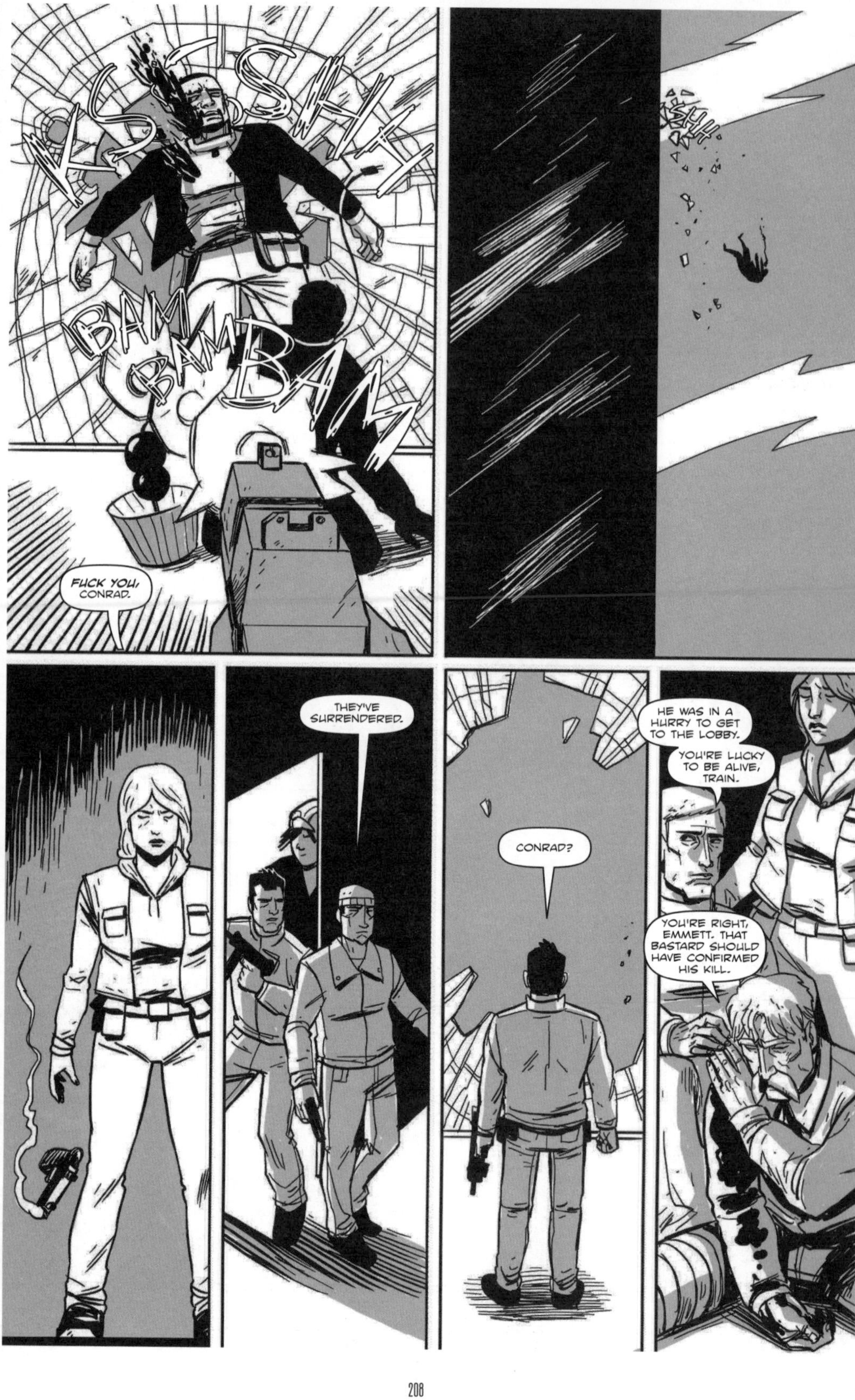
KSSSHHH
BAM BAM BAM
FUCK YOU, CONRAD.
THEY'VE SURRENDERED.
CONRAD?
HE WAS IN A HURRY TO GET TO THE LOBBY.
YOU'RE LUCKY TO BE ALIVE, TRAIN.
YOU'RE RIGHT, EMMETT. THAT BASTARD SHOULD HAVE CONFIRMED HIS KILL.

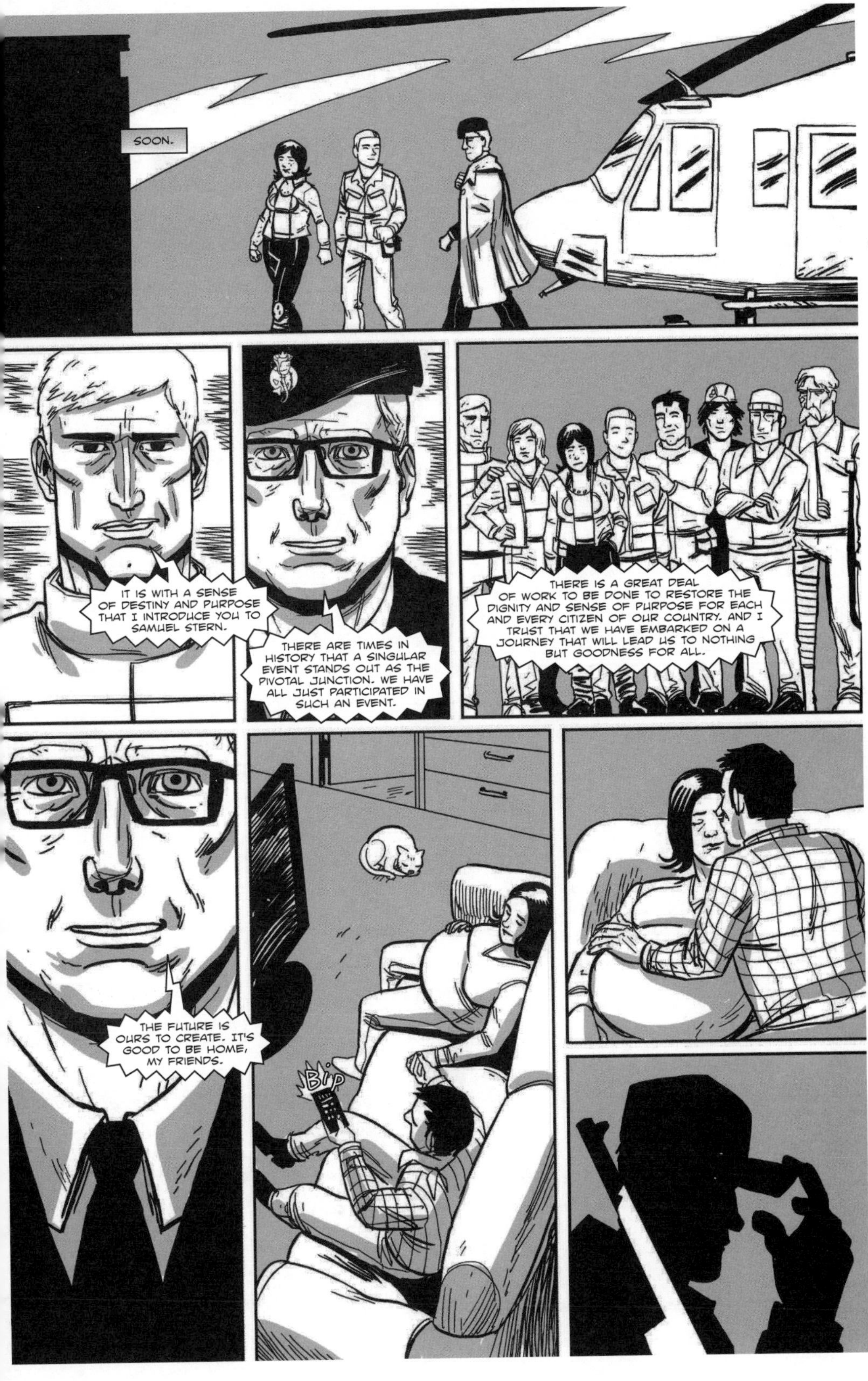
SOON.
IT IS WITH A SENSE OF DESTINY AND PURPOSE THAT I INTRODUCE YOU TO SAMUEL STERN.
THERE ARE TIMES IN HISTORY THAT A SINGULAR EVENT STANDS OUT AS THE PIVOTAL JUNCTION. WE HAVE ALL JUST PARTICIPATED IN SUCH AN EVENT.
THERE IS A GREAT DEAL OF WORK TO BE DONE TO RESTORE THE DIGNITY AND SENSE OF PURPOSE FOR EACH AND EVERY CITIZEN OF OUR COUNTRY. AND I TRUST THAT WE HAVE EMBARKED ON A JOURNEY THAT WILL LEAD US TO NOTHING BUT GOODNESS FOR ALL.
THE FUTURE IS OURS TO CREATE. IT'S GOOD TO BE HOME, MY FRIENDS.
BIP

RRRRRRRRRRRRRRRRRRRRRRRRR

WHAT THE...

RRRRRRRR

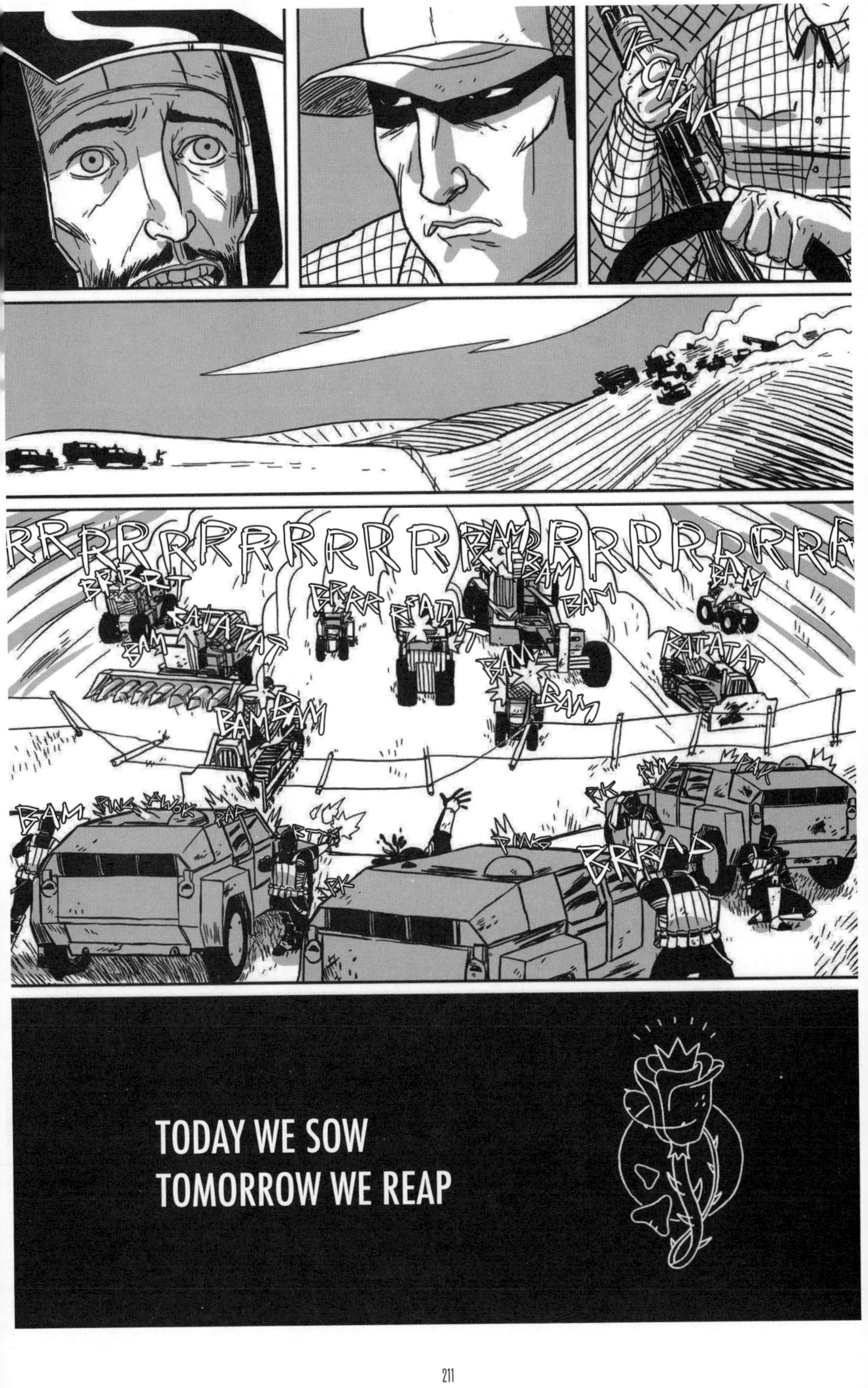
K-CHAK
RRRRRRRRRRRRRRRRRRRRR
BRRRT
RATATATAT
BAM
BRRR
RATATATAT
BAM
BAM
BAM
BAM
RATATATAT
BAM
BAM
BAMBAM
BAM
PING
PAK
PING
PING
BRRAP
BAM
PING
PAP

TODAY WE SOW
TOMORROW WE REAP

The Writers

The Reel Write Bros.: David Longworth, Harry Kalensky and Allan Stanleigh

The Reel Write Bros. collectively represent a century of film, television and musical experience. They have been contracted by film and television producers to develop scripts, treatments and character profiles and one page outlines. Their full-length animated screenplay, 'The Adventures of Mowgli,' a feature based on Rudyard Kipling's 'Jungle Book' stories, has been broadcast on HBO and YTV Canada's youth network. It features the voices of Charleton Heston, Sam Elliot and Dana Delaney.

Harry Kalensky

Harry Kalensky has been in the eyes and ears of Canadians for over four decades. As the original bass player of Canada's Trooper, his contributions have enjoyed multi platinum awards. Many of the songs have become Canadian Rock standards, airing over 250,000 times. These include: 'Two For The Show', 'Boys In The Bright White Sportscar' and 'Santa Maria.' Harry and Cecile Larochelle have just re-released their children's album "Friends Friends Friends", available at Reverb Nation and iTunes. As an actor, Harry has appeared in numerous television and movie productions. However theatre holds a special place in his heart. Harry was a principle actor in Ken Mitchell's play "Cruel Tears," performing in every major city in Canada.

Davy Longworth

Davy has been active in the arts community for over 40 years. As an actor, he has over 90 credits in film, television and stage performing. He is an active cowboy poet and has produced two cowboy poetry and music CD's: 'Bards and Pards – Outstanding In Their Field', and 'Pick-up Pomes."

Allan Stanleigh

Allan has had an eclectic career working as a writer, producer and in the film industry. As a writer for film, he is the author or co-author of nine feature length screenplays. Three have been optioned. Allan has produced live performance events and taught film-making and writing to kids at the Ailanthus Arts Centre for Youth in Vancouver, B.C. Allan is the writer, producer, recording engineer and a voice actor in the comedy podcast, 'No Shirt, No Shoes, Pants Optional.'

Illustration and Design

Dave Casey

Dave lives and works in New York City. Find his portfolio at http://www.dave-casey.com